The story of the
AUSTRALIAN
PEOPLE

The story of the
AUSTRALIAN PEOPLE

Donald Horne

Published by Reader's Digest, Sydney

Contents

First edition
Published by Reader's Digest Services Pty Limited
(Inc. in New South Wales)
26–32 Waterloo Street, Surry Hills, NSW 2010

This book is a revised, expanded and illustrated edition of
The Australian People, first published in Australia in 1972
by Angus & Robertson Publishers.
© Text, Donald Horne 1972, 1985
© Reader's Digest Association Far East Limited
Philippines copyright 1985 Reader's Digest Association
Far East Limited

Edited and designed by Mead & Beckett Publishing
139 Macquarie Street, Sydney NSW 2000

Art editor Barbara Beckett
Editor Bryony Cosgrove
Art assistants Leonie Bremer-Kamp and Carolyn Stafford
Picture researchers Don Chapman and Joanna Collard
Researcher Myfanwy Gollan

National Library of Australia
cataloguing-in-publication data
Horne, Donald, 1921 –
The story of the Australian people.
Rev. edn.
Previous ed. published as: The Australian people:
biography of a nation. Sydney: Angus & Robertson. 1972.
Bibliography.
Includes index.
ISBN 0 949819 67 0

1. Australia – social life and customs.   I. Horne, Donald,
1921–   Australian people: biography of a nation.
II. Reader's Digest Services.   III. Title.   IV. Title: The
Australian people: biography of a nation.
994

Typeset by Asco Trade Typesetting Ltd, Hong Kong
Reproduction by Bright Arts (H.K.) Ltd, Hong Kong
Printed by South China Printing Company, Hong Kong

Page one: Grose Farm from the Toll Gate, *painted by F.C. Terry in the 1860s.*

Page two: elegant Melbourne in the 1940s – the 'Paris' end of Collins Street.

Foreword

The aim of this book is to tell the story of Australia's past in a way that may suggest some answers to the question: *How did Australians become what they are?* It is not a narrowly political history: I have tried to provide a general history that tells of the variety of ways in which Australians lived, the variety of ways in which they saw things, and what the relations were between types of Australians.

It is a story about people, but not about personages. The real participants are not individuals but types of people – whether the 'dungaree settlers' of the 1790s or the 'trendies' of the 1970s. I have tried to turn types of people – 'selector' or 'black hat', 'new woman' or 'digger', 'native' or 'ethnic' – into the kind of characters who make up the collective biographies of a nation. One of the functions of history-writing can be to bring new social types on to the stage and tell what happened.

The names of some individuals appear in the text, of course – especially those who, from poets to politicians, have been among the nation-definers, telling Australians what they seemed to be. But throughout the book there are also dozens of small biographies, separate from the text itself, to give some reminders of the kinds of public personages – the rebels as well as the masters – that have influenced Australia's history.

There are hundreds of pictures, and these are a very important part of the book. They are not meant to 'illustrate' the story, but to help tell it, or, more exactly, to tell those parts of it that can be better told in pictures than in words. To these there have been added maps and statistical tables.

Although the style is narrative, the book is composed of overlays of themes. It is divided into three main chronological divisions, but within each division one theme is developed right through the period, then another, then another. The cumulative effect is intended to provide a memory rather like the kind of memories we have of our own lives: we know that we go on year by year, but we also know that the themes of our lives have histories other than those suggested by the calendar.

There are no footnotes. Either there would have been thousands of footnotes, or none. But not having footnotes has one embarrassment. It is not possible to make acknowledgments. The direct quotations are contemporary voices chattering away, and who they are (or whether they are right or wrong) is of no significance; they are just conversation. Some are named. Some are not. But there is another problem: since the writing of this kind of book necessarily depends on exploiting the devoted work of a great number of historians, it seems unfair not to be able to acknowledge them. Yet to do so in the text would impede the book's narrative style. The best I can do in individual tribute is the bibliography at the back; and in general I can add the observation that history-writing seems well in advance of some other aspects of social investigation into Australia. If that were not so, this book could not have been written.

DONALD HORNE
Sydney, 1985

Sydney in the early 1820s appears neat, substantial and orderly in an engraving by Major James Taylor. In the foreground is the handsome military hospital built by order of Governor Macquarie, where convalescent soldiers in nightshirts stroll in the grounds. At the rear is the Anglican church where all convicts were forced to attend Sunday services. To the right stands one of Sydney's flour mills.

Part one

The age of Authority

1788 to 1850

For tens of thousands of years the lands we now think of as 'Australia' were the home of the first Australians, a black race from the north. Then, a few decades after the founding of the British convict colony, these lands had become 'a new Britannia in another world'.

When the time came for Sydney to get a new Government House in the 1840s, it was built in 19th-century style, with turrets and battlements, like a castle. In the long ballroom there was a medieval-style musicians' gallery.

Black settlement

History

Tens of thousands of years ago, before the ancestors of the American Indians had left Asia for the Americas, in what may then have been the longest sea voyage in human experience, after a slow progression across successions of islands, some black people discovered Australia.

Little is known about the first Australians, except that they probably came at a time when an ice age had so shrivelled the oceans that the shores were extended far beyond their present position. We know nothing of those long walks in which groups of people spread across the continent and adapted to its diverse demands; a continent with a strange vegetation and roamed by giant animals that were to die out. It is only over the last ten thousand years that the seas have risen and the vegetation and the climate have become similar to today's.

By then the first Australians were to have as their own a land much of which was rainless, but in which they had shown much stubbornness and inventiveness. On the coasts they sailed bark canoes and fished; in the forest lands and mountains they were a hunting people of the bush; in the dry interior, they were a people of the plains, who might have to travel so far to find something to eat that they owned only what they could carry, and who, to drink, might collect the early morning dew from leaves or squeeze water from the pouches of frogs. These people all developed cultures that told them what the world was like and how to behave: each tribe's territory was explained, and justified, by a special theory of creation. It made the land sacred to its ancestors, who were believed to live as rocks or trees or waterholes, and it provided a sense of common experience in which land and tribe and ancestors were one, their distinctiveness maintained by two or three hundred languages and thousands of ceremonies, fables and rituals.

The 300 000 Australians were to spread over nearly eight million square kilometres and be divided into 500 or so tribes, some of less than 500 people, few of more than 1500, connected only by an intricate system of trade routes in which an object could be exchanged at several hundred bartering places until it had crossed the whole continent.

The tribes further broke down into smaller groups of several families, and it was in these smaller communities that the first Australians spent most of their lives: each day the men would hunt, or fish if they were near water, and the women would gather vegetables and fruits and seeds from which to make meals; they would leave their food-gathering areas only to visit relations, or to attend the occasional tribal gatherings for games, feasts and ceremonies.

Each tribe lived in a spirit of communality with itself and saw the balance of reciprocity as the correct mode of human conduct – in friendship, a gift was exchanged for a gift; in enmity, sometimes in long, subtle blood feuds, an injury was to be rewarded by an equal injury. But although there were blood feuds, duels, and sometimes large-scale fights, there were no predatory wars. Each tribe was sure of its rights and habits without challenging the rights of others; there were no drives into other territories to seize slaves or land. Land was so sacred to each tribe and each tribe was so sacred to its land that it was not possible to imagine claiming the land of another tribe. There were no leaders. The old men of each small group were supposed to provide its wisdom, and their wisdom did not include the arts of organised warfare.

There was a common thread in many of the creation myths of the Australians; the belief that things began with the sudden materialisation of creatures that did not look like humans but acted like them and wandered aimlessly around the country performing marvels. This was the way, from the 17th century onwards, in which the Europeans materialised in Australia. First there were some apparently meaningless landings, followed by years of nothing. Then in January 1788 eleven strange ships anchored in a bay on the east coast of the continent, and out of them came scarcely human creatures who began moving here and there for some unknown purpose.

White settlement

The purpose was clear enough to the 'scarcely human creatures'. They intended to found a penal settlement at the bay where the English naval captain, James Cook, had first landed almost eighteen years before, when he had voyaged along the east coast of New Holland and found it better favoured than the coasts already explored by the Dutch.

It was an age when any part of the world whose inhabitants could not fight the Europeans was considered European property; so later, as Cook was leaving the northern reaches of New Holland, he ordered the Union flag to be run up and, just as the black Australians might clap bits of wood together to give special solemnity to an occasion, he ordered muskets to be fired to make his claim sound real. He announced that the whole east coast now belonged to Great Britain, and for some unknown reason he gave it the curious name of 'New South Wales'. Soon, Europeans began printing this new name on their maps.

London gentlemen from time to time would urge that the unknown land be turned to some new English purpose. That purpose proved to be the emptying of the prison hulks that had been crowded since transportation of convicts to North America had ended in 1776. The hulks were a nuisance and transportation a habit: it seemed ridiculous that a country should house its own convicts. There were questions in the House of Commons and committees of inquiry. To a cocky, newly arrived power boasting that it ruled the waves, the decision became obvious: start another colony. It might also prove useful as a centre for growing flax to make sailcloth and ships' ropes. Tropical products could be grown there – spices, coffee, cotton, tobacco – and trees could be forested from New Zealand to provide masts and ships' timber for the British fleets in India. It might have some use as a trading base; even a naval base.

As eleven ships lay at anchor in Captain Cook's 'Botany Bay' on 20 January 1788, there was self-congratulation that an eight-month voyage had ended with so few deaths, and curiosity as boats explored the bay and land parties gave beads to the natives. But it was obvious to Captain Arthur Phillip, Governor of the colony, that he had been sent to the wrong place. Too much of the land was low and boggy. The supply of fresh water was poor. The grass was coarse. The soil was black sand. There was no shelter for ships.

Phillip went up the coast with three boats to look for something better. He found 'a large opening or bay' which at first seemed unpromising. But after the three little boats had passed between two high, rugged stone cliffs Phillip saw opening before him 'the finest harbour in the world, in which 1000 sail of the line may ride in the most perfect security'. His main difficulty was to decide at which of the inner harbours he should found his colony. He chose a bay into which a stream ran and with water deep enough for ships to anchor close to the shore. He named it 'Sydney Cove' after Viscount Thomas Townshend Sydney, the English politician who had sent him to New South Wales. By 26 January the whole fleet was anchored off the cove. Early in the morning a party began clearing a space for a flagstaff. Shortly after noon the officers and a party of

marines landed. The Union flag went up. Possession was taken for King George. At sunset a salute was fired. Phillip and his small staff drank to King George's health.

The next day Phillip marked out lines for an encampment. His portable house was to be on one side of the stream; most of the encampment was to go up on the other. Some parties netted for fish; others cut down trees; others unloaded the blacksmith's forge, the cookhouse and tools, and some of the colony's flour, rice, beef, pork and peas. Tents went up. Two days later the Governor's house was erected, a convict had been lashed for insolence and the colony's nine horses, six cattle, 44 sheep, three goats, 28 pigs and diverse poultry were landed.

It began to thunder, with lightning and rain. For the next eight days there were thunderstorms, except on Sunday, when the chaplain preached on the text 'What shall I render unto the Lord, for all his benefits towards me?'

There were complaints of the heat, of the indolence of the convicts and of the ineptitude of their overseers (who were also convicts); a party of natives threw stones at a fishing party; several convicts ran away; a number of others got drunk. The hospital tents were filled with people suffering from dysentery and scurvy.

On the night of 6 February there was a violent storm. The lightning, not letting up the whole night, killed five sheep and a pig; on the ships the sailors were excited to drunkenness ('some swearing, others quarrelling, others singing – not in the least regarding the tempest, though so violent that the thunder shook the ship'), and on the shore the storm was background to a dark carnival in which the women convicts, who had landed that day, got with the men and celebrated the birth of the colony, with lightning flashing and thunder roaring, in 'debauchery and riot'.

It was after this remarkable night that on 7 February the official beginning of the colony was proclaimed. Assembled around the Governor or sick in hospital or in one of the ships were 736 male and female convicts, 17 convicts' children, 211 marines, with 27 wives and 14 children, and the few officials of the colony. After Phillip had been proclaimed Captain General and Governor in Chief he warned the convicts that men found in the women's tents at night would be shot at, and that anyone who stole food would be hanged. Three volleys were fired. Phillip received the honours due to a Captain General and retired to a large tent, where he and the officers dined on a cold collation. 'The mutton,' said one of those who ate it, 'was full of maggots. Nothing will keep twenty-four hours in this country.'

1. New world – old world: 1788 to 1820

In the convict societies that settled in New South Wales and Van Diemen's Land there was an attempt to turn thieves from the cities of the old world into forced labour in a new world. It was a man's society – with only one in seven convicts a woman – and a brutal one. English architectural styles, farming methods and sporting pursuits were introduced and social divisions were cultivated, based on degrees of 'gentlemanliness' and on wealth. The little settlements spread slowly, driving the blacks out of their own lands, but the interior remained a mystery.

A European city

'I looked on the wonderful sight of a European city thriving in the bosom of a country all but wild,' wrote a French explorer who came to Sydney in 1819.

Some of the thousand or so buildings of this town of 12 000 people were still wooden huts, but there were enough brick or even stone houses, and a sufficient sprinkling of bigger residences and public buildings, for it to have some small sense of presence. And it had a certain look of industry about it. Timber was being sawed, beer brewed, hides tanned, salt dried, shells were being burned into lime, clay turned into brick, wheat ground into flour, wool woven into cloth. The town even had a steam engine. Men and women had come from one part of the world to another, and had again built what they knew.

The great diversions of this small, new community may have been gambling, drinking, feasting, prizefighting, cockfighting and bullbaiting, but by 1819 its leaders had learned to comfort themselves with the familiarity of ways of filling in time that were theirs alone. They retained what they could of the pleasures of a provincial English town – musical evenings, cricket, horse riding, occasionally a horse race or a ball and in a few cases, of which picnicking was the main example, things could be run even more pleasantly in the colony than back home; a pleasure party

John Eyre, convicted for burglary and sent to Sydney, worked as a sign writer and painted four now-famous views of Sydney, published in 1808. The east view (above) looks over 'the Rocks' that gave part of Sydney its name.

An early view of Sydney (right) taken from A History of New South Wales, *published in 1802, shows that Sydney's houses were already spreading out, with room for gardens.*

beside the waters of the harbour allowed the extra indulgence of feasting from oysters growing on the rocks. For the leading women there were the familiar tasks of dispensing benevolence by serving on 'Ladies Committees' that conducted sewing classes for female convicts, or taught female orphans household virtues and skills, or cared for sick or destitute women.

The colonists had to do without a theatre, however. The first play went on in a mud hut decorated with coloured paper, and a playhouse was built in 1796, but later it was pulled down because there were too many robberies on play nights. There was only one newspaper, started in 1796, at first mainly for the Governor to issue his instructions, and always subject to his censorship; and the colonists produced no general reading of their own – the first book printed in the colony was a summary of its standing orders, and it was not until 1819 that a local periodical was contemplated. But there was a large supply of imported British periodicals and books to tell them about the part of the world they most cared about.

The small pretension of the bigger public buildings was in the English style of the late 18th century, less well done than similar derivations in Virginia, but familiar. Sydney's main distinctiveness was how it spread out. With most houses on their own plots of land, Sydney took up more space than towns of similar population in Great Britain. And the dominant verandaed style was producing one of the first towns of predominantly single-storey residences in the history of European urbanisation.

By English standards society was thin. There were no aristocrats, no old gentry families (although those who had been in the colony for some time had formed a closed world of their own; a dozen of the leading families were already interlocked by marriage). The best the colony could produce was the small gentry of the principal civil and military officers and a few others who had come to the colony to get something out of it; to these were added those who had made themselves gentry; and in a small community they could seem big. There was an extra distinction a man could boast of: in one generation a unique caste system had been created – between ex-convicts and others – that could also be applied to their children, an attitude not softened by the Church of England, whose chaplain, the Reverend Richard Johnson, showed little

The first Australian landscape paintings: *in 1815, John Lewin, a natural history painter, crossed the Blue Mountains with Governor Macquarie to inspect a site for a new town. The paintings he made on this expedition, titled* Campbell River *(above) and* Springwood *(right) were the first attempts by a European artist to convey the feeling of Australian landscapes.*

Christian charity to the penitent. This new caste system could not work at the lower levels of the colony, but at the top it was pursued by some with zeal.

The higher officials were all 'place men' of English politicians; some, in the fashion of the day, held several offices at once; many squabbled with each other; most were not much good at their jobs; and at times almost all of them seemed to be arguing about what there was to be in it for them. Some disputed the Governor's power, seeing themselves as directly responsible to particular authorities in London; the military and civil officers who sat in the courts sometimes used their independence as a weapon against the Governor; and some of the colony's officials – most notably the chaplain – were in a state of almost continued campaign against him. The petty officials, who were nearly all convicts or ex-convicts, saw bribery and fraud as part of their natural reward.

As comforting in its familiarity as the administrative muddle was the parsimony of the time. Although New South Wales was a convict colony there was not enough government money to build even a jail. When the thatched wooden jail of one of the early governors was burnt down he

Founder: Captain Arthur Phillip

Captain Arthur Phillip, the first Governor of New South Wales, was born in London in 1738; his father was a language teacher from Frankfurt, and his mother had connections with the Royal Navy. Phillip embarked on a seafaring career that took him both on active service, including a period as a captain in the Portuguese Navy, and on survey work; he also farmed in Hampshire after the end of an unhappy first marriage in 1769.

An 18th century rationalist, sensitive and self-sacrificing, with a solid rather than an outstanding record, Phillip was a suitable choice to found a colony, although some say he was a hurried appointment to a position no one else wanted. Sadly, he did not see eventuate his vision of New South Wales as a settlement of free colonists; only 13 emigrants sailed from Britain in the settlement's first five years, and none arrived until after his departure.

Phillip's policy was to try to reform the convicts; to treat the Aborigines kindly; to be just and humane, and to be fair – in the lean, early years he insisted on rations being shared equally. Unlike many of his contemporaries he understood the importance of rewarding good conduct as well as punishing bad.

But scarcely anyone shared Phillip's vision in a settlement described by one of his enemies as 'the outcast of God's works'.

Builder: Governor Lachlan Macquarie

Scottish-born Lachlan Macquarie became Governor of New South Wales unexpectedly. Although he was a cousin of the 16th and last chieftain of the Clan Macquarie, the family into which he was born in 1762 was poor, and he had to make his way in the world. This he achieved through the army, marriage to a rich heiress (who died, to his great grief, three years after the wedding), a charming personality and an assiduous eye for promotion.

Shortly after his second marriage, in 1808, to a kinswoman, Elizabeth Campbell, Macquarie's regiment was posted to New South Wales and by a combination of luck and influence he went as Governor rather than just a regimental lieutenant colonel: Major General Miles Nightingall declined to accept the position of governor and Macquarie successfully promoted himself as a suitable replacement.

After his 12 years as Governor, when he left in February 1822 Macquarie was pleased with the mark he had made on the colony: he had initiated an adventurous building program, encouraged exploration, and played a part in introducing a proper coinage and setting up the first bank.

But his most spectacular contribution to the colony was, unexpectedly for him, to make his retirement an unhappy one. He had been instructed to improve the morals of the colony, which he sought to do by re-admitting certain ex-convicts, the Emancipists, to society. But Macquarie's practical-minded humanitarianism enraged the Exclusives with their powerful friends in London.

Macquarie was shattered when Commissioner John Bigge, who had been sent to conduct an inquiry into the colony, released his report in 1822: he accepted the evidence of Macquarie's enemies and was critical of his governorship.

Sydney's Government House – to be invited to dine there was to have arrived in society.

had to impose special levies to finance the building of a stone one. Fed by special fees, levies and licences, the Gaol Fund he established became one of the colony's two sources of independent revenue, the other being the Orphan Fund, which was similarly provided. The Gaol Fund then became the principal source of money for public works, the Orphan Fund for public schools. It told something of the nature of the colony that its two departments of exchequer were called the Gaol Fund and the Orphan Fund. Sydney Hospital was built by giving three contractors a semi-monopoly in the sale of rum. There was no purse for civic pride: for a while, using Francis Greenway, an ex-convict, as architect, Governor Lachlan Macquarie tried to give a sense of order to Sydney and its smaller towns by erecting public buildings; but attacks on such extravagance were among the reasons for his recall.

Whatever attacks there were on the Governor, to be invited to dine at Government House was to have arrived (even if, as the colony's first brick building, put up at a time when the mysteries of turning Australian clay into true English bricks had not altogether been solved, it was in danger of falling down). A governor was something

different from what offered in a provincial English town, and if less than a lord he was more accessible. The colony was short on official ceremony and belief, but such official ritual as it had was the expression of its loyalty to the British monarch, and to the mysteries of this loyalty a governor, whatever one thought of him as a man, held the key. He presided over celebrations of the royal birthdays and national days; one governor ordered the colony into a week's inactivity to mourn the death of an English princess.

But a governor was less a social arbiter than were the transient English regimental garrisons, which could more easily despise any habits that had become peculiar to the colony. Boasted of as the biggest and best outside Britain, the newly built Barracks was much larger than Government House and dominated the town; the garrison's band played in the park, its red coats gave colour to the streets; its officers defended their position at the top of the colony's hierarchy with a militant attitude of snubs to all colonial upstarts. In particular – although the officers, like their men, took convict mistresses and enjoyed the gambling dens, grog shops and brothels run by ex-convicts in the Rocks area of Sydney – they were the leaders of

The Antipodes observed:
European naturalists were amazed as drawings began to arrive of the new continent's wildlife. Australia seemed to be a very strange place.

those who enjoyed the distinction of having come to the colony as free men.

It was the officers of the five successive military garrisons who provided the governors' most public opposition. Only a few months after the settlement began a captain of marines wrote to an English lord saying of Phillip, 'I do not think (*entre nous*) that your three kingdoms could produce another man, in my opinion, so totally unqualified for the business he has taken in hand as this man is'. The specially formed New South Wales Corps (the Rum Corps) that followed the marines boycotted Governor Hunter and secured his recall; later it went so far as to depose Governor Bligh, and for a while ran the colony. When the Corps was disbanded and replaced in turn by three conventional regiments, officers of each of these took sides against Governor Macquarie and attempted to humiliate him.

Nevertheless, by 1820 the colony had more confidence in itself. For one thing, in London the House of Commons was beginning to take an interest, in 1819 appointing Commissioner John Bigge to go to New South Wales and recommend what should be done about it. Amateur collectors sent plants to London, where they became exotics in English glasshouses; birds were described and new specimens made known through European publications; hundreds of drawings were done of native plants, fish, insects, animals and humans; whole landscapes were painted, presenting the colony as an English nobleman's park or as a drab, monotonous wilderness. In 1819 the first book by a native-born colonist was published in London. In the same year a colonial official, who had been a friend of Leigh Hunt and Charles and Mary Lamb, published in Sydney the colony's first volume of verse. He described the south land as not part of the work of initial creation but 'an afterbirth, not conceived in the Beginning . . . but emerged at the first sinning'.

'Thus we hope to prosper' was the motto of the colony's one newspaper, The Sydney Gazette and New South Wales Advertiser, *first published in 1803.*

With its excellent harbour, Sydney (below) soon became one of the busy ports of Britain's maritime empire. The colonists seemed destined to become a maritime and trading people.

Images of progress:
Governor Macquarie commissioned the convict forger Joseph Lycett to paint a series of views illustrating colonial progress. They included the penal settlement of Newcastle (above left), established as a place of secondary punishment in 1801, and Hobart Town (left), established in 1804.

It had taken years for the colony to be sure it would not starve. The soil was mostly water-hungry sand or hard clay. The seasons were upside down. There were no native crops, and what there was of native game was difficult to shoot, and fish were hard to catch.

'In the whole world there is not a worse country than what we have seen of this,' wrote one of the first officers. 'The colony is never likely to answer the wishes and expectations of Government,' wrote another. 'The Nation would save money by feeding the convicts at home upon Venison and Claret – clothing them in Purple and Gold.'

The plain that had limited the horizons of settlement ran about 64 kilometres along the coast, and at its widest almost 55 kilometres inland, all of it hemmed in by the foothills and cliffs of a bushy sandstone plateau. Within the plain, among the sand or clay, there were isolated stretches of useful soils, but they quickly lost their goodness and the richer river flats were often flooded. Settlement had hopped desperately all over the plain. As each new area proved disappointing, another was tried. For a season the river flats

As settlement slowly spread, a settler's success or failure could be indicated by the type of house he lived in. Some settlers lived in primitive huts (above), and others set about carving for themselves a picture of English order from the surrounding native bush (below).

The land frontier: *scarcely any land exploration had been undertaken when John Oxley attempted to follow the Lachlan River in 1817. He found himself in impenetrable swamps – the first of many such frustrations. A travel book engraving (above) by Jacques Macarthy portrays Oxley bringing 'civilisation to the wilderness'.*

of the Nepean-Hawkesbury – an arc almost completely surrounding the landward side of the plain – were compared with those of the Nile, but when there were four floods in two years another hope was washed away. Dominant for 30 years, the inhospitable plain on which the colony was established was a frontier that could make human endeavour seem absurd. Of the whole population of 24 000 in New South Wales, half stayed in town.

To the north of Sydney a couple of dozen farms had spread along the black flood soils of the Hunter River; to the south, where timber getters were felling the rain forests, there were a few grants for grazing, as there were in the west, opened up when a way had been found across the ridges of the sandstone mountains. But the interior was still a secret, the mystery of its westward-flowing rivers unsolved. Did they turn and flow into the ocean? Did they flow into a great inland sea? Two exploring parties lost their answer in swamps and reeds. There seemed an impassable limit to further expansion.

For farmers, there were the consolations or sorrows of a sardonic luck – the good luck of a governor's favour or of suitable soil, the bad luck of a flood or a drought. Many

The sea frontier: *the real expansions were by sea. Sydney had its own shipyards (right) and the merchant Robert Campbell had established his own warehouse and wharf (left). The colony's first substantial exports were the skins of seals clubbed by sealers (above).*

farmers failed and lost their farms. Those who failed but stuck it out lived in tiny bark huts, growing potatoes and running pigs and goats, perhaps supplementing this by also working for wages. They were so poor that the colonists named them the 'dungaree settlers', after the cheap Indian calico of their clothes, and if their wives, who worked beside them, came to town, they were likely to be recognised and pointed out. They walked barefoot and wore homespun clothes. Most of the other settlers lived in slab cottages from which, if they were married, husband and wife ran small holdings on which there might be some sheep or cattle. But the main concern was growing grain: wheat to sell to the government store for money or credit that would buy tea, sugar, tobacco, spirits and perhaps a little salt meat, and maize, from which to grind their flour.

Whether settlers saw themselves as successes or failures depended on their own expectations. The few who had been favoured lived in comfortable verandaed houses of brick or stone, surrounded by gardens and orchards, with their work done by convicts. Originally, all the land had been government grants – big grants for big men, little grants for little men – but how the land was first granted no longer

mattered. Those who had lost their chances had lost them.

More immediate opportunity had come from the sea. To the south, the islands of Bass Strait swarmed with seals; the business of clubbing and skinning tens of thousands of them had set small associated enterprises going in Sydney – shipmaking, provisioning trading. When most of the seals had been clubbed, merchants looked to the Fiji Islands where muskets or axes could be bartered for sandalwood incense and bêche-de-mer, or to Tahiti, where there was trade for salt pork.

Most of the expansion even of land frontiers had been by ship. In 1801, when Sydney decided to set up its own colony 160 kilometres north on the coast, it was by ship that the expedition had set off for what was to become Newcastle. The next two sub-colonies, established in fear of the French, were also on the coast, on the island of Van Diemen's Land, 800 kilometres south of Sydney. If the 27 000 people of New South Wales and Van Diemen's Land were to become anything, it seemed that, in the British tradition, it would be as a maritime and trading people.

The habits of trading had been harsh, beginning with even a scarcity of coins. Since in the late 18th century Great

Britain was generally short of coins, it was more than ten years before any official consignments reached New South Wales, and then they were only batches of pennies, halfpennies and farthings. Ducats, guilders and rupees drifted into the colony from trading vessels but it was not until 1813 that the first big consignment arrived – $10 000 worth of Spanish dollars from India – and this was so insufficient that the Governor ordered that 'dumps' be stamped out of the middle of them so that each coin could become two. For their own buying and selling the colonists had to rely mainly on IOUs, or on receipts from the Commissariat, the government store; receipts and IOUs passed from hand to hand, more or less as banknotes. In the early days rum was all that many would accept as wages, and it became an important form of currency. When the use of spirits was later brought under control, a currency crisis occurred. What was there worth working for now?

To buy foreign goods, foreign currency was needed and with hardly any exports the colony had hardly any foreign currency. This made the colony's officers its first traders: they were the main holders of internationally negotiable paper, in the form of Treasury bills from London, obtained

privately as pay, or by fiddling regimental funds; and with it they alone could buy the cargoes that came to Sydney. When it became clear that ships' captains were using their monopoly to extort high prices, the officers formed a buyers' ring, which forced down the price of cargoes by making only one offer for them; then they would split the cargoes, mark up the prices and, to avoid despoiling their rank as gentlemen, sell the goods through some of the 'pedlars, dealers and extortioners' of the colony, who marked up the prices again. The success of this monopoly increased when, during an interregnum between governors, the officers helped themselves to other privileges. News of it attracted to Sydney merchants looking for new ways of making money.

By 1800 the officers' trading ring began to break, partly because of the arrival of the professionals, partly because the Commissariat was now issuing more Treasury bills than the officers could monopolise and partly because some of the ex-convict dealers of the 1790s, formerly intermediaries for the officers, had accumulated enough money and skills and more than enough nerve and energy to emerge in their own right. From then on most military and civil officers tried to make or increase their fortunes by farming rather than by trading; and most exceptions were junior partners of the new men. Trade was becoming too tough for amateurs.

By 1820 the survivors of the colony's many commercial disasters were grouped into 12 main mercantile houses. As well as trading, they experimented in manufacturing and, by purchase or by supplying goods against secured mortgages and then foreclosing, they built up some of the biggest landed properties in the colony. They dined with each other in their town houses or on their country estates, and their children tended to intermarry. An ex-convict was the most prominent of them, two other ex-convicts were important. Below them on the money scale there were several hundred petty dealers, shopkeepers, innkeepers and

promissory note

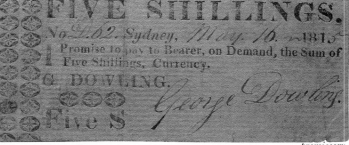

promissory note

French écu

Dutch guilder

Finding a currency: *for decades the colony was short of coins and used whatever came in, from Dutch guilders to French écus. When in 1813 the first big consignment arrived – of Spanish dollars – the Governor ordered that 'dumps' be stamped out of the middle of the dollars. Each coin became two – a 'holey dollar', and a 'dump'. The colony relied more on bills of exchange and promissory notes than coins. On occasions, payment was in rum.*

front of a dump

holey dollar

back of a dump

bill of exchange

rum mug

self-employed tradesmen. Below these, about a fifth of the total work force (including convicts) claimed to know some sort of trade; then came the unskilled, who if free took their work where they could find it, mainly in building, timber working or shipping.

In a colony which was half town, traders and dealers were an important part of its frontier. There was an unusually high amount of litigiousness, harshness and fretfulness as, to the atmosphere of a convict colony there was added the 'prevailing impulse of truck and cavil' of a commercial society of enormous risk. A significant part of its tone was hardheaded and individualistic. This individualism further inflamed the colony's peculiarly autocratic character. There was no other colony with such a despotic constitution. New South Wales enjoyed none of the oligarchic freedom of Britain. The rule of law was that of court martial; the Governor was the sole legislator, the chief executive and the only court of appeal. He could forbid public meetings; there was no religious freedom; and the colony's one newspaper came out at his pleasure. He could parcel out land, and as the main controller of labour he handed out human beings like a slave master. The Commissariat was the colony's largest trader and biggest employer; its buying, selling, price-fixing, lending and control of international currency made it the central part of the economy. Even if this had not been so, the inadequacies of the soil and the seasons would have demanded strong action from the governors.

Although they were masterful individualists, those who were making the most money out of the colony did not oppose government; they saw it as something that was expected to assist them and be put to their purposes. In this they added to the frustrations of the governors. There had been four after Phillip, three naval officers and an army officer, each appointed to clean up the mess his predecessor had left, each frustrated and living out the rest of his time in England with a sense of resentment. To the shortage of money, the lack of experience of the principal labourers, the inadequacies of the land, the corruption of petty officers and the quarrelsomeness of great ones, the masterful individualists added the exploitation of a governor's greatest weakness; his despotism was limited by the fact that his proclamations had to be countersigned in London, and they were often queried. Before a reply was given it might have to take into account the demands of other departments of government, theories in the British Parliament about how the colony should be run, or pressures from groups such as the whaling interest or the East India Company. Only then could the Governor of New South Wales learn the reaction in London to some action he had taken more than 12 months before. And to these lobbying groups were added the conflicting factions of the colonists who were building the biggest holdings in the colony.

As well as the local insults of the military there were disagreements between traders and the larger landowners. Some would support the Governor because he supported them, others would attack him because he did not take their side. Increasingly, the insults offered by the passing military merely gave public colour to these domestic contentions. One of the true 'frontiers' for the 'individualists' of New South Wales was in the exploitation not of its soil but of its government.

Most of the hard work of transplanting Western European civilisation to Australia was done by thieves. Some of those transported were Luddites who had tried to smash the new machines, Irish rebels or other kinds of political prisoners, but 80 per cent of those transported had been sentenced for larceny.

By 1820 almost three-quarters of the total adult population were convicts or ex-convicts, and at least four out of five of the colony's young were the children of convicts.

The process of turning a thief into a colonist began when a convict transport sailed into Sydney Harbour. The convicts were lined up on the quarterdeck, questioned by the Superintendent of Convicts, exhorted to improve themselves by the Governor or the Judge Advocate and then sorted out. Most of the women were assigned to domestic service; those remaining were sent to the Female Factory at Parramatta. The few gentlemen convicts and convicts with special talents or money were usually given a ticket of leave as soon as they arrived, which considerably increased their prospect of self-improvement. Of the others,

First businesswoman: Mary Reibey

Mary Haydock, as a high-spirited 13-year-old dressed as a boy, was arrested in 1790 for horse stealing and sentenced to seven years transportation to New South Wales. In the colony she worked as a nursemaid, and at 17 married a young Irishman, Thomas Reibey, who had been in the service of the East India Company; he was apparently the first free settler-trader who was not a member of the military. Widowed at 34 with seven children, Mary continued to expand the business interests her husband had established – in hotel keeping, ship owning, trading and farming – and developed some of her own, mainly as a property developer and investor.

In her forties, she took her daughters back to her birthplace in Lancashire and was reported to have been received with 'interest and admiration'. She was respected in the new Emancipist society of Governor Macquarie for her involvement with religion, education and charity.

She was a model of improvement, but it was improvement based on hard, practical common sense: the only conviction against her in the colony was that in 1817 she was found guilty at Windsor, New South Wales, of bodily assault – ironically upon one of her debtors.

those judged most useful would be picked as petty officials, overseers, superintendents, police or clerks, or to work in the government establishments or construction gangs. (Thus, how a convict was treated depended not on his offence, but on his capacity to work.) Those expected to be most troublesome were usually sent to Van Diemen's Land.

In their home cities most thieves understood best the criminal's morality: that virtue consists in trickery and sharpness of wit and its reward is the freedom of idleness. But although, in the criminal manner, used to a life of heroism and leisure in circumstances of extreme poverty and squalor, when they arrived in Sydney they were put to *work*. Since opposition to work was the whole ethic of many of them it is not surprising that there were complaints of their indolence. Many of their offences against the authority of the colony were those of cheeky high spirits – they got drunk; they were absent without leave; they pretended to be sick when they weren't; they lay around in bed; they poked fun at people; they didn't salute; they refused to put out the light. And they resisted work with sufficient subtlety to force the authorities into two concessions – that the afternoons were 'their own time', which they could spend in leisure, or 'on their own hands' (working away from their masters). Even at work there were unofficial agreements about the limits of how much they might be expected to do.

The reaction of many to the system was to try to cheat it; the reaction of the system was to flog them. Although most masters preferred to try kindly firmness, floggings became an essential part of the colony's business, and as such they had their own system of control: only magistrates could order floggings; only authorised floggers could do the flogging; and in the towns the floggings were carried on behind the walls of barracks or jails. About two out of five of the convicts were flogged at least once. A short hearing before a magistrate and then a quick flogging cost the colony nothing and allowed the victim to be put back to work fairly quickly.

Symbols of oppression: *only magistrates could order floggings, and only authorised floggers could administer the punishment (left). A cat-o'-nine-tails (above) was the usual instrument of flogging, but other methods, such as stocks, were also used. At Parramatta (below) the stocks were at the bottom of the hill by the road that led to Government House.*

The rebels: *in England, a popular view of the convicts was provided by the visiting artist Augustus Earle in A* Government Jail Gang, Sydney *(left).*

About one convict in ten was not caught doing anything wrong and received no punishment; the majority offended authority a little and received some punishment, if only an admonition; another group ('the flash mob') did everything wrong. Lost in a hell of rebellion and retribution, they were flogged, sentenced to labour in road gangs, or abandoned in chains on the beaches of Newcastle to burn shells for lime. About one in a hundred was hanged, in a public execution where great attention was paid to 'the kind of death' a convict 'made'. People would discuss this later – was it cowardly? shameless? penitent? brave? – as if they had been to a play.

Since only about one in seven were women, the convicts' was a man's society, depending mainly on prostitution or homosexuality for its shared sexual pleasures. Its language was thieves' slang, providing some of the first contributions to the English that was spoken in the colony. (The dominant group were the cockneys, flash-talking 'townies', adept at collective bullying.) It was a society of desperate gambling (convicts staking the clothes off their backs even stood naked while the game went on) and hard drinking. It could be presented as one of the most foul-mouthed,

licentious and drunken societies ever to have existed, although possibly it was no more drunken or licentious than society back home; it may have been only the fact that it was convicts who were indulging themselves that made the colony appear uniquely depraved.

To these rebellions of the flesh there was added a rebellion of race. Within the suppression of the convicts there was another suppression – of the Irish. About a quarter of the convicts were Irish and, although in their court convictions they tended more than the English to crimes of violence and acts of insubordination against the State, even the jailers sometimes pitied their bewilderment and felt sympathy for their anxiety to oblige and their desire to make something more of their lives. There were fewer

The bad luck of the Irish: *in the early 1800s the Irish, many of whom had been transported for political offences, were a suppressed race among the convicts. The Catholic Mass was illegal and the Irish were regarded almost as foreigners, with a different culture. There was a tradition of rebellion in Ireland, and when, in 1804, Irish convicts mutinied at Castle Hill in New South Wales, it was just what the English had expected.*

The passions were still high among many Irish convicts with memories of the defeat of the Irish rebel army by the British at New Ross in 1798, when the Irish charged into the cannon's mouth (left). A contemporary sketch of the uprising of Irish convicts at Castle Hill in 1804 (below left) is a reminder that six years later the Irish had hoped to win, at Castle Hill, the victory they had failed to win at New Ross in Ireland.

A beggar's badge (above) issued by the authorities of St Patrick's Parish, Dublin, to the deserving poor. It was the equivalent of a local licence to beg.

professional criminals among them; the predicament of many was that of destitute or near-destitute peasants who lived in the most poverty-stricken country of Western Europe, in such deprived circumstances that it was natural for there to be an understanding and pleasantness between persons, and also a violence. Of those transported in the first 15 years about 600 (three priests among them) had been sentenced for riot and sedition, most for taking part in the Irish uprisings at the end of the 18th century. In the colony there were from time to time rumours that the Irish were planning revolt: the rumours proved true in 1804 when it was heard in Sydney that a group of them had armed, seized Castle Hill and, with the cry 'Death – or liberty and a ship to take us home', was planning to take Parramatta, then Sydney. Fifteen were shot, nine hanged, a number flogged and

Sydney was not a jail, it was a penal settlement in which the convicts moved around freely at their tasks. Major James Taylor's panorama of 1820 shows, on the left, a government gang working under supervision. On the right are 'assigned' convicts working for a master; one of them, a female convict in mob cap and apron, acts as nursemaid.

50 others were sent in chains to the beaches of Newcastle.

Living under English laws, and for the most part illiterate and bereft of property, the Irish convicts held to the Catholic faith: to many even this lacked much particular meaning, but it was what they had. Yet as Catholics they were forbidden the Mass. Two priests had volunteered to go as chaplains to the colony at its beginning, paying their own expenses, but their offer was refused; apart from a brief period of toleration, which ended in mutiny in 1804, the celebration of Mass was illegal and Catholics could be forced to attend Church of England services. Probably with authority's connivance, ex-convict priests did perform some surreptitious Masses, but after 1808 there were no priests until one arrived in 1817. He was without civil authority and when he began to celebrate Mass he was arrested and deported. It was not until 1820, after the House of Commons had been stirred by this deportation and after Rome had finally designated a vicariate stretching across the Indian Ocean from Cape Town to Sydney, that two Irish chaplains arrived, their salaries paid by the British Government. They were greeted with friendship; they might help keep the Irish in order.

Some convicts were insubordinate, indolent or drunken, but among others there was a contrary drive to respectability that was pursued with such success that the conformity of some received as much comment as the rebelliousness of others. The drive to respectability was aided by the opportunity for most convicts to live some sort of a civilian life. The colony was only a jail to the extent that it was surrounded by bush and sea. The majority of convicts were assigned to private masters, who provided lodging, food and clothing in return for their labour. (A married convict could be assigned to his wife.) If a convict was assigned to a well-to-do master he might live comfortably, by the colony's standards; if the master was poor his assigned convict would live as badly as he did. But since an assigned man could work for someone else in his own time he could add to what he was given by his master. Most convicts ate more and worked less than most working men in England. For much of this period even the government-employed convicts did not live in barracks in Sydney: they were given time off to work for private masters, paying for their lodging out of whatever extra they earned. Convicts wore no uniform at the time; there was no

way for the innocent observer to judge by dress or place of living or by manners who were convicts, who were ex-convicts or who were the few who came free.

By being sent to New South Wales young criminals were given another chance to adopt the habits of the law-abiding, and this time it was made easier because of continuing labour shortages. Many were pardoned before their time was up and, like those who fully served their sentences, they could take up a small land grant of 12 hectares, plus eight for a wife, plus four for a child, with convicts assigned to them for labour. Some paid their passages home; others absconded; most stayed. Of those who stayed, almost all gave up crime. It is true that for most of them honesty had to be its own reward and they had to live out their lives on short measure – there were not enough wives to go around and they worked as labourers for masters, many of whom were themselves ex-convicts – but a significant minority did better themselves by becoming farmers or tradesmen. A few, who arrived when the colony was full of pickings, did very well; one became the colony's second biggest landholder, another became one of its biggest merchants. (Having been transported for

stealing muslin and calico, he ended his career as a textile manufacturer.)

Some ex-convicts found it easy to make an honest living because they were really law-accepting people who had merely broken the law. ('All a man has got to mind is to keep a still tongue in his head and do his master's duty and then he is looked upon as if he were at home.') Others, although criminals by belief, accepted the opportunity to take up a working life. By 1820 these two classes of people had gained sufficient economic strength to provide an implicit challenge to the older standards of the colony; they included a few rich merchants, they provided most of the tradesmen, and although they held only about a third of the total land granted they were producing nearly three-quarters of the colony's grain, half its cattle and a third of its sheep. Whether they were big men or small, those who had hoisted themselves up in the world of the colony's economic activity were now beginning to see its development as mainly *their* work and its future as mainly *their* business.

Great tact was used to avoid the word 'convict' – 'government men' and 'assigned servants' were preferred,

and the term 'ex-convict' was never used. 'Settler' applied to ex-convicts as much as to other farmers, and, as well as 'freed man', the euphemism 'Emancipist' had been coined, suggesting by its suffix not so much one on whom a freedom had been conferred as one who himself conferred freedom. It was to Emancipists with social pretensions that the garrison and its civilian associates were most hostile: the officers of one regiment bound themselves by oath to have nothing to do with successful Emancipists; when Governor Macquarie invited some of them to his table the regiment snubbed the Governor. But the Emancipists enjoyed a compensating pride in Macquarie's presumptuous belief that it was the Emancipists who had made the colony what it was and the Emancipists who held an exclusive right to the possession of whatever it had to offer. When this was linked with social success it created a unique concept of a self-made man. The Emancipists who had made it had made it twice over.

On the whole, as a place of punishment, the object is scarcely gained; as a real system of reform it has failed, as perhaps would every other plan, but as a means of making men outwardly honest – of converting vagabonds, most useless in one hemisphere, into

A convict pass, permitting the bearer, 'a Sawyer employed at the Lumber yard', to go from Parramatta to Sydney.

A Spanish visitor's view of Parramatta: *the comparative orderliness of the convict system was a constant wonder to visitors (above).*

'In their own time' (left) convicts could do what they wished: washing, gardening, grind wheat into flour.

active citizens of another . . . it has succeeded to a degree perhaps unparalleled in history.

Charles Darwin's comment was made at a later date, but it applied even more aptly to this earlier period. The British Government had found a way of turning thieves into honest or more or less honest workers. Beneath the superciliousness and snobberies on top, there was underneath, as well as the drunkenness and gambling and whoring, a contrary drive to achieve a degree of respectability. In a society in which an officer of the colony who had not done particularly well for himself might find it tempting to allow his daughter to marry the son of a merchant who had come to the colony as a convict, or in which an ex-noncommissioned officer who failed as a small settler might find himself in much the same situation as an ex-convict who also failed as a small settler, some were of necessity developing a tolerance of a person's past. It was a society in which even the very least people could achieve respectability.

There was little other impulse: in the whole history of European expansion there were few other European settlements founded with such an official indifference to

Christianity as New South Wales. The Church of England held a monopoly, but this was merely a convention of state: in the style of a sceptical age no importance was given to religion as a mainspring. Only one chaplain came out with the First Fleet, and he had to wait five years for a church. He conducted services under a tree, in a storeroom, in a boatshed, and when he was able to build a church it was only a wattle and daub affair with a thatched roof that convicts burned down five years later in protest against a new rule demanding compulsory church attendance. His successor was the only chaplain for nine years, and had to make do with chatachists until three assistant chaplains were appointed. But towards the end of the colony's third decade there was a small flourish of church building. Other than this, the Wesleyans had a chapel, put up in 1819, and immigrants from the Scottish border built a Presbyterian Church, which was without a minister. For most of this time the Catholic Mass was still banned.

Such official religious drive as existed was of the evangelical kind, and along with squabbling and anxious clinging to expatriate prestige, evangelical moralism began to set some of the tone of the colony, or at least some of its

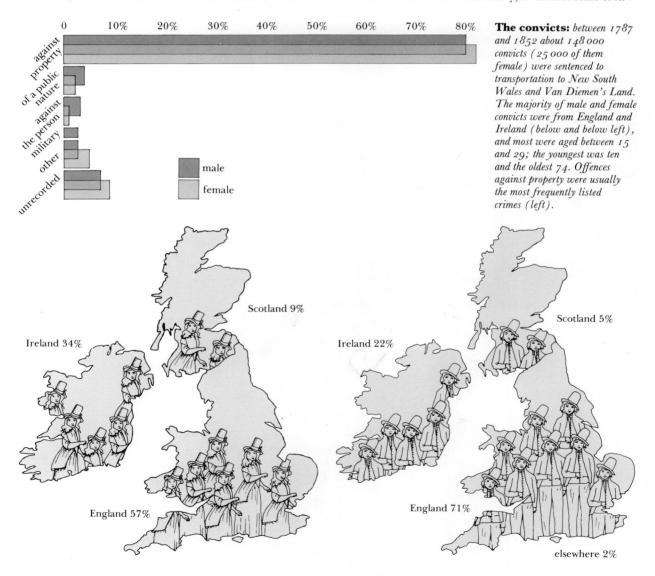

The convicts: *between 1787 and 1852 about 148 000 convicts (25 000 of them female) were sentenced to transportation to New South Wales and Van Diemen's Land. The majority of male and female convicts were from England and Ireland (below and below left), and most were aged between 15 and 29; the youngest was ten and the oldest 74. Offences against property were usually the most frequently listed crimes (left).*

male
female

Scotland 9%
Ireland 34%
England 57%

Scotland 5%
Ireland 22%
England 71%
elsewhere 2%

ambition. Two of the first five governors and both the chaplains were evangelists; the headmasters of the two Orphan Schools were Wesleyans; there was a sprinkling of evangelists among other colonial officials; the one newspaper, when it moralised, did so with exhortations of self-improvement.

Religion was a matter of reaching a state of personal grace by reading the Bible, respecting the Sabbath and following abstemious habits: some of its main drives were regulations and prohibition. In the third decade there were official attempts at an enforced Sabbatarianism, rules against gambling, reduction in the number of inns, and attempts to reduce the use of women convicts as concubines. The evangelicals paid special attention to the women convicts, whom they could find 'highly disgusting' in their immodest dress and 'violent and indecent language' and whom, unlike the men, they wanted to lock up in institutions to keep them from temptation. One evangelical went so far as to speak of the women arriving in the transports with their 'rich silk dresses, bonnets à la mode, ear pendants three inches long, gorgeous shawls and splendid veils, kid gloves and parasols in hand and

dispensing sweet odours'. Yet, as with the perceptions of drunkenness, these may have been exaggerations that existed mainly in the eyes of the beholders. What was common in Britain could seem outlandish in the colony because these women were convicts. Or perhaps it was because these convicts were women.

In a convict colony a stress on self-improvement was understandable. With the spread of evangelism, to the convenience of such a doctrine (reform made it easier to run the colony) there was added moral belief. Not a great deal else was added. There were three Benevolent Societies, a Sunday School movement was started, and in addition to the colony's 11 private schools there were 15 government schools – although only one in eight of the colony's children went to them. Perhaps the greatest success in the drive for self-government was the establishment of a savings bank in 1817, designed to tempt 'poor settlers, mechanics, servants and labourers' not to waste their money on drink and gambling, which would leave them 'poor, vicious and unmarried', but to bank it and so learn the pleasures of 'economy, industry and matrimony'. It was by such means, after a long silence, that the faith of the colony was proclaimed – as one of respectability.

Although most of the convict men died without leaving families the convicts were not to prove an extinct race. They were to found what was quickly accepted as a new kind of people. From the marriages into which about one in ten of them entered, or from the taking of mistresses or from prostitution there came the first generation of native-born Australians, the Currency Lads and the Currency Lasses (to distinguish them from the 'sterling' of the British-born) at once believed by observers to be a distinctive type.

As the children of the convicts grew into men and women they were, generally speaking, 'self-respecting, moral, law-

The evangelicals: *there was small concern with religion in the founding of the colonies, apart from the evangelicals with their insistence on respectability as the principal virtue. The most famous evangelicals were Chaplain Samuel Marsden (left) and his wife, Elizabeth (below left). Marsden became notorious among the convicts for his severity as a magistrate at Parramatta and for his bitter opposition to Governor Macquarie.*

An impression of the first church built in Sydney, which was burned down by the convicts.

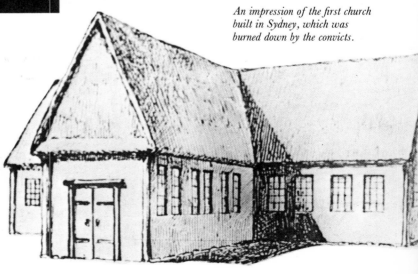

abiding, industrious and surprisingly sober'. Whatever the changes in the convicts themselves, they were not so great as this extraordinary change between the generations. Perhaps this came partly from the not unusual reaction of the children of immigrants, that they should be ashamed of their parents: with, in this case, a special contempt for what was seen as vice and depravity, and with the special circumstances that a large minority of the children were illegitimate. Only a sixth of them went to school; a convict's child could be out in the world at ten years old, earning good wages, and at 13 'a perfect little man, learned in all the ways and byways of life'. In this they were aided by the colony's almost continuous shortage of willing labour. Some of their sense of independence may have come from this economic opportunity for early self-reliance: but perhaps it was also part of their inheritance, freed of the shiftlessness of their parents.

The first native-born white Australians were soon being described as tall, slim, tough and active; although at times awkward and quick-tempered, they were taken to be well-meaning; they were believed to be at all times self-reliant and resourceful; they were the custodians of the colonial style and they knew how one was supposed to behave in New South Wales.

Colonists were now looking for some other name for the huge island in one little bit of which they were living. Naval men had begun to turn the old 'Terra Australis' into the new 'Australia', and by 1817 Governor Macquarie was using this word in his dispatches. At a party of 40 people held in the house of one successful Emancipist on 27 January to celebrate the colony's foundation, a song was sung to the tune of 'Rule Britannia', which, after suggesting that Australia's rise was Neptune's wish, bore the injunction 'Rise, Australia! with peace and plenty crowned. Thy name shall one day be renowned', and concluded with the boast that, 'While Europe's powers in conflict do Exhaust the Flower of the brave, Here peace shall flourish – None conspire with human blood their soil to lave.'

The native-born could hardly describe themselves cumbrously as 'New South Welshmen'. But they needed some way of talking about themselves beyond Currency Lad and Currency Lass; they began to find it in the new word 'Australian'. The belief began to stir that there might be some pride in being Australians.

The Convict Barracks in Sydney, designed by Francis Greenway in 1817.

Arrogant brilliance: Francis Greenway

Descended from generations of stonemasons, architects and builders, Francis Greenway was 35 and practising as an architect in Bristol when, in 1812, he was sentenced to death for forging a document. His sentence was commuted to 14 years transportation. As a privileged convict of the professional classes, he established himself in private architectural practice as soon as he arrived in Sydney in 1814; his wife and three children followed.

Greenway was an arrogant, temperamental, brilliant architect. His graceful but substantial buildings, constructed between 1816 and 1827 in the government service to which Governor Macquarie had appointed him, gave Sydney and its surroundings an air of permanence that would have astonished some of the colony's first arrivals.

Apart from his quarrelsome nature, Greenway's downfall was caused by an extravagant design for a new Government House, which in turn made him a victim of the political jockeying that resulted from Commissioner John Bigge's enquiry into the colony. When Governor Macquarie returned to England, Greenway was left with few friends; he lost his job, and thereafter found few significant commissions. His wife, Mary, opened a small school to help pay the household bills.

Greenway made large claims on the government for architectural fees, and he was discontented with his land grant of 800 marshy acres (320 hectares) on the Hawkesbury River. But he did achieve one victory, sardonic given the circumstances of his arrival in the colony: when he lost his job, he refused to give up the house that went with it, and produced a document giving him the title. The document is now thought to be a forgery.

Pushing away the blacks

The black people whose predecessors had first discovered the continent were now being pushed out of the way. The British Government considered that since the black people did not cultivate the land, it was 'uninhabited' – a kind of no-man's-land – and they had no title to it. It did not have to be conquered, there was no need even to exchange axes or blankets for marks on paper; this land had now become the property of the English king.

The general instructions were to try to gain the friendship of the 'natives', but since they had no tribal structures that could organise or sustain resistance of a kind the invaders would recognise as resistance, or provide some kind of negotiation, the natives could be got out of the way without friendship. But not without trouble; they retaliated with spearings. In the British occupation of the Hawkesbury River district there was a six-year 'Black War', and there were later 'emergencies'.

It was usually incomprehensible to the natives that they could not still take whatever food, including the strangers' animals, they could find on their old hunting territories, but to the settlers, the natives were troublesome and sometimes destructive animals rather than human beings. By decision of the English king, the natives were British subjects, bound to the king's law, with their own laws unrecognised and largely unknown; so if they gave trouble they were treated not as a people resisting invaders, but as criminals. In Van Diemen's Land in 1804 some Royal Marines killed 50 natives because they were armed. They did not realise that the natives were armed for hunting, not raiding.

It had been the British Government's theory that, as part of the lower orders of the colony, the natives would learn the benefits of a superior civilisation and, with industry and sobriety, take their modest place as labourers or as small farmers, converted to Christianity and protected by British law. But what the natives most saw of the new civilisation was its anarchy and barbarity: its land thefts, its peculiar internal institutions such as flogging, chaining men together, hierarchic social divisions, ritual drunkenness, and its individualism that defied the great principles of community and reciprocity. It was not long before it

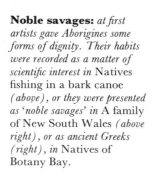

Noble savages: *at first artists gave Aborigines some forms of dignity. Their habits were recorded as a matter of scientific interest in* Natives fishing in a bark canoe *(above), or they were presented as 'noble savages' in* A family of New South Wales *(above right), or as ancient Greeks (right), in* Natives of Botany Bay.

became an alternative amusement to cockfights for the invaders to get a couple of natives drunk and set them against each other.

A Native Institution was set up at Parramatta for children to be introduced to the consolations of the new civilisation. But it did not work. For a few years, annual meetings of natives were held with the Governor bestowing the insignia of chieftainship on representatives of people who, since they did not have chiefs, could not understand what he was doing. In the first year of these meetings, the Governor issued a proclamation, on the one hand offering land grants to natives and on the other permitting settlers to fire on them if they did not leave a farm.

King of the Blacks: *Aborigines were represented sympathetically only if they seemed to be adopting the habits of the Europeans. The visiting artist Augustus Earle painted Bungaree (below) who had been useful to the naval explorers in their relations with Aboriginal tribes. In Sydney, Bungaree became famous for wearing discarded uniforms and aping European manners. He was given a brass breastplate inscribed 'Bungaree, King of the Blacks'.*

Ignoble savages: *after several decades of settlement, the Aborigines were usually represented as a people degraded by their collapse in the face of the 'superior civilisation' of the whites, as shown in* Scene in a Sydney street *(top)*, Natives of New South Wales in the streets of Sydney *(centre)*, and A native family of New South Wales on an English settler's farm *(above)*.

In the mid-1820s the British claimed the whole Australian continent. A settlement was established in the north at Moreton Bay, and a group of free settlers was left forlornly at the Swan River on the west coast, not realising that they were on the edge of one of the biggest areas of arid land in the world. In New South Wales in 1829 the Government declared a limit to the area available for further settlement; two years later land grants were abolished. Small land grants had been discouraged in favour of large holdings, which were made available to the wealthier free settlers – the new 'landed gentry'. A 'free enterprise' seaport civilisation developed in Sydney and Hobart around the industries of whaling and shipbuilding.

A second England

In England, where estates had become larger, it seemed rational to 'divide the country amongst opulent men'. Yet the governments of New South Wales and now the separate colony of Van Diemen's Land were still attempting to encourage small farmers; even worse, they were granting land to convicts, thereby threatening the fabric of British society by weakening the idea of punishment.

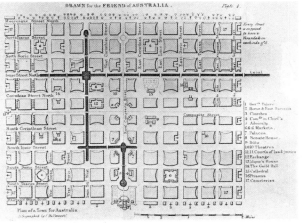

Now small land grants were to be discouraged: land should go to men with capital. By the end of the 1820s a new kind of 'Old Virginia' was being established in the colonies, with British and Irish convicts instead of African slaves.

The latest methods of surveillance were introduced. An office of Superintendent of Convicts was established; boards and committees were set up; forms were filled in. As they arrived in the colonies convicts were now given numbers; records offices were formed in which convicts' names were methodically entered. But to turn convicts into slave labour as well as reducing them to numbers, it was also necessary to treat them more harshly: Norfolk Island was revived as a place of punishment in 1825 and in Van Diemen's Land a penal settlement was formed at Port Arthur in 1830. And it was essential to stop granting land to ex-convicts. Despite the disappointments of a puzzling country, the earlier system of land grants had had some sense of democratic pioneering: even if restricted, it gave the unfortunate a chance to hoist themselves up in the world or – if they failed – it at least offered the self-regard of not working for a master; and the recognition of a possibility of *reform* may have given at least some idealism to a very hard-headed colony. Now, although a ticket-of-leave system still operated and a convict still had a chance to make good, the granting of land to ex-convicts was abolished; and the compassionate hope that people might change for what was seen as the better became even more constricted. For those 'government men' who had to serve their time there were now to be no more easy jobs in town, apart from positions in the hospitals or as servants to government officials, or as constables (a much sought after post, because of the bribes, particularly from sellers of sly grog). Both the use of transportation as a deterrent and the material interests of the colony seemed best served by sending convicts to farms as assigned labourers.

The masters of the plantations were also being assembled: the new settlers attracted by land and forced labour were men such as officers on half pay from the Army, the Navy or the East India Company, or Scottish or Irish small gentry, or sons of English large tenant farmers. In New South Wales the properties of people like these began to spread south from the Sydney plain, west from the mountains, and to the north along the Hunter Valley; in Van Diemen's Land they stretched across the country

Establishing order: *stricter ways of controlling the worst of the convicts were devised. The new penal settlement at Port Arthur in Van Diemen's Land (above left), seen from the commandant's garden, was regarded as a model of modern rationality. Town plans were also prepared for imposing order on unruly Australia. This 'Plan of a Town for Australia' (left) understood local environment in one respect by suggesting that all the streets should be lined with verandas.*

between Hobart and Launceston. On the most ambitious estates little villages were set up by colonial squires. Even the less successful lived with the modest confidence of lesser gentry. Here and there were being built display houses whose formal symmetry and Grecian columns and pediments proclaimed a combination of rationality and learning that, since the Renaissance, had been part of the building style of the European ruling classes. Simple classical ideals of order were now also being imposed on the few small country towns; a direction in 1829 decreed that all new towns would be laid out on a rectangular grid, whose pattern was as controlled as that of a Roman military camp. The landscape was also being brought under civilised control: as well as the simple pictorial naturalism of the early artists there were now painters who contorted Australian landscapes into all of the elaborate stage scenery of the Picturesque school of European painting – or softened them into the mellow reassurances of the European Arcadian school. In Van Diemen's Land, the most talented of the Arcadians, John Glover, discovered how to match even the eucalypt to European traditions of painting.

Now that the colonies were more appropriate to

gentlemen it was useful to restrict the boundaries of settlement, for things to be made more orderly. Since the colonies were penal settlements, right from the beginning there had been an unusually cautious control of settlement, to which was added the poor quality of much of the soil, the caprices of the weather, and the limits of economic circumstances. With a movement out to the frontiers that was slow and constricted and had little aspiration about it except, for the well-to-do, the hopes of foreclosing, there was not much surprise when in 1829 the New South Wales Government declared a limit to the area available for further settlement. Partly to keep things under control and partly to catch up with survey work which was years behind, a border was declared beyond which settlement was forbidden. Two years later land grants were abolished: if people wanted land they could buy it.

In the new colonial upper groups now being created there were divisions based on degrees of gentlemanliness. On one side were those who had arrived first. Now derided by some as 'the ancient nobility', they were the members of the 'respectable establishments' set up by early military or civil officers, the noncommissioned officers, merchants

Images of Australia: *when painters came to Australia they were likely to interpret Australian landscapes by following current fashions of European painting. In his* View of the Illawarra River, about 80 miles from Sydney *(left) Joseph Lycett presented an Australian scene according to the elaborate traditions of the Picturesque style, romanticising the Illawarra River so that it might equally well have been a river in the Scottish Highlands. In* Glover's House and Garden *(below left) John Glover applied to his farm in Van Diemen's Land the Arcadian vision of Europe, with a sense of mellowness and peace.*

turned landowners, and the few early free settlers. They had shown such a quick sense of dynasty-founding that there was already talk of establishing a colonial Order so that with new titles the 'ancients' could be distinguished from other men; but they also distinguished themselves from the rich Emancipist families by seeing themselves as the 'pure merinos', taking the name of a fine-wool sheep to dramatise their freedom from convict taint. However, the social dominance of anciently noble pure merinos was challenged by the immigrant gentry. There were derogatory stories of the ungentlemanly origins of some of the ancients. ('Very strange tales are told of gentlemen of New South Wales.') But, since the aristocratic idea is based on being there first, in a few years even the less-than-ancient might pride themselves on an earlier arrival than someone else.

In the rest of New South Wales and Van Diemen's Land these divisions meant much less. The few hundred landed gentlemen, whether ancient or modern, pure merino or crossbred, made up most of the nobs of the colonies. They became justices of the peace; the few who imitated the great British landed 'improvers' formed agricultural societies and experimented with viticulture, horticulture, the improvement of grain and stock and methods of preserving meat; if public meetings were to be held they preferred to chair them. Power does not seem to have rested lightly on their shoulders. Complaining of their 'supercilious intolerance', one observer warned would-be immigrants that the nobs had 'so long been used to dealing with the poor wretched convicts . . . and to taunt and mock them if they talk about seeking redress for any ill treatment, that . . . they would wish to treat free people in the same way'.

Understandably, the nobs followed the ambitions of the upper classes of the homeland. They wanted to live like English gentlemen. This meant that, as well as establishing

The rulers: *for a period before the large immigration programs in the colony it seemed that it might be possible to reproduce the life style of the English ruling classes. In Sydney, Alexander Macleay (below), the Colonial Secretary and one of the leaders of the nobs, displayed his power and importance by building Elizabeth Bay House (below left). The wife of Captain John Piper (bottom left) was the daughter of a convict, but she became accepted as one of the nobs. At Malahide in Van Diemen's Land (bottom right) an English estate was copied.*

country houses, they wanted the same leisure interests. But there was hardly any system of tenant farmers in the colony – even the least significant farmer preferred to own his few fields rather than to rent them; so, however much the nobs might put duties onto overseers, they themselves, and their wives, usually had to pay attention to the control and working of their properties. Nevertheless they did their best to make New South Wales and Van Diemen's Land 'a second England'. Various kinds of vermin were imported and let loose (joining as pests the house mice, ship rats and sewer rats that had been introduced involuntarily), and hunt clubs were formed to chase them across the bush.

The lesser orders were despised as un-British. A Sydney newspaper said of them in 1826, 'They have lost their English spirit and have degenerated into *Australians*.' However, of the nobs' determined Englishness it was said in London, 'To form a clear conception of the "upper classes" here, suppose all the natives of France annihilated, and the whole country belong to the English residents of Boulogne.'

Associated with the landowners were the town nobs – the court of the Governor, the 'heads of departments', some of the leading professional men, the principal garrison officers. Most of this group was invited more often than anyone else to Government House. Respectability still began at the Governor's table. Connected with them was another (if lesser) town superior class – of civil officers, professional men, property owners and a few ambitious merchants with a sense of education.

Their habits deriving from an English society in which cultivated leisure pursuits were founded in certain economic classes, they were somewhat adrift in a colonial town in which economic classes were developing differently and in which already some of the well-to-do did not attempt – as did arrivistes at home – to heighten their respectability by education. Nevertheless, those who saw themselves as the cultivated lined their studies with books, discussed the novels of Walter Scott and the verse of Lord Byron and went to lectures by gentlemen scientists. In Sydney the exclusive group to which they could belong was the Australian Subscription Library, a privately established lending library in which a blackball could create as great a scandal as in a gentleman's club in London.

It was an affront to these upper groups that the Governor had so much political power and that, except by lobbying and factionalism, they had so little. In 1823, the British Parliament passed an Act for 'the better Administration of Justice in New South Wales and Van Diemen's Land and the more effectual Government thereof', but nothing much was gained. A small Legislative Council was established, but the five members of the first Council were all officials, their meetings were chaired by the Governor, their business was decided by him, they had no control over his executive acts, and they were committed to an oath of secrecy. The Council's greatest use was the opportunity of inspiring officials to act against the Governor.

More hope came from the Supreme Court, now also established. There was provision for a beginning of trial by jury and before a law became effective it had to be 'certified' by the Chief Justice as to its Britishness: when one of the governors instigated measures to restrict the freedom of the new newspapers now being started, the Chief Justice

refused to certify them, thereby in passing granting the colony freedom of the press. He was of the opinion that 'the people are far more intelligent, active and determined than in any of the older colonies; they are newly sprung from intellectual and enterprising England ... To govern them, as one governs ... our Indian possessions, is quite impossible.' The Legislative Council was made a bit bigger; more officials were added to it and to them were added men who were not officials, but were nominated by the Governor. Those who were nominated were the most important of the nobs.

The position appeared to be rounded off in the mid-1820s when the Church of England became the endowed Church of New South Wales. An archdeacon was appointed at £2000 a year; he was put on the Legislative Council, and the government schools were handed over to the Church. The Archdeacon announced that he would be the chief inspector and that teachers would provide detailed records so that he would know what they were doing. For its income the Church was to be given one-seventh of all the settled lands of The Colony of New South Wales.

Woman pioneer: Elizabeth Macarthur

Elizabeth Veale, daughter of a Devon farmer, was 21 when she married John Macarthur in 1788, and the following year, when he joined the New South Wales Corps, the couple left England for the colony. Elizabeth Macarthur was seen as the 'first woman of education and sensitivity' to reach New South Wales. Witty and charming, she held court in society, carefully nurtured her children, presided at Elizabeth Farm, the Macarthurs' family home at Parramatta, where she established extensive fruit and vegetable gardens, and wrote graceful and optimistic letters to her family in England. A devout Anglican, Elizabeth ignored the harsh aspects of colonial life, about which she could do nothing.

Her even life was disturbed in 1809 when her husband was exiled to England because of his part in the rebellion against Governor Bligh. Elizabeth, her social life now limited because of her husband's reputation, became responsible for the Macarthur merino flocks at their most delicate stage. Her intelligent and diligent husbandry in establishing and maintaining the flocks helped found the colony's export wool industry.

When her husband returned, in his increasing fits of melancholy he became obsessed with the idea that Elizabeth had been unfaithful to him. She was to remain a devoted wife, even though the last few years of their marriage were spent in virtual separation.

The new Natives

The first Australians were being called 'blacks' instead of 'natives', and the white colonial-born took the title and spoke of themselves as 'the Natives'.

The Englishness of the 'upper' group was discounted among those in whom pride in colonial birth was extending. There was a magazine called *The Currency Lad*, a boat called *The Currency Lass* and a cricket club called *The Currency Lads*, but now another name was developing for the locally born. When asked in a magistrate's court what his religion was, a 12-year-old boy replied, 'I am a Native.'

To be a Native or, as it might also be put, an Australian, it was necessary to know how such a person might be distinguished from all others. One obvious field of distinction was sport. *The Currency Lad* was mainly a sporting magazine: it was seen as essential that Australians should demonstrate their superiority by displaying excellence in games. Another part of the pride of being an Australian was simply in *being there* (a favourite toast at Native dinners was 'The land, boys, we live in') and the most important part of this was that, like the ancients,

Natives asserted their superiority because they had been there first. Unlike the ancients and other nobs, however, Natives hated newcomers from the British Isles. To the convicts, those who had come free were 'the self-imported devils' but the convicts could feel 'the land was theirs by right' because they had done most of the work. The Natives developed this belief even more stringently: they called immigrants 'the Emigrants' (often 'the bloody Emigrants') as if they were more remarkable for their leaving rather than their arriving. They could say this with a special hatred when land policy became more restrictive and favoured the moneyed Emigrant, with no particular provisions for the Native-born.

Nativeness seems to have been a minor cult of aggrieved ordinariness, its tone set to an unknown extent by convict influence; literate nobs wrote little about it except in disapproval: it found memorable expression mainly in ballads or exemplary tales of rebellion. When the robbers of the bush lost their first description as 'banditti' and became 'bushrangers', they were turned by ballads into heroes displaying some of the Native virtues. The ballad of the death of bold Jack Donohoe, the wild colonial boy, later

Currency: *when the Spaniard Juan Ravenet was in Sydney in the 1790s he sketched* Convicts in New Holland *(left). By the 1830s the children of such convicts, proclaiming themselves Currency Lads and Currency Lasses, had become proud of their parentage. They produced their own magazine,* The Currency Lad *(below), which significantly was mainly a sporting magazine. One of the ways of indicating that one was an Australian and proud of it was by informal dress and manners. In this sketch (bottom) the Native takes his ease while the stiff English-born promenade nearby.*

spread to other parts of the English-speaking world, even if it was to be banned for a while in public houses in New South Wales ('I'd rather roam these hills and dales, like wolf or kangaroo, Than work one hour for Government, cried bold Jack Donohoe'). The story was often retold of a convict who, when challenged by a nob as to who he was, replied, 'I am a man,' shot his interlocutor dead, and then from the scaffold said, 'Good-bye, my lads. I shot the Doctor not for gain, but because he was a Tyrant . . . If any of you take to the bush shoot every tyrant you come across.'

Visitors gave increasingly detailed impressions of the Natives. Some found them as monotonous as the landscapes and as uniform as the seasons; others found the young girls (although mild-tempered and modest) like all children of nature, credulous and easily led into error. To some, although the Natives were very good-looking when young, they soon showed a premature decay and snuffled dreadfully and they spoke with the same nasal twang as Americans; the girls were often very pretty and delicate-looking whilst young (although disfigured by bad teeth) but at 25 or 30 they might seem at least 50; to some it was remarkable that the lower classes were anxious to get into

respectable service or that the girls were all fond of frolicking in the water or that the youths generally married early. But in the more favourable view, Natives were tall, slender and fair; they had extremely good health; they showed a strong independence of disposition and a quality of downrightness that secured truthfulness and sincerity, at least among themselves; they were free-hearted, generous, shrewd and good-natured; every one of them seemed equal with the rest: they were a race with whom one of the worst reproaches was to be a 'crawler'. There were, however, times when they showed a taciturnity proceeding from natural diffidence and reserve. 'They could do everything,' said one writer, 'but speak.'

Bushrangers were one of the curiosities of the Australian colonies. In this engraving for a travel book they provided 'picturesque detail' in an illustration of 'the Australian bush'. The lines under the engraving assured English readers that 'the vigilance of the government and the improved nature of the population have nearly exterminated these ferocious freebooters' although these bushrangers hardly look 'ferocious'.

There was not much attempt to dress up the colonies in the language of new human hope but a rhetoric began to develop, especially in the newspaper *The Australian*, which associated the Natives with the liberal and radical thought of England: the 'Australians', in their struggles, could be seen as part of that great movement of liberation of which some English people had begun to dream. The founder of *The Australian*, William Charles Wentworth, colonial-born nob, and many well-to-do Emancipists used aspects of Nativeness in their general push against the majority of the nobs, whether ancient or imported, who wanted to turn the colonies into a second England: there was particular derision for the idea of 'an English gentleman, *Australian born*'.

But the ideal they opposed to this was often merely that of 'a new Britannia in another world', Britain all over again, with a few faults corrected, so that the colonial-born could become better at being British than the English. Thus, in the more articulate debate about what the colony was, perhaps the main distinction was between the *second* England of the nobs and the *new* Britannia of the better-off Natives and Emancipists.

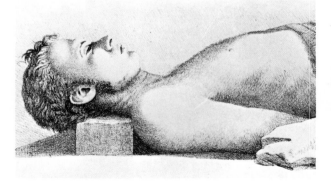

The birth of the bushrangers: *at first the convicts who 'bolted' to the bush and set themselves up as robbers were known simply as 'bolters' or, more grandly, 'banditti', but by the time this sketch was made of James McCabe, Matthew Brady and Patrick Bryant on trial in Van Diemen's Land (top) such men bore the Australian name 'bushranger'. The first of the great hero-bushrangers was 23-year-old Bold Jack Donohoe, sketched by the Surveyor General after Donohoe had been shot dead (above). Donohoe became a legend and the singing of songs about him was prohibited.*

Man of the people: William Charles Wentworth

In 1831 the *Australian* newspaper reported that 'upward of 4000 persons assembled at Vaucluse to partake of Mr Wentworth's hospitality and to evince joy at the approaching departure' of Governor Ralph Darling.

William Charles Wentworth was born in 1790. Both his parents arrived with the Second Fleet: D'Arcy Wentworth, surgeon and magistrate, and Catherine Crowley, sentenced to seven years transportation for stealing. Wentworth was sent to school in England, where he was admitted to the bar. He was to be author, politician, pastoralist and, briefly, an explorer, but above all he was to make a reputation as patriot and believer in parliamentary control over autocratic authority. It was because of this that Governor Darling's departure was celebrated so enthusiastically – a bullock and 12 sheep roasted on a spit, and 4000 loaves of bread washed down with casks of Cooper's gin and Wright's strong beer, at Wentworth's stately mansion at Vaucluse.

Wentworth had been critical of the New South Wales political system since at least 1824, when with Dr Robert Wardell he lauched the *Australian* ('independent, yet consistent, free, yet not licentious – equally unmoved by favour or by fear'). In 1827 conflict erupted with Governor Darling over the question of freedom of the press. Repressive legislation proposed by Darling was met by inflammatory declarations from Wentworth.

But as he became older, Wentworth grew more conservative. He increasingly saw property owners as the only people able to handle political power and even spoke of the need for an hereditary aristocracy in New South Wales. He continued to acquire land, and in 1840 he and some associates bought – very cheaply – nearly one-third of New Zealand from seven Maori chieftains. If this scheme had not been blocked, Wentworth might have become the greatest landowner on earth.

But the colonies were becoming too radical for him: he spent the last years of his life in England, where he was a member of the Conservative Club. After his death in 1872 his remains were brought back to Sydney for a State funeral. They were buried in a vault on the Vaucluse property where 42 years before celebrations had marked the departure of Governor Darling, who had seen Wentworth as 'a vulgar, ill-bred fellow', 'a demagogue', 'anxious to become a man of the people'.

To begin with, the British had claimed less than half of the 7.8 million square kilometres of the continent. Then in the mid-1820s, when more than two and a half million square kilometres of what had already been claimed was still quite unknown to them, they drew a new line on the map and said they owned some hundreds of thousands of square kilometres more.

On the northern edge of this new claim, on a tropical island off the mainland coast 3000 kilometres northwest of Sydney, they built a log fort. The Union Jack was run up in front of an assembled 57 soldiers and 44 convicts; then, after five years of scurvy, tropical diseases and food shortages, and after two ships had been captured by Indonesian pirates and most of their crews slaughtered, the flag came down and the settlement was abandoned. In the meantime, 320 kilometres to the east, a stockade and a log tower were built, thatched huts went up and a palisade was constructed. This settlement of 77 people was perhaps intended to be another Singapore, but just when, in 1829,

regular contact seemed possible with the Indonesian bêche-de-mer fishing fleets that visited the northern coast each year the settlement was closed.

In the south Union Jacks went up at two other little settlements – one near the southeastern tip of the mainland, and the other 2500 kilometres away near the southwestern tip. Then the flags came down and the people in the settlements packed up and sailed away. Despite these failures the remaining two and a half million square kilometres of the continent were claimed, and just before the end of the decade, on the west coast about a month's sea voyage from Sydney, a new colony was conceived.

The Swan River Colony, to be established without convicts, was set up on a five-year trial, on the prompting of a syndicate of speculators (who had broken up before the colony started). The new settlers raised the tents they had brought with them from England, abandoned some of their possessions on the beach, and waited for the surveyors to come back and tell them what kind of land they had come to. They did not know that they had been left on the edge of one of the biggest stretches of arid country in the world – the Gibson Desert.

A new colony: *in May 1829, the British claimed 'New Holland' (what remained of the Australian mainland after the claim for New South Wales), and in June the Swan River Colony was proclaimed by James Stirling, its Governor. Although Swan River was not a convict colony the small settlement at Fremantle (above) was dominated by the jail on the hill.*

Moreton Bay: *in 1824, when the Sydney authorities wished to establish a new penal settlement, they chose a site on the Brisbane River (left). By 1831 the small settlement had become the centre of 'the Moreton Bay District of New South Wales'.*

Whalers, missionaries and traders had been visiting New Zealand for some decades before a Resident was appointed in 1832. New Zealand also attracted artists, such as Augustus Earle, who painted Range Hue, *a New Zealand fortified village (left).*

The first steamship to sail from England arrived in Sydney in 1831 and began to service between Sydney and Newcastle. By sailing up rivers and along the coast small steamers began to help strengthen and then extend the coastal settlements. Newcastle had ceased to be a convict jail, becoming instead a company town controlled, with nob support, by an English company with a monopoly on Newcastle's coal and consignments of convicts to work it. In its place a penal settlement had been established at Moreton Bay, 720 kilometres north of Sydney, after an explorer found some shipwrecked sailors there who took him to the Brisbane River and displayed its commodiousness. To many people in Sydney and Hobart the sea still seemed easier going than the land. Operating with a ruthlessness for which a few of them were killed and eaten, traders continued to infiltrate the South Pacific islands, and some adventurers joined the courts of chiefs. Enough people moved into New Zealand as traders and settlers for a Resident to be appointed in 1832.

Whaling became a big business for Sydney and Hobart. Prices were going up for the wax in whales' heads that could be made into candles, for the bones in their mouths that could be shaped into corsets and umbrella frames, and the blubber that could be turned into lamp oil. Sydney merchants now had enough money to go into the whaling business for themselves. Ships were built for deep-sea whaling; whaling stations, with whaleboats and boiling-down works, were set up on southern Australian coasts and New Zealand. While exports of wool were increasing, whale products increased more; they were the colony's biggest export: the long eluded export staple seemed to have been found and the first impression of visitors when they landed in Sydney or Hobart was that the colonies represented a seaport civilisation.

Dependent on government allocation neither of land nor of convicts, ships providers furnished the Australian whaling fleets and visiting whalers from America and Britain; shipbuilders constructed sloops, brigs, schooners, whaleboats; merchants bought and sold; and hundreds of families lived on the earnings of the whaling crews. To the careful control of the government-sponsored landed society with its forced labour, the 'free enterprise' of the sea frontier was distasteful. Some of the nobs, like the governors, preferred, as far as they could, to keep out of town.

As trading grew, Sydney and Hobart developed more wharves and warehouses. Frederick Garling, the Sydney customs official who executed this scene of a new wharf and bond house in Sydney's Darling Harbour, made paintings over a period of 40 years of most of the big ships that entered Port Jackson.

Whaling: *for a time, whaling was the major business for the Hobart and Sydney waterfronts. In the bays (below) whales were hunted by parties that used boiling down works on the beaches. In deep-sea whaling (below left) the boiling down was done at sea.*

3. The Improvers: 1830 to early 1850s

The introduction of assisted emigration helped to redress the imbalance of the sexes, and by outnumbering the convicts, the new arrivals helped to overcome the dominance of the convict system. The Emigrants brought with them new institutions – friendly societies, temperance societies, mechanics institutes, building societies and trade clubs – which promoted a belief in human improvement.

The age of Improvement

'At last we anchored within Sydney Cove ... In the evening I walked through the town, and returned full of admiration at the whole scene. It is a most magnificent testimony to the power of the British nation. Here, in a less promising country, scores of years have done many times more than an equal number of centuries have effected in South America. My first feeling was to congratulate myself that I was born an Englishman.'

When Charles Darwin said this, after his visit to Sydney, it was not merely chauvinism that made him attribute Sydney's material success to its British origin, but the evidence of his own eyes – by a comparison between the material success of what he saw in New South Wales and the material failure of what he had recently seen in Latin America. The material achievements of the colonists of New South Wales did not come from new talents that sprang uniquely from colonial circumstances; they came because the colonists brought certain characteristics from the British Isles which reacted to those circumstances. They were part of a society that was on the move.

In Britain it was, along with other and opposite things, the age of Improvement with its optimistic faith that things could be made better and better; there was enough of Britain in New South Wales for it to take over many of Britain's improvements. Steam engines had been invented

The founding of South Australia: *on 28 December 1836, the founding colonists of the Province of South Australia assembled under a huge tree to hear the Governor's secretary read the proclamation of South Australia as a Province, a ceremony painted by Charles Hill (above). William Light sketched the camp that was set up near the site for the proposed town of Adelaide (left).*

in Britain; so Sydney put steam engines into some of its flour mills and steamboats ran across Sydney's harbour as ferries; when roads were macadamised in Britain they were later macadamised in Sydney; when omnibuses were introduced in Britain they were later introduced in Sydney; when streets were lit by gas in Britain, streets were later gas lit in Sydney. By 1850 Sydney had begun to build its first railway. One of the few mechanical improvements that Sydney was able to export to Britain was its invention of the pre-stamped envelope. In agricultural improvement there were colonists who experimented with crops – cereals, fruit, cotton, the vine, sugar cane – and with the selective breeding of sheep for fine wools; Australian Improvers were producing a curly fibre whose resilience and intergripping scales made it uniquely useful in spinning.

When the Emigrants began to come in large numbers the colonies could seem to have the makings of a thoroughly modern society in which there seemed no impediment to the spread of sturdy British common sense as it developed new ways for the British, and even the Australians, to make money. For those who preferred social or intellectual advance through 'moral enlightenment' the idea of

Improvement also expanded. As well as steamboats the colonies imported friendly societies, trade societies, temperance societies, building societies – and the faith that human beings could be bettered through the rationality of 'institutions'. As well as omnibuses they adopted Catholic emancipation; as well as using gaslights and macadamised roads they contemplated new systems of education and even the hope that ordinary people might, by gaining the right to vote, choose their own masters. Just as, by careful breeding, sheep could be made better wool producers, so by opening accounts at savings banks artisans could become better persons, and by education all might reach excellence.

Both the material and the moral ideals of Improvement seemed to reach one of their climaxes under a gumtree on an alluvial plain on the southern coast in 1836 when a proclamation was read announcing the establishment of the 'British Province of South Australia'. The assembled

The railway boom: *in the early 1850s railway building began, by the mid-1850s producing such powerful symbols of progress as railway bridges, tunnels and viaducts.*

Shares were offered in the first of the colonial railways (above) to run from Sydney (left) to Parramatta. The line was begun as a private railway but, as happened in all the colonies, it was taken over by the Government.

Other signs of progress: *modern sewers were being laid in Sydney by 1855 (left), and the West Melbourne Gas Works (below left) was established in 1856. The first issue of adhesive postage stamps in New South Wales, in 1850 (below), showed the Spirit of Industry welcoming convicts to Sydney.*

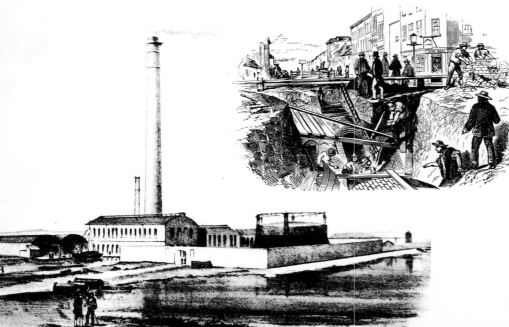

immigrants sang the British National Anthem and 'Rule, Britannia!', and then, as had happened at Sydney Cove in 1788, went off to eat a cold collation. This time the collation was better prepared. And this time there was high formal hope. The word 'colony' was not used. South Australia (by which was meant only the central strip of territory of the continent) was to be a 'Province' of Britain.

It was also to be an Improvers' model of rationality and liberty. Its rationality was to lie in its practical expression of the new theories of 'systematic colonisation': land would be divided neatly into adjoining lots and devoted to agriculture, which sharpened men's minds, rather than straggle out in sheep runs, which depraved their manners. The Province's liberty was to lie in the absolute equality of the various denominations of the Christian religion; there would be neither monopoly for one, nor the corrupting equality of government subsidy for all. And there would be no convicts. Overall, the Province suggested a return to the 17th century, when chartered companies started colonies in North America and there was an expression of religious conviction (although not of religious equality). Perhaps this was why, as an expression of hope, the Province failed.

There seemed too many people in the British Isles: the unemployed were destitute, and at times in parts of Ireland and Scotland there was not enough to eat. The new use of coal and iron, the new ways of making textiles and the new steam engines were destroying old habits: in the new towns there were disorders and dangers of a kind no one knew what to do about.

Periods of riot were followed by spasms of coercion. Except in Ireland there were pauses of reform (there was no pause in the coercion of Ireland), but dreams of redress or perfection faded; the imaginings of frustrated hope floated overseas. While in 1815 less than 2000 emigrants left the British Isles, the average annual emigration was 65 000 in the 1830s; by the late 1840s a quarter of a million or more left each year.

In the first small rush of the 1820s, hardly anyone had emigrated to New South Wales or Van Diemen's Land; a four-month voyage was too long and costly. North America was quicker, cheaper, and seemed to offer more. Then in the early 1830s it was realised that the decision to sell land

Early planner: Colonel William Light

When Colonel William Light arrived in South Australia in 1836, as Surveyor General of the colony charged with finding a site for the new settlement, he decided upon the entrance to the Adelaide River, with its surrounding fertile plains and mountain ranges. Light's experience of cruising in the Mediterranean (his wife, the illegitimate daughter of the third Duke of Richmond, was rich) influenced his choice of the natural harbour at the river mouth.

Light was born in 1786 in Kuala Kedah, Malaya, the son of an English trader who persuaded the East India Company to take over the island of Penang. Light's mother was described as a princess of Kedah, but was probably a Portuguese Eurasian.

Light joined first the English navy, then the army, and as a junior officer on the staff of the Duke of Wellington, to which he was appointed in 1812, he learned the art of mapping and reconnaissance. These skills gave the Colonisation Committee for South Australia faith in Light's ability not only to choose the site for the first settlement, but also survey it, divide the rest of the country into sections, select suitable areas for secondary towns and map 2500 kilometres of coastline.

But it was for his famous plan of Adelaide, sketched in a hot week over Christmas, that Light was to be remembered. The siting of Adelaide caused some dissension and Light resigned. He later wrote: 'I leave it to posterity ... to decide whether I am entitled to praise or blame.'

The voyage to Australia could give the Emigrants a sense that they were particularly enterprising to leave the Mother Country.

in the Australian colonies would provide a fund to pay people to get out of Britain without expense to the British taxpayer. For the next 20 years there were various schemes of assisted emigration to the Australian colonies – for one period two different schemes were tried at once – and, although there were punctuation points when emigration was suspended because of depression in one colony or the other, 200 000 people emigrated to Australia. (During this period 1 750 000 people emigrated to the United States.)

Almost two-thirds were 'bought' by assistance schemes; there was fear that the best Emigrants would go to North America, leaving the Australian colonies to make do with second best. 'Who, we ask, would be so foolish as to emigrate to New South Wales?' demanded an English magazine in 1835, comparing the uncertainties of Australia with the 'decency of manners and comfortable life' of Upper Canada. (Perhaps the reply was contained in the heading of an Australian propaganda pamphlet: 'Comfort for the Poor! Meat Three Times a Day!'.) Many assisted Emigrants were paupers, gathered from workhouses, orphanages, mendicity societies, refuges for the destitute. For two years there was a special hunt for Irish orphan girls; at another time children were collected from the Ragged Schools (70 out of 178 children in one emigrant ship died of measles). Parish officers sometimes put forward those they least wanted, and ships' brokers, keen for the county money, were not always careful about whom they picked – of the first 14 shiploads of women sent out in the 1830s to redress the balance of the sexes, a high proportion were said to be prostitutes.

The nobs, although wanting labourers, complained about what was coming out. But sometimes it seemed they were complaining that the quality of the Emigrants was too high. Paupers were simply men or women made destitute by unemployment and many were trained for better jobs than those the nobs wanted to give them. It was said that to the nobs the ideal Emigrant was 'an able-bodied single man from an agricultural county – humble, ignorant and strong'. For most Emigrants the idea of working for wages on Australian farms was repulsive, and many of them stayed in town. Paupers wanted to return to being human beings.

In 20 years, by outnumbering the convicts, the Emigrants wiped out the freakishness of the convict system, and the emphasis on female Emigrants soon began to balance the numbers of non-convict men and non-convict women

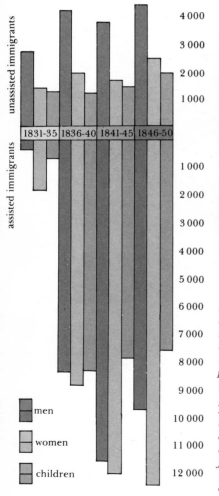

A voyage of experience: *after farewells in England, the Emigrants found themselves on a steerage deck where they lived and slept without dividing partitions (right). Eating (above) was equally communal.*

How many new chums?: *the majority of Emigrants who came to New South Wales between 1831 and 1851 had their fares paid by assistance schemes (left). The Emigrants outnumbered the convicts after 20 years.*

(although most of the ex-convicts were left with no consolation but themselves). And some Emigrants began to think they were the true makers of the colonies, a sense of importance that came partly from the sea changes that happened to them on the way.

Small sections of the populations of the three nations of the Union – some destitute, some poor, some lower-middling – were put into emigrant ships and for months subjected to the shocks of a crudely enforced equality and fellowship. They were mixed up on a steerage deck which, to begin with, had no dividing partitions; and even when bulkheads sorted out single men, single women and the married into three odd lots, only a low fence separated berths (sometimes with four people to a berth), and meals were taken in further odd lots, groups of ten or so sitting on the deckboards to eat the food dished out from the galley. After a voyage which for many may have proved a critically self-defining period, these batches of haphazardly drawn together people were deposited in seaports in Australia and, either from spontaneous self-congratulation or from what they heard around them, could come to see their act of emigration as a sign of particular independence and enterprise, which now deserved some reward.

Perhaps even more important than this new sense of independence were the already established habits they brought with them. For those who grappled with the harshness and oddness of rural life many of the old ways would be destroyed; but an Emigrant who got a job in town somewhat similar to work at home might continue in some of the former habits of Improvement. Since so many stayed in the town it was their Improving ways that helped change the colonies, because some of the ways of the Emigrants were newer than the traditional ways of Van Diemen's Land and New South Wales, and in South Australia and the Swan River Colony it was the Emigrants who had arrived first.

What many of them now brought was an acceptance of 'work', in the sense of paid labour, as a central and acceptable, or at least unavoidable, part of existence. In the 18th century an 'Irish temperament' was often attributed to the English poor, but in the 19th century the temperament of some of the working class was seen to be changing to new and more methodical habits that matched the changes brought by the new industrial machinery. Until mass emigration started, the colonies' population seems to have been more traditional than methodical. Thieves were a highly traditional class, and, whether Irish or not, given to the 'Irish temperament'. But free immigration brought a much bigger proportion of those who represented acceptance of the methodical in the British Isles.

For some of them, with this acceptance of the new, methodical approaches to work, there also went another acceptance of the methodical – in the belief that Improvement was to be found in the 'mutuality' of collective action. The habit of getting together to do something in common had been established in English manufacturing towns, and Emigrants from these towns brought to Australia this new sense of group morality, in which those who did not conform (either through treachery or eccentricity) were treated with intolerance. In certain ways this was a repetition of convict exclusiveness, but the institutions of thieves' honour did not have chairmen or secretaries, minute books or points of order.

Of the 'mutual' groups, the oldest were the friendly societies. A small group of people would contrive to try to protect themselves against the costs of sickness, unemployment and funerals. From meeting together in an orderly way, in arranging to keep funds safe, in working out rules by which they could disagree without splitting up, they would learn much self-discipline and collective purpose. In the new 'mutuality' even having a good time was made more methodical – with organised club nights and annual outings. There were more than a million friendly societies in Britain before mass emigration to the Australian colonies, and in the colonies small friendly societies soon grew beyond measure, in little groups who worked together, or lived near one another, or shared some other common interest. When the big amalgamations of friendly societies began in Britain, great names began to echo in the southern hemisphere: the Manchester Unity Independent Order of Odd Fellows was established in Sydney in 1839 and members began meeting emigrant ships to help British members of the Order; the 1840s saw the foundation of the Independent Order of Rechabites, the Ancient Order of Foresters, the Grand United Order of

Emigrants' friend: Caroline Chisholm

Born in England in 1808 to a well-to-do Northampton farming family, Caroline Chisholm possessed a strong sense of philanthropy. In 1832 she accompanied her army officer husband to India where she established at Madras the Female School of Industry for the Daughters of European Soldiers. But it was in New South Wales, to which she came in 1838 on leave with her family, that her most celebrated work was done.

At a time when there was no formal policy for dispersing assisted emigrants, Caroline Chisholm met every ship and provided new arrivals with support and shelter. In 1842, when an economic depression affected town employment, she mounted her white horse, Captain, and took unemployed emigrants from Sydney to rural areas where there was a need for labour.

Her emigrant settlement program, and the papers she wrote on the subject, were so notable that she became an acknowledged expert on colonisation; she was often in opposition to government policy and wealthy landed interests. In England in 1849 she established the Family Colonisation Loan Society. Charles Dickens supported the society in his magazine *Household Words*, although the unattractive character Mrs Jellyby, in *Bleak House*, was partly based on Caroline Chisholm. However, other contemporary poems, articles and cartoons gave a more sympathetic picture of this tall, serene, yet determined woman who was a legend before she was 40.

Odd Fellows. Native improvisation waited until 1849 for the formation of the Australian Mutual Provident Society.

There was a similar transplanting of the early institutions of trade unionism. In the first half of the 19th century the early trade clubs and trade societies of Britain, probably growing out of the habits of mutuality of the friendly societies, were organised by skilled artisans who wanted to keep their status while things around them were changing; such organisation was not known to the farm labourers or domestic servants who made up the larger part of the British work force or to most of the workers in the new factories. Their skills were not scarce enough, nor their wages high enough for them to be able to take a stand against their masters. In the Australian colonies, where a workshop might consist of only ten hands, the trade societies were equally confined to the traditional skilled trades, but they were active on questions of status, work conditions and margins. Individual trade societies came and went, but they were replaced by others. By the late 1840s there were a couple of dozen trade societies in Sydney, with others in Hobart and Melbourne, and at one of the protest meetings that had become popular in Sydney a Chartist Emigrant

was able to say with some meaning, 'I belong to the largest class of men in the colony – the working class.'

Starting in the United States at the beginning of the 19th century, temperance societies, devoted to the ideal of mutual Improvement, spread to Ireland and then to England; in the 1830s they were transferred to the colonies. Temperance halls were built, providing general community centres; magazines were produced; festivals and processions were arranged (in which, to symbolise the universality of the movement, the marchers might wear rosettes made up of the national colours of England, Ireland and Scotland). Oratory was one of the entertainments of the age and a special temperance oratory developed, promising a brighter future for mankind. To show that 'national enjoyment and merry-making can be kept up well without the aid of stimulants', 'tea parties' were held, sometimes with dancing till dawn. In the 1840s the battle within local temperance movements between adherents of moderation and the newly powerful Total Abstainers provided great issues of the time, with opportunity for group activity, political contest and the display of rival views of the meaning of life.

Since, except during the great depression of the early

Cultural baggage:

Emigrants brought with them not only their physical possessions, but also 'cultural baggage' in the form of new habits and new beliefs from industrialising England – methodical habits of work, belief in the 'mutuality' of organisations such as friendly societies, support for the temperance movement, and a belief in land reform and democracy.

Mantraps (right), by which English landholders protected their property, had become one of the most hated symbols of inequality. The Emigrants hoped that in Australia they would gain the right to own their own land.

An English spinning mill in the 1830s (below). In such institutions workers had acquired methodical and obedient habits.

A meeting of three of the mutual benefit societies formed in Australia in the 1830s and 1840s (below). The societies had distinctive emblems, such as the clasped hands (top) and the crossed oars (above) of the United Watermans Benefit Society of Sydney.

For democrats, the Massacre of Peterloo in Manchester in 1819 was becoming a sacred memory, and unofficial medals (below) were struck in honour of it. At Peterloo troops broke up a demonstration for democratic political rights; 11 people were killed and 400 were injured.

1840s, jobs were not scarce, the hostility of the Natives was practised mainly against those Emigrants who did remarkably well out of the colony. The Improving ideas and methodical habits that the Emigrants brought were also known to some of the Natives, but the huge increase in the proportion of Emigrants probably made the growth of a methodical and institutional approach to 'mutuality' stronger than if it had been left to the Natives, and it may have strengthened that faith in respectability that had already emerged alongside the licentiousness of the colony.

Sydney, said Charles Darwin, 'may be faithfully compared to the large suburbs which stretch from London'. And while in the bush the Natives might begin to seem to have special wisdom, and to provide metaphors of independence that seemed to give a unique sense of locality, in the towns it was the Emigrants, expressing the hopes of the suburbs of London, who seemed to express wisdom. Prompted by impulses that came from Britain and were perhaps in some sense 'artificial', they strengthened the institutions of mutuality, while what mainly prevailed in the bush was nomadism, dominated by men who showed the crassest kind of individualism.

A sense of moral shock was common to both Emigrants and Natives: that in a colony it required money to be a farmer. The Natives saw the land as 'theirs by right'; the Emigrants thought not getting land easily an affront to a myth that had quickly grown in the new manufacturing towns of the British Isles – that in the old days there had once been a happy time when every true man was his own landowner. Town workers in England might dream of working their own farmland; their offspring might transfer that dream to Sydney. It was a dream that the common people had a right to lead some life of their own, on land that was their own, and escape the rest of the world. In Sydney this dream might seem almost as hard to realise as in Britain.

But now they could at least grow things. In the new softening of leisure pursuits, in which amusements such as cockfighting were giving way to gentler pastimes, gardening was taken as morally good; and if they could not be yeomen farmers, Emigrants could at least tend their gardens. Although speculators were cramming terraces into the main towns, there was still the detached cottage style, with its veranda: and in 1829 there had been a government requirement that all houses should be at least 14 feet (4.9

The Tolpuddle Martyrs: *six of the great heroes of the early working-class movement were agricultural labourers from the Dorset village of Tolpuddle; they were sentenced to seven years in the Australian colonies after they tried to form a trade union. This contemporary cartoon (below left) is entitled 'The Dorchester Unionists Imploring Mercy !!! of their King'.*

A procession in London (left) on behalf of the Tolpuddle Martyrs.

A warning (below) threatening seven years' transportation for anyone who took an 'illegal oath' to join a trade union.

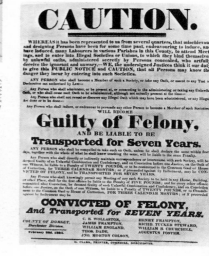

metres) from the front alignment. So as well as the fruit and vegetable garden at the back grouped around an outhouse kitchen (where cooking was done on an open fire), in the front, behind the paling enclosure and perhaps a geranium hedge, there was room for a flower garden of the English country farmhouse kind, where a family could arrange honeysuckle and sweet peas, mignonette and roses, wallflowers and hollyhocks in rectangles and circles of reassuring formality.

Even more important, if families could not own a farm, some of them might now be able to think (or their children might) of owning a cottage. The building society movement had been slowly developing in England, mostly in the Midlands and in the north, but it exploded into popularity in the mid-1840s. In the colonies building societies began to form from 1847. Meanwhile savings banks for 'the industrious poor' had opened in all the main towns. It is

doubtful if 'the industrious poor' had any money to put into them, but small-scale artisans, and tradespeople did; so did some of the domestic servants and some of the better-off working people. In Sydney, through this form of self-help some of the ordinary people were financing the building of 'the humble cottages springing up in thick clusters in the Surry Hills, at Chippendale, at Pyrmont, at Balmain'.

A few years later the British economist W.S. Jevons saw how a labourer or mechanic might have 'his own residence on freehold or leasehold land', a couple of rooms often built by himself, to be added to later. A suburb of that period might have looked like the wooden huts of a military encampment, but nevertheless 'unpretentious as it is to any convenience or beauties, it yet satisfied him better than the brick built, closely packed, and rented houses of English towns'. With framed certificates of membership of a friendly society, perhaps also of a temperance society, on their walls, a sense of their right to the dignity of independent existence in their hearts, and of the right to respectability of every person in the society around them, some families could walk out into their own backyards and feel that an ambition had been met: they owned some land.

The Australian style: *although speculators were now putting up terraces, there were still plenty of houses, detached, with verandas, in the Australian style.*

Holding things together

New South Wales and Van Diemen's Land were England, Ireland and Scotland all mixed up into one, and it was feared that maintaining old divisions would provoke new disasters.

It was this dread of division that caused the *No religion! No politics!* rules in some of the mutual societies; the rosettes worn in processions sometimes included all three of the national colours of the colonies' three founding nations. For the same reason Improvers' ideas of tolerance as a creative force in human conduct achieved much faster realisation in the colonies than they did in Britain. Tolerance was a useful way of holding things together.

A most remarkable result of the new tolerance was the quick destruction of the special position of the Church of England. Even when it was the established church some of the nobs had worshipped with more than one denomination, not finding religious dogma and denominational disputes important enough matters to split a colony. It was only within the church itself that there was much concern when in the early 1830s it ceased to be the State church: to have kept it as the endowed government

church would have risked dangerous tension. Even in the British Isles the Church of England was 'in danger', so, with a government of Whig Improvers in London and the Improving Governor Bourke in Sydney, there was a chance to display the now fashionable religious tolerance.

The Government cancelled the grant to the Church of England of a seventh of the colony's lands and the monopoly of its public education, and instituted instead a system in which Anglicans, Romans, Presbyterians and Wesleyans – the four main divisions of religion of the British Isles – were all to be subsidised by the Government with stipends to 'duly appointed' clergymen and grants to match money voluntarily raised for the construction of church buildings. There were now to be four 'established churches'. (The Independents and the Baptists later also took government money.) There were envious complaints against 'turtle and port for the overfed preacher', and in 1842, because of a depression, a limit to the total amount was fixed, but the subsidy was to last for another 20 years. Each new suburb and country town could look forward to four churches going up, from which it could take its pick.

Governor Bourke also tried to set up a system of non-

Reformer: Sir Richard Bourke

Sir Richard Bourke was given a joyous, enthusiastic welcome by the people of Sydney as he sailed down the harbour in December, 1831. Although possessed of charm and a sense of purpose, even he was only occasionally able to mend the rifts in the quarrelsome, factionalised colony to which he had been appointed Governor. The conflict between Exclusives and Emancipists remained bitter, although the situation did start to improve after Bourke's arrival, when the increasing number of assisted passages meant that free settlers were beginning to outnumber those whose blood was 'tainted with the convict stain'.

Born in Dublin, Ireland in 1777, Bourke saw active service in the Grenadier Guards, and was promoted to the rank of colonel before retiring to his estate in Limerick. There he encouraged public education and local industry and, as an Anglican and magistrate, he was aware of the pitfalls of a religiously divided country.

Bourke's income from his estate and half pay from the army were not large enough to maintain his growing family, and his physically frail wife (who was to die soon after reaching New

South Wales) also needed a healthier climate; so Bourke sought official appointments.

He was made Acting Governor of the Cape Colony, South Africa, in 1825, where he dealt successfully with problems ranging from tension with colonists of Dutch descent and with blacks, to freedom of the Press.

Bourke was the first liberal Governor of New South Wales. Although he did not succeed in establishing an elective government or government schools, he did introduce trial by jury, and greater religious freedom by giving government subsidies to churches other than the Anglican. He also limited the power of magistrates to punish convicts – a reform which was to bedevil Bourke. It was continuously, sometimes stridently, blamed for a perceived increase in convict misbehaviour.

His enemies were the Exclusives who were not to be soothed by increased economic growth or orderly territorial expansion. When they won a political skirmish over an appointment to the colony's Executive Council, Bourke resigned. He left the colony in 1831, a figure so popular that a fund was set up to pay for a statue of him – the first statue to be erected in Australia.

sectarian government schools, with non-denominational scripture lessons. The Church of England defeated him, but the Governor replied with a system of subsidy for *all* church schools that lasted for 15 years. At the end of the 1840s non-denominational 'national' government schools were finally established, but the subsidised church schools were kept as well. Two boards were set up, one for each kind of school. Now New South Wales had one of everything.

With its sense of monopoly outraged, the Church of England seemed to lose its self-possession. It set up a hierarchy of bishops, but the first of them was humiliated at Government House by having to contest his precedence over the Catholic bishop. He had both to write a complaint to a tolerant government in London that Anglicans, not Wesleyans, should have been sent as missionaries to the blacks and then to his own tolerant flock ('A letter of Vindication of the Principles of the Reformation') warning them that they should not contribute money to help put a roof on an unfinished Catholic church.

It was now the emancipated Catholic Church that began to prosper. Its growth helped change the colony. In the 1820s the Catholic Church had not one proper church building, no prominent laymen, and for a while only one priest. By 1850, although its congregation was still predominantly poor and mainly Irish, a few of its best-known members were among the nobs, and, helped by government money, its churches, schools and clergy had grown to match its position as the denomination of more than a quarter of the colonists. With an archbishop in Sydney and bishops in other towns, it had established the first Catholic territorial hierarchy under the British crown since the Reformation. The Catholic Mrs Caroline Chisholm was one of the most influential private persons in the colony; priests were in the forefront of movements for self-improvement and respectability.

In Melbourne's biggest procession, the Father Mathew Total Abstinence Society was followed by the Rechabites; after the German Union came the St Patrick Society; after the Freemasons came the priests. The Catholic Church saw itself as an integrated (if different) part of the community, even if the Protestant Irish had set up Orange Lodges. But now that the Anglican ascendancy was destroyed the Catholics had become the main enemy of the other denominations. The growth of the Catholic Church led

Symbols of toleration: *although there was much sectarian bitterness in the colony, there were also signs of a toleration not then to be found in Britain. But religion was nevertheless seen as an expression of nationality. An 1840s sketch of three churches (left) does not identify them by their denominations, but as '* THE IRISH, ENGLISH AND SCOTCH CHURCHES'. *Although the Irish were distrusted, the annual St Patrick's Day dinners (below left) were one of the great annual events of the colonies. Toleration extended to the Jews, who opened a new synagogue in York Street, Sydney (right), and Nonconformists, who established a Free Chapel at Angaston, South Australia (below right).*

many non-Catholic clergy to believe that Rome was planning domination of Australia; a hypothesis that seemed confirmed when the Catholics, although professing, and in other fields practising, a determination to join community activities, set up their own temperance societies, which flaunted their independence in street processions with brass bands and regalia. The Romanist plot seemed even more fully established when the Catholic bishop came back from Britain as Archbishop of Australia, and was escorted from wharf to cathedral by 2000 Catholics, with a Temperance band playing 'See the Conquering Hero Comes'. Nevertheless, despite whatever hostility existed, and however wide or narrow it was, the priests could follow the Freemasons in a procession.

It is difficult to estimate how much of the anti-Catholic agitation was a matter of pulpits and clerical pamphlets that did not reach far into the community. There may not have been much readership, for instance, of a pamphlet one Anglican clergyman produced under the title 'Are the Catholics of Port Phillip Tridentine Romanists?'. What at first may have been more significant than anti-Catholic feeling was feeling against the Irish of 'Pat-*riot*-ism'. As one

Sydney newspaper put it, 'The Irish are ignorant, turbulent, mentally debased and totally unqualified for the elective franchise.'

Nevertheless here, too, there was integration. The Irish may not have been liked by some, but they were sharing the colonial experience; they did not see themselves with quite such separateness as did the floods of Irish emigrants who were settling themselves in various cities of the United States.

Reverend rebel: *the Reverend John Dunmore Lang (below) tested the toleration of the colony. As a Presbyterian clergyman he established the Presbyterian Church in Australia, but later quarrelled with the Presbyterians and was deposed from the Presbyterian ministry, although maintaining a church of his own. As a member of parliament, he declared himself a republican and even proposed rebellion. As editor and writer, founding the weekly newspaper the* Colonist, *he fought many libel actions – on one occasion being sentenced to imprisonment. He also founded the Australian College, having secured a Government loan to do so on a visit to England, but he quarrelled so regularly with the masters that, finally, the College was closed down.*

The faith of the Improvers

It was an age when the Press could seem of more significance than the pulpit. Some of them half-magazine, some denominational, some temperance, some political, newspapers came and went at a rate that usually had ten existing at once in Sydney alone; newspapers were active in all the other capitals and now they were being founded in the principal country towns.

Their very presence, diversity and obsessive vindictiveness seemed to cry freedom – in different languages. When a paper in the Swan River Colony attacked the Governor as 'corrupted by the flattery of the adulterers in the Government House clique', or a paper in Adelaide attacked their Governor for governing 'in the interests of vanity and his own pocket', or a Sydney paper attacked *their* Governor as a 'despotic radical given to claptrap and maudlin sentiment', these newspapers were criticising their Governors not for the sake of absolute freedom, but for the right of the big men in the colonies to replace the governors and take over. As one paper said, 'They were not concerned with the fanciful and metaphysical rights of man but the unquestioned and undeniable rights of property.' But, in the name of the people, other newspapers attacked 'the pure merino and high Tory establishment' and made broader claims for liberty, freedom and improvement of the human condition. Several papers spoke (if politely) for the 'working man' – of achieving 'the moral and social improvement of citizens of the humbler classes', of 'the right of the labourer to his fair share' and of 'the right of the emigrant mechanic to rise above his condition'. One of these papers lasted for seven years.

The Press flourished. But even by 1850 the number of people likely to be at church on Sundays was about half that in the British Isles. In Sydney the Legislative Council had no prayers, an innovation that caused one critic to complain that the Council was 'under the stigma of being the only legislative assembly in the world which, as such, makes no recognition of Divine Providence'. There was no new sustained religious enthusiasm like the revivalism that gave Methodists and Baptists big new congregations in the United States and caused the creation of the new sects on the North American frontiers.

To the official indifference to religious impulse that had marked the colony's founding was added the private indifference of many of the convicts, and of the immigrants who came from the 'heathen' cities created by industrialising Britain. In this climate the transplanted churches seemed to loose some of their sap. To the more tolerant nobs the clergy could appear mere chaplains of respectability, their emphasis on respectability both reflecting a newly growing belief in the British Isles and meeting the needs of a convict colony. Diaries and letters show that some of the prominent persons in the colony did not lack faith, but their faith was often almost private.

It was only when the Government began subsidising the Churches that the number of church buildings began to match the population. Within five years the number of church buildings doubled; then doubled again. But faith remained thin. The Churches struggled bitterly for pupils and school subsidies, but it seemed mainly a matter of possession; there was not much religious instruction given in the church schools and the poorer people who were their main customers often did not care whether the school a child attended was run by the denomination to which he belonged. Often the Presbyterians were favoured because of their better reputation as teachers.

The Catholics provided the greatest community sense of religion, providing not only religious faith but also, although the Church was led by English Benedictines, a sense of Irishness. As 'the Church of the Penitent' the Catholic mission to the convicts combined old compassion (even if at times affronting with what seemed an overzealous soul-snatching at the gallows) with some of the new Improvement. The Anglicans and the Presbyterians had fallen into the same internal divisions that were occurring in England and Scotland. The English Church was not sure whether it was Catholic or Protestant. Did it rely for its spiritual power on consecration or conscience? Congregations of largely Evangelical origin were puzzled by the tolerance of the ancient nobility who saw *any* religion as useful in a prison. The other established church of the British Isles, the Presbyterian Church, split into four groups, partly because of the turbulence of personal relations, but mainly as a reflection of schism in Scotland.

What religious revival there was came mainly from 'shop-keepers' Methodism'. The Wesleyans had four good years from 1840 to 1843, during a depression, and they trebled

It was a time when newspapers were easy to found (and easily went bankrupt). They could seem the main form of opinion. The Port Phillip Herald *became the* Melbourne Morning Herald *in 1849 and the* Daily Evening Herald *in 1869; The Sydney Herald became The Sydney Morning Herald in 1842.*

their numbers. But their usual state was summed up by a Methodist minister who said, 'We have at times appeared just on the eve of revival amongst the people, and then something has transpired that has appeared to put an extinguisher upon the gracious flame.'

Next to the thinness and divisions of religious belief the Improvers juxtaposed the faith that only the spread of knowledge would improve the general human condition. Under the Improving Lieutenant Governor Franklin and his even more Improving wife, Van Diemen's Land was for a season seen as a centre of learning. It had its Society of Natural History and its *Journal of Natural History*. Its Botanical Garden bore a name from classical Greek and its Museum of Natural History was housed in a Greek temple. Patronage was given to several natural historians and there were attempts at literary and intellectual periodicals. To John Glover's Arcadian landscapes were added the efforts of Benjamin Duttereau to provide, in several paintings in the grand style, the first suggestions that Australia might have an Australian sense of history (even if what came through most strongly – a suggestion that a compact had been reached between whites and blacks – proved disastrously untrue). It was also in Van Diemen's Land that the first system of state schooling was established.

It was Franklin's hope that more schooling would improve the ways people lived in Van Diemen's Land, and soften their relations with each other. In discussion on colonial education the view that elementary education was mainly a matter of preparing the poor for suffering the indignities of this life with hope of reward in the next had quickly yielded to such views as that it was a 'sacred and necessary duty' to use education for moral reform in a convict colony, or that 'a child must be taught to reason', so becoming a better or more useful person (a view expressed as early as 1803), or that 'the diffusion of knowledge' was good in itself or a basis for good citizenship or success.

Views like these were expressed most clearly by the colony's Scottish schoolmasters. In England, education was more backward than in most other parts of Western Europe, but Scotland had had an education system for more than a century, and it was probably no accident that

The Normal Institution, a school mainly for boys who wished to become teachers, was founded in 1834 with high educational aims.

Giving a lead: Jane Franklin

When Sir John Franklin was made Lieutenant Governor of Van Diemen's Land in 1836 his wife, Jane, was determined to be more than merely the Governor's wife.

The daughter of a wealthy London silk weaver, she had travelled a lot and developed her intellectual curiosity by the time of her marriage at the age of 37. In England she belonged to the circle of women, of whom the prison reformer Elizabeth Fry was one, who saw their role as leading the general improvement of society.

It seemed obvious to her that in Van Diemen's Land, a penal settlement, there were great opportunities for human improvement, but when she tried to form a 'Tasmanian Ladies Society for the Reformation of Female Prisoners' in 1841, she was frustrated: two years later, however, she had her way.

Her ambitions rose above those of a penal settlement; she made Van Diemen's Land the intellectual centre of the Australian colonies. The first Royal Society outside Britain for the advancement of science was instigated by her, and she established botanical gardens, a museum of natural history and a scientific library. She made plans for a state college, established an agricultural settlement on the banks of the Huon River and won popularity with the convicts by paying one shilling for each snake's head she received, in an attempt to rid the island of them.

But it was vipers of a different sort she had most to fear. She was drawn into bitter colonial faction fighting, provoking strong attacks on her and Sir John by the *Van Diemen's Land Chronicle*, which was partly responsible for her husband's recall in 1843.

in New South Wales, despite their smaller numbers and their schisms, the Presbyterians ran the second biggest proportion of church schools; and about a third of their pupils were not Presbyterian. The most notable of these Scottish schoolmasters, Henry Carmichael, a reformer who had experimented with several ambitious private schools in New South Wales, including an *école normale*, saw the teaching of religion as 'no part of the duties of an ordinary schoolmaster'; the Bible should be present in schools, but only as a 'book of reference and voluntary perusal'.

On his voyage out, he found that after shipboard lectures some immigrants had mastered logarithms, the first six books of Euclid, and the first two books of *The Wealth of Nations*. Impressed by this industry, he responded to the Improving Governor Bourke's invitation to help found a Mechanics School of Arts in Sydney, the idea of mechanics institutes and schools of arts having become popular in Scotland, then England. It was opened in 1833, and by 1841 it was reckoned that one in every 14 adult males in Sydney belonged to it. Mechanics institutes or schools of arts were to be established in almost every town in the colonies, often with a government subsidy. In Britain, the

idea was 'to impart instruction to workers in the rules and principles which lie at the basis of the arts they practice'; but with so few industrial arts practised in the colonies, there was not much occasion to explain the theory that lay behind them. Instead, at their most ambitious, the institutes concerned themselves with public lectures, at first with a leaning towards science, and then with a dominant concern for the literary. It was as much the age of the public lecture as the age of oratory and the procession, and lectures were part of the amusement available.

The Sydney School of Arts became the strongest intellectual institution in the colonies. Attacked by Charles Harpur, a Native intellectual, as the 'School of Charlatans' because it was controlled by Emigrants, it reflected the changing nature of emigration; at its beginning it was dominated by non-political sections of the superior town class and reflected their cultivated interest; with the Emigrant rush it became more a means of diversion for the middling, but from it, and reflected in some of the other institutes, came a hope of a national civilising mission that, by improving minds, would improve morals and spread the gospel of an enlightened humanity. In this sense its

Teaching aids: *an 1830s sewing sampler (above) and two pages from an 1830s illustrated alphabet book (above right). About half the schools had insufficient books.*

The first professors inspect the building of the university at Sydney in 1858 (left), which was spoken of by some, in the Sydney manner, as the national university.

The Black Hats

function, like that of the temperance movement (despite the backing of this by clergymen) was in effect an attempt to provide a secular substitute for religious faith and a sense of community.

A minor belief grew that a sense of common purpose was to be found in a common culture, or more narrowly, in a national literature. Carmichael said, 'If we mean to rise in the scale of nations, we must possess a literature and science of our own.' There were suggestions that to this end the arts should be given government support, although to some the moment of national liberation through cultural achievement seemed already at hand. 'We do not believe there is a town or province in Europe possessing the same number of inhabitants ... that can boast of more extended benefits accruing from literary institutions than can we of New South Wales.' In 1845 it was predicted that the colony was 'on the verge of a glorious cultural advance'.

Uplifting minds: *for a while, great hopes were expressed that mechanics institutes and schools of arts (below and bottom) would uplift minds by adult education.*

It took New South Wales 62 years for the Legislative Council to pass an Act to incorporate a university in Sydney (spoken of by some, in the Sydney manner, as 'the national university'). Perhaps even more to the point: while the first of the North American public high schools started in 1821, by the end of the century most Australian colonies did not have one public high school. Between the language of the Improvers and their achievement was a large gap.

Even in the elementary schools little was achieved. Many teachers were themselves scarcely educated. About half the schools had insufficient books; three-quarters did not have enough furniture. The usual schooling period averaged only two years, with irregular attendance even within that short time; in any case, fewer than half the children attended school. Most elementary schools still practised the old system in which pupils of different ages sat in one class, learnt off set questions and answers, and went up one by one to the teacher's desk to be catechised, although some

The phrase 'Black Hats' was used to describe the elites of the colonial cities. This particular black hat is on the head of Osmond Gillies, Esquire, one of the most solid of Adelaide's early citizens.

larger schools, particularly in Sydney, were using the newer monitorial system, whereby a teacher taught the brightest pupils and they taught the others. Something was known of more experimental methods being tried in parts of Western Europe – for a while infants' schools were run on a principle of 'gentleness rather than coercion' – but on the whole not much. Attempts to introduce vocational training failed.

There was a general drive in the United States in the 1830s for people's schools subsidised by taxes, but there could be no parallel in Australia, because of the lack of local government. It irritated the British that in the colonies the central government accepted such unusual functions as constructing all the roads, controlling all the police, and subsidising all the schools and churches. To save money and to introduce what was seen as the basis of all civil liberties the idea of local government with local taxes was regularly pushed from London. The colonists preferred to express their civil liberties by boycotting attempts to make them use them, which they saw as a trick to make them pay extra taxes. By 1850 it was clear that education would remain a central responsibility. Among other things, this meant that not enough money was spent on education.

In the colonies there was not much drive towards the education of the children of even the better-off. Most of what did exist was served by the 250 or so little schools, most of them bad. Parents often treated them with contempt, sometimes speaking in front of their children scathingly of their teachers, sometimes telling the teachers (with a 'low-bred malice') how to run their schools. In the United States there was no lack of parents who despised education, but there was a contrary attitude that was based on a sense of religious mission derived from a very different beginning of settlement, and that found one of the symbols of human aspiration in the schoolmistress. There may have been something else: the idea of accepting one's station in life as a matter of divine providence was being discarded in the colonies, but its replacement by the idea of success as the reward of industry and merit was not altogether accepted. It was spoken about and written about because it was a growing idea in the English-speaking world: but the history of the colony, so different in its land settlement from the United States, seemed to suggest that success might be also a matter of special government favour, or of cheating, or gambling, or luck.

Perhaps there was an influence even more profound. The United States was an independent nation; seeking its own character was essential to its survival. Australia was a series of British colonies. It didn't need its own character: in fact it might be desirable if it did not have one. In the main cities, gentlemen's clubs had been set up on the London pattern and for most of those who ran the colonies they provided the true standards of existence. It was said of the one in Sydney that 'all the aristocracy of the colony belong to it'. In an appealingly exclusive dream the 'Black Hat' life of the Government House set and of the clubs gave to the powerful the truest indication of what life was about. But if their standards were to affect the schools there was a serious weakness: if education were to be a matter of learning the manners and cultivated interests of those of higher status, most of the colonists were not interested.

There were experiments in setting up corporate schools to turn Native sons into English gentlemen, but although there were usually three of these at any one time, they survived only feebly. Ambitions of imitating the gentlemanly uselessness of the English schools did not come off because colonial hard-headedness sensibly preferred imitations of the

Scottish or nonconformist academics as more appropriate to the colonies. But unlike the United States, where the public schools soon became comprehensive schools, there was no official sponsoring of the idea of useful vocational education in the Australian colonies.

Even if the standards of the Black Hats and superior town classes had been more suitable to the colonies, they had themselves been weakened. The manners and cultivated pursuits of an upper class were only feebly represented and they were in any case very largely swept away by colonial economic circumstances. Those of the superior town classes who wished for some of the life of a cultivated gentleman were often frustrated. 'Amongst the higher orders, wool and sheep-grazing form the constant subject of conversation,' said Darwin.

Cultivated aspiration remained, but, instead of spreading the gospel of humanity, the mechanics institutes became libraries for lending light novels. What most strongly survived were the stiff, outward forms of colonial exclusiveness – the invitations to Government House, membership of the gentlemen's clubs, and, of course the black hats.

Gentlemen's clubs: *an essential part of upper-class life transported to the colonial cities were the gentlemen's clubs: the exclusive Melbourne Club (above) and the Australian Club in Sydney (right).*

Joseph Fowles, a drawing master at Sydney Grammar School, made a number of paintings of Sydney to 'remove erroneous and discreditable notions' of the town and present it with proper dignity. He titled this scene (left) of a Sydney gentleman in black hat Rider on White Horse in Macquarie Street North.

4. The land grabbers: 1830 to early 1850s

In the wake of explorers, who discovered vast grasslands beyond the mountains of the east coast, came adventurers driving great herds of cattle and sheep – the overlanders. They waged war on the blacks, seized their rivers and water holes and spread new diseases. Soon, almost all of the southeastern arc of Australia was under the control of 'squatters'.

The rush to the grasslands

Cedar cutters opened up much of the coastal settlement of New South Wales. They would establish a camp; the logs would be hauled by bullocks to the nearest river and then rafted to a port from which they would be shipped to Sydney and, finally, perhaps even to London. As the trees were felled, small farmers, often dairy farmers, would move into the cleared spaces. But the settlement of the grasslands beyond the mountains was the scene of something more dramatic than this: in 15 years – over roughly the period of the Emigrant rush to the towns –

there was one of the greatest pastoral rushes in history. This was to create a unique society within the general society of the colonies, a society whose leaders were to challenge the existing order.

The scouting parties of this advance were the ex-soldiers, naturalists, surveyors, geologists or bushmen who took up exploring – a tedious, debilitating and, on several occasions, fatal task in a country where looking for water could take up much of the time and where familiar food was so hard to find that the early explorers took live sheep and cattle to eat on the way; the later explorers, although travelling lighter, allowed for the possibility of eating their packhorses or camels on the way back.

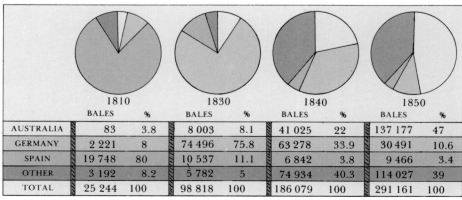

	1810		1830		1840		1850	
	BALES	%	BALES	%	BALES	%	BALES	%
AUSTRALIA	83	3.8	8 003	8.1	41 025	22	137 177	47
GERMANY	2 221	8	74 496	75.8	63 278	33.9	30 491	10.6
SPAIN	19 748	80	10 537	11.1	6 842	3.8	9 466	3.4
OTHER	3 192	8.2	5 782	5	74 934	40.3	114 027	39
TOTAL	25 244	100	98 818	100	186 079	100	291 161	100

Squatters' rush: *one of the decisive influences on the rapid spreading of the European occupation of Australia developed in textile towns such as Bradford (above) in Yorkshire, England, where the demand for wool prompted the great rush of squatters and their sheep over southeastern Australia.*

The golden fleece: *by 1850, the Australian colonies were Britain's principal supplier of wool (left).*

What first impelled them was the puzzle of the rivers that flowed away from the ocean. When they discovered that these flowed into two main rivers that joined together and headed southwest to an outlet on the southern coast, there appeared on the map a river system that looked almost as extensive as those on the maps of other continents; but there was not enough water in it. Nevertheless, by the mid-1830s the unravelling of these rivers led the way to what was to prove much of the most useful land in Australia. The explorers were to have few further successes. They searched for an inland sea, and found deserts; they searched for a great river system in the tropical north, but it did not exist. In the south, one explorer, Edward John Eyre, travelled west for 2400 kilometres without passing any running water.

Even some of these who were successful could be melancholy in their reports; because of the unfamiliarity of the strange continent or because it was a time of drought, some dismissed as difficult or useless territories that were among the best Australia had to offer. But whether the explorers were optimists or pessimists, pastoralists were soon driving sheep and cattle into the new country: in one case they followed tracks left by an explorer's bullock drays. By the 1840s sheep and cattle were eating the kangaroo grass over a huge crescent in the southeast, 2200 kilometres long in its inner curve, 650 kilometres broad at its widest, with the southeast coast on one side and the arid regions on the other. By the middle of the century there were 16 million sheep and two million cattle on what was to prove the better part of the hospitable land of the continent.

In a couple of decades there had occurred one of those great annexations that since the 16th century had been turning the whole world into a storehouse for Europe.

At a time when 100 000 sheep might be moving to new runs on the same track, the most heroic form of this expansion was that of the 'overlanders', a pastoralist and his men and a whole pastoral property moving on the hoof and on bullock drays; perhaps thousands of sheep, hundreds of cattle, several score of horses and working bullocks, and drays packed with boxes of tools, and sacks and chests containing 12 months' supply of food. The driving belief was that there was 'something better further out'. Some of the pastoralists moved everything, looking for new and bigger runs; others split their flocks or herds, dispersing them in different parts of the colony. More cautiously, others would ride off to the borders of settlement, notch some trees, try to get their new neighbours to take this as meaning something, and then go back for their animals.

What moved them was not the romance of empty spaces but the existence of a gambler's avarice: flocks of sheep could quickly double and re-double, and an ambitious man might try to snatch 20 times as much land as he needed to be ready for the later re-doublings of his stake.

The boom was so great that for many woolmasters the most money was made simply by expanding flocks so that they could sell stock to other woolmasters who would in turn expand flocks so that they could sell stock to others. As the runs spread along the river banks those who had staked claims became apprehensive of 'run hunters' attempting to bluff their way into part of a run. Scouting parties found information harder to get. It was like a gold rush.

Many of those who raced each other across the wilderness knew nothing about sheep until they had set up their runs.

The pastoral rush in Australia arose from a limiting problem, and a sudden opportunity. The limiting problem was that the main form of land transport consisted of drays pulled by teams of six or more bullocks yoked in pairs, and these were too expensive to transport grain more than 80 kilometres or so. However, meat could be driven to market on the hoof. And so, to begin with, expansion meant sending cattle or sheep to graze on up-country runs. The smaller settlers went off on their own; the nobs might have several runs in different parts of the colony, looked after by overseers and a few shepherds while the proprietor stayed on his comfortable estate nearer town. In the 1820s the money to be made from sheep was in mutton. Then came the seizing of sudden opportunity; as part of that rise in demand (that was later to send flocks of sheep across large stretches of North America, southern Africa and Argentina) mills in Yorkshire were increasing their demand so quickly that sheep farmers in Australia, 19 000 kilometres away, began switching from mutton to wool. A dray load of wool could be worth ten times a dray load of wheat, sometimes 20 times: it could be produced profitably almost any distance from the ports. At the same time, sea freights came

Rise and fall: Benjamin Boyd

Vantage points around Sydney Harbour were crowded on 18 July 1842 when Benjamin Boyd (financier, entrepreneur, adventurer and later pastoralist, whaler and trader) sailed through the heads in his schooner the *Wanderer* from Plymouth via Port Phillip.

Boyd had set his mind on making a fortune, and the colonists had already heard about him. He first established a branch of the Royal Bank of Australia (which he had set up in London in 1839) at Church Hill in New South Wales and rapidly extended his investments. By 1844 he was one of the largest landholders and graziers in the country; he established his own port, Boyd Town, on Twofold Bay, to handle the produce of his Monaro grazing lands and nearby, East Boyd, a whaling station. He entered politics to look after his interests.

Boyd's recruitment in 1847 of labour from southwest Pacific islands angered some colonists, and his restrictions on rations to his shepherds – no 'luxuries' such as tea or sugar – along with other attitudes provoked a contemporary to describe him as typical of 'the haughty gentlemanly, selfish class he represented'.

By 1847 Boyd had overreached himself financially, and his complicated business dealings were in trouble; by 1849 his Royal Bank was in liquidation.

Boyd left for the Californian gold fields, but had no luck, and in June 1851 the *Wanderer* left San Francisco; it had reached the Solomon Islands by 15 October. Boyd left the schooner to hunt game, but was never to return. It was speculated that he may have been killed and eaten by cannibals.

down so that it was cheaper to ship wool to Britain from Australia than from Germany. From 1830 to 1850 British imports of wool trebled and the Australian share of this increasing market went up by six times. By the middle of the century Britain's principal supplier was Australia.

To some, money from wool seemed as quick and easy as finding gold: it was only necessary to have enough cash to 'put it into four legs' and then watch it grow. In the 1830s, when the volume of bank loans increased by 600 to 700 per cent, gamblers floated on a sea of English credit: they put all their own money into sheep and borrowed up to three times as much again. According to theory, receipts from wool would cover costs, and rapid increases in flocks would make a gambler's fortune. Apart from the merchants and other speculators in town, many of those who went out and controlled their own runs often saw this as just a quick bet: they would make a killing and then go back to Great Britain. But fortunes were lost on the sheep runs like stakes at cards. The oddities of flood, bushfire and drought, the diseases of sheep, the uncertainties of credit, and plain ignorance, led to many disasters. With such a reliance on credit, a man was usually ruined if something went wrong,

and his creditors would take over his run; if *they* were also ruined, *their* creditors would take over. In a world of get-rich-or-bust more may have been ruined than got rich.

A depression hit New South Wales in the early 1840s. Banks failed or shut down. In its own exaggerated view of itself the whole colony seemed bankrupt. Total wool production continued to go up but those whose credit had flown too high fell down. When colonial ingenuity set up 'boiling down establishments' which bought sheep at five shillings a head and turned them into tallow, in one year pastoralists who needed cash sold two and a half million sheep to be boiled down. A moratorium and more sensible credit saved those who were not in too much of a mess, but many pastoralists had been cleaned out.

As often happens after the scourgings of a depression, what then emerged was a new efficiency. And this time there was a greater sense of permanence: as exports continued to increase there developed around the wool industry the first beginnings of commercial and financial sophistication in the colonies – 'pastoral houses' began holding wool auctions in Australian wool ports; there was a growth of banks and merchant financiers and foreign

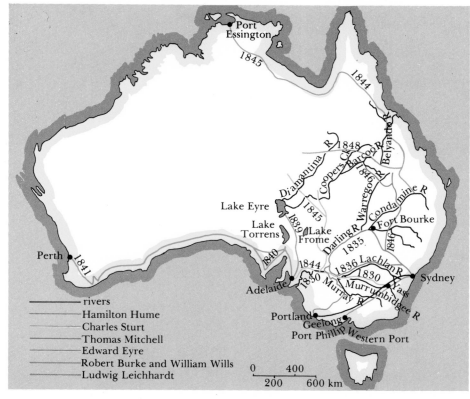

A whole new economy: *the rapid spread of the squatters produced a whole new area in the economy. After sheep shearing (above right) the wool would be sent by bullock wagon (centre right) to wool stores in one of the seaport towns (below right). If the worst came to the worst, and drought threatened the squatters' livelihood, there were 'boiling down establishments' (left) where sheep were boiled down to tallow.*

The tracks of the explorers: *the puzzle of rivers that flowed away from the ocean inspired the early explorers (left). They did not find a great inland sea, but the river system led to some of the most fertile land in Australia.*

rivers
Hamilton Hume
Charles Sturt
Thomas Mitchell
Edward Eyre
Robert Burke and William Wills
Ludwig Leichhardt

exchange markets. New types of notables had arisen and they gave more texture and diversity to the colonial hierarchies, but there was no disguising that they flourished through their dependence on the woolmasters and their British customers. It was necessary for British world trade that these small groups of local specialists should exist.

The rush to the grasslands had seized millions of hectares – both within the official borders of settlement and beyond them – and respectable people had become land thieves or 'squatters'. The most audacious land-grabbing episodes occurred when groups in Van Diemen's Land sailed sheep and whatever else they needed over to southern New South Wales and established three wool-growing settlements, each with its own port, at what became Geelong, Melbourne and Portland. Meanwhile, the Surveyor General in Sydney made a triumphal march across the Murray River into what he named 'Australia Felix' and proclaimed it as 'a country ready made for the immediate reception of civilised man, destined perhaps to become eventually a portion of a great empire'. He had scarcely returned to Sydney before overlanders occupied the territory he had surveyed. Soon emigrant settlers, many of them Scottish, were arriving at

Geelong, direct from Britain, and marching into Australia Felix to find their fortunes. In a few years almost all of southern New South Wales was settled. The Government of Sydney had to accommodate itself to this illegal settlement. It declared the area the 'Port Phillip District of New South Wales' and appointed a Superintendent, with his headquarters in the new town of Melbourne. When squatters moved into pastoral lands outside Brisbane, the Sydney Government declared Brisbane the administrative headquarters of the 'Moreton Bay District of New South Wales'. New South Wales now had an official area of settlement, two special 'districts', one in the south and one in the north, and between them 'the squatting districts', on all of which there was not supposed to have been any settlement. A large part of the most valuable land in Australia had gone for grabs.

A portion of the sheep owners were city credit institutions or absentee speculators (one of whom piled up 47 runs totalling two million hectares) with overseers working for them, and most of the working squatters had started with some money. It is true that some had begun as prudent overseers who had raised their own stock on the side, or

New social types: *the sheep rush introduced new social types into the colonies' structure, from the humble shepherd and the 'treacherous black' (above) to the venturesome drovers (left), and the squatter himself (right), who liked to see himself as 'monarch of more than he surveys'.*

been staked by a city investor, and others had established themselves by stealing someone else's animals. But most had started with money. Money was needed to buy sheep and provisions, and to cover costs for the 18 months or two years before the first wool cheque; and credit went only to those who had cash to begin with. The colonial dream that a property-less man could get some land and lift himself up in the world by his own efforts became weaker still.

Some of the colonial-born got into the rush – mainly the sons of successful officials and settlers – but the typical squatter was someone fresh from Britain with some money and some education who had come out with the intention of getting rich and then going back home. The discomforts of life on a run, living in a slab hut with its bark roof and mud and manure floor, were regarded as 'a few years of banishment'. On the other side of the picture, almost two-thirds of the bush workers in 1840 were assigned convicts, ex-convicts or colonial-born. The pastoral society was dominated by the new arrivals, but most of the work was done by those who were stuck in the place. Just as the black Australians were pushed aside in the first invasion, the sons of the first white Australians, the new Natives, were pushed aside in the second.

The centre of this society, which had been created in a few years, was made up of several thousand up-country slab huts. These were the 'head stations' where the working squatters lived, or, in the case of runs belonging to absentee speculators, the overseers. If the head station hut were distinguishable from others on the run it was because it was a little bigger, and perhaps because it had a veranda (a bark awning over an earth floor). Its furniture might consist of a bush bedstead of saplings tied with green hide, with sheepskins or possum rugs, a sea chest, a few iron pots and tin plates. According to the ethos of the wool rush, all a working squatter needed was something to eat and something to lie on while waiting for his new wealth. The human part of his domain consisted of the 'out stations', other bark-roofed slab huts, each usually with two shepherds and a hutkeeper, and with a rigid demarcation of duties: each shepherd had a flock to watch during the day while the hutkeeper did whatever cooking or cleaning suited his personal style. At night, when the sheep were folded in hurdles made of split palings, the hutkeeper slept nearby in a simple shelter of laced-up hide, with collie dogs beside him to give warning of native dogs or blacks. Shepherds

were despised by other bushworkers as 'crawlers after sheep'. Shepherds, however, often despised hutkeepers, although they had to be polite to them because the hutkeepers did the cooking.

For most shepherds, squatters and hutkeepers, life tended to be lonely and male and monotonous (except when monotony was relieved by catastrophe); breakfast, lunch and supper were all the same meal, cooked over an open fire – mutton, damper and tea. Pannikins of sweet tea, brewed in quart pots and drunk through the haze of pipe tobacco, seemed all that a man needed for solace. The impermanence of the squatters' tenure led to a stylisation of improvisation: the expected thing was for a squatter to live on his run like a tramp putting up for the night and to do no more than was necessary for survival. Whatever old aspirations he had to English standards of gentlemanliness were washed away by new colonial circumstances. A run might have been established for years without anyone bothering even to dig a vegetable garden: it was as if the huts were tents, the run a nomad's camp, and everyone would later pack up and go away. In such a cult of crudity and impermanence there was no place for wives or display mansions or cultivated leisure interests, not even for fences.

The same sense of movement impelled other members of this new society. Timber splitters, hurdle makers, shearers and dealers roamed through the bush from one run to the next. The main representatives of government in the areas beyond the officially settled territory, the Commissioners of Crown Lands, dressed like army officers and sometimes adjudicated from the saddle. Attached to them were the border police, dragoons whose concerns with blacks and bushrangers kept them on the move. In the ballads that began to celebrate this society, naming its parts and making it real, the heroes were usually going somewhere else. At times it seemed the only people who stayed still were the keepers of the grog shanties. The pastoral expansion did not throw up significant inland towns: a 'town' might be little more than a courthouse, an inn, a store, a few huts, a police barracks. What mattered were the bullock drays, filled with wool as high as a hay stack, and the city ports where the wool was shipped for England and where the intricate social webs of credit and middlemen were now being spun.

Crudity was the fashion: even in Sydney or Melbourne the squatters might still dress as bushmen, and back on the run, slovenliness was an essential part of style. Getting away for a while was one of life's rewards. Working squatters would sometimes hang around in town from the Squatters' Ball in January to the horse races in March; in the same way, when a contract was up, the shepherds might 'drink their cheques', sometimes a matter of a walk of up to a hundred kilometres to the nearest grog shanty where a week's drinking (and being cheated) could get rid of six months' wages.

Hospitality was equally obligatory, and whether with a squatter or with shepherds it might be much the same: an evening in a hut with pannikins of tea, pipes, yarns, ballads (clean and dirty), chaffing, bush news and talk of the performance of bullocks, horses or dogs. The required approach between two men meeting for the first time was one of frankness and cordiality, but for the convicts and ex-convicts there might be some reserve behind this outward

THE LAND GRABBERS / *THE RUSH TO THE GRASSLANDS*

openness. According to observers, their *esprit de corps* was an exclusive one, with a reckless internal generosity but a readiness to despise those outside the group.

Homosexuality was common among the convicts, and presumably it spread to some of the other colonists. Usually the only other shared sexual activity available was with black women, who were paid in tobacco and food (and sometimes further rewarded with syphilis and a half-caste baby that might be murdered for the sake of tribal purity). What affection existed was usually that between men, particularly that between a man and his 'mate', who was usually the man he worked with, with whom he might even divide his earnings. It was said that 'a man ought to be able to trust his own mate in everything', and these occupational associations, based on the habit of working in pairs, could become so permanent that although shepherds were always on the move ('a full two thirds of the labouring population of the country is in perpetual migration') they often moved in pairs. They could leave a run, drink their cheque, hump their blankets and clothes on their backs, and walk off to another part of the colony.

The squatting area made nonsense of orthodox classifications of frontiers: since it relied partly on forced labour it began as something of a 'plantation' frontier (yet with many modifications and quick changes); it was also something of a 'small farm' frontier because, although its units were big, its manpower was small and, except for the properties controlled by absentees, the owners of the flocks themselves worked. And, in a strange way, it was also something like the 'camp' frontier of a gold rush – a temporary settlement in search of quick wealth.

Farming was seen as a gamble for quick profits, with something approaching contempt for the land itself. Expansion had meant not improving the land or flock techniques, but getting more land. The squatters saw themselves not as farmers, but as something bigger. The sheep and cattle runs were not called farms. 'Farmers' were little men who grew wheat or maize or ran dairy herds, the most despised still being the 'dungaree settlers' living scarcely above the level of barter, selling their wheat for enough meat to keep them going and enough tea and rum to give them solace. On the pastoral runs the cattle and the sheep nibbled and trod down the native grasses. Weeds flourished. The native grasses were never to grow again.

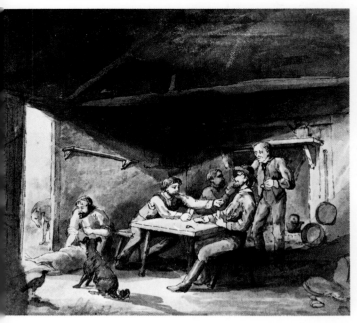

Station life: *within a few years, the squatters' rush produced a new social order that distinguished between the head station, where the squatter or his agent lived, and the outstations of the shepherds, many of whom were convicts or ex-convicts. Inside a head station (below left) a squatter takes his ease in front of the fire, which would also be used for cooking. By the early 1850s some head stations had achieved a modest standard of comfort (below). Outstations provided basic accommodation (left), which was preferable to the cramped movable 'watchbox' (above) from which shepherds kept watch on the sheep.*

The destruction of the blacks

A rate of economic progress greater than any other British possession was made possible in the colonies by taking land from the blacks, and by the use of convict labour. It is difficult to see how the pastoral rush could have kept up its thrust without the supply of ex-convicts and assigned convicts to man the shepherd's huts.

The wool rush coincided with the period of mass transportation of convicts and these extra labourers increased production out of all proportion to their numbers: while fewer than 30 000 convicts were sent out in the first 30 years, four times that number were transported in the following 30 years, at the time when Australia was becoming Great Britain's biggest single supplier of wool.

The convicts also built roads, important in reducing graziers' transport costs. The Great North Road, the Great West Road and the Great South Road stretched across New South Wales. Some convicts (those being punished for secondary offences) worked on the roads in 'iron gangs', iron bands riveted around their ankles and connected with a foot chain suspended from their belts; but even if they were without irons convicts could be shut up at night in stockades or in large portable boxes on wheels. Ring bolts were driven into trees to fasten the chains of recalcitrants; flogging posts were put up along the roads. In one month in 1833, 9000 lashes were ordered in New South Wales and 4250 in Van Diemen's Land. It became a children's game to lash a tree, pretending it was a convict. Discipline became more deliberately degrading: for a time there was a fashion for treadmills, then for solitary confinement.

But discontent with the convict system in the colonial towns, along with doubts in London, had political effects. Transportation to New South Wales was suspended in 1840, although it continued to Van Diemen's Land. Almost at once the graziers complained of a labour shortage. There was an experiment with a small consignment of Indians; then with some Melanesians; then a couple of thousand Chinese. The anti-transportation cry extended to *No convicts! No coolies! No cannibals!*, but the squatters complained that none of these new labourers was as satisfactory as the convicts they had complained about so bitterly.

For the blacks, the rush to the grasslands was a guerilla war in which the enemy seized the key rivers, creeks, lagoons and water holes, drove away the native game, despoiled sacred places, set up dissension by pushing one tribe into the territory of another, and killed insidiously by spreading new diseases.

To the *Sydney Morning Herald* it was clear that it was not the Creator's intention when he caused 'this great continent' to rise from the seas that it should remain 'an unproductive wilderness'. The British people took possession 'under the Divine authority, by which man was commanded to go forth and people, and *till* the land'. God had not allowed for nomads. To the blacks, the continent was merely 'a common – they bestowed no labour upon the land – their ownership, their right, was nothing much more than that of the Emu or the Kangaroo'.

To the whites, the 'Black Wars' that were fought across the grasslands could be seen as a struggle for control of territory, but for the blacks the white invasion was not only of territory; since for the Aborigines the land was part of themselves, the invasion was also an invasion of their souls. To a people who could believe that 'every living animal that roams the country and every edible root that grows in the ground are common property' it was a spiritual war (if not in these words) between modern individualistic competitiveness and traditional communalism and reciprocity.

In these Black Wars, using their bushcraft, the Aborigines could be guileful in spying out the enemy and stealthy and swift in ambush or raid; they had great successes in appropriating livestock (some of them even ran sheepyards in the back country with what they had appropriated) and in conducting terror campaigns of looting and burning; and at times they could believe they had superior magic on their side. But their magic could not match the self belief in the minds of the whites. In wars in the open grasslands their resistance was always, finally, defeated; their longest successes were where they could retreat into difficult country ... among extinct volcanoes ... along the Coorong ... in mountain ranges. Here they could keep up resistance for years. Then they were defeated.

At times the whites sent in the military; sometimes there

Some of the possibilities of horror in the relations between whites and blacks are evident in the story of the wreck of the Maria, *off the Coorong in South Australia. When blacks murdered the 26 survivors, the white authorities sent out a punitive party, chose two blacks as an example, then hanged them in front of the tribe, with orders that the bodies were to remain hanging. The Surveyor General made a watercolour titled* Two blacks hanged for murder, September 1840.

were declarations of martial law. In one such episode, when a hundred Aborigines were massacred in a swamp, the heads of 45 of them were boiled down to the bone and the skulls sent over to London; phrenologists held that it was enough to examine the Aborigines' craniums to know that they lacked intelligence. On their own initiative, the settlers often formed armed patrols which in reprisal might slaughter whole groups, perhaps quite innocent, in the scrub; when a force of Native Police was formed it became a new instrument of murder. It was almost impossible to get court evidence against killers of the blacks since blacks were not permissible court witnesses: settlers might shoot blacks in the scrub without anyone knowing, or leave them gifts of flour mixed with arsenic, or sheep carcasses spiced with corrosive sublimate. There were promptings to greater kindness from London and in Sydney protests against the spilling of 'black blood', but there was only one significant case when evidence could be brought against the murderers: seven settlers who killed a group of blacks were brought to Sydney, tried and hanged.

In Van Diemen's Land, in an attempt to clear the blacks from settled areas, a governor organised a drive lasting seven weeks and costing £35 000, but this human hunt found only a woman and a boy; what was left of the tribal Aborigines was later placed on an island. In a minor art vogue they were portrayed with the nobility of a dying race, in Roman busts with kangaroo skins draped like togas, or in sombre paintings reminiscent of a Greek tragedy – in a neo-classical style that matched the sofas and the silver tea services of the gentry. One group of them was still, in its own way, surviving: this was made up of the descendants of the black women who had done most of the work on the sealing islands; but that was not the kind of way in which the whites wanted to remember the blacks. In New South Wales some settlers were charitable; others found the blacks more useful in odd jobs than they cared to admit; some explorers depended on the blacks more than they said; but usually any benevolent policies of government were taken as meddling, likely to encourage an ungrateful violence. Towards the end of the 1830s the settlers saw themselves in danger along an 1200-kilometre front from what they saw as an organised rising. This mirage of fear was a mirror projection of their own conduct. It was the blacks who were the victims of a rising.

The Black Wars: *as the squatters' rush expanded into the Aborigines' lands, they fought back – but in these Black Wars the blacks always lost. Aborigines could be arrested and jailed for trespassing, even on their own land (above). Skirmishes between whites and blacks were often presented in the heroic style of European battle scenes (left).*

In London in 1837 a Select Committee, having examined means of protecting the civil rights of those who had been displaced by the spread of British power and of introducing them to British Christian civilisation, recommended that in Australia there should be protectors, missions, reserves, schooling and special interim codes of law for the blacks. Protectorates were set up in the Port Phillip District in 1838: the blacks would be taught how to work and in return they might get rations and clothing. At the same time Christian missions were to be given government money. Turned sober, industrious and God-fearing, the blacks might, after all, rise to the lower orders.

The remains of tribes, often the remnants of several different tribes, were put together in the protectorates and missions. But, dispossessed, their society shattered, and their new masters determined to take the young away from the old, many of the blacks responded with cynicism and despair. By the mid-century it was decided that the experiment had not worked. By that time whole populations were obliterated as surely as the Tasmanians and, in effect, Aboriginal society, as such, was destroyed in New South Wales.

The dying race: *for most Australians, the Aborigines seemed doomed to die out. In the terms of the theory of the survival of the fittest, they were inferior. Robert Dowling, in his* Aborigines of Tasmania *(above), tried to show them dying out with dignity.*

The conciliation: *the Australians had no paintings in the 'historical' style until Benjamin Duterreau painted* The Conciliation *(top) to give a sense of historic occasion to the conquest of the Tasmanian Aborigines. The survivors are shown with their white protector – Truganini is on his right – as if there were now about to be an end to their degradation.*

The innocents: *there were still some paintings of Aborigines as innocents. The style of John Glover's painting* Natives dancing at Brighton, Tasmania *(left) presents them in a mellow scene.*

The squatters take over

At first there were only five high officials – the Commissary, the Head of the Convict Department, the Judge Advocate, the Surgeon General and the Surveyor General.

Then a Colonial Secretary was appointed ... then an Inspector of Government Works ... a Postmaster ... a Superintendent of Police ... a Colonial Treasurer (for a while he kept some of the colony's funds in his bedroom) ... an Attorney General ... a Solicitor General ... a Controller of Customs ... a Collector of Internal Revenue ... an Auditor General ... a Government Printer. A Superintendent went to Port Phillip, and a Resident to Moreton Bay; Land Commissioners, with the Border Police, ran the squatting districts and police magistrates, with the Rural Constabulary, supervised the districts of official settlement. For the more spectacular work (bushrangers, blacks, cattle thieves) there was the Mounted Police. These new officials created around them their own small departments of clerks, copyists, attendants and messengers, as well as those with specialist roles.

The Governor could himself make appointments to all government jobs of up to £100 a year, and he recommended to the Secretary for the Colonies in London appointments to jobs of from £100 to £200 a year. Sheafs of papers moved backwards and forwards between heads of departments and the Governor as part of the compromises of patronage; an appointment once made might give its holder an opportunity to enjoy 'gross and outrageous corruption'. The Secretary for the Colonies still appointed all the top officials, his choices sometimes so disastrous that one governor described New South Wales as not only a colony of convict 'rogues and vagabonds' but also, as far as some of its civil officers were concerned, 'an excellent asylum for fools and madmen'.

'HE'S OFF! THE REIGN OF TERROR ENDED', said a Sydney newspaper when an unpopular governor was recalled.

As the squatters felt their strength they sometimes hired painters to immortalise their land. Eugene von Guérard was commissioned to paint two canvases of Koort Koort-nong, a grand Victorian property, one showing the homestead with a flock of sheep grazing in the foregound and the other showing cattle, including Master Butterfly, the property's prize bull.

Attacking governors was one of the most exciting political activities the colonists had, and throughout the 1830s public meetings, deputations, petitions and newspapers enacted a drama of protest, threat and intrigue that was followed by continuing concessions.

In these uproars there were two main factions: the Emancipists and the Exclusives. The Exclusives hated convicts, Emancipists, Catholics, Irish and anybody else who upset their nobbish ideas. Although in some way they could be Improvers, the interest in constitutional reform of most of them was merely that they alone should enjoy all of what they saw as the rights of Englishmen. They wanted to take over so that they could live like English gentry. In distinction from them the Australian Patriotic Association, formed in 1835, put up a Native and Emancipist view of life, with some touches of democracy. The Patriots wanted full civil liberties for ex-convicts and general social acceptance of their children, and from some of them came the belief that Emancipists and Natives were the only true Australians. (*Australia for the Australians . . . The land is theirs by right.*) But poor Emigrants were sometimes accepted as honorary Natives and in general the Patriots also became

for a while one of the main vehicles for liberal ideas brought from Great Britain.

As a political force the Emancipists and their allies made up a city connection. Most of the Emancipist factions belonged to the town, and they attracted other self-made townsmen, including Emigrants who came to the colony low but rose high in the town. This grouping of forces had its greatest success with the formation of the Sydney City Council. It gained control in the first council elections in 1842, overwhelming the nobbish interests, the first check to the nobs' idea that it was they who should take over. Their second check came in the same year – from the squatters.

On the face of it, the nobs were to gain much of what they wanted now that the greatest of the changes that had followed the colonial uproar was about to be put into practice: although the Governor would still control the bureaucracy and the colony's land policy and could also veto the Legislative Council's measures, the Council was now to be given the power to determine its own proceedings and there were to be elections to it, the elected members having a majority over those put in directly by the Governor; at the same time there was to be no great experiment with democracy – in fact on the day of the polls the unenfranchised in Sydney were so outraged that for an afternoon their riots seemed to give them control of the city.

Despite fear of the votes of some 'Romanists and liberals', it was to prove an assembly of the well-to-do, with a useful bias against Sydney which, with a quarter of the colony's population, secured only a twelfth of the representation. But the new Legislative Council was not the body the nobs had hoped for in the 1830s. It was a squatters' council. The squatters' men won most of the seats, and so many members were themselves squatters that the council usually adjourned for the wool-shearing season.

The political idea of the rebellious squatter now swamped all other political activity. The Australian Patriotic Association disbanded, broken after the success of the squatters, and when the squatters formed the Pastoral Association in 1844 to fight Governor Gipps's land policy, most of the colony's best-known political performers trooped into it as auxiliaries to the squatters' rebellion. The insults governors had previously suffered now seemed small. The word 'humble' was cut out of the Legislative Council's first 'humble address' to the Governor, and on the first day of the Budget debate it was moved that the Governor's salary be reduced from £5000 to £3000.

Most ordinary townsmen hated the squatters, but the squatters were too strong for them. Against town hostility, and despite their own divisions between absentee and resident, and large and small, the squatters were an efficient collective force demanding special government protection. Believing themselves surrounded by envy and malice, they would meet to discuss common action or to make threats, and they had the support of the city spokesmen who shared in their interests. Rather like desperadoes taking over a town and appointing their own sheriff, they now wished to become the government; they channelled other feelings of discontent to serve their purpose.

In the mid-1830s the Government had tried with a makeshift system of licences to give some legality to the squatters' land grab. In the 1840s when Governor Gipps wanted the squatters to pay more for the land they were

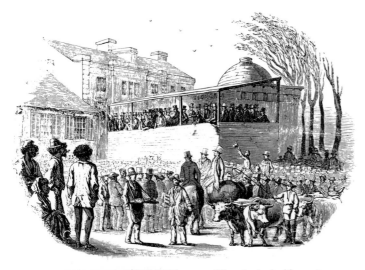

The colonies had begun to develop the habit of the public protest meeting, open to all (above), although when elections for the Legislative Council were first held in 1842, voting was restricted to those with wealth. However, the public meeting would later take on a life of its own. There seemed no limit to the vituperation with which unpopular governments were treated. When Governor Arthur was recalled from Tasmania a special celebratory poster was issued (left).

using they used their monopoly of political power – grabbed as quickly and spectacularly as their land – to defeat him. Governor Fitzroy, his successor, gave in. The squatters got what they wanted, a combination of grazing licences and rights to purchase strategic lots within a run. There was a last scramble and in the rush for the new leases some squatters lost their runs. Then, except for those who had been thrown in this last gamble, the squatters had secured both tenure of land and political power. At first some nobs, believing that a gentleman should own his land rather than lease it, had opposed the squatters. But nobs also speculated in squatting – if they did not they lost their significance in the rush – and, as a distinct and significant economic class, by 1850 they had largely dissolved.

Once the squatters had what they wanted they moved from rebellion to conservatism. Out on the runs life had already lost some of its peculiarities as the new hands from Britain began moving in as bush workers among the old hands. The new hands were less restless: many would stay put on the one property, and they did not disdain taking an interest in its future. Married couples were sometimes hired – the squatters found them cheaper – and children began to

appear among the sheep. With a security of tenure that was an asset they could sell, some squatters sold out to go back to Britain, but most stayed; they saw greater wealth 'further out' into the future. 'Head stations' became 'home stations', huts were replaced by weatherboard cottages and plans were made to build comfortable houses, some as ambitious as those of the disappearing gentry. Native trees and plants around home stations were cut down or pulled out and exotics planted in their place.

In town the squatters looked forward to a complete self-government, controlled by them, with a restricted and country-biased voting system giving them the main voting power. The successful ones tended to enjoy club life and some joined the Government House set, taking over many of the attributes of the nobs they had helped to destroy; but the special circumstances of the strange frontier where they had gambled and won meant that even if they wore the black hats of nobbishness they did not usually wear its gentlemanly sense of culture or responsibility.

Nevertheless, since in all countries the great landed interests could still seem the natural ruling class, it seemed to be the squatters who were now to be the rulers. And as well as their material and political success they were also winning an important moral victory: Improvement could be seen as 'moral enlightenment', but it could also be seen as developing 'the resources of Australia' into 'a smiling seat of industry' so that 'teeming millions' from Britain might find new 'greatness and glory'. In this profitable enterprise staple exports were the essential underpinning, and although Hobart and Sydney were still important ports in the world whaling industry, wool was now king. The opinion was strong that what mattered most in economic life was what could be drawn from the land; those who developed these 'resources', and above all those who exported wool, were called 'the producers', as if the rest were parasites. 'Let the producing interest be destroyed and the active fabric of society must crumble in ruins.'

Search for glory: Sir Thomas Mitchell

Thomas Mitchell was a restless, ambitious man with a poor but educated Scottish background. While serving as a second lieutenant in the Peninsular War, he learned how to gather topographical intelligence. He was promoted to the position of major in 1820, and the following year, aged 35, he and his wife arrived in New South Wales. He was appointed assistant to John Oxley, the Surveyor General, whom he succeeded in 1828.

Mitchell set about reorganising the Survey Department and initiated a successful road building program; but it was in exploration that he saw his chance for glory.

On his first expedition, in 1831, he went north to Tamworth in search of a large river flowing northwest: then in 1835 he attempted to trace the unexplored parts of the Darling River. His third expedition, in 1836, established his reputation when, after mapping the junction of the Darling and Murray rivers, he marched confidently southwest, down to the coast, and was so delighted by what he saw that he named the area Australia Felix.

Still inspired by the thought of a great north-flowing river, Mitchell began a fourth expedition in 1845 in search of an overland route to Port Essington but found neither.

Mitchell pursued other interests while employed as the colony's Surveyor General: he published accounts of his expeditions, produced *The Australian Geography*, for use in schools; took part in one of the last recorded duels in Australia; and developed such a record for insubordination to governors that, just before he died, he was about to be dismissed.

James Macarthur, John Macarthur's fourth son, was seen as the leader of the Australian 'aristocracy'. He managed the family estate at Camden Park, was involved in a number of business interests in Australia and played an active part in the colony's politics.

5. The Austral–Asiatics: 1830 to early 1850s

By 1850 there were five colonies established around the continent, and six settlements in New Zealand. With the spread of systematic colonisation by free settlers came ideas of political and social equality. Legislative Councils were constituted, and under pressure from the Anti-Transportation League *the British Government stopped dumping convicts in New South Wales and Van Diemen's Land.*

Taking over

Whether all the inhabitants of all the Australian colonies wanted to be called 'Australians' was not decided by the mid-century. And in any case the term did not include the New Zealand settlers. There were other possibilities.

That Australia, New Zealand and the smaller islands were south of Asia seemed obvious enough; to some they seemed the southern part of it. A publication called the *South Asian Register* had been started in Sydney in 1827 and the terms 'Austral-Asian' and 'Austral-Asiatic' were invented to encompass the Europeans who lived in this imagined South Asia. By mid-century there were more than 400 000 Austral-Asiatics in five colonies that, including deserts and

ocean, stretched from tip to tip across nearly 6500 kilometres of the Southern Hemisphere.

When the Swan River Colony had begun in Western Australia in 1829, the hope had been that a well-to-do squirearchy would appear almost at once, with large estates, fine houses to live in and plenty of willing labourers to do the work. But they found themselves in 'a miserable region, scarcely more valuable for the purposes of cultivation than the deserts of Africa'. Some of the settlers went home. Others moved to the convict colonies. When better land was found most of those remaining had run out of resources. There were no convicts to build roads and bridges; there was no Commissariat expenditure; much of the trading was barter; wages were often paid in kind; there were too few land sales to subsidise immigrants. Throughout the 1830s

Port Essington (above), established in northern Australia as a 'second Singapore', was finally abandoned, after 11 years of failure.

By 1842, when this view of Perth was painted (right), the Western Australian colony had been established for 13 years, but its failure was so great that it was still saddled with the name of 'the scarecrow colony'.

72

the colony was a settlement of 'sand, sorrow and sore eyes – the scarecrow colony'.

A new breed of British colonial reformers of the new school were delighted. Now *their* theories could be tried. So that it could start all over again with a proper scheme the British Government attempted to get back much of the land it had granted. But the colony's main success was not planned. Although there was reluctance to create 'a nation of Bedouins', sheep runs began to spread out, and they made money for those who ran them. However, in a colony whose potential stretched across two and a half million square kilometres they suffered from a unique sense of isolation: in a settlement separated from the others by desert, it was not only London that was far away; it took up to a month's sea voyage to get to Sydney. Sceptical of new schemes, the colonists petitioned for convicts. In 1850 the British Government obliged them.

In 1838 there was another attempt to set up a 'second Singapore' on the intractable northern coast, to be both trading centre and a place to show the flag so that the claim to the continent could seem more secure, and so that there could be a base, if one was needed, from which to protect the British world. A flat piece of land on the extreme north-central tip of the continent was chosen and named Victoria Town. Its sea frontage was called Port Essington. Troops were sent, a Commandant appointed; a wooden fort was built; flag poles went up; a jetty went out. A land route was explored across the continent to Port Essington. After 11 years of failure Port Essington was closed down.

In the province of South Australia, founded with so many rational hopes for Improvement, aspirations disintegrated. When confronted by a new environment and the old cupidities, the proposed 'systematic colonisation' became mainly a way for speculators to make money. Too many settlers stayed in the new town of Adelaide; there was not much development of agriculture; in 1841 the province was pronounced bankrupt and the British demoted it from a province to a colony. Expenditure was cut, immigration was suspended, Adelaide was partly emptied. South Australia could not even avoid 'the convict stain'. Immigrants from the 'pickpocket colonies' of New South Wales and Van Diemen's Land – stockmen, shepherds, whalers, builders – came to teach South Australia how to do things in the colonial manner, and some time-expired and pardoned

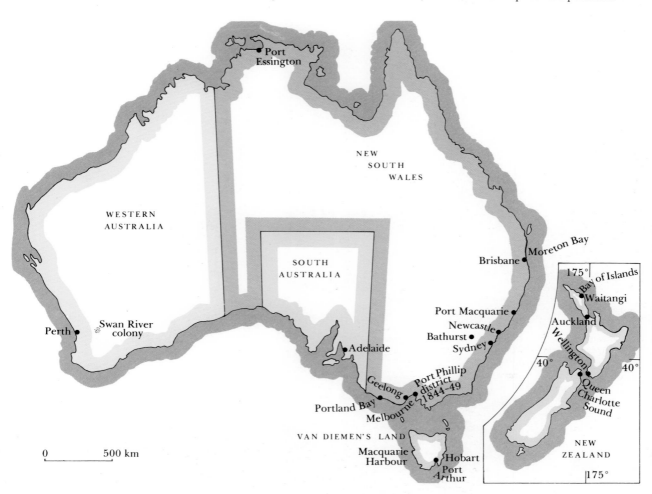

The map in 1850: *free settlers established the Swan River Colony in Western Australia and Adelaide in South Australia, and troops and a commandant were sent to Port Essington in the north. Some of the settlements in New Zealand's south island were sponsored by* churches, *while those in the north island tended to be despised as the mere overflow from Sydney. Meanwhile, the Port Phillip and Moreton Bay districts were beginning to press for separation from New South Wales.*

convicts were among them, and even some runaways. (The best South Australia could do in return was to transport to Van Diemen's Land some of those who were found guilty of crimes in Adelaide.) Even worse for those who had put their faith in planning: economic success first came to South Australia from the unplanned expansion of the squatters who came over from New South Wales, and although the squatting interest was not so dominant as in New South Wales, it could still seem that it might be about to take over South Australia. Further prosperity came to Adelaide with another unplanned and irrational process – the 'coppermania' that followed the chance discovery of copper. With the copper boom and the wool boom the value of South Australia's exports quadrupled in five years.

In its aspirations towards religious liberty, South Australia was also disappointed: it was achieving no more than New South Wales. The opposition to government subsidy led at first to a state of 'religious destitution' and then to years of bitter dispute, after which, for a while, all except the most dissenting denominations abandoned their principles and accepted the government money for which the Church of England had been fighting (letting the others

have some so that it could have more). There was an equal disappointment in political ideals. Adelaide was the first colonial town with a municipal council. It collapsed, however, two years after its incorporation because of lack of interest.

Nevertheless South Australia continued to see itself as different, and in a more complex manner than did the Swan River colony with its grudging sense of neglect and isolation. There was the consolation that South Australia was less Catholic and less Irish than New South Wales – to a Protestant Improver this at least could be seen as a token of the success of the values of rational civilisation – and there was, among the Protestants, an unusual diversity. With as many German Lutherans as Catholics, South Australia was the only colony with a sizeable proportion of emigrants not from the British Isles.

But it had been part of its founding dream that it should be a society based on the civilising virtues of agriculture, rather than on the gambling and plunder of those who saw Australia as 'one great sheepwalk'. Despite the founding failures in small farming, the desire persisted that South Australia should be 'one of the first agricultural colonies in the world' and by the mid-1840s this prospect could at last

South Australia booms:
Hindley Street, Adelaide, 1846 (left). After its early disasters, by the mid-1840s South Australia was beginning to enjoy some taste of success.

The Kapunda Copper Mine, South Australia (below left). The development of sheep-raising in South Australia, and then the discovery of copper, helped raise the colony from its early disasters.

The stripper-harvester (below), invented in Adelaide in 1843, was the first significant machine developed in Australia.

seem real. When markets for wheat were found in Adelaide after the successes of squatting and copper mining, and later, in Singapore and other regional ports, there began to spread out of Adelaide the comforting sight of the neat and rational fences of small family farms; at the agricultural shows, ploughing contests began to replace the shearing competitions. A South Australian Agricultural Association was formed. Above all, as a sign of Improvement, was the invention by John Ridley, Australia's first miller, of a stripper-harvester. It was not of much immediate practical use, but as a symbolic act it was of great importance: an Australian had invented a machine.

At first European settlement in New Zealand was part of the expansion of the settlements in eastern Australia. There was a township, and elsewhere sawmilling camps, whaling stations, mission settlements, small traders, totalling about 2000 Europeans by the end of the 1830s. When plans for 'systematic colonisation' spread to New Zealand it became a colony on its own. By the mid-century, there were about 25 000 Europeans in the six main settlements, more than half of them in Auckland and Wellington.

In the southern settlements there was something of South Australia all over again. Once again colonists saw themselves as 17th century North American settlers, and in fact three settlements were sponsored exclusively by individual Protestant churches. Wellington had three times as many Methodists as Catholics. The north, however, was seen (and by the south despised) as 'Australian'; Auckland was described as 'a mere section of the town of Sydney transplanted to the shores of New Zealand', and when a New Zealand pastoral movement began, the sheepmen's clothes were those convention demanded for squatters in New South Wales. On their runs they acted in some of the same ways, although their huts were an adaptation of Maori dwellings, and they were more likely to let their Maori women live with them instead of fornicating with them and then dismissing them.

The strongest differences between settlement in New Zealand and in Australia were enforced by the Maoris. Perhaps this was where the parallel with North America lay: like the American Indians and unlike the Australian 'blacks', the Maoris had traditions of warfare. Their lands were not seized by the Europeans as were those of the

Lutheran settlement: *the Lutheran settlements, such as the one at Bethany (top), were peculiar to South Australia. The South Australian Lutherans produced* Die Deutsche Post *(above), Australia's first foreign language newspaper. The Lutheran Johann Gramp (left) established the first vineyard in the Barossa Valley at Jacob's Creek.*

75

Australian blacks. There were instead attempts to cheat them with respect, paying for land purchases with blankets, nightcaps, pipes, beads, sealing wax, or with what the Maori chiefs most prized – muskets, kegs of powder, casks of shot and boxes of cartridges, the possession of which produced an immediate technological revolution. Many of the Maoris picked up reading and writing from the missions (they would sometimes scorn illiterate whites) and the adoption of the new religions gave inter-denominational rivalry some of the zest of tribal disputes. In some districts Maoris took up European-style farming and trading. They soon discovered the enormous profits to be made from the resale of land, and became shrewd salesmen.

From the beginning of systematic colonisation people theorised about racial amalgamation, sometimes suggesting that the Maori chiefs should be turned into 19th century English landed gentry. Land was allotted to Maoris in some of the new systematic settlements, but in a way senseless to them. A Commissioner appointed by the British Government to inquire into land disputes found for the Maoris, but with 4000 Europeans spread over the disputed territory, nothing was done. By the mid-1840s the Maoris

and the whites were at war in some districts. Garrison troops from New South Wales were rushed to New Zealand and a local militia was raised. The final act occurred when the Lieutenant Governor reduced a Maori stockade with a force of 60 officers, 1100 troops, 450 Maori auxiliaries, five cannons, four mortars and two rocket tubes.

The second oldest of the colonies, the island of Van Diemen's Land, was, with 70000 people, the second largest in European population. It was also the whitest, since the blacks had been removed from the mainland – and, externally, with its greenness, it was the most like 'Home'. Its landed gentry lived an assured life in their neo-classical mansions, and there was a civilised tone to its farming, with wheat-growing as well as sheep grazing. With no useful land 'further out', there was a need to increase production by making better and more intelligent use of what there was. It remained a 'plantation' economy, still built on convict labour, since throughout the 1840s at a time when transportation had been suspended in New South Wales, convicts still flooded Van Diemen's Land. But while there were those who wished to rub out the convict stain, to those

New Zealand: *in 1839 New Zealand was declared part of New South Wales. Two years later New Zealand finally succeeded in having itself declared a colony in its own right. The two principal towns were Wellington (right) and Auckland (below right) both on the north island.*

The Maoris as fighters were better organised than the Australian Aborigines. The first of several 'Maori Wars' (below) ended in 1845 when the British attacked a Maori stockade with cannon, mortars and rockets, killing most of the people inside it.

who did well out of it convict labour seemed as natural and as necessary to civilisation as serfdom or indentured labour or slavery. With its flour mills and breweries, its tanneries and soap and candle factories all meeting its needs and its own forges beating ploughshares it could feel a certain self-sufficiency. Like Melbourne, Hobart was a wool port, but it was also a whaling port – and a port of cooperage, rope making, sail making, and shipbuilding. The first marine engine manufactured in Australia was made in Hobart.

Along the southern coast of the Port Phillip District of New South Wales, at several of the beaches where bay whalers had camped with their boats and boiling down plants, small settlements were now forming, serving the squatters; but the main squatters' port was Geelong, where the first of them had landed on the beach with their stores in 1836, now laid out as a town, with its own small suburbs, and its mechanics institute, its friendly societies and savings banks and its two theatres. By 1848 Geelong had outstripped Melbourne in the value of its wool exports. It was described as the 'pivot' on which the prosperity of the Port Phillip District would turn.

Hobart Town in 1851 (above), the year Van Diemen's Land was given a partly elected Legislative Council. It was not until 1855 that the name 'Tasmania' was proclaimed officially.

The rise of Melbourne:
Geelong (right) was threatening Melbourne as a wool port but Melbourne was nevertheless growing, not least in its hatred of rule from Sydney. Two views from the early 1840s show the cottage of the first commandant (below) and Melbourne as a frontier town (below right), complete with tavern, theatre and town crier.

Melbourne itself had quickly grown from a few huts into a town of merchants and dealers, servicing the squatters and living on them, but, by and large, hating them. Its Town Council, made up mainly of Scots and Ulstermen, professed a radicalism less Native and more Emigrant than Sydney's. The pastoral districts had more worker-owners than the rest of New South Wales, more middle-sized men with less of a gambler's wastefulness. But the squatters, whose actions had created the Port Phillip District, appeared more dominant than in Sydney, which had been created by other means.

Whatever the tensions between Melbourne and the Port Phillip squatters, both detested rule from 'the Sydney side'. The Port Phillip District elected six men to the Legislative Council but since Sydney was 960 kilometres away it was almost impossible to find candidates other than absentees. In derision, in the 1848 election, Port Phillip elected the British Secretary of State for the Colonies as one of its representatives. In the local press 'freedom', above all, meant freedom from Sydney.

Things moved more slowly in the Morteon Bay District of New South Wales. Until 1840 there was a penal settlement among the mangroves and mosquitoes of Brisbane, but even when a Prison Commandant was replaced by a Government Resident, Brisbane still languished. The Moreton Bay squatters despised it and attempted to set up their own rival port. They were still on a frontier of expansion. A 'flood of gentlemen' had claimed the Darling Downs for their sheep and cattle runs; now gentlemen were looking to the unoccupied north, where there seemed new prospects of *something better further out*.

The same Surveyor General whose explorers' party had opened up Australia Felix to the squatters now moved out with an explorers' party from Brisbane into land that would 'rejoice the heart of a stockholder . . . the finest country I have seen in a primeval state'. Another squatters' annexation followed. For a brief period a 'Colony of North Australia' was formed, and then abandoned, but explorers and overlanders were in any case moving north. There was talk of forming three colonies – 'Cooksland', 'Capricornia' and 'Carpentaria' – and of growing cotton and sugar as well as grazing cattle and sheep. In January 1851 there was the first meeting that demanded separation from New South Wales.

By 1850 there were already a few substantial buildings in Melbourne, such as the first Treasury (top) and Customs House (above).

In the 1840s Brisbane was still on the frontier of expansion (top and above). There still seemed 'something better further out'.

In Sydney, 'Anniversary Day', the celebration of Phillip's landing at Sydney Cove, had early taken on a significance given previously only to royal birthdays. In 1838 it became the first public holiday of colonial origin, kept up by a race meeting, pigeon shoots, cricket matches and a regatta on the harbour watched from the foreshores by a crowd with the picnic lunches they had brought, or watermelon, peaches, nectarines and pies bought from vendors.

There was concern in New South Wales and in Van Diemen's Land (where 80 per cent of the colonists lived) about what it meant to be an Australian. National anthems were written (and forgotten) and there was an assumption in Sydney (shown for example, in the choice of 'national' to describe Sydney's institutions) that it was, somehow, the 'capital of Australia' and that if there were to be a nation, it would be a development of New South Wales. But such ideas could seem remote in the Port Phillip District, which had fewer Natives and sought its freedom from Sydney; in

Western Australia and in New Zealand, so far away, they seemed irrelevant; in South Australia, proud of its purity from convicts, they were insulting.

Nevertheless, Sydney at least thought it time for a definition of 'national character' or 'national opinion'. But what kind of a 'national character' was it to be? What sense of special destiny was there for an enterprise that began with the founding of a penal settlement? If God had a purpose in arranging this act, it could only have been that of salvation through penitence; but this view affronted respectability. Nor could any sense of history be respectably appealed to. To those who controlled the debate, Bold Jack Donohoe was not an acceptable hero. Nor were there any great national ideals embodied in the State, since it consisted of London-appointed officials.

Looking back to English history was enough for some, although it could be an affront to the Irish and Scottish. Or could the colonies adopt a fictitious 'British' history, disguising its Englishness, and rename institutions 'British'? Or was it to be 'the land, boys, we live in', a new society? Natives and Emancipists had impulses towards this, but it was hard for them to say what they meant. Was it possible to be a nation that, though lacking a past, could look to the future for its history? This was the Improvers' view. Everyone could be made better. But with what distinctiveness? Would the answers come, as the Improvers who looked to education believed, in the development of a distinctive national culture? If so, it had not yet arrived. In the 1830s several magazines had deliberately concerned themselves with the idea of establishing a national consciousness through a literary culture. But the waves of Emigrants in the 1840s drove this hope away. To meet their tastes, the new magazines were direct imitations of English

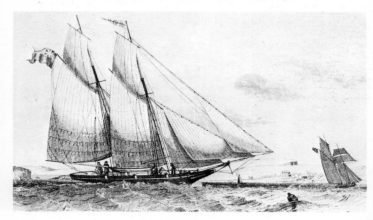

By the 1840s magazines in Australia began to run illustrations. The Heads of the People, *published from 1847 to 1881 (above), projected on its cover a slightly sophisticated image of what it might mean to be an Australian. The* New South Wales Sporting Magazine, *published from 1848 to 1849, saw Australia as a land*

of sporting men, as in this engraving of a racing yacht (top), one of the first registered in the new Australasian Yachting Club in Sydney. The Atlas, *published from 1844 to 1848 (above), whose coat of arms reflected native themes, projected a highly political view of Australia.*

magazines, some put together with scissors and paste. Novels were written about the colonials using the tricks of the day, but giving some description of colonial life; in verse, following the trend in Britain, there was a switch from the Augustan to the Romantic, and some attempts to accommodate the European vision to the Australian landscape. But a great deal of the verse might as well have been written in Manchester. Esteem seemed to be sought more by approximation to the fashions of the homeland than by Native experiment.

Despite concern that colonial society might be 'unfitted, and wholly unprepared, for the establishment of a theatre', one had started in Sydney in 1833; it was patronised by the reforming Governor Bourke and welcomed as a diversion preferable to 'horse racing, cockfights, bullbaiting, skittles, billiards and gaming of every description'. Other theatres went up in the main colonial towns, each with some variation on the royal name: a 'Theatre Royal', a 'Royal Victoria Theatre', a 'Royal Theatre', a 'Victoria Theatre', a 'Queen's Theatre Royal'. Italian opera was introduced in the 1840s; a few plays, some with bushranger themes, were written by colonists. In self-congratulation, one newspaper

suggested that colonial theatre was 'at least equal if not superior to any of the second-rate London theatres', and entrepreneurs went to England to seek suitable second-rate talent. What could matter most in the theatre was that it should be 'the latest from London'. Concerts became popular in the 1830s in Sydney and music schools opened.

Several good second-rate English painters passed through the colonies, and several others stayed. Some of their more ambitious work, particularly of landscapes, had to be shipped to England to sell. For a season, Australia could seem the land of the fern. There were fern and palm devices in silver picture frames and silver presentation pieces, in furniture and pottery; painters looked out for fern gullies; at a fancy-dress ball the woman who went as 'Australia' wore a dress with extensive fern decoration and carried a fan in the form of the tail of a lyrebird.

Even the first colonial architectural style – Georgian with verandas – was losing self-confidence. Single-storey houses with verandas on three or all four sides survived as 'homesteads' in the country, but when blocks of two- or even three-storey terraces began going up in town in the late 1830s there was pleasure that many of them did not

The sublime: *European painters continued to bring a European vision to Australia. For Conrad Martens it was the style of romantic grandeur – whether among romantic cliffs luminous with light in the ranges of New England (above), or in the storm and stress of Sydney Harbour's heads (left).*

In the colonial style there was a tendency to build churches in revival-gothic and courthouses in revival-classical. When it was built in the early 1840s, Sydney's new courthouse at Darlinghurst (right) was the most ambitious reminder of Ancient Greece in Australia.

have ungainly verandas. It is true that shops and hotel verandas spread over the pavements, but what seemed more important was that churches were now in Early English Gothic and courthouses had Classical façades.

Of the poets, Charles Harpur made the most serious attempts to adjust the English vision of William Wordsworth and other Romantic poets to the Australian continent; he was also ambitious in seeking a history for Australia in a future where there would be an extension of the ideas of liberty and human brotherhood. The son of an ex-convict schoolmaster, he led a life inhibited by lack of conversation and frustrated by lack of recognition. (One of his sonnets was 'On the Fate of Poetical Genius in a Sordid Community'.) He was contemptuous of the power of the Emigrants and regretted the failings of the Natives. He said, 'I am not one of the present men of Australia, nor could I mass myself down, endeavour to do so as I might, into the dead murky level of their intellectual grossness.'

Even those who sought a proud future for the colony sometimes expressed despair that the colonials were excessively concerned with drinking, sport, gambling and money-making. In particular, the 'fatal facility' for making

Patriotic table centrepiece: *when Thomas Smart, the well-to-do son of a convict, ordered a silver table centrepiece (above), he displayed his patriotism by including in the design an Aborigine, three tree ferns, two emus, two kangaroos and a cabbage palm.*

Representation of Australia through its animals reached a climax in the seven volumes of John Gould's The Birds of Australia. *These birds (above) are Rose Hill Parakeets.*

The terrace house was now coming into favour (above left), making the colonies seem more 'English' – although the terrace houses maintained vestiges of the colonial veranda.

Charles Harpur (left), now most noted of the early poets, had a romantic and liberal vision of Australia, but suffered much from Australia's realities.

money was usually taken to be the root of all the other evils. The gentlemanly pursuits of money-making, gambling, sport and drinking were now becoming democratised. The same process was occurring in the British Isles, but in the colonies there was no hiding it. Most of the poorer classes lived with less evident destitution than those in the British Isles; they could eat more and engage more freely in some of the amusements of the rich; they seemed to have more opportunity to make money and, if they made it, to buy the kinds of goods previously associated only with their betters. These events seemed so severe an attack on the moral order that some took the 1840s depression as a judgment.

Such obsessions continued, especially among the rich. In a famous debate in the New South Wales Legislative Council, the most illustrious of the landowners warned against the dangers of wealth if it fell into common hands; he saw 'the danger of a deeply rooted, sordid love of gain becoming the prevailing character of the community and obtaining undue influence in its public councils' if, as in the United States, it was combined with 'the democratic spirit'.

In the late 1840s the Colonial Office began to consider giving South Australia and Van Diemen's Land the same system of partly elected legislative councils that New South Wales already possessed, and to turn the Port Phillip District into a separate colony (with a similarly elected Legislative Council), to be named 'Victoria', as if it were a theatre. It also considered allowing the four colonies to make their own constitutions at some suitable future time.

The Secretary of State for the Colonies wanted more than that: he proposed for Australia a perfectly rational constitution, matching the Improving spirit of the age, and expressed with geometrical balance. At the base there were to be strong local government organisations; above them would be the four colonial legislatures, each itself nicely balanced between lower house and upper house, on the English pattern; above them, at the apex, there was to be an assembly, appointed by the four colonial legislatures, so that, like the United States (although with less democracy about it) Australia might become a federation.

The colonies were not interested. South Australia wished to keep clear of the pickpocket colonies and to maintain an independent land policy, and all three of the small colonies were suspicious of the likely dominance of New South Wales; but lukewarm indifference was the overriding reaction. The great distances separating the four main cities gave the scheme a sense of impracticability and, apart from the tariff disputes already begun between New South Wales and Van Diemen's Land, there did not seem to be any special purpose served by a federation. Surrounded by apathy, the Secretary of State stuck by his plan for three years, but when the Bill reached the House of Lords there was a great deal of opposition, ranging from allegations of impracticability to allegations that this kind of arrangement would usurp the power of the British Government and lead to the dissolution of the British Empire. The government was weak in Parliament and, to save the rest of the measures, it gave in on federation. As the next best thing, the Governor of New South Wales was to be called the Governor General, but nobody knew what that would mean. Each colony was to go its own way. Except as a geographic term, there would be no Australia.

Manly independence

It was a time when it seemed both ordinary common sense and an expression of divine will that, as lesser creatures, women should lack property rights and general civil and political liberties.

But in the Australian colonies in their opening decades, two classes of women were also open to an almost unparalleled quantity of permissible public abuse. All the women convicts and many of the female Emigrants were axiomatically spoken of as prostitutes. The convict women were seen as 'excessively ferocious' . . . 'all of them, with scarcely an exception, drunken and abandoned'. 'Soon after their arrival they begin to be negligent, and from negligence they turn to pilfering, and from pilfering generally follows drunkedness, and from drunkedness generally debauchery.' Their conduct on the voyage from England made the transports 'floating brothels'; their conversation was 'universally obscene'; in the Female Factories, 'the atmosphere was polluted with the fumes of tobacco and the walls echoed with the shrieks of passion, the peals of foolish laughter and the oaths of common converse'; when they

were assigned as servants 'a great number were drunkards and a still larger proportion thieves'. Similarly, with female Emigrants; when emigrant ships berthed at Hobart 'the most vile and brutal language was addressed to every woman as she passed along – some brutes even took still further insulting liberties, and stopped the women by force and addressed them, pointedly, in the most obscene manner'. Such abuse was also a matter of course in public life: thus it was said by *The Sydney Herald* that on the emigrant ships the women's conduct was 'frequently riotous and immoral' and that 'the great bulk of these creatures add pollution even to a society of convicts'.

In both cases, at the very least, what was said was exaggerated, but what is remarkable is that, whatever the particular truth or falsity of these thousands of rhetorical assaults on women, for more than half a century the colony's males, or the more privileged of them, were allowed an open season to curse women as prostitutes and drunkards. With an irony not unknown in public defences of morality, this enabled many of these men to engage in a titillating indulgence, in which they could publicly castigate women for what their detractors privately themselves did, as

men. To this was added another extraordinary circumstance: for most of the colonies' existence men had abnormally outnumbered women.

Yet, despite these rituals of male arrogance, in other ways the colonies may have been unusually prolific in male-female working partnerships, at least on the farms (if not on the squatters' runs, where the only usual male-female partnership was a sexual one degrading to a black female). On the farms, females and males worked as hard as each other, trying to make a go of it. Even among the better-off, the wives, as well as managing the household (in itself a small business) might also control the distribution of rations and stores and manage the dairy; if their husbands were away they might take over general management of the property. Although nothing was said about this, the 'taming of the wilderness' in Australia was (except in the squatting districts) as much a matter for women as for men: perhaps, among themselves, at least some of the women and men recognised this, even though it was not spoken of in public. In the towns there was a difference: household skills were, of course, essential to women and these could include various kinds of manufacturing – butter making, cheese making,

Images of women: *the most popular view of the women convicts was that they were uniquely licentious, as shown in this contemporary drawing of women farewelling convicts leaving for Australia (above left); yet occasionally there was a different view, as in the portrait of the convict nursemaid in James Taylor's panorama of Sydney (below left).*

Women appear in colonial paintings and etchings: a woman and her daughter come out of a Hobart shop (above left); a woman is seen stooping to pick up her shopping basket (above); a squatter's wife rides proudly along George Street in Sydney beside her husband (left). But there are very few illustrations of women working.

baking, preserve making, dressmaking and so forth – but 'toiling' was now being seen as producing goods and services for money – at least if men did it: women might work as domestic servants or as dressmakers or governesses, or run shops or taverns, but this was not 'productive'.

Yet not even in Britain were female factory workers seen as 'workers'. The habit had grown and it had spread to the colonial towns in Australia, of imagining that 'work' was something done only by men. Of the first three newspapers that were produced in New South Wales for 'the humbler classes' one described itself as 'a peculiarly Working Man's Paper' and another as 'the Working Man's Guardian'. There was no reference to Working Women. Despite the realities of colonial life in which so much work was shared, books were now coming from England explaining that 'the sphere of Domestic Life is the sphere in which female excellence is best displayed'. And while in these new writings the family was seen as the basis of society – the theoreticians of 'systematic colonisation' in South Australia and New Zealand had seen the participation of 'young couples' as an essential part of their foundation – when it came to extolling the virtues in the humbler classes

establishing homes of their own it was not the women who were exhorted towards this, or husbands and wives together: controlling one's own home was seen as one of the principal forms in which the humbler classes could display 'a *manly* independence'.

Meanwhile, women were active in the civilising missions of the temperance societies; some female friendly societies were formed; and, as well as running the 'Ladies Committees' of the benevolent institutions, wives of the colonies' rulers had begun to form institutions of their own. Thus, in response to the irrationality of bringing out shiploads of women to meet the demand for servants and wives without making proper plans for establishing the newcomers, Caroline Chisholm set up four Homes for female emigrants and established an employment-arranging (and sometimes a marriage-arranging) service.

In a society in which one of the benevolent institutions could proclaim in its annual report that most of those in distress had become destitute 'through their own immorality' and were 'unworthy of the smallest consideration', Caroline Chisholm saw the essential

Among the few illustrations of 'women's work' are an S. T. Gill painting of a cosy, well-equipped kitchen (above) and another Gill painting of a woman hanging out some washing (left).

improving role as one to be carried out by 'good and virtuous women'. It was women (whether they were good and virtuous is not recorded) who received letters from the English prison reformer Elizabeth Fry and attempted changes in the Australian Female Factories, and it was women who founded various Female Schools of Industry, institutions that were intended to reform young women and make them useful. Working with daily timetables that told the girls when to wash, when to sew, when to learn and when to pray, the organisers wished to instil into their charges 'every hour, every day, regularity, industry and cleanliness'. By these means they hoped to make young women 'more serviceable in the sphere of life in which they are likely to move'. They were making life safe for 'manly independence'.

Good works: Eliza Darling

What shoot little birds with a great big gun. Poor dear little things! And they say 'it's all fun'.

These words were written by Governor Ralph Darling's future wife when she was a young girl. Strong opinions, philanthropic purpose and a sense of duty to use her 'God-given talents' were bred into Eliza Darling by her devout mother, whose religious faith sustained her when her army officer husband was killed in 1804 during the Napoleonic Wars.

Eliza Darling's talents for good works were given opportunity for expression soon after she arrived in New South Wales in 1825, as wife of the Governor. As well as producing four children in the six years she and her husband were in the colony, she became involved with the Female Orphan School, the Ladies' Committee of the Female Factory and the Benevolent Society, and founded the Female School of Industry and the Female Friendly Society. She encouraged the setting up of public amenities for children and supported the Sunday School movement. She and her husband were patrons of the new Sydney Dispensary for the provision of medical advice to the poor.

At a time when women were the unpaid organisers of much charity work, Eliza Darling showed a strong, practical interest in the female convicts and persuaded other women in the colony to assist her. Elizabeth Fry, the English prison reformer, saw Eliza Darling's work as being ahead of penal reform in England.

When she and her husband retired to England, she wrote *Simple Rules for the Guidance of People in Humble Life, More Particularly for Young Girls Going Out to Service* and dedicated it to the inmates of the Sydney Female School of Industry. The book went through three editions, so that even when Eliza Darling had gone, her words still carried authority in Sydney.

Divisions as to what life should be about give existence a sense of shape and urgency. To many of the colonists the great division of the day, for which one group of people would contest with another, was whether one should drink alcohol only in moderation, or totally abstain. To others it was whether the mechanics institutes should be controlled by the Emigrants or the Natives. To others what mattered was the humbling of the ascendancy of the Anglicans; to others the frustration of Rome's invasion of the colonies.

For a short season in Sydney, the only colonial town with elected politicians, once concern with the rebelliousness by the squatters had subsided when they got what they wanted, the most significant sense of political difference lay between the Legislative Council of New South Wales and the City Council of Sydney.

In aggregate, despite its internal disorders and factional formlessness, the Legislative Council still stood for an English view of life. The squatters had been graceless in their declarations of self-interest, but there they were, members of the gentlemen's clubs and, if anything, their political ambitions were even more oligarchic than those of the old nobs. On the other hand, the first Sydney Council included three butchers, two publicans, two builders, a druggist, a cabinet maker, a merchant tailor, a linen draper, a tanner and a miller. About half of them were Natives. Several were sons of Emancipists, and the first Mayor was married to the daughter of the colony's richest Emancipist. When one prominent alderman, who had come to the colony as a mere sergeant in a garrison regiment and had grown rich and become associated with gentlemanliness by marrying the daughter of a lieutenant, went to a Queen's Birthday Ball at Government House, he was asked to leave, because of his earlier non-commissioned rank. (The alderman subsequently got his own back by attending the Mayor's fancy-dress ball dressed half as a sergeant, half as an alderman. The next year he was made Mayor.)

The governors complained of the quality of the debates of the Legislative Council. But the Legislative Council looked down on the debates of the Sydney Council as 'noisy, contentious and meaningless'; its language was 'indecent'; its meetings were like 'the burlesque and beer garden ruffianship of American legislatures'; it was considered to be in the hands of the liquor interests; it put too much emphasis on equality; it was shameless in its use of patronage as a way of helping the needy. It was considered excessively and crudely chauvinistic, and spoken of contemptuously as Emancipist and 'Australian' – second-rate, non-British. To the scorn for the idea of the Emancipist as self-made man was added scorn for any fellow who had risen above his station.

Along with their sense of brotherhood found in the institutions of mutuality, the Emigrant Improvers had also brought with them the view that Jack might not only band together with the other Jacks in a friendly society; he might also seem as good as his master. It was a view already present in a colony where bushrangers were becoming examples of rugged independence; but while the sense of equality of Bold Jack Donohoe was expressed by roaming hills and dales like wolf or kangaroo, some Emigrants brought with them more ordered and institutionalised ambitions for equality; the secret ballot, manhood suffrage, payment of MPs. Some of the new idealism of political equality in the British Isles emigrated to autocratic Australia and tried to set itself up in the same forms, with some wish to realise in the new world the frustrated idealism of the old. Although taken up now and again, the question of separation from Britain lacked wide appeal. It did not seem as familiar an idea as the secret ballot.

In the towns in the 1840s the phrase 'the people' began to be used to harness to political ambition the dreams of those who hoped to go up in the world. In the manner of the age, 'the people' did not include domestic servants or unskilled labourers. 'The people' were roughly those in that part of the economic scale stretching from skilled workers and clerks to small 'masters' and shopkeepers. As the decade went on there grew a belief that 'the people' were frustrated only by the power of the squatter 'monopolists' and that their simple goodness was corrupted by this evil.

In 1843 the Mutual Protection Association, formed during the economic depression to express liberal and

radical opinion, supported the Sydney Council as a true voice of 'the people', but the Association collapsed when the squatters had their short season as leaders of rebelliousness. However, liberal and radical newspapers continued sporadically, and in 1848, with the squatters satisfied, the Constitutional Association was formed, with a full program of English radical political reform. By now there were two populist impulses: the older, deepest-felt and more original, if less coherent and articulate, was based on Nativist ideas of a true Australian-ness; in political rhetoric it was now being replaced by the Emigrant idea of 'the people', defined in orthodox-English terms and combined with ideas of mutuality and political equality.

'Revolution in France. Flight of the King. Republican Government Elected.' When the news came on 19 June 1848 of a new European disorder, there was fear that a European war might mean the French would attack the colonies, particularly New Zealand. For that matter, what effect would a successful uprising in Ireland have on the Irish in the colony? A week after reading reports of the overthrow of the French, Governor Fitzroy issued writs for the second Legislative Council election which was not due

Elections were still mainly in the hands of 'the nobs', who could present themselves with patriotic pride (below). However, several newspapers that professed to speak for the working man had, by now, begun to appear (left and above).

THE
C O N V I C T S H I P
HAS ARRIVED!

———

THE GREAT MEETING will be held on the CIRCULAR WHARF, TO-DAY, at Noon, to Protest against the Landing of the Convicts.

The Chair will be taken by Robert Lowe, Esq., the Member for the City.

Let all places of business be closed !

Let every man be at his post !

Revolution in Sydney: *the year 1848 saw many revolutions in Europe – in Berlin (below left) as in almost all of the European capitals. Despite some fears, the year passed quietly in Australia, but in 1849 there was some concern about an uprising when the British tried to restore the convict system. When the first convict ships arrived a 'Great Meeting' was called at Circular Quay (left). It produced many fiery speeches, if no revolution, but from it came the radicalising Anti-Transportation League, established in Melbourne in 1851, which produced its own flag (above) and a wave of protest and democratic aspiration. The League's members pledged to stop the establishment of English prisons or penal settlements in the Australian colonies.*

until September: he wanted the election out of the way before there was more inflammatory news from Europe.

It was in this election that some of 'the people' began to imagine that they might rise higher than the City Council and perhaps go so far as to put a man into the Legislative Council. There was a meeting in the Royal Hotel to discuss it. A few of those there had connections with the Sydney Council – one was an ex-mayor, a leather, soap and candle manufacturer who was the son of a minor official in the Commissariat; but others were entirely new to official politics – shopkeepers, tradesmen, a Scottish schoolmaster, a few radical journalists. A few were Chartists, seeking democratic rights for the working man; a number were Irish; almost all were young. For safety's sake they chose as their own candidate for the Legislative Council Robert Lowe, a nob lawyer who had come to the colony to make his fortune and then return home, and to whom the expediencies of politics now suggested a new political force in 'the people'.

The nomination was done modestly. This was the 'first time the citizens of Sydney have ever dared to nominate a candidate of their own, and it has created a great deal of surprise and indignation that we should have the impudence to nominate one not introduced to us by our betters'. There was confidence in the campaign. ('Let this be a commencement of a new era, in which the people shall ... be looked upon ... as a mighty and self-acting power.') And their victory was hailed as 'the birthday of Australian democracy'. 'The glory of a new era in the political history of New South Wales is ours ... Our watchword is "Onward to national freedom and happiness".'

Other than the election to the Legislative Council of a man who, even if a nob, was the first to be successfully nominated by the unnobbish, the European turmoils of 1848 found little echo, beyond an intensifying of rhetoric. A newspaper could remind its readers that 'while Europe is striking off the fetters which despotism has forged for the people', New South Wales labours under 'a government more despotic, and more oppressive than any in the world'; but it was not until 1849 that the new radicalism enacted a drama that in matter was unique to the colonies, and in manner within the central tradition of European street politics.

Transportation of convicts, suspended at the beginning of

Parkes has his first election victory.

The young Henry Parkes

Henry Parkes, poet, visionary and romantic, left England for New South Wales in 1838, aged 33, because he could not get work; he left behind him a poem for publication condemning a society that forced so many men to seek the means of subsistence in 'a foreign wilderness'.

In Sydney he found it just as difficult as in Birmingham to earn a living. Home for his wife and the child born on the voyage from England was at first a small, squalid room, while Parkes, with only threepence in the world, went up country looking for work. Slowly he built up some substance – enough to buy tools and set up business in Sydney as an importer and ivory turner, the trade at which he had served an apprenticeship.

He was to have continuing financial difficulties, but by the early 1840s, in spite of his little schooling, he was developing a reputation as a writer, reader and thinker with Chartist sympathies for working-class political rights. His intellectual associates were most of the colony's radical patriots – but his radicalism had defined limits.

In his first public speech, made in January 1849 at the City Theatre, he advocated universal suffrage as a way of avoiding 'the excesses of Paris and Frankfurt', a reference to the European revolutions of the previous year. Although he was associated with the Australian League and its work for a 'Great Federal Republic', he regarded the liberal movement as most effective in eroding the power of the colonial conservatives whom he described as 'the dunghill aristocracy of Botany Bay'. He was a strong supporter of Federation, believing that 'these colonies should be united by some federal bond of connection'.

In 1850 Parkes received the financial backing to start the *Empire*, a newspaper that was to unite radicals and liberals with Parkes at the centre. He was elected to parliament in 1854 as member for Sydney, and later held the seats of East Sydney, Kiama, Mudgee and then Argyle. He was to marry three times, father 11 children, survive three bankruptcies, be five times Premier of New South Wales and be remembered by Australians as 'the father of Federation'.

the decade, was to be resumed. A cargo of ticket-of-leave men was to be dumped in New South Wales. When the convict transport anchored at Sydney, guards with fixed bayonets stood behind the locked gates of Government House. Reserves of soldiers waited in the stables. Police hid in the kitchen. A 'Great Protest Meeting' was held on the waterfront with the top of a horse omnibus as the speakers' platform. Between this and the second Great Protest Meeting the Superintendent of Convicts organised the unloading of some of the 'exiles' and their dispatch up country, but almost every town in the colony had its protest meeting. There was a sense of crusade; it was an issue that overwhelmed all others and seemed to throw light on the colony's whole social condition, with a transcendant radicalism that illuminated many other issues. 'Let us send across the Pacific our emphatic declaration that we will not be slaves ... the time is not far distant when we shall assert our freedom not by words alone. As in America, oppression was the parent of independence, so shall it be in this colony.' Some of this radicalism was laced with caution, and comparisons with America in 1776 were deplored as 'erroneous'. But in politics the colony was now doing something for itself.

Anti-Transportation Leagues were formed in all three eastern colonies, and then in South Australia. An Australian League came together in 1851, with the flag of the Southern Cross – five stars set on a Blue Ensign – as its symbol of revulsion against the convict system. There were protest meetings in cities and towns, and petitions, pamphlets and threats of separation from Britain. The league organised a prize for an Australian national anthem; there was talk of organising an Australian national day, even of writing an Australian national history ('Why not have an era – a chronology of our own?').

The British Colonial Secretary tried a last compromise – that a new penal colony be started in the north. Then the British Government changed and the British gave in: there were to be no more convicts. When the last transport arrived in Hobart, the town took a holiday to celebrate the end of its shame. Two years later its Legislative Council asked that the name of the colony be changed from Van Diemen's Land to Tasmania, since the old name was blackened with embarrassing memories.

It had not been nobs or squatters leading this radical movement but city merchants and professional men, with support from shopkeepers and artisans and other voices of 'the people'. Now that the colonies were demanding the self-government already given to the Canadian colonies and to New Zealand, it was these new liberals who wanted to shape this future. The battle for self-government was fought and won in New South Wales, then extended to the others. It was won partly with nobbish leadership, but when the new constitution was debated the new liberals, speaking in the name of 'the people', wanted a constitution that was amenable to them. They wanted self-government not only to overcome British influence, but also to overcome the influence of the squatters. The squatters and other conservatives were opposed to 'democratic and levelling influences' ('Who would stay while selfishness, ignorance and democracy held sway?') and it was suggested that the upper house should be hereditary, to provide a 'strong

check to the arbitrary will of the multitude'. And, since wisdom was believed to accompany the ownership of property, there was special concern for the 'great interests' in the colony. But the new liberals won their victory: although the 'great interests' were still to have a grip on the upper house, the lower house was to be elected on a wide franchise. Now that the itch to struggle had been ennobled by the participation of men who saw themselves as tribunes of 'the people', the colonies, so weak in faith, had acquired a belief that it was through politics that the human condition could move closer to perfection.

Brilliant Dan Deniehy

In 1853, at a public meeting at the Victoria Theatre in Sydney, Daniel Deniehy, 'the boy orator', denounced W.C. Wentworth's proposed colonial aristocracy as a 'bunyip aristocracy' and so helped ridicule it out of serious consideration.

Deniehy was a 'currency lad', the native-born son of two Irish convicts. In the colony's 1828 census his father was listed as a labourer owning 18 horned cattle, although he eventually became a successful merchant, able to afford a sound education (including a period in England) for his talented, quickwitted son.

Deniehy had a great love of literature, and he was able to indulge his taste for books while articled to the solicitor Nicol Stenhouse, who had an impressive library; he later established an enormous library of his own.

Deniehy did well when he was admitted as a solicitor, but he soon became involved in radical politics and was elected to parliament (although doubting that he had yet achieved 'the requisite spiritual and mental proportions'). He became a noted debator and writer, flinging himself into the great issues of the day.

But the glittering genius, so remarkable to his contemporaries, soon began to fade. In his early thirties he took to drink, and at 37 died in poverty, after a street accident, from 'loss of blood and fits induced by habits of intemperance'. He was survived by his wife (whose rich father had disowned her when she married Deniehy) and three daughters.

Charles Harpur, another currency lad and the first notable Australian-born colonial poet, portrayed Deniehy at the time he illuminated the political sky:

> Little Dan Deniehy!
> Brilliant Dan Deniehy!
> Dear is the light of the spirit to me!

The railway line between Adelaide and Port Adelaide was opened officially on 19 April 1856, and South Australia became the third colony to introduce the steam engine.

Part two
The age of Improvement
1851 to 1914

It was an age of 'Improvement', and nowhere else did certain forms of Improvement spread faster than in the six Australian colonies. For a period, Australia may have been the most prosperous society in the world. And it was not only material improvement that spread to Australia: for a time it could also seem the most liberally progressive country in social reform.

6. Australia unlimited: 1851 to 1855

No sooner had the new colony of Victoria been separated officially from New South Wales in 1851, than a gold rush began. By the end of the year at least 20 000 people were on the gold fields – businesses closed, ships were left unloaded, work stopped on farms. The population boomed, and Melbourne became the fastest-growing city in the world, and for a while, Australia generally may have been the most prosperous country in the world. Public works were planned and built on a grand scale, while in the new suburbs and country towns, for some of those in regular employment, there was the prospect of a 'home of one's own'. With the building boom, Melbourne itself became one of the first places in the world where some workmen gained an eight-hour day. Meanwhile, another great ideal was taking shape: sport was being democratised in what one English visitor called 'the most sporting country in the world'.

The diggers

When Melbourne learnt that it was to be separated from Sydney, the celebrations lasted five days. Hilltop fires and rockets, thanksgiving services and sporting events, a procession, a fancy-dress ball and a Separation Anthem welcomed the birth of the new colony.

Then it settled down to what seemed a predictable future in which the first step was to be the election of a Legislative Council in September 1851, to meet in November. But by November, Victoria had reached such a state of gold fever that its Governor asked London for military reinforcements: normal ways of running things were about to collapse.

Gold had already been found in the colonies, although for various reasons nothing had happened. But early in 1851, when a New South Wales prospector back from California

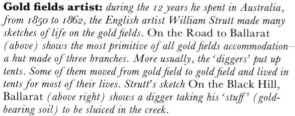

Gold fields artist: *during the 12 years he spent in Australia, from 1850 to 1862, the English artist William Strutt made many sketches of life on the gold fields.* On the Road to Ballarat *(above) shows the most primitive of all gold fields accommodation— a hut made of three branches. More usually, the 'diggers' put up tents. Some of them moved from gold field to gold field and lived in tents for most of their lives. Strutt's sketch* On the Black Hill, Ballarat *(above right) shows a digger taking his 'stuff' (gold-bearing soil) to be sluiced in the creek.*

A gold fields brooch (right) in 18-carat gold, designed in 1860, has a miner with picks, shovels, revolver, gold bag, winch and bucket set against a panel of mine dumps in a border of foliage.

turned a small gold discovery into a rush, the Government gave in. ('It would be madness to attempt to stop that which we have no physical force to put down.') Goldfields Commissioners were appointed and a system of licences improvised to cover expenses and to try to limit the number of gold diggers. There was a drift of men from Victoria into New South Wales – a bad start for a new colony – so rewards were offered for a Victorian strike. By July a few hundred men were at two Victorian diggings; by August, at what was soon to be Ballarat, the diggers began to strike it a bit richer; in September, in one dig, 27 kilograms of gold were discovered; by October Ballarat had between 6000 and 10 000 diggers. Then new finds at Castlemaine caused a rush of 10 000 more. In Melbourne, 'When are you off?' became the normal beginning of a conversation.

There was a run on the banks. Many businesses closed down. Ships were left unloaded. Work stopped on farms. Wives and children were deserted, and some fell into destitution. Men turned their cash into tents, shovels, sieves, cradles, buckets, pickaxes and cooking pots and set off along the bullock tracks to camp on the diggings. The Governor wrote, 'Cottages are deserted, houses to let, business at a standstill and even schools are closed. In some of the suburbs not a man is left.' By December 20 000 diggers were spread out across the hills, gullies and flats of the midlands in what could seem hostile camps threatening Melbourne. When several thousand of the luckier ones invaded the capital at Christmas, drunken parties went on night and day, horses were shod with gold, cigars lit with £5 notes, champagne bottles used as skittles; prostitutes rode in carriages. To the pious, God's intentions seemed clear. Melbourne was being punished.

In the new year thousands of diggers came in small steamers from Van Diemen's Land and thousands more walked or rode overland or sailed in from South Australia. About half the men of these two colonies tried their luck in Victoria. Later in the year, fortune-seekers from the British Isles floundered in, looking for quick riches and a first-class ticket home. The poet Alfred Lord Tennyson said he would have gone if he hadn't been married, and depressed by the reception of their paintings, the Pre-Raphaelites almost went as a group. Nearly 300 ships came to Port Phillip, and by the end of 1852 Victoria's population had increased in 18 months from 77 000 to nearly 170 000. In the next year

On the diggings: *many gold-digging teams were family affairs. Zealous Gold Diggers (right), painted by S.T. Gill in 1852, shows a digger's wife at Castlemaine nursing her baby while she rocks the cradle in which miners washed and sieved soil from gold. The whip, a kind of wooden crane, was one of the devices used for hauling the 'stuff' from a shaft (below). Another device, the whim, a large, slatted drum suspended from a wooden frame, had been designed in the Middle Ages. Windsails, another medieval invention, were turned into the prevailing wind to ventilate deep shafts. A section of a shaft, at Bendigo in 1853 (below right). One man broke the clay with a pick and shovelled the dirt into the bucket. Another turned the windlass that then pulled up the bucket.*

900 ships came, bringing men from the United States, China and Germany as well as the British Isles. The population jumped to within a few thousand of New South Wales's total, and in the following year it was 40 000 more. Later in the decade, the rushes became even bigger as up to 50 000 men would stampede to a valley, loot it and then rush somewhere else.

At the diggings at night, with hundreds of fires shining outside the tents, it looked as if an army had taken over the gullies. In some ways the gold rushes were like the kind of safe, minor military campaign for which a man would volunteer and remember with growing affection for the rest of his life: there were not many deaths; there was plenty of fresh air; and there were the excitements of failure or success, the bonds of exclusive comradeship, and the feeling of free choice that can come from an unpredictable event.

There were enough hardships and tediums to test manliness. Although some put up bark or slab huts and some even brought their wives, most lived in calico tents with only an outside fire for cooking, with boxes, chests, saplings, sacks or tree trunks for furniture; and for meals mutton chops, damper and pannikins of tea, with only

Founding feminist: Louisa Lawson

When she was 15, Louisa Lawson's father, Harry Albury, went to the gold diggings near Mudgee, where as a carpenter he earned enough money in a year to set himself up in a small pub on the edge of the shanty town he had helped to build. To escape from the tedium of such a life, at the age of 18 Louisa married a 32-year-old Norwegian seaman, Peter Larsen, who was passing through the diggings. However, almost at once, Larsen joined the rush to new diggings at Grenfell, where, on a black night of wind and rain, Louisa gave birth, in their tent, to a son, Henry. In 1871, when Louisa was 23 and had borne a second son, the family moved to the Gulgong gold fields.

Peter finally returned to Mudgee and became a farmer, and at 28 Louisa was living in her first solid house, a small weatherboard cottage, one room of which became a post office and general store. The family moved from one disaster to the next, and in 1883 they eventually broke up.

Louisa Lawson, as she then called herself, went to Sydney and became one of the first Australian feminists. In 1888 she started *Dawn*, Australia's first women's magazine, which she ran for 17 years; in 1889 she founded the Dawn Club, a social reform club for women; and two years later she helped launch the Suffrage League. Louisa was one of Australia's most significant feminists, but until recently was remembered only as the mother of Australia's famous bush poet, Henry, who hated her.

pipes of tobacco to make the food seem better once it was swallowed. Inflation raged like a fever: in Melbourne the cost of things had doubled in three years; out on the diggings the cost of foodstuffs could go up by three times, six times, ten times. Even the price of water could be high. In a ruined landscape, stripped to its gravel or clay, the winter mud brought colds, rheumatism and cramps; the summer dust brought diarrhoea and eye infections.

Many diggers were to be ruined. Gentlemen from England could go down in the world irretrievably. But these very trials added pride to the thought that the diggings were 'a wonderful place to take the conceit out of men who expect much deference'. It did not matter what people had been before: what mattered was how they would react to the challenges of the diggings. In this sense they were a test of individual self-reliance, but the group solaces (and demands) of comradeship could be more important, in particular how men fitted in as members of the four to six partners who usually worked a claim. The term 'mate', formerly an occupational term for a two-man partnership, was now extended to describe this slightly larger group. In a wider solidarity, a feeling of difference could come from being an 'old hand' instead of a 'new chum', or a white man rather than a Chinese; but above all the distinctiveness was in being a *digger*, whether American or Irish, Australian or Scot, English or German; and with moleskin or corduroy trousers, blue or red jersey, leather belt and knife, there was even a special uniform.

'Happy days ... glorious freedom from all the restraints of home life' ... The diggings gave a wonderful chance to have a good time ... fiddles, banjoes, accordions ... pipe bands, brass bands ... and an improvised main street, much of it still in canvas, that might go on for some distance, with saloons, sly-grog booths, brothels, theatres, eating-houses, shooting galleries, boxing booths, bowling alleys and gambling dens. At night, lit by tallow lamps, with the hucksters shouting and so much canvas, it looked like a carnival. As ever, there were also strong tides of respectability, especially on the Sabbath when the Methodist meetings boomed, the bands played politely as if the diggings were a park, and the diggers dressed in their Sunday best to make their Sunday visits. But good times were there to be had – given more excitement by the overwhelming fantasy that people might make their fortunes, if not from a lucky strike, then at least from running a saloon, or winning a two-up game. It was always a *man* who might 'strike it lucky'. Yet by the end of the decade almost a third of the adult population of the gold fields were women – most of them not prostitutes or sly-grog sellers, but wives keeping things going, cooking, cleaning, perhaps taking in washing, bearing children, and sometimes helping with the gold-seeking. It was said of the women in Bendigo as early as 1852 that they were 'mostly young wives, recently married and content to share the fortunes of their husbands; they cooked and washed, split wood, swept out their tents; in the afternoon they smartened up, often with the innate tastefulness of ladies, "to do the shopping"'.

The larger diggings had a wooden barracks with the Union Jack above it, where the troops and the police were quartered and the log jail was guarded. 'The traps', hastily recruited, many from 'the very lowest class', some ex-

The Eureka uprising: *unlike most other nations, Australia has scarcely any great legends of freedom gained by struggle. In terms of casualties, the bloodiest was the Eureka uprising on the Ballarat gold fields in 1854, when 29 men were killed. The remains of the Eureka flag (above) have become a national treasure.*

Italian exile: Raffaello Carboni

The Italian author Raffaello Carboni was already an exile from Italy when he came to Australia in 1852, aged 32. He had been wounded during the fight for Italian liberation in 1849 and had exiled himself in London, where he worked as an interpreter. When the uprising began at Eureka he was put in command of the foreign diggers at the stockade. They formed themselves into a company ready 'to put a pike through a tyrant's heart'. After the collapse of the revolt Carboni was one of the 12 diggers tried for high treason – and then acquitted. Carboni's greatest contribution to the Eureka episode was the publication of *The Eureka Stockade* on the first anniversary of the uprising; he was the first person to turn it into an heroic tale.

Having published his book he left Australia and from then on seemed to show only an intermittent interest in the country – his obsession was with Italian liberation and with play-writing and composing music. Italy was liberated, Carboni was then abandoned by those whom he had served. None of his plays was acted, and none of his music was performed publicly.

A watercolour of the storming of the Eureka barricades (below) was painted by H.B. Henderson, who was at the scene four hours later.

convicts, had become the hated representatives of the incompetent and corrupt administration of the gold fields. The miner's licence, renewable monthly at £1 a time, became the diggers' symbol of grievance; for the traps it gave the opportunity for licence hunts, organised in surprise attacks, ambushes and encircling movements, 'a good deal like a rat hunt'.

Protests sometimes burst into disorder, but surprisingly it was at Ballarat, in 1854, that there was a brief set piece of rebellion – surprising because the Ballarat digger had been spoken of as 'a man of capital, able to wait the result of five or six months' toil before he wins his prize' so that 'he will always be a lover of order and good government'. But when the owner of the Eureka Hotel at Ballarat was let off by a magistrates' court for a killing in which there was prima facie evidence against him, thousands of the small capitalists held a protest meeting, in what they saw as the best traditions of British freedom. At the end of it some of them burned down the hotel.

Some diggers were now gripped with the feeling that 'moral persuasion is all humbug, nothing convinces like a lick in the lug', but most followed the promptings of

Improvement. A Ballarat Reform League was formed, in which the Chartists added to the special grievances of the miners some more general recipes for the betterment of humanity. Oratory flourished. Deputations moved in and out of officials' rooms. A Royal Commission was set up.

It turned out it was to be a lick in the lug after all. The Governor sent more troops. Stones were thrown as they marched through the diggings with fixed bayonets. A drummer boy was shot. There was a public burning of licences, then a retaliatory licence hunt at which the Riot Act was read. A few shots were exchanged. At the Eureka lead there was talk of rebellion: pit slabs were piled into breastworks and men began to drill. A thousand or so diggers gathered in the stockade, with the flag of the Southern Cross hoisted above them. ('We swear by the Southern Cross to stand by each other, and fight to defend our rights and liberties.') Two days later only 120 were still truly standing by each other (most of them asleep) when before sunrise 400 troops and police marched up to the stockade and fired. Ten minutes or so, and it was done.

Twenty-four diggers were killed, and five soldiers; a hundred diggers were taken prisoner. The flag of the Southern Cross was hauled down, bayoneted, trampled on, and dragged through the dust tied to a horse's tail.

The small capitalists were satisfied with the reforms that followed this event – replacement of the monthly miner's licence by an annual 'miner's right', and the setting up of locally elected miners' courts in each mining district to make the district's mining laws.

The Eureka uprising became connected with political reform, and even republican sentiment, but what precipitated it was a bread-and-butter matter – discontent with police demands to inspect miners' Gold Licences, and a monthly tax that was paid in addition to the Miner's Right (left). A year after the Eureka episode, Victoria had its first would-be democratic elections. There were candidates from the gold fields. At Bendigo (above) the diggers cheered the success of their candidate, who addressed them from the balcony of the Criterion Hotel.

Quartz king: George Lansell

Kentish soap and candle maker George Lansell was 30 when he came to Australia in 1853 to try his luck on the gold fields. After a few weeks as a digger, he and his two brothers set up shop in Bendigo as butchers and soap and candle makers; their shop became a meeting place for Bendigo sharebrokers. When the boom in quartz mining began, Lansell became a shrewd and bold speculator in mining shares, in spite of many early failures. He became a director of 38 companies, a millionaire, and known to the newspapers as 'the Quartz King of Bendigo'. Like others who had struck it rich, he returned to England to enjoy the fortune he made in Australia, but when the citizens of Bendigo petitioned him to return, he did. He built himself a 40-room mansion which, with its conical tower, stained glass windows, ballroom, chapel, gymnasium and swimming baths, set in a park of smooth lawns, ornamental lakes and trees imported from five continents, became the centre of Bendigo's new-rich society. When Lansell died, Bendigo put up a statue of him, which looked as if it were striding towards the doors of the Bendigo Stock Exchange.

The greatest disorders in the gold fields then came in outbreaks of persecution by the diggers against the Chinese, whose numbers were moving up towards ten per cent of the adult male population. Feeling lost in this remote place at the very edge of the Southern Ocean, the Chinese, like the early squatters and most of their fellow immigrant miners, hoped to get their loot and return home. But to the others they were 'a swarm of human locusts', and there were riots against them in both Victoria and New South Wales, with violence and burning.

Some of the diggings were deserted after they were plundered, leaving behind wrecked shaftheads and mounds of muck, rivers clogged with sludge, hillsides scoured down to clay or bedrock, or river flats so sluiced that they had become fields of stone. But out of other diggings grew respectable towns where things could seem new and hopeful, with the soft swish of a new printing press, the clean façade of a bank, and the branch office of one of the new, efficient American-style coaching firms. The refreshment rooms dazzled with modernity; there was fresh timber in the veranda posts and, in the mechanics institutes, hopes for progress. At Bathurst a courthouse went

up that was grand enough to be the palace of an imperial governor ... in Bendigo, to become the largest quartz-mining town in the world, public buildings arose like *palazzi* around a Renaissance square.

There were always new strikes. Some diggers, some of them with their wives, moved from one new gold field to the next for the rest of their lives. In the 1850s they tried their luck along a 1600-kilometre stretch of the Great Dividing Range in Victoria and New South Wales. In the 1860s they swarmed off when gold was found in some of the roughest parts of New Zealand, and moved on again when there were reports of new strikes in one or other of the Australian colonies. Whenever there was unemployment in a colony its Government would hope that a gold find might provide the answer. But in the big rushes half the diggers would give up

Continuing rush: *gold rushes went on for the rest of the 19th century, and into the 20th, still creating instant towns, as in Gympie (left) where this main street had formed only a year after the rush began in 1897. Much of the equipment could still be primitive, as it was for this team at Gulgong (below) in 1872, with their simple windlass and leather bucket.*

While some gold towns were deserted as soon as a rush was over, others boomed. Bendigo in particular was noted for its grand buildings, such as the Bendigo Benevolent Asylum (above) of which it was said that Australians 'lodge the recipients of public charity in just such mansions as the estated gentry are in the habit of erecting for their private residences'.

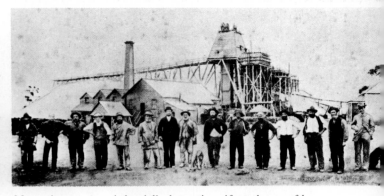

Many mines were now industrialised operations, if not always safely so. Twenty-two men were killed in a disaster at the New Australasian Gold Mine at Creswick (above) in 1882. A hundred or more miners were killed in accidents every year.

after a few weeks. If luck did not come at once, capital was needed and most of the rest found that after six months or so they lacked the money to go on.

Quartz-mining towns like Bendigo or Ballarat became industrial areas. In the late 1860s, with 300 mining companies in Ballarat, a thousand 'stampers' in the crushing batteries battered the quartz, throwing a haze of dust over the town and rumbling so loudly that the whole town could seem like a factory. Despite its Italianate public palaces, Bendigo was dominated by shaftheads, sand dumps, mullock heaps and yellow, swirled earth. Shaftheads stuck up right in the middle of town; along with the statues and the *palazzi*, one shafthead rose beside the city's central square. In these towns the miners were no longer 'little capitalists' but wage earners, and the uprising at Eureka now became part of their view of themselves as 'toilers'. This view began to spread to coal miners, copper miners, tin miners, as an example of the kind of thing miners could do if they stuck together.

So a dormant memory of this brief rebellion remained, but the rebellion was transformed into an uprising not of 'little capitalists' but of wage-earning 'toilers'. It was

there as an heroic tale, if an heroic tale were needed. In the same way, as part of the memory of the gold rushes, there remained the idea of 'the Chinaman' as a threat. For a while colonial governments tried to restrict the entry of the Chinese; to avoid the Victorian restrictions, 16 500 Chinese landed at Robe, South Australia's second largest port, and walked 500 kilometres to the diggings. But by the 1860s, as the number of gold finds diminished, Chinese immigration dropped, and governments worried about other things. The idea of the Chinaman as a threat was still there, however, if also temporarily dormant. Another idea had come up – that of 'the digger' himself, independent-minded but fraternal, above social pretension, a man who had stood a test; the legends of the uniqueness of the digger had no mention of the women of the gold fields. To have been a digger, even if only for a few months, gave a man a sense of being unique. Even if what they saw in themselves was much the same as what the successful Emancipists, Natives and Emigrants had already congratulated themselves on, the diggers could imagine they were a new kind of person. Overall, the colonies' population almost trebled within the decade, and some diggers felt that with them things had really started.

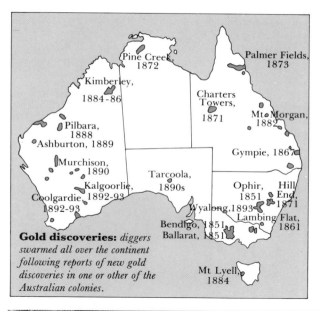

Gold discoveries: *diggers swarmed all over the continent following reports of new gold discoveries in one or other of the Australian colonies.*

Pine Creek, 1872
Palmer Fields, 1873
Kimberley, 1884-86
Charters Towers, 1871
Mt Morgan, 1882
Pilbara, 1888
Ashburton, 1889
Murchison, 1890
Gympie, 1867
Tarcoola, 1890s
Kalgoorlie, 1892-93
Coolgardie, 1892-93
Ophir, 1851
Hill End, 1871
Wyalong, 1893
Lambing Flat, 1861
Bendigo, 1851
Ballarat, 1851
Mt Lyell, 1884

The Chinese invasion: *some Government notices (below right) were printed in Chinese. Fears continued of a Chinese invasion: in 1875 Chinese were shown landing at Cooktown as if it were a military landing (above). The Chinese were usually represented as leading depraved lives, and those who had settled down respectably with families (below left) were ignored.*

Apart from the economic boom, the gold rush's greatest significance was that it peopled Victoria, making it the biggest and most progressive colony. In ten years its population rose from 77 000 to 540 000, more than half as big again as New South Wales, and holding nearly half the total of the Australian population. In those ten years, from being a district of New South Wales, Victoria had become the most celebrated of the British colonies. It consisted predominantly of immigrants: of the 230 000 who came to Victoria from the other colonies, only about one in ten stayed, but of the immigrants from other countries only about one in ten went home. They were to set much of the tone in Victoria for a generation, a generation in which Victoria was to be the most important of the colonies, seeing itself as setting the pace for the rest.

The idea of 'the digger' soon entered the Australian imagination as one of the ways of being a 'typical Australian'. When Julian Ashton painted The Prospector *(below) in the 1880s, three decades of myth-making already lay behind the meanings that Australians could give to such a painting.*

It was into the pockets of Melbourne tradesmen, saloon keepers, merchants, landlords, property speculators and builders that the diggers' money mostly went, and then it recirculated among workmen as part of the general boom.

While most diggers made at the best no more than a living wage, with perhaps three or four thousand finding more than £1000 worth of gold and only a hundred or so making more than £10 000, publicans could build up fortunes of £520 000 in three years, and those who before the rush had invested small savings in Melbourne land could sell out for a profit of up to £100 000.

Jobs came from new factories, extra demand for farm produce, new roads, new railways and above all from house-building. With the magic of confidence that released all this new prosperity, Melbourne became the fastest-growing city in the world, with land prices to match. Ships were used as dormitories to sleep in. Then whole suburbs of canvas nailed over wooden frames went up. Easily assembled prefabricated galvanised-iron houses were imported from Britain, and the use of 'weatherboards' was developed: two men could put up a timber frame in two or three days, then nail it to the prefabricated 'weatherboard', topping it off with a roof of galvanised iron. 'Weatherboard cottages' of this kind were let out at £1 per week per room. But even in 1861 a third of the population of Victoria was still living in tents or huts, or, at best, canvas houses.

The building boom led to building workers gaining an eight-hour day in Melbourne, a reform still only a dream elsewhere in the world, but proclaimed at a public meeting on 11 April 1856 by the Mayor of Melbourne as such an obvious necessity that he offered a prize of ten guineas for the best address on the subject. The eight-hour movement was slow to spread into other industries and other colonies, but a Trades Hall went up in Melbourne ('This hall is the first ever erected by working men'). The eight-hour day festival became the most important annual event in trade

The 'iron house', prefabricated in galvanised iron and imported from England, was one of the makeshift answers to the housing shortage. This shortage encouraged the development of the distinctive Australian 'weatherboard house'.

union life, promising a new future that, some felt, Victoria would be the first to offer, so that the workers would have the leisure to devote themselves to the pursuit of moral and intellectual Improvement.

There were other aspirations to Improvement. It was Methodism that had captured the biggest attendances at the diggings, and by 1861 a third of those who went to church in Victoria went to Methodist chapels. The repressive side of Evangelicalism had for half a century been unsuccessful in publicly taming the colonies' wildness, but in Melbourne puritanism now enjoyed at least one victory: it took possession of Sunday. An Evangelical Alliance, open to all Protestant denominations, was formed in 1857, and it enthusiastically pursued Melbourne's salvation by controlling what it did on the Sabbath, even if it could not yet control the exuberance of the other six days of the week. There were fanatical protests when Sunday trains ran on the newly built suburban railways, with decency's only triumph a restriction on timetables. When the Public Library was built it was shut on Sunday. So were the saloons, a change not imitated by the other colonies for more than a generation.

The demand for buildings was so great that Melbourne building workers were among the first in the world to gain the eight hour day. The movement spread to other colonies and celebrations of Eight Hour Day, like this demonstration in King William Street, Adelaide (above), became on annual event.

The Melbourne revivalist Dr John Singleton persuades a prospective customer to give a bible reading in a brothel. 'Marvellous Melbourne' was, in part, a city of sin. It was also a centre of puritanism.

Amid the aspirations towards being both an imperial city and a centre of Improvement was the clink of coin, the rustle of bank drafts, mortgages, ledgers. Melbourne was a hard, pushy place. In its get-rich-quick bustle it was said 'a most unbounded spirit of avarice actuates all classes' ... 'to take care of number one is the guiding rule of action' ... 'he who displayed the greatest ingenuity in *taking in* his friend or his neighbour is called a smart fellow'. Although it wished for shops equal to the best in London and clubs that would not disgrace St James's, for many years Melbourne was seen as the 'American-style' city of the Australias. Sydney was believed to be 'quieter, less assertive, more civilised', 'a city of charm with an element of the ideal', with 'an essential respectability' and 'a respect for constituted authority, typical of an old-fashioned crown colony'. Sydney's charm lay in its crumbling past; Melbourne, the 'phenomenal city of Australia', was busy organising its future. 'There is a bustle and life about Melbourne which you altogether miss in Sydney' ... 'The Melbourne man is always on the look-out for business, the Sydney man waits for business to come to him.' 'Victorians of the upper class ... both in their defects and their excellences ... approach nearer to the American than to the British type. And in this respect the Victorian is distinct from the colonist of New South Wales who retains more of the John Bull attributes of the mother country than his younger and more energetic brother in the South.'

This onrush of a city's confidence was soon more attractive to immigrants than the lotteries of the diggings. They came with their wives, wanting to settle in a place with so many new opportunities. On the face of it, Melbourne was a gold rush town, even wilder than San Francisco: the theatres were packed, the hotels boomed, prostitutes provided relief services day and night. But it was not the diggers who set the basic nature of Melbourne. Those who stayed on at the diggings were more concerned with their own affairs as little capitalists. It was the attitudes of those immigrants who were attracted not by the diggings, but by the opportunities of a money-making city.

They were somewhat better educated and had more money-making skills than the colonists of New South Wales; they were better at getting on in the world; they were more given to the practice of religion, Methodism and Presbyterianism in particular. And in their attitudes to their new country they were not prompted by Melbourne's earlier Native moods – its conflicts with the squatters, its fight for separation from New South Wales, its campaign against transportation. 'Australia', as such, did not mean much to them. Their ambition was to rise above the improvisations and the squalor and get on with the job of building a fine British city in the south land, as modern as the mid-19th century.

As early as 1853, in its first flush of confidence, Melbourne decided to have its own university. In the next year Australia's first town hall building was planned, a copy of Inigo Jones's Banqueting Hall at Whitehall, and it was decided to match it by building a splendid public library. Solid buildings of secular and religious hope went up in streets that were nothing more than rough country roads; sewage floated in front of them in huge open gutters. The new Parliament House was one of the boldest inspirations of

Imperial Rome built anywhere in the 19th century. The unemployed marched past it with banners: 'We want bread! Give us work!' The opera was 'worthy of the English metropolis itself'. The shops were 'equal to the best in London'. The new buildings for the gentlemen's club 'would not disgrace St James's'.

It took only till 1852 for one of its legislators to put in a claim for Melbourne as the 'seat of Supreme Government', since it was clearly 'the centre of Civilisation and Christianisation in the Eastern Archipelago'. By 1859 one of its writers not only claimed that Victoria was 'the New York State of Australia' and that Melbourne 'would be the great central heart, regulating all the pulses of the Australian continent', he also suggested that 'here, amidst the Austral-Asian and Austral-Indian group, compact in feeling and action . . . would be a fair scene to which you might shift the seat of empire'.

Marvellous Melbourne: *'The Block' in Collins Street became the place to promenade for the new rich of booming Melbourne, seen as one of the most go-ahead cities of the whole Victorian age.*

For a while the Australian and New Zealand colonies were probably the most prosperous countries in the world. As these things are measured, the Australian economic boom was one of the greatest the world had known.

As well as being a place that shipped out wool, Australia was now seen as a land rich in minerals. Export earnings from gold jumped ahead of export earnings from wool and were to stay ahead until about 1870. The colonies found new markets: Newcastle's export of coal rose from 71 000 tonnes to 368 000 tonnes. The copper fields, copper smelters and copper ports of South Australia seemed essential to the colony's prosperity; in the 1870s Tasmanian prospectors began to open up fields of tin; in the early 1880s a 'silver rush' west of the Barrier Ranges in New South Wales threw up in a couple of years the town of Silverton, with a population of 3000 and another 2000 in the surrounding mining camps. Western New South Wales was seen as 'the new Nevada'. Mining had joined farming as a 'natural industry' because gold also came from the land: all the rest were 'artificial industries'. *The export* was what mattered in

life. Miners joined farmers as 'the producers'. The rest were regarded as parasites.

Internally, the passing stimulus of gold had brought a much bigger work force, a much bigger local market, and a confidence that made capital easy to get. British investors put money into the colonies – through finance houses and government loans – on a scale they had not thought of before. At times half a year's investment capital came from London speculators, and increased British demand in the 1870s helped cause a pastoral boom that brought wool ahead of minerals as the main export. Although, as the decades moved on, other countries were to catch up with Australian growth, the rate of economic growth was double that of Britain and second only to that of the United States and Japan (with Sweden and Germany a slow third).

The most important single internal impetus to the colonies' economic growth was the housing rush, which took up about a quarter of all capital investment, private and government. Although all the honour went to 'the producers' the greatest economic stimulus came from the extension of the towns. The oscillations of the cycle of more immigrants more houses, more immigrants more houses

pumped life throughout the economy. The housing boom – a product of immigrant labour, immigrant demand, a revolution in rising suburban expectations and the development of building societies – was as important a stimulant to the economy as the rushes for wool and gold.

Population went up from nearly one and a half million in 1860 to more than two and a quarter million in 1880: by then there were about 860 000 people in Victoria, 740 000 in New South Wales, 276 000 in South Australia, 211 000 in Queensland, 115 000 in Tasmania and 29 500 in Western Australia. Melbourne was a city of 282 000, Sydney of 224 000, Adelaide of 104 000. Immigrants accounted for almost half the total population increase. When the Northern District of New South Wales became a separate colony in 1859 (called 'Queensland', as if 'Victoria' was not homage enough to the distant monarch) this new colony of 1.7 million square kilometres with only 25 000 Europeans in it was so anxious to catch up with the others that sometimes the recruiting to Australia of immigrants to work as navvies was left to public works contractors. Whenever there was unemployment there was agitation to end assisted immigration – but only until the next boom.

In the 1870s a 'spirited policy of public works' sprang up in all the colonies, bigger than before, providing further stimulus. Often borrowing in London, colonial governments became such big spenders on public works that governments provided up to 40 per cent of total capital investment; wages went up; jobs were even easier to get. Now and again there was a panic: Queensland, most reckless of the spenders, had gone broke – for a while, until another loan from London came in, and there was a gold strike as well. But overall there was the feeling that Australia was unlimited, with 'no price too high to pay for national development'. 'What America has done, Australia can do.'

The colonies now bought almost 20 per cent of Britain's exports; in the 1850s shipbuilders in Britain and the United States of America had enjoyed a new boom because there were so many new ships to build to carry cargoes and immigrants to the Australian colonies. Driven by westerlies, clippers raced from the Irish Sea to the Southern Ocean, bringing British immigrants and British manufactured goods. The colonies seemed as maritime as ever: crews were shanghaied in colonial ports; the flags of 30 shipping lines, many of them Australian, flapped over Sydney. Australian-owned steamers ran a busy coastal traffic, providing the main link between the coastal cities, and traded with Pacific islands. (In Sydney there were dreams of a Sydney empire of plantations spread across the South Pacific.)

Because of high charges, steamship traffic with Britain developed slowly, even after the opening in 1869 of the Suez Canal; steam cut the average passage of mail from 90 to 45 days, but even in the 1880s most cargoes still went by sail. As well as the coastal trade, steam had important effects on the connected river system of New South Wales, Victoria and South Australia where paddle steamers now ran, with plenty of trees on the river banks to chop down in passing and use for fuel. There were shoals and piles of driftwood and overhanging trees, and some rivers did not have enough water in them for nearly half the year – on the Darling a paddle steamer was occasionally marooned and had to wait for months for the water to come back – but the river trade offered cheaper freights than bullock wagons. With their quays and warehouses, river ports flourished on an inland water transport system that ran for more than 6000 kilometres. One of them, Echuca, was Victoria's second largest port; with 35 steamers, 70 barges, a long

Steaming ahead: *paddle steamers now made use of the main river systems of southeastern Australia (above), towing a variety of cargoes, including wool. For a period, Australia may have been the most prosperous country in the world. While steamers traded along the coast and to the Pacific Islands, Australia's main link with world trade was through 'clippers' such as those docked at Newcastle Harbour in 1878 (left).*

In the 1870s, railway construction boomed, and gangs of navvies picked and shovelled their way over the countryside (above right).

One of the boom's most dramatic public works was the construction of 3200 kilometres of Overland Telegraph line. These construction workers (right) were photographed beside the banks of the Northern Territory's Roper River.

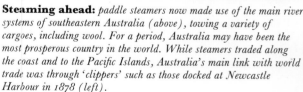

wharf, and hydraulic cranes, it was 'destined to become the Chicago of Australia'. For those not near this system, transport was usually by roads, with bullock wagons for freight and Cobb and Co. mail coaches for passengers (by 1870 offering 45 000 kilometres a week). The driest and most desolate regions were serviced by camel trains, bred from imported camels and run by imported Afghans.

Then railways became one of the most spirited of the public works, in the 1870s making up more than half of all government spending. At first railway construction had been slow, with only a few local lines. (The first line at Sydney was opened to a salute of 21 guns and the playing of the 'New South Wales Railways Waltz'.) Less than 300 kilometres of track were in use by 1859, most in Victoria. By 1875 there were little more than 1600. By 1880 there were 6500. Then the real boom began. Lengths of steel rail became an important import item in ships' cargoes.

Governments found themselves in the railway business by accident: private ownership had failed because the towns large enough to generate traffic were too far apart, and since most were ports they were more cheaply serviced by sea. But having set up departments of railways by chance,

governments found good politics in them. Since railways were not run for profit but as a public service, freights could be kept low to subsidise farmers (in Victoria the extension of railways opened up new areas for wheat farming and the colony became a wheat exporter); railway construction work was sometimes started to provide extra jobs. A thousand or more navvies would arrive, many of them with their women and children, bringing a canvas township complete with stores and saloons. Sometimes a railway line was extended to get political support. Some towns were most prosperous when they were at the head of a line.

The first telegraph line went up in Melbourne in 1854. At once the governments of Victoria, New South Wales and South Australia hired gangs of labourers to set up lines of poles and string single wires between them, connecting each colonial capital with its main country towns. Government and commercial messages passed along them in Morse code and there were reports to the newspapers and, for those who could afford them, personal 'telegrams'. By 1858 Sydney, Melbourne and Adelaide were linked by lines of wire; in 1859 a cable was laid under the sea to Hobart; in 1861 the wires went north to Brisbane. Meanwhile the telegraph line

Modern cities: *Melbourne and Sydney were becoming 'modern'. The first passenger lift in Australia was installed in 1881 in Sydney (above). By 1885 there were trams in Sydney, Melbourne, Adelaide and Brisbane (below).*

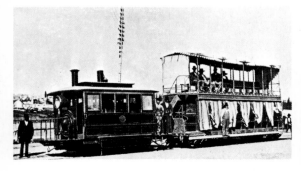

Sumptuous 'grand hotels' in the European pattern went up. The first was the Menzies in Melbourne (above), built in six months in 1867 in the style of a French chateau. Its chef came from Buckingham Palace.

By 1880, private telephone companies were operating in Melbourne, Sydney and Brisbane (left).

from London was moving across land and under water to the Dutch East Indies. Over 3000 kilometres of wire were then stretched between poles across uninhabited dry country between Adelaide and Darwin, with little stone fortresses every 160 kilometres where the relaying operators could work and live. In 1872 the cable from the Dutch East Indies reached Darwin, and through it five of the six colonies. (It was not until 1877 that Perth was linked to Adelaide.) Now trade information and decisions could pass directly between the colonies and London; brief news items could be telegrammed to the colonial newspapers (what the Kaiser was doing, the new policies of the Tsar). The latest sporting results came at a cost of ten shillings and four pence a word. In 1878, only two years after Alexander Graham Bell had invented the telephone, Melbourne installed its first telephone exchange; by 1880 private telephone companies were operating in three colonies. Then they were bought by the Posts and Telegraph departments.

To all this was added a boom in city buildings. Use of the new passenger lifts spread quickly after a lift was installed in a Sydney store in 1881. Buildings went as high as six or seven storeys; in 1885 a ten-storey building went up in Melbourne; city land values went up correspondingly. With lifts, the new 'grand hotels' were being built, with several hundred rooms and flourishes of marble and mosaics, mahogany and plate glass. New theatres went up, equally grand with red plush and gilt; showy town halls sprouted.

In Melbourne, Sydney and Brisbane, intercolonial exhibitions were held where machinery, stock, produce and manufactured goods, among the shrubs and flowers and paintings, expressed confidence in progress. In 1879 Sydney put on the colonies' first International Exhibition in a 'crystal palace' of concrete and steel, built in the Botanic Gardens; the colony's first electrical plant was installed for this, to enable work to go on by night as well as during the day, and the colony's first steam tram ran on the opening day. The next year Melbourne replied with an International Exhibition: the building, a mixture of French and Italian styles, was topped with a dome higher than St Paul's. A cantata was written for its opening, hailing Victoria, Queen of the South.

'You are told constantly that colonial meat and colonial wine, colonial fruit and colonial flour, colonial horses and colonial sport, are better than any meat, wine, fruit, flour, horses or sport to be found elsewhere. And this habit springs from things national to things personal,' said Anthony Trollope after his visit to the colonies in 1871. In Sydney 'it is asked . . . with bated breath, and with something of an apology, "Of course you have been bothered out of your life about our harbour – but it is pretty; don't you think so?"'. But 'the blast of the trumpet as heard in Victoria is louder than all of the blasts – and the Melbourne blast beats all the other blowing of that proud colony'.

In this economic progress 'Melbourne money and Melbourne brains' had led all the rest; but a pastoral boom in the 1870s helped New South Wales, and Queensland was galloping to catch up with South Australia. Although Western Australia stood almost still, and Tasmania was beginning to realise that it might have copper and tin but it was not, after all, to become the Athens of the South, overall in the headlines of material expansion the Australian colonies – or at least those orators who made the speeches – now seemed to have found a meaning for their existence. Even the Catholic Archbishop of Sydney could praise the mining boom. In 1889 he boasted, 'from being a wild, uncultured waste, so poor and barren that the first explorers shrank back aghast . . . Australia has become a civilised land, clothed with loveliness as a garden, rich with unlocked treasures of gold and silver, and with priceless mines, almost beyond parallel in the world's history'. With this faith in economic development there was the increasing feeling that 'free from the class and accumulated hindrances which act as drags upon the progress of other countries . . . we, having nothing to undo, can, if we will, make the last pages of their history the first of our own'.

Great Exhibitions: *the Great Exhibition in London in 1851 set a fashion in exhibitions, expressing the technological confidence of the 19th century. The first International Exhibition in Australia was opened in Sydney in 1879, in a specially erected building, the 'Garden Palace' (above right), overlooking the Botanic Gardens. A souvenir mug of the exhibition (right) shows the exterior of the Palace.*

A home of one's own

In Britain, a vogue had developed for writing about the poverty and misery of slum life, from the novels of Dickens to the reports of parliamentary commissions; in Australia there were no novels to speak of, but journalists wrote reports and, occasionally, a government commission inquired into the social evils of the cities.

During one inquiry in Sydney into 'scenes of filth and wretchedness' the commissioners reported that the smell was so horrible they were obliged to put handkerchiefs to their mouths; members of a later commission vomited during their inspections. What they were inspecting was the secret world of Sydney, where wretched little hovels were crowded around filthy courts or foul back alleys, hidden in the centre of blocks with more respectable houses or shops at their edge. There were 'rooms scarcely high enough for a man to stand erect'; 'a den of two rooms might be occupied by seven men and seven women'; the floor level was 'often lower than the ground outside; the rain came in through the roof and filth of all kinds washed in at the door; everything

was an object of disgust'; 'streams of filth and sewage' ran down the narrow lanes. Others described the cheap, vermin-ridden lodging houses, where people might lie six to a bed, or 'seventy human beings might be found herded together in a house of six rooms'. Of Melbourne, a journalist wrote, 'I do not suppose any city in the world can show such foul neighbourhoods centred in its very heart'; these were the 'one-storey hovels, low, dilapidated and dirty, surrounded by filth and garbage', among which, 'the female population' might sit and 'sun themselves and interchange ideas and opinions, which are generally couched in language which it is euphemism to call merely bad'.

Along with the derelicts who slept in the Sydney Domain or on the banks of the River Yarra, the people who lived in the hidden slums or the verminous lodging houses were the city's outcasts. Some were criminals or prostitutes, but the social sin of most of them, the reason, as it were, for their punishment, was that they were casual labourers. A new

Some of the worst slums in Melbourne and Sydney were centred in city blocks, hidden behind the more respectable buildings.

division was separating humankind, the division between those who had regular employment and those who did not. And only the first class of persons would be offered the consolations of the respectability that had surprised observers when they had found the Currency Lads and Lasses 'self-respecting, moral, law-abiding, industrious and surprisingly sober'. The desire for regular employment and the acceptance of such virtues as punctuality, obedience, cleanliness, sobriety and the readiness to perform set tasks were essential to the modern societies; and other elements in 'respectability' – sexual morality and self-respect – could offset the insults that came from working for a wage. These were the kinds of Improvements in which individuals could feel they were doing something by themselves. Those who had regular work and were respectable could feel that it was the moral depravity of the casual labourers that had reduced them to hovels or verminous lodging houses.

As a description of a place of domestic residence, the word 'home' was gaining a new, spiritual meaning. 'The home' was the citadel of the new self-respect. A woman polishing the front door knob, or washing the front doorstep, or scrubbing the floors, became a deeply moving

symbol of Improvement. For people making household purchases, 'the home' could now become a stage for personal enactments of progress: in the mid-1870s kitchens began moving from outhouses on to the veranda, or even into the house itself, and 'Yankee ingenuity' was producing new objects to put into these kitchens – ice chests, vegetable cutters, jelly strainers, egg beaters and other novelties displayed at the colonial exhibitions. When in the 1880s 'time payment' schemes were introduced, a family where money was coming in might begin to plan improvements in the kitchen. The sewing machine revolutionised dressmaking so that, as expected of them, women could more easily proclaim their status by their clothes. The lawn mower revolutionised gardening so that a husband could construct his own Arcady, in his spare time.

It was within 'the home' that working people in regular employment could begin to carry out those ideals of 'family

Sydney slum dwellers, 1875. A whole family might live in a one-roomed shack. In wet weather the roof might leak and filth be washed in at the door.

life' that had already been promulgated by their betters. The real basis of society could now be seen in family sentiment and a central concern with the care of children. 'The family' became an essential phrase in the speeches of politicians. As one of them said in 1866, 'Our business being to colonise the country, there is only one way to do it – by spreading over it all the associations and connections of family life.' The prime task of women was now to carry out this new concept of the family: 'a woman's work' was seen as 'home duties'. It was a wife's natural task to spend her whole time running a well-managed home; to keep her husband in 'decent comfort' and to 'bring up' her children. While the house was the husband's 'paradise' to which he could retreat from the cares of work, for a woman the house was 'your handiwork, your refuge, your pride, your castle, your very, very own, your actual self, a part of you that was inseparable. It is your heart and brain translated into the arrangement of daily life.'

This was why the suburbs had to be built. For ordinary people who could settle into a house with a name such as *Fernside* or *The Haven* or *Anchorage* or *Sans Souci* or *Nirvanah*, the building of suburbs could seem a profoundly satisfying

victory, even if critics could speak of how 'the houses are all as like one another as peas in a pod – four-roomed squares or six-roomed oblongs built of red brick, with every detail exactly the same'. Terraces and attached houses were becoming 'universally disliked', although not so effectively as to prevent speculators cramming thousands of them into the inner suburbs.

The preferred house was in one of the new suburbs, a single-storey, detached 'cottage' (a word that itself suggested an Arcadian retreat) with a one-metre boundary between one 'cottage' and the next, and in Queensland with elevated floors for coolness and to defeat the white ants. In memory of the past, verandas remained in front, although with the development of Gothic styles with their high gables and intricately carved bargeboards, one of the two front rooms tended to push itself forward flush with what was left of the veranda. In the new working-class suburbs and in the country towns, most of the streets were likely to be lined with four-roomed timber-framed 'weatherboards' with iron roofs, perhaps with a bit of cast iron or Gothic bargeboard in front, for decoration; in the middle-class suburbs, instead of Gothic, there might be a small arcade or a loggia

In the mid-1870s the kitchen, from being an outhouse, began moving into the house itself, at first only onto the veranda, and then into a room of its own (above right). Time payment schemes came to Australia in the 1880s (above) at a time when many new products were becoming available for kitchens, such as sausage machines (top), gas stoves (right) and meat safes (far right).

plastered in the Italianate style. In either case a hall would lead straight through the centre; the back veranda would have a kitchen at one end, and a bathroom at the other. Exotic flowers – geraniums, hollyhocks, roses – would grow in neat beds in the front garden (a display area otherwise not used); there would be vegetables, fruit trees and perhaps a hen run in the backyard.

The paddocks near the big towns were being divided into rectangular grids of streets and marked into allotments, back to back, and then put under the auctioneer's hammer in land sale carnivals that offered free travel and free lunches. Not only was a new world of 'the home' and 'the family' being created, but a new world of ownership as well. In Sydney, almost a third of houses were owned, or being paid off, by those who lived in them; in Melbourne the proportion of home owners was almost half. There had been a unique strengthening and sophistication of the building societies, and an extension of general mortgage systems; along with the South Australian invention of the Torrens Title, which stripped land purchase of its feudal past. These made possible a democratisation of suburban ownership less primitive than the economist William Stanley Jevons had

reported in the 1850s. 'A home of one's own' was becoming the greatest of all requirements in the new self-respect. 'To have a home which he himself raised or purchased – a home which he has improved or beautified – a home, indeed, which with honest pride or natural love, he calls *his own*, will make any man a better citizen.' Even manual workers ('the lower middle class of thriving artisans and prosperous tradesmen') could now look forward to achieving the self-respect of 'manly independence' by 'becoming their own landlords'. Workingmen's railway fares were being introduced: in the 1880s new suburbs spread along the railway lines 'like a lava flow'. An American writer said that in the Australian cities could already be found 'the reproduction of the new order of things towards which the modern world is advancing'.

By 1880, about 57 per cent of the people in Victoria and New South Wales lived in towns (even if some of them were very small). An unusually low proportion worked on farms – less than a third, compared with about 50 per cent in commerce, manufacturing, transport, construction, government and the professions. Manufacturing had risen rapidly from a very low proportion to providing more than

The march to the suburbs: *land sales, such as this one in Sydenham in Sydney (left), were indications that Australia was beginning its historic march to the suburbs. Building societies offered four-bedroom brick buildings (above, below and below left) in the 1880s, for those who could afford a 'home of their own'.*

No class too poor to play

a quarter of the colonies' wealth, and in the reverse of what had happened in the new industrial towns of Europe, industrialisation did not create towns; the towns, having assembled people for government and commerce, began to create industrialisation.

There was said to be a confidence of manner in the towns. 'A man feels himself a unit in the community, a somebody.' To some this showed a dangerous democratic levelling, to others 'a greater sense of self-respect and responsibility'. Even the sons and daughters of the well-to-do were noted for their openness of manner: the girls were seen mostly as of the 'jolly' type, piano strummers, able to cook and make their own dresses, outward going, if dissolving into nothingness with marriage; the boys were a 'caution', school-hating, sport-loving, cheeky, disrespectful.

Although, in the manner of the age, almost one in ten of the work force were female domestics (many of them Irish and many of them working 16 to 20 hours a day, six days a week), there were fewer servants in private houses than in most other countries. A householder on £1000 a year might have to make do with one maid of all work. There was usually a labour shortage, and an employee could afford to display a certain amount of spirit. In the 1860s particularly, there were times of unemployment – processions would march, deputations would form, soup kitchens would become busier – but the numbers were not great. In Queensland when the 1860s financial crash led to a group of unemployed railway navvies marching on Brisbane, the police were given guns, the civil servants batons, and a reserve force of citizens was armed with rosettes; all the shops and banks closed and the Riot Act was taken out, but only 135 navvies turned up. Some stones were thrown, there were a few arrests, then the navvies were headed off and given something to eat.

It continued to surprise visitors that working men should be able to afford to eat so much meat, three meals of it a day, roasted or boiled, hot or cold, served in hunks, washed down by tea, often with potatoes the only vegetable. The deprivations of history were being revenged: the working man seemed determined to cram meat into himself to make up for what his predecessors had lacked. As the eight-hour day spread, and the idea of a half-day off on Saturday was accepted, the colonists' success at cricket was explained as due to the fact that they had more time to practise.

The usual delights of city life were available. Theatres, menageries and circuses, nightly free concerts in inns, public rejoicings (street decorations, fireworks, processions, banquets), photographic studios, skittle alleys, waxworks, phrenological museums, billiard saloons, gambling, prostitutes (one of the bars in a Melbourne theatre was called 'the saddling paddock') and drinking (licences were easy to get and hotels were open till midnight, but drunkenness was less desperate than before – beer was now the principal way of getting drunk).

Successful entrepreneurs had built up chains of theatres, with local companies supplemented by touring companies from Britain; there were theatres in the larger country towns as well as in the capital cities; in one year in Melbourne two Shakespeare seasons were on at the same time. Brass bands and choral societies were forming in towns and suburbs (the aspiration of every choral society was a full performance of Handel's *Messiah*).

The sporting life: *a unique form of football had been devised by the Melbourne Football Club, with rules first consolidated in 1866. In 1870, players were required to wear jerseys in the colours of their club; several years later they were required to wear knickerbockers. In 1877, the Victorian Football Association was formed. By 1881, when this sketch of a Melbourne-Carlton game was made (above), the game was dominated by the 'Reds' and the 'Blues'.*

Elias C. Laycock, like many other Australian rowing champions, came from a river district, where rowing was a part of life. He was a timber getter from the rainforest hills overlooking the Clarence River in New South Wales. Pairs, fours, an eight, and single scullers row with Laycock on a turbulent river which flows past the smoking factories of industry.

'No cards on Sunday' was an almost universal rule (although there was a division between those who played tunes other than hymns on the piano on the Sabbath and those who did not) and Melbourne still kept one of the world's strictest Sundays. But it was said of Sydney's Sunday that it was 'rapidly becoming Continental. Public galleries are open; concerts are given; there are endless trips and picnics about the harbour and to pleasure resorts; boating, sailing in all sorts of yachts' – the kind of activity that prompted an English visitor to remark, 'It is hard to quarrel with men who only wish to be innocently happy.'

A victory was being won that was equal in importance to the growth of the suburban home in giving the colonies an appearance of 'classlessness': ordinary people were gaining access to sport, once the preserve of the privileged. ('There is no class too poor to play, as at home.') Sport had been outwardly democratised, passing from the control of private patrons to that of clubs and associations (controlled by men from the middle classes) and the plentitude of playing areas, the good climate, increased leisure time and perhaps the sheer drive to be egalitarian on a question that mattered, had made sport 'the colonial *carrière ouverte aux talents*'.

Before any European or North American country had generated a wide range of new mass outdoor entertainments for the working classes, ordinary Australians had become 'the most sporting country in the world'.

Up to 80 000 would attend the Melbourne Cup; the crowds ready to watch rowing, sculling, foot racing or swimming were so great that promoters could offer prizes big enough to attract international champions. As soon as a new diversion was invented in England – cycling, lawn tennis – it would be imitated as quickly as a British political principle. The one Australian-invented game, Victorian Rules football, was so popular that in 1879 a night game was played on a field lit by electricity. Melbourne began to divide into football club rivalries with some of the intensity of Romans divided between the racing clubs of the Circus Maximus. An English visitor said, 'The excitement of a Madrid crowd about a bullfight is hardly greater than that of the workshops, offices and warehouses of Melbourne on the eventful Saturday afternoon which decides for the year the football championship.'

It was seen as characteristically Australian that, with 'an absence of lines of demarcation', sport produced a 'fusion of

England won the first and second Tests played in July 1886, in England. The Australian team, captained by H.J.H. Scott, was without its best batsmen, and the legendary Frederick Spofforth, the 'demon bowler', was suffering from an injured finger.

Edward Trickett was Australia's first national hero. The son of a Sydney bootmaker, he quickly established himself as Sydney's fastest sculler and when, in 1876, at the age of 25, he defeated an Englishman in a match on the River Thames and became world champion sculler, he was the first Australian to win world status in any sport. On his return to Sydney (caricatured at left), he was given a hero's welcome by a crowd of 250 000.

all classes', or, if not that, at least 'good feeling and fellowship between all classes'. As well as leading to feelings of classlessness, sport played its part in strengthening respectability: it built 'character'; it prompted 'a laudable ambition to excel' in a 'wholesome spirit of rivalry'; it encouraged 'temperate and regular living'; it cultivated 'a sense of independence and pride in manliness'. It was, however, a spirit of *manly* independence that sport produced. Owning 'a house of one's own' was also a sign of manly independence, but it was acknowledged that every 'home' needed a good woman. Women were not needed in sport. In this sense, the new cult of sport became also a public glorification of maleness in Australia.

At first, sport was British. Playing games was an expression of 'pride of race'; it 'kept the proud old flag of England flying'. Then the colonists began to enjoy another satisfying victory: they were beginning to beat the old country at its own games.

It began with sculling, in 1876, when the Australian Edward Trickett beat an Englishman by four lengths on the River Thames and became the world champion. Sydney rejoiced as if it had won a battle. Winning the championship could be 'a grander national advertisement than all the lectures of immigration agents and agents-general.' Later, Trickett lost to an American, but the title was regained, and held successively by three Australian champions whose 'aquatic fame', according to a patriotic sporting jingle, helped maintain Australia's 'unblemished name'. After an Australian team went to London in 1878 and beat a Marylebone Cricket Club (MCC) team at Lords, it was greeted by a festive Sydney where ships in the harbour were trimmed with flags and bunting was flown in the streets. The team was welcomed by the Premier and the Lord Mayor as returning conquerors, and it was said, 'As Napoleon's soldiers carried a marshal's *baton* in their knapsacks, so the young Australians all remember that they have a chance of becoming successors of that illustrious band of heroes who have recently conquered the mother country . . .'.

In Holiday Sketch at Coogee, *Melbourne painter Tom Roberts caught the mood of 'innocent happiness' that an English historian, visiting Australia in 1885, said was characteristic of Australians.*

7. Almost everyone a liberal: 1855 to 1885

As the colonies adapted to self-government, they were quick to adopt the new liberal ideas being voiced in Britain – vote by ballot, manhood suffrage, free secular education, although economic evils such as slums and sweated labour remained uncared for. The new politicians, who were city men, declared war on the squatters with a series of Land Acts that gave selectors the right to purchase small farms on squatters' leasehold runs. On paper it was one of the most liberal land reform programs in the world. But the squatters partly circumvented it. Certain aspects of society remained unchanged; the business interests of a select few were interlocked, and these men were able to influence the Legislative Councils. The progress of liberalism was also disrupted by the growth of religious sectarianism and by the failure to develop a sound system of secondary and higher education, or technical education. And the liberals, like the trade unions, remained racist.

The liberals

When the colonies were given self-government in the 1850s the new legislators were predominantly 'Emigrants': in the first Victorian Parliament 'Emigrants' outnumbered 'Natives' by fourteen to one. They set up as exact a copy as they could of the British Parliament.

Lower houses played the House of Commons; upper houses played the House of Lords; governors played the monarch; and members of parliament decided whether governments rose or fell, so that the government was 'responsible' to parliament, in the British fashion. Speakers wore wigs, maces were put on tables; before moving on to what he really thought, a member would address his fellows as 'honourable members'; soldiers were 'honourable and gallant', lawyers were 'honourable and learned'.

The old and the new: *the funeral of W.C. Wentworth in 1873 was the largest Sydney had known (below), and the funeral day was declared a public holiday. Despite his early rebellious politics, Wentworth had been seen for several decades as a conservative, but after his funeral he could seem to be a radical again, remembered as a fighter for freedom and home rule. What appeared to rule Australia now was the ballot box (below left). Australia was such a pioneer in democratic reform that the secret ballot was known as 'the Australian ballot'. South Australia was quickest to introduce measures such as adult male suffrage for enrolled voters, one-man-one-vote and triennial parliaments (left).*

'Having imported their whole constitution and law books holus bolus from England,' said the visitor R.E.N. Twopeny, 'the legislative equipment of the young Australian corresponds pretty nearly to the tall hats and patent leather boots which fond mothers provided for the aspiring colonists. An exogenous growth has prevented originality of ideas, for which the most part has been supplied by English thinking.'

For a while there was concern among conservatives whether the new politicians could work this venerable system. Sneered at as 'the wealthy lower orders', these merchants, lawyers, journalists, publicans and traders, risen to liberal leadership in the anti-convict agitation as spokesmen for 'the middling class' and 'the little men', were sufficiently un-nobbish for the question to be raised of whether 'the sudden uprising of persons of subordinate rank to a level with the best society of the place' might mean misgovernment, even tyranny. There were complaints about vulgar abuse in debates, about drunkenness, corruption and favouritism; but governors had earlier complained of the vulgar abuse of the squatter-dominated Legislative Councils, and there had been a great deal of corruption when government departments had been run by gentlemen officials from England who were themselves appointed by favouritism.

Just as they took old ways from England, the new liberals also tried to put into effect as quickly as they could the new ideas of England, most of them not yet even tried in the mother country. In a quick series of liberal amendments to its constitution, South Australia showed the way, instituting adult male suffrage for enrolled voters, the secret ballot, triennial parliaments and a one-man-one-vote rule that gave Adelaide two-thirds of the seats.

As part of his concern for 'the greatest happiness of the greatest number', the famous English liberal Jeremy Bentham had taken up the cause of national parliamentary reform. The dreams of liberal England were now realised in South Australia: it had 'the only thoroughly Benthamite constitution in the world'. Bentham's follower John Stuart Mill began sending letters to colonial acquaintances telling them what liberal measures they might introduce next. When Victoria and New South Wales followed South Australia, the three colonies were among the most democratic societies in existence so far as liberal concepts of democracy went. No sooner was Queensland established than it also set the same modern liberal constitution.

The new liberals were all Improvers. Although they were so far away from the centre of things, they were part of the great, reforming 'middle class' dynamic of the 19th century. (Perhaps it was because they were so far away that they were so successful: in this new world they faced fewer impediments.) They professed belief in 'the people', in land reform, in education, in the capacity of human nature to do good. Their power did not depend on radical support: some of the radicals who had earlier supported them joined them as liberals; most of the rest went into decline; some radical phrases continued, but for a generation republicanism almost disappeared. (Separation from Britain was not so familiar an idea as payment of MPs.) What appealed to them was any policy of Improvement already urged in Britain, and they put many of these policies into practice

'long before they had emerged from the region of theory in their native land'. One of their most famous publicists boasted of 'the carrying out by English, Scotchmen and Irishmen, on virgin soil, of the reforms they had dreamed of at home . . . vote by ballot, the manhood suffrage, the separation of church and state, home rule, free and secular universal education, yeomen proprietorship have all become realities here, while they are for the most part still nothing more than aspirations in England.' With the general change in mood, with the scepticism of the age of Authority gone, and with the new economic buoyancy, even conservatives became optimists. The future suggested that 'advancing with rapid wing's stride', Australia, 'the country of true liberty', with 'no poverty . . . to distress it', would 'build on the wrecks of the Past' and become 'the shelter of Freedom and boast of the world'.

As part of their secular faith, the Improvers looked to education to show the way to achieve social cohesion. The idea continued of a sense of common identity fostered by the culture of the mechanics institutes and schools of arts, 'the Palladiums of our Nationality . . . making us conscious of our brotherhood', but what seemed to matter in particular now were the schools. As one liberal lawyer said, 'The most serious and far-seeing thinkers of our day clearly perceive that the only wise means of averting anarchy is to teach the people their own interests, and to qualify both them and the classes above them to perceive in how many ways their interests may, instead of conflicting, be made to coincide. The people may thus be rendered not only a harmless, but a highly beneficial conducting channel of political power.' It was already becoming evident in Australia, in ways Europe was yet to learn, that the new democracy could be a bulwark, not a threat, to social order.

But education could seem so important that it could no longer be left to the churches. One by one, as part of their secular faith, the colonial governments withdrew assistance to the churches, so that they became more and more dependent on the good works of women, in organising bazaars, raffles, concerts, 'bunfights', to remain solvent. Then, in the interests of a secular unity that could seem threatened by denominational education, the governments made an assault on church schools. Catholics feared that secular schools were 'the seed plots of future immorality, infidelity and lawlessness'; Protestants proclaimed that the Bible should remain the basis of all teaching and Anglicans that everything should go back to the proper state it had been in when the colony began, with the Church of England in command of religion. But governments withdrew their grants to church schools and instituted State systems of education that were supposed to be 'free, compulsory and secular', and to provide a sense of creedless unity. ('Let our children be sent to the same schools irrespective of creed and let them be brought up in the creed of kindliness which will make them forget that other creeds divide them.')

In the interests of unity it was even demanded that God should be a Victorian. A member of the Victorian Parliament said in 1872, 'It should be our constant aim to render our churches less English or Genevese, less Irish or Roman, and more Victorian . . . purer and more patriotic faiths.' Another said, 'In a couple of generations, through the missionary influence of the State schools, a new body of State doctrine and theology will grow up and the cultural and intellectual Victorians of the future will discreetly worship in common at the shrine of one neutral tinted deity, sanctioned by the State department.' By this means would be created 'a united community, the first germ of a nation'.

To help this process, readers in Victorian schools were partly re-written to cut out religious divisiveness. Such changes were made as replacing the words 'the great reformer John Wycliffe' with the words 'the celebrated John Wycliffe', or replacing an article called 'Paul in Athens' by an article called 'Wonders in Cotton Manufacture'. Even English history was suspect because of its potential religious divisiveness.

There was, however, one huge technical flaw in the prevailing liberalism. Above all, liberals were expected to believe in the natural harmony of the market and free competition, yet for English-speaking territories, the Australian colonies showed an unusually centralised system of government; in each of the capital cities there was a remarkable concentration of powers. Governments engaged in land reform; they directly ran the railways and other public utilities; they played an important part in the control of other essential services, and in their 'spirited policy of public works' and in other ways provided a larger portion of capital investment than governments did in any other country except Japan. But these were matters that were simply accepted without being talked about, so that there were no theories about what was original in colonial policies: the self-congratulation was saved for what was derived from Britain.

The main exception was whether governments should adopt protective tariffs, a matter over which there was endless dispute. Victorian governments had made up for a lack of revenue by instituting customs duties and then decided that this would mean, as in the United States or Prussia, a program of protection for 'infant industries'; fighting against the depredations of the squatters and the merchants of Collins Street they would preserve young industrial goodness from attack and rear it to an adulthood of independence and prosperity. In New South Wales, where governments had enough revenue from land sales not to need extra revenue from tariffs, free trade could seem the natural state, the free play of the market part of progressive

Progress: *the Victorian Supreme Court judge, Sir Redmond Barry (left) was seen in Melbourne as one of the finest of Victoria's liberal minds. As chancellor of the university, founder of the public library and patron of charities and mechanics institutes, he was a fountain of Improvement. To some he was to be remembered as the judge who sentenced to death the bushranger Ned Kelly.*

Newspapers had become one of the new hopes for humankind. The Melbourne Age *(below left), founded in 1854, saw itself as one of the colonies' greatest voices for progress. Other newspapers founded at this time included the Hobart* Mercury, *1869, the South Australian* Advertiser, *1858, the Newcastle Morning Herald, 1858, the Brisbane* Telegraph, *1872, and the Perth* Daily News, *1882.*

The exploitation of women: *the clothing industry was seen as one of the greatest forms of exploitation of women. Some worked in clothing factories (above right), underpaid, but with regular wages and conditions. But much of the clothing business was carried out by 'sweating' – putting sewing out to women who worked at home for starvation wages (right).*

destiny, and protection a perversion of the natural order. J.S. Mill was quoted on both sides.

David Syme, owner of the Melbourne *Age*, and the most famous propagandist for protection, wrote a book which was translated into German and given an American edition because of its assault on the pure liberalism of English political economy. Arguing that 'free competition' tended towards monopoly, that trade practices could in any case be fraudulent and could prompt State control and that the ethical element in economic conduct could not be ignored, he attacked the defence of the free market by English political economists as being a rationalisation into universal principles of a special interest that suited British manufacturers.

In this clash between two conflicting ideas of the role of government in Improvement were some of the shapes of later and more general political battles, but for the moment it was confined to protection. In some other matters colonial governments were even less active than in Britain. No colony passed a Factory Act until 1873, and by 1855 Victoria was the only colony with anything approaching a modern, for then, attitude to factory legislation. The

dangers of machinery, the employment of children, overcrowding, bad ventilation and insanitary conditions, were largely unchecked, and the 'sweating system' was the kind of scandal from which a journalist could make a reputation. Standards were behind those of Western Europe because most factories were too small to generate adequate pressure for reform. In the same way, although even by the standards of the age there was destitution in the hovels crowded about the filthy courts and alleys of Sydney and Melbourne, with pavement waifs and daughters sold into prostitution, there was no public policy about it; paupers were left to the Benevolent Societies, which colonial governments then subsidised; although men controlled them, the real work in these was done on 'the ladies' committees', by unpaid women. Pauperdom was assumed to need no other consideration since, except where it was seen as the paupers' own fault, it was believed to be a merely temporary phenomenon. It would have insulted colonial ambition to set up a Poor Law in Australia.

Overall, there was less talk of revolution than in the radical days of the anti-transportation movement of the late 1840s and early 1850s. A section of the Socialist First

Pauperdom: *evidence of it provided sensational material in the illustrated papers, whether as a horror story in itself, exposing the hopeless despair of an immigrant home (above), or as an occasion for illustrating middle-class kindness in the form of a free concert at a benevolent asylum (left).*

International was set up in 1872, but its connections were more with utopian socialism, J.S. Mill liberalism, the mystic cult of Swedenborgism, and a spiritualist cult called 'Harmonialism', than with Karl Marx. It lasted a few months, part of a general desire for Improvement also manifest in groups such as the Spinster Land Association of South Australia, the Eclectic Association of Victoria, the Sunday Free Discussion Society, the Victorian Co-operative Association and the Melbourne Spiritualist and Free Thought Association, all of which were seeking to restore mankind to what was seen as its natural goodness.

Awareness was beginning to grow of that division between 'Capital' and 'Labour' that became one of the most important new ways in which people were beginning to see themselves in the 19th century. The eight-hours movement provided one vehicle in which wage earners might consider themselves to be part of 'Labour' but the most important vehicles for this new kind of definition were the trade unions that, in the towns, were now becoming stronger – first the builders and building materials workers, then the iron workers and allied trades, then others. When in 1882, 2000 Melbourne tailoresses formed a union and, in

a long, bitter strike that lasted into the next year, forced better conditions for themselves, this was said to have further encouraged the growth of unions.

At first the coal miners had displayed the greatest militancy: in Newcastle in 1861 the wives of striking miners had picketed and fought 'scab' labour and 40 police were sent up from Sydney. But it was also the Newcastle miners' lodges that had agreed with the pit owners in 1873 to take over from England the new idea of arbitration in industrial disputes, and also adopt a scale of wages related to profits. The agreement was celebrated by a procession of 4000 with their own brass bands, and for seven years disputes were settled by reference to an arbitration committee of four 'disinterested persons' and an umpire. Various Trades Halls and Trades and Labor Councils ('the Senates of the working class') formed. In 1879 the first Intercolonial Trade Union Congress was held, but many people still hoped, as one liberal had put it, that while 'first came the era of master and slave, then that of capitalist and hired servant', there would now be approaching the era of 'partnership or co-operation' in which the labourer would enter 'a more perfect brotherhood of industry'.

The growth of the unions: *the Eight Hour Day movement (left) continued to be one of the great unifying ideas in the labour movement. The development of photography could show workers as they were (right). But since photographs could not yet be reproduced in newspapers, it was by drawings that the workers were usually represented, whether glamorised in one of the contemporary styles in which labour was dignified (below left) in an iron foundry, or in the new realist style (below) in a meatworks. In either case, the idea of 'The Works' (below right) had become one of the symbols of the age.*

Perhaps there was more antagonism against the Chinese than against employers. From the 1870s, unionists in the capital cities began to agitate against what they saw as a threat from the Chinamen. Most of the Chinese grew vegetables or tobacco, or were greengrocers or servants, and the only industry with any numbers of them was the furniture trade; but they were seen as a threat to living standards, and when the most powerful Australian shipping line proposed to meet competition on the Chinese run by employing Chinese sailors, the threat seemed realised. With the support of the Sydney Trades and Labour Council the shipping unions went on strike; unions in Victoria, Queensland and South Australia sent money in support; coal miners' unions refused to cut coal for the shipping company. There was disorder and violence, and the strike lasted many weeks. The resultant ill-feeling later caused an intercolonial conference to consider what the colonies could do to save themselves from the Chinese.

But while Chinamen might tremble, the well-to-do could sleep safely in their beds.

The pauperdom of England has grown at a rate scarcely less rapid

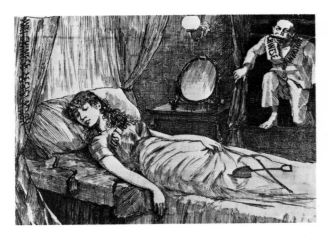

Race hatred: *trade unionism developed in Australia more rapidly than in most other countries. But racism tinged trade union feeling, evident in an anti-Chinese cartoon in* The Boomerang.

than her wealth, and both have reached colossal proportions ... the social condition of this colony is, thank Heaven!, widely different. Here we have no 'dangerous class'. The number of paupers bears an insignificant proportion to the men of the community. Every Australian citizen is interested in defending his just rights of property, and the smallest freeholder will as earnestly maintain those rights as the large capitalist who has invested tens of thousands in the soil.

Within the general political agreement that everything was going to Improve there were no divisions into a true party system, although party names were sometimes used. With almost everyone professing to be a liberal, parliamentary life became a ballet of intricate groupings and re-groupings, with some independents thrown in to make weight (or rock the boat). South Australia averaged a new government a year, New South Wales and Victoria a new government every 16 months.

At the basis of a group was a core of loyalists. 'My dear old Chief,' wrote one of them to Henry Parkes, his faction leader, 'Are you not my chief? I am the only one of the present team who was with you in '72 when you for the first time took your proper place as Prime Minister – first and foremost – *facile princeps* – and unless you sit on my right hand on Monday I shall be miserable.' But more gritty matters could also attract loyalty – expectations of office, hatred of other leaders and new, if sometimes temporary, adherents might be gained by specific promises.

No sense of general ideology bound a faction together, although sometimes a particular principle might be a cohesive force. There were no party organisations, although when a coalition of factions was in office the cabinet system usually combined the ministers in loyalty to each other. A group seeking a share in office would try to increase its numbers by expediencies, and when the mating of two groups seemed near there would be a hunt for independence to bless the union with enough numbers to give legitimate birth to a government. The groups and independents making up the opposition would then seek out the weaknesses of a governing coalition and try to break it.

The number of voters in each constituency was small, and as there were no party machines, and for most elections no defined issues, 'appropriate attention to the needs of the district', whatever they were, might help swing a seat, unless it was a time when special principle (trade, education) might do the trick. Since there was no choice of parties, it could make sense for an elector to vote for a candidate on the basis of purely local issues. Candidates were chosen in a form of democracy where what settled whether they were elected or not might be one issue – land reform, perhaps, or protection, temperance or sectarianism, or the extension of a railway or the building of a bridge.

Although there were no true parties, political leaders might patch together primitive and highly secret personal political machines, dealing with local men who might seek reward in promises of local public works, or jobs for local boys. Relations between a leader and his local man were kept private from the others, so that no consistent pattern emerged publicly from a series of separate bilateral obligations. A local man might suggest that a certain candidate, who looked like a winner, might give limited support on specific conditions: he might also deal with local conspirational groups, of which the most common were the Orange Lodges and the Catholic Church. The most talented of all the New South Wales faction leaders, Parkes was for a season able to get support from both the Orange Lodges *and* the Catholics, because the Catholic conspirators were delivering the Catholic vote secretly.

'The curse of the Australian politics is that ... there are no parties in the strict sense of the term, but merely cliques or groups,' wrote one governor. But the result was not an apathetic electorate, it was an electorate that was more interested in issues – sometimes vehemently so – than in politics. The world could still appear to divide into forces of light and forces of darkness but it did so not on party lines. However, it seemed wrong that while so much British aspiration seemed to have been achieved, the colonies could not imitate Britain by dividing themselves into a party system. Observers sought signs of infant parties with the eagerness of a boy searching for the pimples of adolescence.

The war on the squatters

It had been a scandalous affront to the progressiveness of the age that the colonies should resemble a great sheep walk without a 'numerous, industrious and virtuous agricultural population'.

When the new representative forms of government brought in new politicians – city men, with support from the country towns – one of the greatest of all reforms could seem the overthrow of the squatters. With Europe and Latin America still dominated by great landholders, land reform was seen as one of the world's most radical programs. Yankee notions of land reform had shown the way: the new liberal politicians now took up the cry of 'unlock the lands'. In any case, the small farmer could seem to be one of the greatest expressions of the liberal ideal. There were dreams of how 'the deserted interior was to present a beautiful scene', a thousand farmhouses with flourishing English gardens along each creek, if the monopoly of 'the squatting lords with their serfs' could be overthrown. And there was the sharp consideration for the liberals that if a colony were to be one great sheep walk, what place was there for them?

'The earth is the gift of God to all, not a few. It was never intended that one portion of mankind should starve while others revelled in idleness and luxury.' After rhetoric such as this at huge meetings, mass torchlight processions were held in the streets, the crowds singing the 'Marseillaise' and songs from the American Revolution; in Melbourne the crowd twice invaded Parliament, demanding 'a vote, a rifle and a farm'. In the 1860s, using their new parliamentary power, the liberals then declared their parliamentary war on the squatters with a series of Land Acts – first in New South Wales, then in the other colonies – that gave a right of selection for lots of up to several hundred acres on the squatters' leasehold runs, with five shillings an acre down and easy terms. When a district was about to be declared open for selection, selectors would gather and, at midnight, rush off and peg their claims. Within a few weeks, hundreds of their wooden huts would be up, and there would be the sounds and smells of clearing and burning off. Within one week of the first Victorian Land Act, 360 000 hectares were selected.

Dreams of a rugged independent yeomanry seemed about to come true. But defects in the Land Acts meant that a

On their selections: *with the dividing up of much of the land into smaller holdings, Australia became the scene of one of the 19th century's greatest land reform movements. One of the great ideals was that there would be established a sturdy, independent yeomanry of small farmers. Charlotte Rushby made a model of her father's cottage at Mudgee (below), using local clay for the figures. The house of a selector on the Upper Burdekin in Queensland in the 1870s (left) was considerably more comfortable than the poverty-stricken dwelling of the widow Stockdale, near Maffia in Victoria (below left).*

squatter could use fraudulence, sometimes backed by bribes, to extend his stake. He could 'pick the eyes out' of his own run, snapping up the best bits by faking a land use that did not exist and by using stand-ins. At other times he might be the victim of a land shark who got control of some of the most important parts of a run and then blackmailed him into paying a high price to get them back. To these illegalities were sometimes added violence, arson and theft. Two hostile groups were warring over the same territory.

Even worse, most selectors were misled by their belief that 'anyone can be a farmer'. Even established farmers could be up to a hundred years behind English practice; many 'cockatoo farmers' knew nothing at all about farming. With no knowledge of soils or seeds or rotation of crops, hostile even to the use of manure, and with no capital, the 'cockies' happily acquired too much land. Even if they had been experienced they would have found it difficult to set

The first stage of 'selecting' was the building of a camp; in this case the selectors are establishing themselves in the Gippsland district in eastern Victoria.

themselves up and tide themselves over with no money. Lacking anything tangible to offer the banks, the cockies borrowed from moneylenders at up to 27.5 per cent, and paid up to 50 per cent extra to merchants who gave them credit. (Some managed to get their own back by getting money twice over on the same security.) They sold out or were sold up – to the squatters, to the moneylenders who built up big holdings by foreclosing on debtors, and sometimes to the 'boss cockies' who, by accumulating other selections, were able to put together holdings big enough to carry sheep and make a living.

Little help came from governments. No credit arrangements were made, no Departments of Agriculture were set up. Governments subsidised local pastoral and agricultural societies to spread knowledge, but this failed. Above all, the fault came from a misunderstanding of the land itself; the best use for large parts of it was as grazing land, organised in big economic units using only a small amount of labour. The lack of a huge class of semi-subsistence peasants was the greatest single reason for the colonies' extraordinary prosperity; if the ideals of land reform had been met, that prosperity would have lessened.

More often than not, the result of so much enthusiasm was failure. After 20 years of free selection in New South Wales, only 222 000 of 16 million hectares sold were under crop, and fewer than one in eight of the 190 000 selectors remained on the land. In Victoria, of six million hectares sold only 607 000 were under crop, and half of the best land in the colony was in the hands of squatters. Though they were patched and repatched to cover loopholes, the greatest single effect of Land Acts that were intended to help the little man was to pass land into the hands of the big man.

Paradoxically, there was continuing improvement in agricultural techniques. In South Australia, where a quarter of the breadwinners were farmers, the success of the Ridley stripper was followed by the first burst of technological innovation known to the colonies. Inventions in agricultural machinery led to the 'stump jump' plough, the 'mulleniser' (a log roller that cleared the tough scrub of the Mallee country) and later to the designing of a complete harvester, which stripped, winnowed and bagged in one process. South Australians also developed 'dry farming' techniques of working the soil into a good tilth, conserving nitrates and moisture for the next crop; in 1884

Australia's first agricultural college was established, in South Australia. When this sense of innovation spread to Victoria, dry farming, along with new implements and the spread of the railways, caused a rush of wheat farmers inland. But it was in South Australia that wheat farming most seemed the harbinger of civilisation. South Australia saw itself as becoming 'one of the first agricultural colonies in the world'. Neat little wheat towns, each laid out like Adelaide, each with its flour mills and stone farmhouses, and each connected by bullock wagon or railway with one of 28 small wheat ports, seemed to provide the beginnings of that European orderliness that Australia had lacked.

But most cockies did not have such images of civilisation. In New South Wales, selection worked only when it opened up market gardens and dairy farms (for 'cow cockies'). Success usually came only to the more experienced farmers – the families of the older 'dungaree settlers', the 'boss cockies', or others with holdings big enough for mixed farming. The cockies' role had been to clear the scrub, break up the virgin soil, and then go broke and hand it over to those who knew how to use it. If they stuck it out, they lived in bark humpies with beaten earth floors, with sugar

Staking a claim: *like any other social struggle, the land reform movement produced pictorial representations of struggling heroes – in this case, the Australian selectors. One of the most famous of these became* Victorian Land Selectors Pegging Out Allotments at Midnight, *from* The Illustrated Sydney News, *in which the heroic settlers are shown pegging their claim on a squatter's run at night before he could set his dogs on them.*

Although in many economic fields Australia simply derived its ideas from other countries, it was highly successful in the invention and use of farm machinery, like this portable steam engine on a Western Australian wheat farm.

bags for beds and packing cases for furniture, with their wives working even harder than they did and bearing the babies that, at times, could seem to be all they could produce successfully. As 'the selector', the small farmer continued to ride large in the colonies' rhetoric as a figure of manly independence, but as the 'cocky' the small farmer became one of the colonies' figures of fun.

Meanwhile, the squatters, although they may have failed in their ambition to be a sole ruling class, rode as large as ever in the colonial imagination. Now they were putting their business on a better basis. Ring-barking trees could double stock; pastures were improved; earthen dams were built; artesian water was discovered and a distinctive type of windmill was designed to pump the water out. New types of merino sheep were imported; more care was taken in breeding; stock horses were improved; the kelpie, a new smooth-haired, prick-eared sheep dog, emerged; mechanical wool presses and mechanical shearing machines were invented; the preparation of the clip for the market became less primitive; shearing was done by contract teams. In the 1860s the city institution of the pastoral house developed, providing long-term finance, large-scale wool assignment,

and other services. Clearing rivers for paddle steamers opened up large parts of New South Wales to pastoral expansion; then railways moved into the sheep districts. By 1880, ten years of experiment in methods of refrigeration began to open markets in England for colonial meat.

Perhaps the most important of all was a technological change that began in Victoria in the 1850s, then spread through New South Wales in the 1860s and reached Queensland in the 1870s: this was the discovery by the squatters of the use of the fence. Shepherds were no longer needed; sheep could run free over the big fenced 'paddocks', with a few boundary riders to keep an eye on them. The saving in wages soon repaid the cost of fencing; it was then found that with these healthier conditions more lambs lived, sheep and wool were in better condition, and more sheep could be run on a property.

Buying out the cockies had made many squatters freeholders, but the cost of this, along with the cost of improvements, had put many squatters in the hands of banks and mortgage houses, and this meant a loss of some personal initiative. But they were now living better than before, and the grandest of them were living very grandly.

A grand life: *a large sheep station would have a permanent staff and a transient population, of whom the most famous were the shearers, lining up (above) to be photographed outside the shearing shed.*

Although no longer a 'ruling class', on their own stations the squatters did the best they could to live in the manner of English lords (above right).

The stately offices of the large pastoral houses, like the Squatter's Exchange, in George Street, Sydney (right) became some of the most imposing buildings in the capital cities.

Their wives had joined them on their properties (and they showed a remarkable propensity to marry among themselves); the wooden 'head station' had become a substantial homestead surrounded by rose gardens, oaks, willows and elms (and the whole property was now known as the 'station'); the richest built mansions of 30 rooms or more, towered and turreted, with a village of retainers attached to them, peacocks on the terraces, and vistas of landscaped parks. Some of them also bought mansions in the city; all of those who could afford it sent their children to the Rugby-type corporate schools where they learnt nothing about sheep or cattle stations and little about anything else – except something of the manners of an English gentleman, which some of them wore with special arrogance.

On the largest 'stations' (100 000 sheep or more) the woolsheds could be as large as cathedrals. Stations of any size were run by a stereotyped but economic hierarchy of

manager, overseer, book-keeper, stockmen, boundary riders and jackaroos that left many station owners with not enough to do. Some of the richest contrived some smartness in living, but most lived like a working man grown rich – chops for breakfast, cold joint for lunch, hot joint for dinner, washed down with tea. Their most regular household pleasure was to enjoy tobacco and brandy and water after dinner on a wide veranda made comfortable with lounging chairs, tables and sofas. In town they might spend most of their time in their clubs, waiting for the gas to go on so that the gambling and drinking could begin.

Wool did not contribute a huge part of the national income, nor did it provide a great proportion of employment – less and less, in fact, as management became more efficient. But after 1870 it was the most valuable single export, and the prosperity of the pastoral industry encouraged further growth in the city ports. The squatters saw the cities as their towns, and the bigger stations themselves provided small townships of their own. The squatters' main community service in the cities was to be patrons of the turf, and in the country to play a part in the hospitality system, now institutionalised so that a traveller

Station hands on a South Australian station – the permanent staff settled in comfortable quarters.

who was a gentleman, or could pass himself off as one, gave his name and was put up in the homestead, and travellers who were not gentlemen went to the kitchen for their rations and were put up in a hut. In this the squatters served the rural character who had most emphatically dropped out of orthodox society – the 'swaggie' who passed from station to station doing odd jobs for his rations, walking with billy in one hand, waterbag in the other, with a swag across his back, with blanket, clothes, soap, towel, flour, tea and sugar wrapped up inside his tent.

English visitors were disappointed in the squatters' failure to provide a landed class with a sense of social responsibility beyond feeding the swaggies. Perhaps, they decided, 'by the fourth generation there will be a true aristocracy'. One favourable omen was that although the younger generation gambled more than their fathers, they drank less.

In the 1860s in Victoria several of the original owners of the land – now called the 'blackfellows', from their own word for themselves – had been given places in intercolonial cricket matches, and in 1868 an Aboriginal cricket team had toured Britain, playing altogether 47 matches (of which they won 14, lost 14 and drew 19). Scarcely anyone drew from this the lesson that, when they wanted to, the blacks could pick up the skills of the white people: in rural Australia they had often demonstrated this – but what they would not acquire from the whites' culture were the white disciplines of work. In the southeast, where their lands had

now been conquered, there was no attempt to allow them to take their own initiatives or make their own compromises. Increasingly, they were being seen as a disposal problem. Ideas were put up for reserves and missions, but in practice, they languished: of the 42 small reserves in South Australia, for instance, 35 had been leased to Europeans. With the growth of Social Darwinism and belief in 'survival of the fittest' it seemed clear enough that the problem would soon be solved because the Aborigines were 'a dying race'. For humanitarians there were Anthony Trollope's comforting words: 'Of the Australian black man we may certainly say that he has to go. That he could perish without unnecessary suffering should be the aim of all who are concerned in the matter.'

But in the 1860s there had begun a new wave of conquest, up from southern Queensland and South Australia into tropical Australia, and here there were new frontier wars. In some areas raiding parties from the blacks kept up the struggle for as long as 20 years. Things were working differently on this frontier: the progress of the whites was slower; there were fewer of them; and, lacking convicts, they were more likely to seek black labour. But since this new frontier was far away from the capital cities the putting down of the blacks could be a more ruthless procedure , especially when it was in the hands of the Native Police. 'No,' said a witness in a Brisbane inquiry, 'I don't think they understand anything else than shooting them.'

The last Tasmanian Aborigines. Truganini is seated at the right.

A survivor of failure: Truganini

When Truganini died in 1876 she was labelled, falsely, as 'the last of the Tasmanian Aborigines', an assertion based on the belief that the only true Aborigines were 'full bloods'. Some saw her as spending her last years 'apparently without bitterness . . . enjoying a daily glass of beer, followed by a pipeful of tobacco', but others saw her enduring the night 'with sips at a glass of hot ale . . . prey to a mixture of the superstitions of her own people and those she had learned from the Christians'.

She was part of a society that was being destroyed: her mother was killed by sailors, an uncle by a soldier, her intended husband by timber getters, her sister was abducted by sealers, and she and four other blacks were later to be charged with the murder of two whalers (the men with her were hanged). After the Black Wars in Van Diemen's Land in the 1820s Truganini and her father, who had been a tribal leader, joined George Augustus Robinson, travelling with him as guides and interpreters, helping in his attempts to resettle remaining blacks in one settlement. In 1835 Truganini, whom Robinson had renamed Lallah Rookh, went to join a hundred captured blacks on the settlement at Flinders Island where they were to be Christianised, Europeanised and turned into farmers. By 1847 the 40 or so survivors of this failed settlement were taken to Oyster Bay near Hobart – in 1869 Truganini was the only one left.

Truganini was most concerned that after her death her body would be properly buried, and not treated as a scientific curiosity as had been others of her race. Promises were made and in spite of demands by the Anthropological Society of Tasmania the Government buried her secretly, but two years later her skeleton was exhumed and in 1904 put on display in the Tasmanian Museum. It was not until May 1976 that her remains were given the dignity she had requested, when, in a ceremony conducted by Aboriginal rights workers, the ashes of her cremated bones were scattered over D'Entrecasteaux Channel, near her presumed birthplace.

In their shiny frock coats and ill-brushed hats, and with their heavy gold watch chains and diamond rings, many of the businessmen of the cities, along with the professional men they might meet at their clubs, were members of parliament, sometimes providing some of the underpinnings of liberalism.

The Victorian Parliament became a kind of businessman's and land speculator's club, with chances for quick profits. These new men upset many of the traditions of 'society' with its court-like emphasis on government officials. Now the highest officials were 'not infrequently the least esteemed socially', although what was left of the 'ancient nobility' was respected, the Church of England still had some social *éclat*, and the black-hat cliques most favoured at Government House continued to see themselves as an inner circle. The new men tried to keep up English manners (if sometimes disturbing English visitors by their drunkenness and swearing); but it was wealth not position that established importance, although retail traders were beyond the pale.

The richest of the city rich were still mainly merchants and financiers. Most manufacturing concerns were small, with primitive production processes; many were in country towns. In any real sense Australia had not yet developed a factory system or an industrial working class. One of the most solid forms of business remained what it had been in the beginning: importing English goods to sell to the colonists, exporting colonial products, arranging credit within the colony, and putting money into speculations on the side. What was most sophisticated – the pastoral houses and the financial institutions with which they were interlocked – was tied to the wool industry. Other levels of Australian capitalism remained primitive, and derivative.

A couple of dozen men in Melbourne and another couple of dozen in Sydney among them shared the directorships of most of the main business institutions of each colony, and about four times that number were important minor figures. Interests interlocked: the directors of the main pastoral

The masters of an engineering works in Sydney pose in their top hats in front of the men they employ (below).

houses were also directors of some of the main insurance companies, banks, mortgage companies, mining companies, shipping lines, island trading companies, newspaper companies, gaslight companies, shipyards, flour mills, iron foundries, sugar refineries and breweries. The pastoral interest tended to run through everything that mattered.

Set up in large suburban estates, hidden by trees from their neighbours, with aggressively ostentatious houses complete with banqueting halls, ballrooms, coats of arms and four-poster beds to assure themselves of their significance, some of these central figures in the colonial economies, along with the squatters, provided much of the opposition to some of the Improvements of their lesser business colleagues and others in the lower houses in the colonial parliaments. Their spheres of interest were in the upper houses, the Legislative Councils, maintained at the time of constitution-forming in the 1850s with members who were either nominees, or elected on a restricted property franchise, said to represent 'the interests' as against 'the masses'.

At that time of constitution-building one of the governors had written home, 'There is an essentially democratic spirit which activates the large mass of the community: and it is with the view to check the development of this spirit and of preventing its coming into operation that I would suggest the formation of an Upper House.' The upper house did this job well. Proving to be more vigorous in their assertion of rights than the House of Lords, its members emasculated or threw out Bill after Bill. Parliamentary crisis between the two houses – with appeals sometimes to the Privy Council, sometimes to the people – became as normal to colonial politics as the faction system. By these disruptions the upper houses, although not representing 'the people', began to weary some of the energy of the liberals and to stale their appetite for Improvement.

There were other frustrations. God was not only a Victorian. He was also an Irishman. Catholics were being urged 'to build up in Australia an Irish Church that in the coming time will rival in sanctity and learning the unforgotten glories of the ancient Church of Ireland'. Like the churches in the Unites States and Canada, the Australian Catholic Church had become a dependency of the Archbishop of Dublin: not one appointment was made to the Australian dioceses without reference to him; not one

Many of the business houses in the cities were built in the style of the palaces of Renaissance merchant princes (above).

There was still an obsession for the simple life, which had shown itself early in the colonies with the fondness for the picnic. William Ford painted the genteel Picnic at Hanging Rock *near Mount Macedon in 1875 (above left).*

The land interest ran strongly through business institutions in the cities. Executive members of the Australian Agricultural Company pose for one of the newly fashionable group portraits (left).

A beautiful life: Thomas Mort

Thomas Mort came to Australia in 1838, aged 21, hoping to make his fortune, and in the process helped make the fortunes of many others. He pioneered the regularisation of wool sales in Sydney, and was the first to develop a 'pastoral house' which, with its credit facilities, arrangements for wool consignments to London and other services, provided an essential backing for pastoralists of a kind that was imitated by other firms and became part of the reason for the success of the Australian wool industry.

Mort indulged many interests: railways, sugar, silk, cotton and alpaca production, mining for gold and copper, engineering, and refrigeration for perishable goods to Britain. The last became an obsession into which he invested £100 000 for little return. In 1875 he gave a dinner for 300 at his Lithgow freezing works at which everything had been prepared weeks before, and the meat had been stored for 18 months. During the years of experiment he said, 'I now feel that the time has arrived when . . . the over-abundance of one country will make up for the deficiency of another.'

He sought to solve industrial unrest on one of his projects by having workers as joint owners, but this failed because most workers did not earn enough to buy shares. Mort also supported cheaper funerals for the working man, and he pulled the plumes from his first wife's hearse because he thought them ostentatious.

Mort's large warehouse at Sydney's Circular Quay was a landmark, as was his dry dock at Balmain, built to accommodate the largest vessels Sydney then expected, and extended into an engineering works. As well as the statue erected by public subscription after his death, these buildings remained monuments to a man who spent a fortune on his enthusiasms, but remained shrewd enough to die with an estate still worth £600 000.

In the manner of the age, the city rich crowded their mansions with lavish displays of possessions, such as those in the drawing room of Fairlie House, South Yarra, Melbourne, photographed in the 1880s.

	NSW	VIC	SA	TAS	QLD	WA	UK
RESPONSIBLE GOVERNMENT	1855	1855	1856	1856	1859	1890	
ADULT MALE SUFFRAGE	1858	1857	1856	1900	1872	1893	1884
SECRET BALLOT	1858	1856	1856	1858	1859	1893	1872
MPs PAID	1889	1870	1887	1890	1886	1900	1911
END OF PLURAL VOTING (SO-CALLED ONE MAN ONE VOTE)	1893	1899	1856	1900	1905	1907	1948
MEMBERS OF LOWER HOUSE NEED NOT OWN PROPERTY	1893	1857	1856	1900	1859	1893	1858
VOTES FOR WOMEN	1902	1908	1894	1903	1905	1899	1928

Towards democracy: *the new liberals tried to put into effect as quickly as possible the new ideas of England, most of them not yet even tried in the mother country.*

recommendation by the English-born Archbishop of Sydney was accepted. As the Irish bishops, Irish priests and Irish nuns took over, they provided a sense of folk as well as of faith, and even their faith was expected to follow Irish devotional practices and Irish Church discipline. They were scandalised by the statement of their first Archbishop that a mixed marriage was better than none at all, and hastened to make their church insulated and exclusive.

Catholics began to appear more credible as 'aliens, enemies of the English crown, of English laws'; the counter-bigotries of the Orange Lodges took on new strength in secret organisations designed to exclude Catholics from positions of power or influence. In 1868 – a year in which there was regular news of violence in Britain – an Irishman fired a pistol at the first English prince to visit New South Wales, and the colonial parliament became demented in its fear that the Irish were forming a secret society to overthrow Queen Victoria in New South Wales.

God was also becoming an Italian. Pope worship became an alternative to Queen worship, and when the Vatican Council debated the infallibility of the Pope, not one Australian bishop opposed the idea. Pius IX's attack on liberalism in his 'Syllabus of Errors' seemed so strange in a society based on what the Pope saw as 'the principal errors of the age' that initially even Catholics did not respond to it; but by the late 1870s 'liberal' was being given Pius's meaning, and as well as episcopal assaults on the godless conspiracies of Freemasonry there were forays against materialism, progress, modern civilisation, and other matters that to many colonists gave existence a great deal of its meaning. Catholics began to seem more peculiar.

As the State systems of education were fabricated, the Catholics built their ramparts higher and fired off bigger guns. 'A system of national training from which Christianity is banished is a system of practical paganism, which leads to the corruption of morals and loss of faith, to national effeminacy and to national dishonour.' The Australian Catholic Church began to establish an independent comprehensive system of education parallel to the State schools. There had been no plans for such a system (more than half the Catholic children were attending State

schools), but the bishops felt forced towards it because the State system was being set up just as the Australian Church had found that Rome's anathema against liberalism might after all be applied to Australia. Nuns and brothers were recruited (some from Ireland, some from Australia) and to the commitments of faith were added an increasing commitment to raffles, jumble sales, fêtes and socials, as a second education system was improvised. When the Archbishop, in a pastoral letter, thundered against the errors of secular education, 20 per cent of the Catholics with children in State schools took them away in a week.

Even the State schools were proving disappointing. They paid lip service to the new Swiss educational principles of developing a child's personality; but they also imitated the English system of elementary education, which, apart from those of southern Italy, Portugal and Spain, was the worst in Europe. Officials might claim that the intellectual and moral development of the individual child would release his will to goodness, but when the English system of 'payment by results' was copied in the 1860s, Her Majesty's Inspectors, instead of helping teachers, became examiners who would descend on a school, set the children a test, and mark the results into one of ten grades on which depended the teacher's level of payment. By the 1880s most of the inspectors were overworked bureaucrats playing a routine part in an established system. Some of the old ideals were still given formal expression: 'object lessons' meant to encourage a child's sense of the concrete and natural curiosity were continued, but now they were learnt from textbooks.

The system developed one characteristic – a high degree of centralisation that was more French than English. The local school boards had failed and, following their failure, to the standardising effect of the inspectors' examinations was added the detailed control of each colony's schools from its capital city. Teachers filled in forms to assure the Department that they were all the same.

With so much government activity, departments proliferated. A Department of Land and Works might be formed from the old Surveyor General's Department, then it might split into two separate departments. The new

Anti-Irish and anti-Catholic feeling reached one of its climaxes in 1868 when an Australian Irishman fired at the Duke of Edinburgh, the first English prince to visit Australia. Catholics were attacked as 'enemies of the English crown'.

Department of Lands might then split into three more separate departments of Mines, Lands and Forests, while the new Department of Works might split into two separate departments of Works and Railways. The colonial civil services were increasing at rates of up to four times the general rate of population increase.

Since the patronage system still applied, the power of appointments to the civil service was one of the delights of office, and sometimes an essential part of the process of gaining local political support. Each minister could run his department according to his own ideas of how conditions, promotion and salaries should be regulated. If money had to be saved, salaries could be cut, or there could be dismissals of some of the large numbers of temporaries and supernumeraries. However, there were opportunities for greater flexibility than in more rigid bureaucratic systems: if one man were no good at his job it was possible to leave him in the function in which he most assisted administration – that of doing practically nothing – and appoint someone else to do the work; for a minister who had an eye for talent, promotion of it was possible.

It was a time when new theories were developing in the

industrialising countries about what kind of education government officials should receive. There was scarcely any such concern in Australia. Lacking the educated elites of the European countries, and lacking the deeply ingrained belief in education of the United States, the Australian colonies saw little connection between educational institutions and work in the departments. The rate of administrative activity was high. The concern about who should do the administering was low.

Ostensibly, Victoria imitated the new British system in 1862 by setting up civil service examinations, and Queensland and South Australia imitated Victoria; but New South Wales did nothing; and in the other colonies an escape clause that 'persons of known ability' could be appointed to the civil service as well as those who passed examinations was abused so flagrantly that in Victoria, 20 years after selection by examination was instituted, nine times more people had been admitted on 'known ability' than by examination. There were agitations for more orderly methods – but they were mainly on questions of fairness, predictability and precedent. And when in 1883 Victoria ended patronage by setting up a Public Service

Three kinds of Australians: *Australia was developing three education systems. For the rich, there were the 'colonial Rugbys', such as Newington College, set up in imitation of English public schools, complete with rugby teams (left). For most Catholics there was convent education, although there were a few Catholic 'Rugbys', such as St Joseph's College (below). The majority of young Australians were State school children (below left).*

Board to control the civil service, it was the question of fairness that prevailed: it is true that entry, except for specialists, was to be exclusively by competitive examination, but educational standards were low (they had to be), and there was no inducement for the entry of the better educated.

Throughout the colonies little direct relation was seen between education and usefulness. A continuing discussion in England about how 'both the masters and foremen of foreign countries are more scientifically educated than ours' meant a continuing discussion in the colonies on technical education. But the results proved as whimsical as in England. At a time when in the United States, following the example of the new German *Technische Hochschule*, there was a proliferation of technical schools, there was not one technical school in the Australian colonies, apart from several mining schools in Victoria. There were evening classes at the mechanics institutes, and later a technical college was set up in Melbourne and then one in Sydney, but they were devoted mainly to spare-time classes in subjects like languages, arithmetic or political economy. Only a few classes were devoted to subjects like mechanics

The Government schools were highly disciplined organisations, with their chief disciplines based on annual inspections of schools to assess the work of teachers and the standards of their classes. The inspections were carried out by Government school inspectors and Education Department officials (above).

or mechanical drawing, and there was a blank refusal to provide any straightforward trade training. Following aristocratic, pre-industrial English attitudes, there was an emphasis on 'mental culture': if practical subjects were to be taught, it was to be theoretically, so that the principles underlying a craft might be studied, but not the craft itself. 'Schools of design' were favoured – degenerating into little more than drawing schools – but not instruction in the use of what had been designed. In the United States there were many agricultural colleges; in the Australian colonies, when Victoria followed South Australia, there were two. Education seemed to have as little to do with prosperity as it had with the government departments.

As State universities proliferated in the United States and the faith of Americans in education reacted to the demands of a new age, the old emphasis on 'classical' curricula was destroyed and replaced by a broader, elective and more democratic system. But in so far as the Australian colonies provided university education (by 1885 Sydney, Melbourne and Adelaide had small universities) there was still a considerable concern with classical studies. There were three professional schools at Melbourne University, but Sydney did not get its first two until 1883 and 1884; in both universities Greek, Latin and mathematics were compulsory. The universities were 'too timid to boldly make themselves samples of the modern education theory; they have limited their appeal to the exhausted Anglo-Australian tradition'. In 1880 there were only 263 undergraduates in Melbourne, and in Sydney after nearly 30 years of existence there were only 76, and the staff had been reduced to six.

At a time when State high schools were appearing everywhere in the United States, the Australian colonies had none. Some New South Wales elementary schools were developing 'grammar classes'; the other colonies had no State secondary education. In England there was no State system of secondary education; so it was also to be in the Australian colonies. There were a number of private schools, but in these, according to Francis Adams, a follower of Matthew Arnold, 'A good three-quarters of the knowledge acquired by an average boy [was] of no subsequent use whatever to him, either in the culture of himself or in the prosecution of his business or trade.'

By the 1880s those of these schools that had survived were turning into little Rugbys (although with very few boarders), increasingly devoted to the theory that the important aim of Australian education was to mould boys' characters into the ideal of an English gentleman. The prefect system was introduced ('If boys could be gradually schooled into subordination to the intellectual and moral leaders among them, the habits of obedience thereby created would be of immense benefit themselves.'), and to it was added the hearty comradeship of the house system, school colours, school uniforms, cadet corps, and organised team games (which at once took on more vigorously than had been imagined possible in England). The result was that 'the moral tone . . . in some cases almost rises to that of a second-rate public school at home'.

Before the 1880s, such fee-charging secondary schools as there were in the colonies had been influenced by the academies and city high schools of Scotland and by the private and dissenting academies of England, so that a wide variety of courses was offered. But now courses were being narrowed into 'dry intellectual knowledge'. At a time when even in England the old classical curriculum of Greek, Latin and mathematics was being weakened and broadened, in the Australian colonies it was now being given emphasis.

'So far as I am aware,' said Adams, 'there is not a single colonial politician who seems to realise that if the education of the People, the rulers of the future, is of vital importance to us all, the education of the Middle – or, as we should say now, the Upper class, the rulers of the present – is of importance at least quite as vital.' The liberals had not worked out a way of educating the people who were going to run the country.

8. Looking for Australia: 1870 to 1885

While British immigrants continued to outnumber the colonial-born, their ideas dominated an Australia they wished to see as their own. In 1885 New South Wales went to war for the Empire in the Sudan. The native Australian could be seen as an insolent larrikin, but there was also affection for the larrikin, and the bushranger, whose acts were glamorised in songs and pamphlets as the bandit who seemed to speak up for the people. The bushranger became a subject for poets and artists, along with the melancholy, wild bush itself, which was beginning to seem the main symbol of Australia. But even as attempts to convey Australian-ness were beginning, intercolonial rivalry was creating divisions, in particular between Sydney and Melbourne, and in Queensland there was a threat from the use of black, indentured labour, and some talk that the North might break away from the rest of Queensland.

Members of the Empire

Among the age groups with power, and in the towns that were the centres of initiative, immigrants still outnumbered the native-born. It is possible that at the top, cities had become *more* British than they were before the gold rushes, when the ideas of the Emancipist and of the Native had some life in them.

National anthems were written less frequently, until the habit seemed to die; people from Britain dominated the little Rugbys, the universities, the churches and the professions. In 'an infant community' English ideas of accent, manners and deportment were taken as best; knighthoods and other honours came from 'home'; the dominant town cliques of loyal Anglo-Australian clubmen, judges, barristers, rich squatters, professors and merchants were mostly English-born, and the others imitated the British. The novelist who did best out of Australian themes

Coming to the aid of the empire: *the killing of the British General Charles Gordon in the Sudan in 1885 created as much indignation in the Australian colonies as it did 'at Home'. New South Wales showed its patriotism by sending an expeditionary force of 750 men to the Sudan (left). Victoria showed its patriotism by putting up a statue to Gordon (below left). Beneath the statue, among the many inscriptions, the most famous is: 'This is the happy warrior, this is he, that every man in arms should wish to be.'*

was Henry Kingsley, a visiting Englishman, who portrayed Australia as a sunny, wide-open society of landed gentlemen where an Englishman could enjoy a little adventure, make a fortune and go back to England to spend it.

When General Charles George Gordon, Governor of the Sudan, was trapped in Khartoum while trying to suppress an insurgent rebellion, hopes and anger swept the Australian cities as fiercely as they did in London; and with his death in February 1885 there was an hysterical impulse for revenge, given material substance by a decision to send a military contingent from New South Wales to the Sudan. 'As members of the Empire we are defending ourselves and all most dear to us just as much in Egypt as if the common enemy menaces us in this Colony. The Queen's enemies are ours wherever they are.' 'While we have a gun, a ship or a shilling, England shall never want assistance.' Volunteers marched through the streets to the tune of 'The Girl I Left Behind Me'; hotel balconies budded into red, white and blue for mayors' patriotic addresses; after 13 days' drill, when the volunteers marched to their ships it was under banners reading 'For England, Home and Gordon'.

Beyond guarding a railway line near Suakim, the colonial troops took part in only a few village skirmishes, but they earned their Commander a CB and their Premier a KCMG. In the rhetoric of blood and sacrifice the disgrace of Botany Bay had been washed out in the waters of the Nile.

It was mainly when England lagged behind the colonies' version of the imperial dream that it was most likely to be criticised. From the late 1870s colonial governments, disturbed by French activity in the New Hebrides, and by the extension of German trading from Samoa to New Britain and New Ireland, urged British annexation of these areas. In 1883 the Premier of Queensland decided to settle the issue: he ordered the magistrate at Thursday Island to run up the Union Jack and claim New Guinea as a British possession. When the British Government disowned this action there were protest meetings, and at the end of the year a convention met with delegates from the Australian colonies, New Zealand and Fiji. The next year, when Otto von Bismarck, as part of a complicated world play, sent a German warship to north New Guinea to hoist the German flag, Britain gave in and proclaimed a protectorate of what was left of New Guinea. The three eastern colonies agreed to pay some costs. The colonies now had a share in a colony.

With the exception of Western Australia, which chose a black swan, the colonies put Queen Victoria's head on their stamps.

Australia gains a colony: *after prompting from Queensland, Britain proclaimed part of New Guinea as British, and later handed it over to the Australians. The flag-hoisting ceremonies showed the New Guineans who were now their masters (above).*

Amid all these imperial concerns, carried on mainly by the British-born, the locally born Australian could be seen as a kind of insolent native who did not make way on the streets.

'The Australian boy is a slim, dark-eyed, olive-complexioned young rascal, fond of Cavendish, cricket, chuckpenny and systematically insolent to servant girls, policemen and new chums . . . His face is soft, bloomless and pasty . . . He can fight like an Irishman or a Bashi-Bazook; otherwise he is orientally indolent, and will swear with a quiet gusto if you push against him in the street, or request him politely to move on.' But fortunately the natives still kept their place: 'Such a young gum-sucker must not be confounded with the ordinary middle-class Englishmen who form the majority of the professional and businessmen one comes into contact with in the present day. The native Australian element is still . . . in the minority in everyday life, and the majority of adults are English-born colonists.'

The idea of the Australian as a 'town tough' found its most convincing practical expression in the 'larrikins' who, in bell-bottom trousers, broad-brimmed slouch hats and high-heeled fancy boots, provided enough nuisance and at times enough vandalism to be compared with the b'hoys of New York, the hoodlums of San Francisco and the blueskins of Boston. But there was also a certain respect in the towns for the wildness of the larrikins. If some successful man confessed that he had been 'a bit of a larrikin' when he was young, his audience might praise him for it; he had followed the colonial style. It was what there was to offer against English manners.

To the larrikin was added the bushranger. In his earliest forms he had been made a hero for the benefit of convict resentment and Native sullenness. When Victoria saw a revival of bushrangers during the gold rushes in the 1850s, they were still mainly ex-convicts, but when New South

It had become fashionable all over the world to look for 'national character'. One of the ways Australian illustrators, balladists and short story writers found of identifying Australians was in the character of the 'larrikin'. They were much the same as hoodlums in other modern cities, but in Australia they were gradually given a certain sentimental respect as typically Australian, shown in this Bulletin drawing of a 'larrikin' and his 'donah' (girlfriend).

Young heroine bold: Kate Kelly

If a disreputable police force so harassed Ned Kelly that a wayward youth was turned into a self-righteous murderer, Ned's brothers and sisters were victims twice over. First, because the sour eye of the law was turned on their Irish family background of petty crime, and second, because their lives were forever affected by Ned's notoriety.

Kate Kelly, Ned's younger sister, remains a shadowy figure. Was she the Belle of Benalla, sweetheart of Aaron Sherritt who was killed by the Kelly gang when he turned police informer; was she the lover of Ned's companion Joe Byrne who died in the siege at Glenrowan; and was she the cause, because of his advances to her, of the alleged attempt to murder Constable Fitzpatrick, which was to destroy the Kelly gang? Was it she, or her sister, Maggie, who took supplies to the gang in hiding?

During most of Kate's early life either her mother or one or more of her three brothers (Ned first when he was 14) was in jail, and she tried desperately to gain public support for an attempt to have Ned reprieved when, aged 25, he was sentenced to death in 1880. After he was hanged she put on 'The Ned Kelly Show' in Melbourne, which was closed by the police because of the fear of public disorder. But was the show to clear Ned's name or was it to make money for Kate?

Kate apparently spent the rest of her life in New South Wales in various jobs and relationships. No one knows if her death, in her thirties, by drowning, was suicide.

Wales had its turn in the 1860s, the new generation of bushrangers were mainly failed or struggling selectors. Sympathy for them broadened. Settlers gave them some support, passing on information of police movements by the 'bush telegraph', and in the towns their acts were glamorised in songs and pamphlets, and their forms immortalised in waxworks. Even respectable people despised the police, very few of whom were native-born; their drunkenness, brutality and incompetence made it credible that some bushrangers had been hounded into crime by police persecution. Bushrangers were almost a national institution; 15 000 people signed a petition to reprieve one bushrangers' gang, and when after eight years of peace from bushrangers the Kelly gang had its two years of notoriety, those who wanted to could feel themselves in the presence of a living legend. Ned Kelly himself had sufficient of the Robin Hood rhetoric to become that extraordinary impelling folk creation, a bandit who seemed to speak up for the people.

Although there were some commercially successful Australian-written melodramas in the theatre, there was little reflection of Australian life. Of the few locally written satirical comedies, one was banned by the Victorian Premier because it lampooned him, and another, about families of a squatter knight and an upstart iron founder, lasted only five nights. The Press put on a more impressive performance; some daily newspapers achieved high provincial standards, and at last there were a number of successful weekly and monthly journals. These included weekly news magazines produced by the daily newspaper companies – original in form, and with a strong Australian emphasis. Most capital cities had imitations of London *Punch*, the best-lasting of which, Melbourne *Punch*, achieved a distinctively metropolitan wit, being joined in the 1880s as a magazine of metropolitan vision by the Sydney *Bulletin*.

Cartoonists and illustrators saw Australia as mostly metropolitan, but some painters found the freedom of the open air and the relaxed ways of drovers and stockmen distinctively Australian; some discovered a familiar sense of adventure in gold diggers and bushrangers, or in droughts and bushfires. One began to paint Australians as men of sardonic humour, with a careless contempt for authority.

The cult of the bushranger: *in the search for national character one place to look was among the bushrangers. In his* Bushrangers on St Kilda Road *(above)*, William Strutt *found one way of projecting bushrangers as a national type. But it was Ned Kelly, ironclad at his last stand (left), who was most satisfactory to the myth makers.*

As well as the bushrangers, there were now developing respectable national heroes. In national myth making the most widely respected of these were the explorers, and of them, the most honoured were the ill-fated Burke and Wills. The Arrival of Burke, Wills and King at the Deserted Camp at Cooper's Creek *(right) was painted by* John Longstaff.

With the great excitement caused by attempts to cross the continent, the deaths of explorers became a subject for painters. Art galleries were founded in Melbourne, Hobart, Sydney and Adelaide, and with the current European obsession to find the character of a nation in its landscapes, these became among the most sought-after paintings. Two of the most prominent artists – one an Austrian and the other a Swiss – found a majestic, but somewhat melancholy Australia in the fashionable image of the sublime. However, another Swiss painter, following a new European fashion, found cosy, charming, domesticated Australian landscapes in which the eucalypt could seem as familiar as the oak.

Amongst the writers, some found friendly landscapes, others a sullen despair in the 'melancholy gum' and the 'frowning hills'. Even the animals could seem grotesque or ghostly in 'that wild dreamland termed the bush'. Work songs, boasting songs, bushranger songs and funny songs had become popular in the bush, accompanied by concertinas, accordions, Jew's harps, gumleaves, or a piano brought to a property on a bullock dray. The Irish, English and United States derivation of these songs and the printed concert music form of most of them had shaped their nature, but they were felt to be of a particular kind that belonged to the bush, and they did not become so popular in the cities, where the bush could seem a dull place without cricket teams or brass bands. These songs were generally cheerful – if hardship were described it was usually with dry humour – but when their subject matter did take on in the cities, its style became more melancholy.

Adam Lindsay Gordon, the agent of this change, was an English expatriate, a daring rider who tried his luck in the bush and saw himself as a second Byron. Not much of his verse had an Australian setting but it gave the colonies their first idea that they were a people with a poet. In 1870, on the day after the publication of his latest volume, *Bush Ballads and Galloping Rhymes*, depressed by his lack of recognition and his inability to pay the printer's bill, Gordon shot himself dead. The book was an instant success. His work seized 'a place in the heart and mind' of the people, in the cities as well as the bush, although not among Anglo-Australian cultivated circles. His extraordinary popular appeal came partly from the way he described sport and violent action, but also from his scepticism about life's journey, which he saw as almost meaningless except for helping the weak, and from his stoic message of living uncomplainingly and being ready to die game. 'No one has sung our modern woes more healthily,' said Francis Adams.

Ten years later, Henry Kendall, a poet who had suffered a breakdown from alcoholism, won a newspaper prize on the subject of the forthcoming International Exhibition in Sydney (with one of his worst poems). His next book made money and he enjoyed celebrity for two years before he died. He had taken metaphors from the inland to express his own unhappiness and frustrations, and metaphors from the coastal scenery to express his longings, so that from him as well as Gordon the townspeople of Australia were able to commemorate themselves as a people of rural virtue; and thus, by seeking to identify their condition, to conceal it.

The character of Australia: *impressions of character continued to be projected in painting styles. The Swiss Louis Buvelot found a domesticated Australia, with a settled, familiar countryside. His* Mount Fyans Woolshed *(above) shows his affection for the Australian eucalypt. He was the first of the great 'gumtree painters', helping to make the tree an Australian national symbol. The Austrian Eugene von Guérard painted his* Mount Kosciusko *(right) after he had visited the Australian Alps as part of a scientific expedition. He found an Australia that best expressed its sublimity in mountains. In 1864 the Swiss Nicholas Chevalier won first prize from the National Gallery of Victoria for* The Buffalo Ranges *(below right). The gallery was trying to encourage Australian landscape painting, and was impressed by the sublimity of his view.*

In New Zealand, despite a central government, the six provincial governments had largely followed their own ways; the sea was so much their chief highway that news sometimes passed from north to south by means of journeys to and from Australia.

In the 1860s the South Island was jolted from a population of 50 000 to 159 000 as Australian diggers swarmed across the Tasman in the gold rushes; in the north the frontier sporadically became a battlefield between whites and Maoris, with the whites finally breaking the Maoris' grip on the land. In the 1870s a boom equal to that of the Australian colonies – and partly an extension of it – was accompanied by the abolition of the provincial governments, with some of their power going to local authorities and the rest to the central government.

The 450 000 white New Zealanders had achieved a form of common government, but the 2.3 million white Australians were passing through a period of disintegration. Each blasting its own trumpet, each fighting the others by trade restrictions, shipping regulations and freight rates, each competing for British capital and immigrants, the colonies had refused co-operation, apart from the occasional colonial conferences. When the British withdrew their military garrison in 1870, leaving only naval protection, an intercolonial conference decided to re-establish units of militia, but whatever pride was served by bodies such as the Victorian Volunteer Yeomanry or the South Australian Troop of Mounted Rifles, it was the pride of each separate colony. Few businesses except financial houses and shipping lines operated in more than one colony; many businessmen and politicians had not set foot in another colony.

Overriding all other discords was the rivalry between Sydney and Melbourne. In Sydney, Victorians seemed 'a people to be distrusted' and Melbourne 'the city of stewpans and stockbrokers'. In a kind of retrospective irredentism, Victorians laid claim to part of New South Wales, wishing to spread to at least this part of the backward-looking colony some of Victoria's 'moral, conscious power'. Even the taste in entertainment of the two cities was seen as different: 'The play that succeeds in Melbourne rarely succeeds in Sydney, and vice versa.'

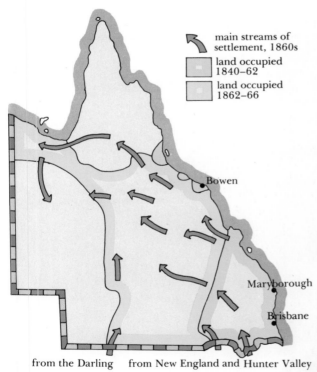

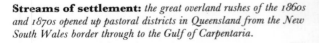

from the Darling   from New England and Hunter Valley

Streams of settlement: *the great overland rushes of the 1860s and 1870s opened up pastoral districts in Queensland from the New South Wales border through to the Gulf of Carpentaria.*

One of the symbols of the separateness of the colonies and their differences with each other was that they could not even come together in a common defence policy. Each had its own small army. The Victorian Cavalry ranked first in the Victorian Army. It had 58 active members and nine reserves. The New South Wales Mounted Rifles had four companies. The Adelaide Lancers were distinguished for one act of military service: they attended Queen Victoria's Diamond Jubilee Celebrations.

From being the second largest colony, Tasmania was now second smallest, and from a sense of its own importance it had passed to a fear of Melbourne's power. South Australia aloofly took pride in a mastery of agriculture that would have pleased Virgil, and Adelaide was so firm in its respectability that it had no larrikins. There was also, however, an imperial wildness of imagination. Adelaide took over the Northern Territory when the explorer John McDouall Stuart boasted of what he had seen up north; then came the imperial grandeur of Adelaide's establishment of Darwin . . . and, after the building of the Overland Telegraph Line, the beginning of a Great Northern Railway to cross the continent. ('If the railway only goes to Darwin' it would be worth constructing, said the Governor in the ceremony of turning the first sod. 'But in going there it will go to Java, India, Siam, China . . .') Western Australia had remained remote and resentful: the transportation of convicts had ceased, but there were hardly any free immigrants.

A new kind of Australia seemed to be developing in the tropics and subtropics of Queensland. After the great overlanding rushes of the 1860s and then the 1870s, the great holdings of semi-arid steppes of those who had become the cattle kings of the west reached dimensions not previously imagined, while at the ports freezing works were being built in the hope of a boom in refrigerated meat. The gold rushes of the 1860s and 1870s threw up new boom towns; for a while there were fears that the Chinese, brought by gold, might take over Queensland; in one remote field the 17 000 Chinese outnumbered the whites several times over and there was talk that the 100 000 Chinese on the United States west coast might come to Queensland if they were expelled from there. In the Northern Territory the railway built to the mining town of Pine Creek (believed to be one of the biggest minerals-producing areas in the world) was constructed by 3000 Chinese coolies. It had seemed self-evident that white men could not work in such enervating heat. In the short cotton boom of the 1860s there was talk of bringing in Indian coolies. When sugar plantations later spread along the hot coast, black men ('kanakas') were brought in by traders, bought or kidnapped from Fiji and other South Pacific islands, and used, or abused, as indentured labour. In

Developing Queensland: *the Pioneer Sugar Mills at Mackay (top) were part of the development of the sugar industry in Queensland that led to much of the indenturing of 'kanaka' labour from the islands of the Southwest Pacific. Many of the kanakas (above) were recruited from the New Hebrides to work in the Queensland cane fields. Gold rushes continued to open up Queensland. These Gympie miners (left) take their ease outside their hut while the lone woman cleans boots. But Queensland's development was at the expense of the Aborigines, who were sometimes fobbed off with a 'King Billy' plate, such as the one worn by a tribal elder in Bowen (below).*

Brisbane both conscience and economic expediency denounced this as slavery. A doctors' report to the government in 1879 announced that death rates on some plantations from overwork, malnutrition, bad water, lack of medical attention and general neglect were as high as ten per cent.

Would the north break away from the rest of Queensland? If it did, there were fears that other new colonies might form along the north coast of Australia, setting up planter-slave communities in what might prove a tragic parallel with the Southern States of America.

Manipulator: Sir Thomas McIlwraith

Boundless optimism, ambition and apparent availability of capital for development marked Sir Thomas McIlwraith's term as Premier of Queensland from 1879 to 1883. One of the new class of Australian businessmen-politicians, McIlwraith, who controlled 29 pastoral runs of his own and shared eight others, had no interest in supporting squatting as an idyllic way of life: development, increased productivity and return for investment were his goals.

He was a shrewd, pragmatic investor. Born in Scotland in 1835 he migrated to Victoria in 1854, where he was successful, but at the age of 28 he was attracted by favourable land terms being offered in Queensland. One of the motivating factors in his business life was financial manipulation – a talent he displayed as Premier. However, his plan to pay for a railway line to the Gulf of Carpentaria by a system of land grants along the way (thereby saving on interest repayments), and his proposal to bring in Indian coolies to work the sugar plantations, brought about his defeat in the 1883 elections.

McIlwraith's business life did not run smoothly. His financial and commercial integrity had been questioned since a select committee had enquired into allegations of corruption against him in 1881, and he was eventually forced to retire temporarily from politics in 1886. In 1888 the London directors of his Queensland Investment and Mortgage Company were complaining about flimsy security and illegal titles to land. Finally, in 1897, after a committee's report on mismanagement in the Queensland National Bank, his political career ended in disgrace.

It was not only in his public life that things went awry for McIlwraith. His first wife became an alcoholic and he himself was seen as an excessive drinker. A contemporary described him as 'an able bully with a face like a dugong and a temper like a buffalo'. Others, who knew him as a Calvinist, thought him a hypocrite for having fathered an illegitimate child.

In the mid-1890s in the eastern colonies a drought began, which was to last for eight years. Thousands of sheep and cattle died, the soil disintegrated and blew away, and introduced plants, insects and animals ravaged the land. At the same time, Melbourne experienced a drastic financial crash caused by falling farm prices and the subsequent withdrawal of money by British investors, and there was depression in the other eastern colonies. Meanwhile, Western Australia boomed on the profits of two of the biggest gold discoveries in Australia's history. Assisted immigration had almost ceased during the depression, but by 1910 it was once again in full swing and prosperity seemed to have returned. But although farming was improving, and Australia was now producing engineers and other professionals, the business class was weak. The emphasis was on government, and in government Australians boasted that they were an example to the world.

We are all floundering

As surveyors continued to make neat marks on maps, and wheat farms, towns and ports spread around the South Australian gulfs, there were warnings that they were moving into an area of low rainfall. But, in the belief that 'rainfall followed the plough', settlers pushed on.

In an outburst of 'railway mania' the 28 wheat ports began to contest with each other as to which of them would become a great port in the world wheat trade. Then, with that sense, as some saw it, that God was striking down their wicked pretensions (a sense that for the next ten years was to return again and again) there came drought and such disaster that in several years over 600 000 hectares were abandoned. The stone houses and the mills that had seemed to mark the advance of civilisation crumbled into ruins.

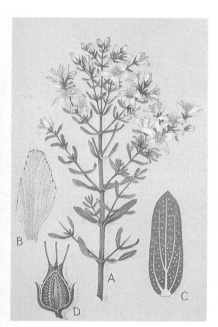

Destroying the natural balance: *presented as a botanical specimen,* Hypericum perforatum *(above) could seem a beautiful plant. But as the introduced weed, St John's Wort, it infested large areas of Victoria. Most notorious of all the introduced plants that ran wild, however, was the prickly pear (above right), which by 1900 had devastated over four million hectares. Farmers were urged to use the plant for stock feed, but it spread remorselessly.*

Rapid development of Australia had upset the natural balance and caused enormous damage to the topsoil, which dust storms, like the one in Narrandera, New South Wales, in 1903, blew away (left).

Then in the mid-1890s there began in the eastern colonies the eight years of the Great Drought, culminating in the 'Sahara year' of 1902, when half the sheep and cattle died. Accompanied by a big drop in world prices, the Great Drought led many outback squatters to walk off their properties; it was cheaper to give up. In the west of New South Wales the land would never be restored. Cattle and sheep had ripped out the grass. Axes had chopped out the scrub. When no rain came, stock stripped the soil even of its roots, and died: the soil disintegrated and blew off as dust.

Almost everywhere the natural balance had been destroyed. When the trees were axed, the soil lost the sponginess that had easily held rainwater so that, instead of being absorbed, rain scoured away the topsoil into the rivers and so silted them that they flooded more quickly. Introduced insects ate introduced crops and infested introduced animals. Introduced plants spread as weeds. By 1900, prickly pear, introduced originally as a pot plant, and then used as a hedge, had infested four million hectares and was spreading in a way that seemed uncontrollable. Worst of all were the rabbits. Rabbits had become a pest in Victoria in the 1860s; by the 1880s the governments of four eastern

companies constructed edifices of hope on new heights of credit. Melbourne was seen by its most hopeful boosters as the centre of an area which in 50 years time, Australia's population by then being bigger than Britain's, would be ready to take over the government of India. But although it had seemed an important part of the purpose of life that rich men should become richer by buying and selling land, the banks suddenly put up their interest rates, and then cut their overdrafts. New financial institutions had to be improvised: for a season the boom became more frenzied, but now there were more houses for sale than money to buy. Prices fell. The market collapsed. Immigration ceased.

This failure was part of a more general disaster that came when a financial crash in Argentina frightened British investors and they began pulling their money out of Melbourne. The Government added to the panic by stopping public works. There were runs on the banks. Then in 1893 the whole Melbourne financial system fell to pieces. In January one bank suspended payment, in April another; within a month 11 more. The Victorian Premier declared a week's bank holiday. His only comfort was the statement, 'We are all floundering'. Melbourne had lost 50 000

The wheat lands: *the spread of railways and new farming techniques boosted the wheat industry, previously the preserve of South Australia, in Victoria and then in New South Wales, which became the leading wheat producer.*

colonies were building great lengths of fencing to stop them spreading, but the rabbits were crossing New South Wales at the rate of about 100 kilometres a year, and by the 1890s they had reached the coast of Western Australia. When the rainfall was low the rabbits would not only eat the grass but also kill the edible shrubs that were a standby for sheep.

At the height of its confidence, 'Marvellous Melbourne' sprawled across 260 square kilometres as municipal councils tried to outdo each other, and land and mortgage

Melbourne loses faith: *the bank crashes and other incidents in the 1890s depression were a psychological as well as an economic disaster in Melbourne, typified by the grimness of the scene in Collins Street during a run on a bank.*

population; houses stood empty; unemployment grew. Processions, mass meetings, deputations, armed police and soup kitchens testified to the crisis. God's hand had struck at Melbourne's wickedness. The Presbyterians declared a day of public humiliation and prayer.

Through a bank of which he was a director, the Premier had lent himself and his associates nearly £750 000; he retired to London as Agent General. The Speaker was arrested, but government delays helped him get off. Another MP announced debts of £1 500 000, on which he paid a halfpenny in the pound; when he died in London in 1907 his estate was worth £250 000. Enough came out in the courts and in Press exposures to reveal that cliques of those belonging to 'a worldly Presbyterianism' had falsified balance sheets, paid dividends out of capital, manipulated the share markets, given each other unsecured credit and, by their control of banks and other financial institutions, helped themselves to other people's money. A Solicitor General declared them 'an aristocracy of criminals'.

A general crisis had seized all the eastern colonies. As confidence vanished, with fallen farm prices and withdrawn British funds, the previous banquet of unproductive investment left no sustenance. Throughout there was the kind of unemployment and distress not known since the early 1840s. New South Wales also knew scandals during the depression: companies failed; the Mines Minister was jailed; the building industry collapsed; there was much unemployment. But New South Wales had not been so taken by surprise as Victoria. When the financial crisis came, instead of announcing a policy of 'floundering' the Government helped tide over financial institutions. But it was in Melbourne that the crisis was most serious. Melbourne was not again to seem the clearly dominant city.

While the others were suffering their worst economic disaster, Western Australia made up for time lost and rushed into its golden age. Given self-government only in 1890 (when its greatest explorer then became its Premier) it almost at once boomed from the gold discoveries that began in the northwest and then, at Coolgardie and Kalgoorlie, produced two of the greatest rushes in the colonies' history. Not only that: at Kalgoorlie it was the most intelligent gold rush Australia had seen. In Kalgoorlie's testing laboratories and treatment plants were being worked out

Explorer and politician: Sir John Forrest

Sir John Forrest, Western Australia's first premier, was one of the richest Australian parliamentarians. He was born in 1847 at Bunbury in Western Australia, one of ten children. He was apprenticed as a surveyor, and was asked to join Ferdinand Mueller in 1869 on the search for the missing explorer Ludwig Leichhardt. When Mueller was unable to go, Forrest led the search over 3000 kilometres. He made such a success of it that he became one of the colony's heroes.

He married into one of Perth's most 'social' families, and within a few years had become Surveyor General with a seat on the Governor's Executive Council – an unusual honour in Western Australia for one who was colonial born. When Western Australia gained self-government, Forrest was elected Premier, a position he held for 11 years.

During those years gold brought a boom to Western Australia while the other colonies were sunk in economic depression. Forrest maintained his position through personality, popularity, and the luck of gold. However, when he entered Federal politics in 1901, faced by a competition he had not known in his own State, Forrest always came off second-best.

The 1890s depression provided material for realist illustrators; (above left), an unemployed protest march, from the Sydney Mail. *Even after the depression began to clear, poverty remained, evident in illustrations to an article 'Waifs of our streets' in the women's magazine* The New Idea *(left).*

new metallurgical techniques that were exported to the world's gold industries.

The money that poured into Western Australia helped subsidise farming developments: railways were built, ports improved; an agricultural bank was set up; new wheat lands attracted many of the farmers who had failed in South Australia, and in the north there was a spread of cattle stations and the setting up of isolated pearling ports. Perth's population increased tenfold; the colony's population jumped from 48 000 to 179 000, bringing it ahead of Tasmania. In 1890 Western Australia had the smallest public debt of the colonies; by 1900 its growth was so great that, proportionate to population, it had a debt twice as high as that of any other colony.

By 1900 all the colonies had staggered out of the depression, but assisted immigration was still abandoned and private investors and banks were still cautious. New South Wales passed Victoria in population: by 1900 it had 1 360 000 to Victoria's 1 196 000; and although, with 496 000, Melbourne was still ahead of Sydney, it was by only 15 000 people. A Sydney magazine said that Victoria should be declared an infected province.

By 1910 Australians had made new records in prosperity and all the capital cities were again bidding against each other for immigrants. More than a quarter of a million were to arrive in the next four years.

The normal march of economic progress appeared to have resumed. But to visitors, used to the idea that prosperity should be deserved, it could seem to be economic progress without intelligent leadership either in country or city.

In the country, after the Great Drought some saw the squatters as 'almost extinct', but in fact some squatters had done well out of the catastrophes of others. From failures of squatters' mortgage repayments, one cattle man built up control of 3 500 000 hectares. There were still enough squatters left to be both hated and held in awe for their wealth and for the isolation they maintained both from the country areas where they lorded it and the cities where they took most of their diversions. Prospering on their overdrafts, devoted to 'wealth, senseless leisure, or the stupid adoration of titles and royalty', the only civic duties they accepted were to maintain a black-hat Anglophilia in their clubs and

Western Australia's boom: *while the rest of Australia suffered depression, Western Australia at last began to prosper: from gold rushes (above) aided by the invention of new metallurgical techniques, expansions in farming, the timber industry, small manufacturing and pearling.*

The greatest expression of Western Australian confidence was the laying of 60 000 pipes from a weir near Perth to Kalgoorlie (left).

Government House attendances, and to be patrons of the racecourses. They saw the maintenance of racing stables as their particular public service, and race meetings as the important ritual of the State. For some, the culmination of both Anglophilia and horse racing was to join 'the rich racing set in England', and for most of them the proper division of society was between those who went to the Members' Stand, those in the Paddock, those in the Leger Enclosure, and those who could afford only the Flat.

Their partners in dominating, or appearing to dominate, economic life had been the merchant families, whose homes were in some of the suburbs' largest neo-Gothic or neo-Classical mansions and whose warehouses were in some of the cities' most ornate neo-Renaissance palaces. Their dominance, going back to the beginning of the colonies, was being challenged by the new system in which foreign exporters commissioned their own agents in Australia who would then deal direct with retailers, and by the growth of the new 'department stores' (on the American model) whose ornate style of building was soon to take over from the magnificence of the warehouses. But the merchant families tended to go into other forms of business, thus

remaining rich – some of them went on to the land, thereby compounding their respectability – and while the retailers who succeeded in establishing department stores also became rich, there were social ambiguities about them, since, according to English snobberies, they were 'in trade'.

What passed for 'society' in the cities, with its charities, its system of formal calls, its 'At Homes', its picnics and its balls, continued to be dominated by the womenfolk of the (now intermarrying) squatting and merchant families, along with the Government House ladies and the ladies from some of the richer professional families. The men from these families continued to command the citadels of male prestige – racing, and the gentlemens' clubs, where they would relax over dominoes and cigars for so long after a lunch of soup, joint, sweets, cheese and salad that one observer regarded the atmosphere as more Mediterranean than Northern European. To visitors, they could seem 'the commonplace rich', with 'an intransigent opposition based on the defence of their profits', little concerned with public affairs and even less with the intellect; they had not learnt to clothe their self-interest in even a pretence of acquired culture or social responsibility. 'Aggressive in manners and

For the people who saw themselves as the basis of fashionable society, Cup Week in Melbourne became the most sustained annual festival (left).

Social pages: *the newspapers and magazines were now illustrating their social pages with photographs of society weddings (below). And it was likely to be society people who took up expensive novelties such as the horseless carriage (below left).*

blatant in dress', with 'neither homeliness nor splendour; only bad taste and cold indifference ... *money-making* and *racing* seem their only concern.'

No system of education, except an imitation of the English, had been found for the children of those who through wealth controlled many of the colonies' affairs. To learn the assured arrogance of lucky birth, the children of the rich and the well-to-do went to the now proliferating colonial Rugbys: even the Catholics and Methodists set them up. There was no provision for a useful education; the emphasis was on honour. After learning their assured manners, the squatters' children went back to the land; many of the brighter children of the rich or well-to-do went into medicine or law; to those who went into family businesses their theory of management was English – that only a gentleman could command. It was said in 1910 of the education of the colonial Rugbys: 'It breeds a certain kind of man – a man who can rise to the top, who can face difficulties, who can lead others, who can manage affairs successfully; a man who may be neither smart nor doctrinaire nor scientific nor original, but in whose hands any piece of business is safe which entails management of

men.' That seemed all that was necessary in Australia: if innovation was needed, the English would show the way.

Given the self-assurance of gentlemanliness, even the technical training of wage earners seemed unnecessary. While the practice of technical education had previously been perfunctory, even derisory, and often non-existent, there had at least been a lot of talk about it. Even the talk had now subsided. Neither manufacturers nor trade unions were interested; students from the government schools were not usually sufficiently educated to follow technical courses; there were no classes in the higher levels of trades. The supply of skilled workers declined. In 1910 the Associated Chambers of Manufacturers of Australia demanded large-scale immigration to fill the gap.

So far as wealth was measured in the great age of financial and manufacturing expansion that was occurring in Europe and North America and now beginning in Japan, the Australian rich were not very rich. And most of those who had some wealth were merchants or retailers or farmers. They were making their money in ways that existed long before there was an industrial age. There were no great

Ideas on the functions of education remained English. Classes were large (right) and Australia did not see any need to expand higher education or research. Even technical training was neglected. By the beginning of the 20th century, apart from Victoria, there was scarcely any 'manual training' in the schools (below right).

Where the colonial elites were strongest was in traditional fields, deriving income from landed estates or merchant houses; in finance capitalism and industrial capitalism they were weak. Almost all the manufacturing works were small, and in very simple forms of production, such as jam-making (below).

financiers, as there were in the innovating industrial societies: the Australian financial system worked as a kind of branch office within a worldwide financial system whose headquarters were in the City of London; where Australia was innovative it was in relation to the primary industries, as befitted its role within British world trade.

And although manufacturing was the great industrial dynamic of the age, there were no great manufacturers. There had been some growth in manufacturing: with so much money wasted on unsuitable pastoral expansion or ridiculously high prices for city properties, there was such a gap in investment in manufacturing that after the depression it was one of the main places where money could go. The use of electric power rapidly expanded, and the number of factories and factory workers was to double, with New South Wales now moving faster than Victoria, and both colonies together controlling about three-quarters of manufacturing activity. But most of the 'factories' were small workshops, many of them simply backyard affairs, and what they manufactured was mainly at a technologically low level. Mostly, they were brickworks, sawmills, furniture factories, textile mills, small clothing workshops (often

dependent on putting work out) and a great number of small places making food (with a remarkable concentration on lollies, soft drinks and pickles). A quarter of the registered factories were in the area of 'metals, machines and carriages' but most of these were small foundries, repair shops or low-grade engineering works. The first novel written in Australia depicting the industrial working class, Edward Dyson's *Factory 'ands*, was set in a small stationery factory: Dyson had based it on 'jam, pickle, lollie and biscuit factories, shirt factories, rope works and paper mills'.

Where there was innovation, it was likely to be in agricultural machines. It was not that Australia lacked innovators in other fields (there were innovations in the use of reinforced concrete, for example, or in new techniques in welding), but Australia lacked the kind of financiers who could get behind new ideas or the kind of businessmen who could turn them into profitable activities. There were Australian capitalists, but in world terms most of them were second or third rate. If one looked at the mansions of the rich it could seem that Australia had a strong elite, even a 'ruling class'; but if one looked for signs of financial and industrial enterprise the elites could seem colonial-minded.

The Broken Hill boom:
the opening of the Broken Hill mines was to start a new stage in Australian industrial development. Wherever one looked in Broken Hill, the scene was dominated by the smokestacks of the smelters (above and right).

The mining industry was an exception. The big gold mines had their scientists and technologists (and at the beginning of the new century Australia was the world's largest gold producer). The copper mines of South Australia, Tasmania and New South Wales developed new skills (in 1893 the Mt Lyell Copper Co. in Tasmania proclaimed itself owner of the world's richest copper mine). For a period the tin fields of Tasmania and New South Wales made Australia the world's largest producer of tin. In New South Wales the opening of new coal fields almost doubled production; and after silver-lead was discovered in 'the broken hill' in the Barrier Ranges in the west of New South Wales, Australia became one of the world's main suppliers. Head frames, powerhouses, workshops and winder houses went up along the top of the ridge of 'the broken hill' . . . on the slopes of the hill, smelters were built. Then in 1892, the Broken Hill Proprietary decided to dig a whole hill out so that they would miss nothing.

By 1898 all the smelting had been moved to Port Pirie, a failed wheat port set among mud flats and mangrove swamps but now able to again believe in itself as 'the Liverpool of Australia'. What was critically important was that in 1886 the newly formed BHP had decided to import foreign mining experts to tell them what to do; this example was followed by other mining companies, and there were already in Australia those who had been trained in the Schools of Mines. Australia became known as a place of innovation in metallurgy, as it already was in farming; pyritic smelting was developed in Australia; new processes were devised for roasting lead ores; when the 'flotation' process was developed to separate zinc from zinc sulphide, the Broken Hill companies could re-work their dumps to extract zinc. To find a use for the sulphur extracted from zinc separation, the BHP built a sulphuric acid plant and began producing superphosphates.

Overall, the men running the various Broken Hill mining companies acted with enterprise, but they benefited from government support. It was the drive of the politician W.M. Hughes which forced the base metal industries into marketing effectiveness, and when the BHP acquired two mountains of iron ore in South Australia and decided to go into the steel business, it was with government encouragement.

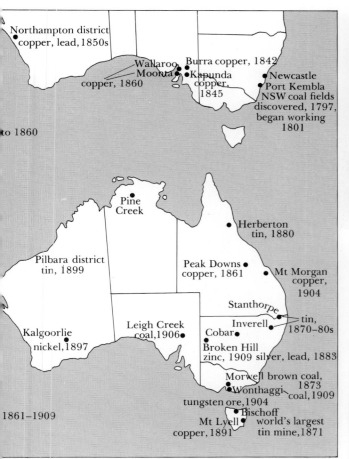

Mining developments: *at various times Australian colonies were the world's biggest producers of gold, copper, coal, tin and silver-lead (above). In the mining industry there was development in metallurgical research, with Australia as a world leader.*

Class struggle: *some of the most bitter class conflict in Australia's history occurred at Broken Hill in its earliest days. The strike of August-September 1892 provided dramatic material for the magazine illustrators, with the arrival of troopers (top) and women attacking 'scab' labourers (above).*

Every farmer a yeoman?

In the United States, Canada and the Australian colonies, at about the same time, new techniques and expanded world markets gave wheat farmers sudden ideas of their own importance.

In the Australian colonies the wheat farmer had already been honoured in South Australia as a rational agriculturist compared with the squatter-depredator: rash expansion and subsequent disaster dulled some of his brightness, but now he came into his own in Victoria when the rush into the mallee, backed by railways and new farming techniques, made Victoria the main wheat colony. Then from 1894 to 1899 New South Wales doubled its wheat production. It doubled again in the next decade. By 1911 the wheat crops were roughly ten times as big as those of 1891. New South Wales was now the leading wheat producer. The railways had opened up virgin farmland and, after so many failures, Governor Phillip's dream had been resolved: New South Wales could grow wheat.

Country towns had already grown up, with no special form to them other than the rectangle and the straight line, but usually with railway station and post office, police station and courthouse, churches from the four main denominations and often a masonic temple as well to keep watch on the Catholics; there would be a school of arts or a mechanics institute and a convent school and State school; a park might be established and there might be a show ground; the hospital and the cemetery were likely to be on the edges of the town. In the biggest wheat-growing areas new towns now grew up; if towns were already there they were made to pay honour to wheat. Wheat trains joined other symbols of prosperity as they rolled on to the city ports, and the wheat ships paid honour to the importance of *the export*.

In the 1890s an idea began to grow that was new to an Australia where the squatters had been dismissed as greedy gamblers and the selectors as 'cockies': this was the idea of 'the pioneer' as someone who had followed in the footsteps of the explorers, worked the land and tamed the wilderness. Frederick McCubbin painted a patriotic triptych of pioneers, as if they were Christian saints; the novel *We of the Never Never* became one of Australia's greatest best sellers; the myth-making poet Banjo Paterson's 'Song of the Future' eulogised the pioneers:

Country towns: *they had gradually assumed a pattern of their own – luncheon adjournments on livestock sale days (left) and even sometimes the regular flooding (above) were opportunities for social intercourse.*

The Australians gained new myth makers, of whom the most commercially successful were the Sydney solicitor A.B. (Banjo) Paterson (above), whose The Man from Snowy River and Other Verses *was an immediate best seller, and Mrs Aeneas Gunn (above right), whose* We of the Never Never *had world success.*

Expanding world markets brought a new boom to wheat farmers and increased their political power and social importance (left).

148

> Their faces were westward bent
> Beyond the furthest settlement
> Responding to the challenge cry
> Of 'Better country further out'.

There was a place for women in this new pioneer legend –
McCubbin included them in his paintings; they were
central to *We of the Never Never*; and one of the greatest poets
of the pioneers, as well as writing 'The Man Upon the
Land' also produced 'The Women of the West'. But the
hardest work was seen as being done by men, and among
the men the wheat farmers saw themselves as the sturdiest of
the pioneers. They could begin to imagine that they might
provide the most admirable characteristics of a nation
whose goodness was otherwise being sucked dry by the evils
of the cities and the excesses of the wealthiest squatters.
They began to organise in dissident, sometimes radical,
groups and to plan new political parties in which some of
the smaller graziers also showed interest. Even some of the
dairy farmers, the despised 'cow cockies', now began to
claim respect as, like the wheat industry, dairying was
modernised. They too became interested in new political
parties. They could all believe the refrain of 'The Man

The pioneers: *although the selectors could be derided as 'cockies',
they were now also praised as 'pioneers'. Frederick McCubbin raised
them to an almost religious veneration when he painted his triptych,*
The Pioneer *(below), in 1903–4. George Lambert in his* A Bush
Idyll *(above), reduced Australian bush life to mere prettiness .*

Upon The Land': 'And the men that made the Nation are/The men upon the land.'

Further honour was given to small farmers when the problem of lack of water began to be amended by United States technology. Two American exponents of 'scientific irrigation' were brought to the exhausted sheep station of Mildura, Victoria on the River Murray to start an irrigation colony: the red, silver and blue pump was installed, the irrigation canals were dug, and after the tensions of adaptation an unprofitable sheep station was turned into a cultivated area providing a living for 3000 settlers. Avenues of triumphant palms were planted in celebration. Another irrigation colony, at Renmark on the Murray River in South Australia, also succeeded. Other irrigation settlements started, and soon there seemed no limit. 'Gold will eventually become exhausted, but water will continue as long as the world lasts.'

The desire to establish a class of 'virtuous and industrious' small farmers was now so strong that during the depression, utopianism about the virtues of rural life prompted the three eastern colonies to pass laws enabling autonomous cooperative communities to be set up, with the rights to govern themselves. One of humankind's old dreams – the right of self-organisation in small units of common wealth – had now been enacted by Australian laws; but very few village communes were formed. (The most famous of them, 'New Australia', was set up not in Australia but in Paraguay, where several shiploads of utopian Australians emigrated to found 'a community where all labour in common for the common good'. It was a disaster.)

Governments turned to buying success. 'Free selection' had failed; more costly schemes of land reform were developed, given the name of 'closer settlement', and government money was put behind them. Governments bought large estates to subdivide and sell off on easy terms as small holdings; large estates were taxed; government banks were told to give cheap credit for improvements. Holdings were often too small to be economic, but governments were now prepared to subsidise them. Backed by government research and agricultural colleges, by government sponsorship of cheap land, irrigation, trade and pest control, and by the readiness of government Departments of Railways to cut freight rates, an independent Australian yeomanry was at last produced.

When Arthur Hoey Davis, writing under the pen name Steele Rudd, wrote On Our Selection, *he had intended to convey something of the heroic as well as the comic in the life of small farmers. But as his commercial success increased, and sequel followed sequel, he was seen mainly as the creator of the comic figures of 'Dad and Dave'. The artist Norman Lindsay gave them visual form in his illustrations for* On Our Selection.

The boss: William Chaffey

Canadian-born William Chaffey and his brother George were successful irrigation developers in the United States. In 1887, they sold their Californian interests cheaply and moved to a drought-stricken Victoria, intent on making a fortune by using irrigation to develop arid land. It was not to be achieved easily; but the Chaffeys persevered for the next few years at Mildura, and Renmark in South Australia.

By 1890, after an expensive sales promotion, 3300 people were settled at Mildura and 1100 at Renmark, about half of them recent emigrants. Problems soon developed with the quality and supply of water, and they were compounded by the Victorian depression and the decline of land sales. Some of the settlers decided that the Chaffeys' Mildura Irrigation Company had no authority to sell irrigation water and succeeded in getting the government to take over. Chaffey Brothers Ltd went into liquidation, the Mildura Irrigation Trust replaced the Mildura Irrigation Co., and in 1897 a Royal Commission report largely blamed the Chaffeys' insufficient capital and their errors in plan-

ning for the problems that had subsequently developed at Mildura.

George Chaffey returned to the United States and rebuilt his career as an irrigationist. But William persevered at Mildura. As a farmer he developed 80 hectares of orchard and established a winery; as a community leader he promoted better marketing for Mildura fruit and helped start the dried fruit industry. He became known affectionately as 'the boss' in Mildura, a title earned by leadership rather than money.

The development of wheat farming had not come only from railways and new markets. The establishment of Departments of Agriculture had led to a scientific approach.

There were careful experiments in breeding new strains; the study of the importance of superphosphate was continued; machinery continued to improve; more agricultural colleges were founded. With science, technology and education now showing the way, yields per hectare almost quadrupled. It was the same with dairying. Australia had imported butter from New Zealand, but cold chambers on ships made chilled Australian butter available to British markets, and refrigeration and the spread of the railways increased markets at home. Swedish cream separators appeared in Australian dairies, co-operative butter factories were set up, pasteurisation was introduced. From 1900 to 1910 the amount of machinery on dairy farms doubled. In the 25 years after 1890 the production of butter quadrupled. Refrigeration had also provided an opportunity for an alternative industry to wool-growing. Freezing works had been set up at the city ports and refrigerating machines in the holds of the fast mail steamers. With New South Wales mutton and Queensland beef on the British market, sometimes at a quarter of the price of British meat, one ninth of export income came from frozen or chilled foods.

Specialists were needed for the new Agriculture Departments. Veterinary science and agricultural science faculties were established at the universities, and these and other demands led to an extension of science teaching at the universities. In this new age with its new demands, the colonial Rugbys, although offering no training, except in arrogance, for the 'management of men', nevertheless had to show some concern for the 'smart' or 'scientific', or even the 'original', because of the uses that had been found for universities after they had been forced to abandon their dreams of providing a classical education for Australian gentlemen. Since no one else, apart from the Schools of Mines, had provided technical and professional schools, the universities had stepped in, with considerable efficiency.

To meet new demands in technique, the university engineering faculties expanded. Large parts of the new Australia were put together and held together by engineers: men with hard-bitten faces and military moustaches,

The entrance to the most respected professions was through the universities, and the entrance to universities was mainly through wealth; but it was also necessary to pass the matriculation examination, sometimes held in the town hall (above).

Useful education: *law and medicine were the most prestigious professions. A few graduates began to engage in research (above). An Australiasian Association for the Advancement of Science was formed in the 1880s, and badges were struck for the Association's congress meetings (below). The 1902 meeting of the congress in Hobart was held in the Tasmanian Museum (below left).*

conservative in disposition, suspicious of idealistic excess (unless it was the idealistic excess of the rhetoric of development), but keenly competent in adapting to Australia what had already been thought of in some other country, or sometimes, trying something out themselves. As well as the expansion of the engineering faculties at the universities, faculties of architecture and economics and chairs in education were founded to meet other demands. Original research was done in geology, biology and anthropology. Most practitioners of the older professions of medicine and law were now Australian, so there was expansion of those schools as well. The medical faculties began to produce highly competent graduates, a few of whom produced original research. The New South Wales Government set up a Bureau of Microbiology; an Institute of Tropical Medicine was established at Townsville. Dentistry and pharmacy faculties were instituted.

By 1910 little more than a quarter of university students were studying arts; the biggest single faculties were medicine. Useful at last, the universities were training specialists, producing new kinds of people, the 'professional men' – engineers, scientists, dentists, economists, architects, agricultural scientists, veterinary scientists. The arts faculties were still given the highest honour in lists of precedence and academic processions but, palely derivative of British institutions, they provided neither a meaningful cultural background nor a useful general education for those who were to exercise the generalist arts of administration in business or government. It was their production of 'the professional men' that gave the universities meaning. Without them, Australia's prosperity would not have existed.

It was not to the commonplace rich but to their own governments that the colonies looked for progress. And here, despite the opposition of the Legislative Councils, change was so remarkable that a few social scientists from other countries came to Australia and New Zealand to write books about them.

'Australasia has not contributed much to social philosophy, but she has come infinitely further than any other country in the practical field ... Western Europe is richer in doctrines, Australasia in realities,' said one of them.

South Australia, in particular, may for a period have been one of the most progressive places in the world. By 1893, the year of financial collapse in Melbourne, a new government, uniting both liberal and radical elements, was to institute women's franchise, a State bank, factory inspection, progressive land and income taxes, death duties, among other measures. By the end of the century Adelaide was to seem like a German *Residenzstadt*, the neat capital of a little principality, 'with its parks and gardens, its little court societies and its general air of laying itself

Annual Intercolonial Trade Union Congresses helped to pioneer initiatives such as compulsory arbitration, seen as the most advanced in the world. Two women delegates from the Victorian Tailoresses' Union, seated in the centre of the third row, attended the Melbourne Congress in 1884 (above).

Stock Exchange: *trading in stocks and shares began in the 1840s – the Brisbane Stock Exchange (above) was founded in 1885 – but it was several decades before properly established stock exchanges were in existence.*

out to enjoy quietly a comfortable life', but devoted to the well-mannered pursuit of democracy. In population and economic activities, however, it had been out-traced by the cruder vigours of Queensland, with only 357 000 people to Queensland's 493 000.

Overall, Australia's labour laws were seen as 'not matched elsewhere in their number, boldness and stringency': compulsory arbitration in industrial disputes was unique; Factory Acts had become more extensive; early closing in shops had been instituted everywhere except Tasmania; several colonies had adapted English worker's compensation legislation; New Zealand and New South Wales were two of the first places in the world to set up government unemployment bureaus; wage boards were concerned with maintaining minimum living standards; graduated income and land taxes and death duties introduced a mild redistribution of income. When New South Wales imitated New Zealand and legislated for old age pensions in 1901 the only other place with a non-contributory scheme was Denmark. (The German contributory scheme was seen as not suitable for 'a free country like New South Wales and impossible of accomplishment in Anglo-Saxon countries'.) New South Wales introduced a non-contributory invalid pensions scheme in 1908, the first place in the world to do so. The divorce laws of New South Wales, Victoria and New Zealand were among the most advanced in the world; payment of members of parliament and women's suffrage were introduced ahead of most other places. Governments were the main landlords, with intricate rules for land administration, land reform and subsidising of farmers; some saw the tariff as the basis of all human progress. Governments owned the railways, controlled central education systems, pursued active policies of immigration, and ran homes for neglected children and the aged and infirm. 'Australia,' said a trade union newspaper, 'has ever been an exemplar to the old lands ... it has steadily forged ahead, initiating and perfecting, experimenting and legislating, on new lines.'

Yet, while State action could be seen as the basis of progress it was not sustained by a reservoir of talent. Scorned by the rich and well-to-do, the government bureaucracies reflected the 'muddling on, with a high standard of honour and a low standard of efficiency [that] is the dominant note of Australian public life'. Recruiting policies showed no concern for attracting talent; there was no recruitment of people with higher levels of education, and attempts to relate advancement to tests of ability were defeated by concern for the 'decent duffers' who might otherwise miss their promotions. Everybody had to start at the bottom, and after that the slow climb through the hierarchy usually depended on seniority. Heads of departments tended to be elderly men of a kind found only in the lower divisions of the civil service of other countries. In an annual report one Public Service Board wondered if something more might be needed; it raised the question of 'the desirability of introducing to the Government Services young men who had secured a full university training'.

State action had come in a series of improvising reactions to difficulties for which imported political ideologies, except un-Anglo-Saxon ones, were of little use, but no distinctive theory developed to sustain it. 'Australian politics concerned themselves with day-to-day affairs ... The poverty of the theoretical basis ... is astonishing to those used to the polemics of Europe.' Phrases such as 'State socialism' and 'colonial socialism' were sometimes used, but *étatisme* seemed un-British and no phrase caught on that enabled people to imagine what their style of government was. 'Colonial governmentalism' was a phrase invented by an observer who later became head of the London School of Economics, but that was scarcely a phrase to stir the human heart. And he was a New Zealander.

Radical Premier: Charles Cameron Kingston

When Charles Cameron Kingston died, *The Bulletin* praised him as 'Australia's Noblest Son ... a good Australian all the time, and a good Democrat all the time'. Those who preferred good manners to democracy, however, had vilified Kingston as 'absolutely unscrupulous', a bully and a lecher.

Kingston's government, in power in South Australia from 1893 to 1899 as a coalition of liberals governing with Labor support, was at the time one of the most radical governments on earth. Kingston had to his credit the starting of a progressive land tax and a progressive income tax, the extension of votes to women and the institution of full adult suffrage, Australia's first arbitration system, the foundation of co-operative settlements along the River Murray, and the establishment of a State bank and a high protective tariff. He refused a knighthood and fought the Adelaide 'establishment' and the colonial governor, trying to restrict his powers and even cutting his salary and allowances; and he tried to reduce the powers of the South Australian upper house and widen the franchise for it. It was this concern that brought him down when some of his supporters, afraid of an election Kingston was trying to force, voted him out of office.

He resigned from State politics to enter the Federal arena and assisted with the drafting of a constitution for the proposed Commonwealth. After the first Federal election in 1901, Kingston was given the portfolio of Trade and Customs.

The Australian colonies seemed to be leading the world in liberal democracy, and of them South Australia, which planned a new parliament house for the 1880s, seemed to lead the rest.

10. The modern age: 1885 to 1914

The modern age heralded the 'new woman': a beneficiary of the Married Women's Property Acts; able to enter university and a larger part of the work force; a suffragist campaigning for women's votes. Yet many areas of employment were still exclusively male, and female wages remained low. Socialism was adopted by an enthusiastic minority as the answer to inequality, but the trade union movement gathered a much larger following, campaigning successfully for workers' rights. A sense of belonging to the working class became important, as did the distinction of being an office worker or a public servant. Away from sporting pursuits the concept of classlessness was a myth; the rich moved out of town, and the office workers and manual workers settled in separate suburbs.

The move to improvement

'Box-like ... gigantic ... hideous ... grotesque ... gruesome ... ugly ... monumental without being sublime.' The new city buildings, towering up ten or even 12 storeys brought protests; limits were soon placed on their height.

There were other signs of the 'modern age': the Marconi Company set up two broadcasting stations in 1905 for communicating across the Bass Strait; horseless carriages passed the stage of seeming an expensive public nuisance, and by 1910 there were 5000 of them; a flying machine built on a Victorian sheep station flew six metres above the ground for 180 metres at 40 kilometres an hour; in 1912 Australia was to see its first air race.

As part of 'the modern age', in that continuing move to human improvement that had been one of the great concerns of the 19th century, there was now the 'new woman', who could seem to have achieved some of what

The new woman: *by the turn of the century there was a belief in 'the new woman'. The 'new woman' wore loose, one-piece dresses – and was satirised for it (above left). She had taken on the new leisure habit of cycling (above) and she was likely to be an admirer of Australia's most publicised new woman – swimmer Annette Kellerman (far left). In Australia Kellerman had won many records and given a number of public exhibitions before she went abroad, where she built a career as swimmer, vaudeville star, dress reformer and fitness advocate. In the United States she was voted 'the world's perfect woman'.*

The exploitation of women in advertisements had begun – often as sex objects (left).

J.S. Mill had hoped for when he had written his influential book *The Subjection of Woman*. The 'new woman' was seen as independent-minded, well-informed and competent. As an advocate of dress reform, she had abandoned tight corseting, wearing instead loose one-piece dresses. Both for the sense of freedom it gave her and because it helped produce that healthy womanhood that was seen as essential to 'maintaining the race', she might play tennis, or cycle, or go swimming. Before she married she might, for a while, be a 'bachelor girl', leaving home and, in demonstration of her industry and self-respect, supporting herself through work. As a wife she might speak of the need for the study of 'domestic economy' (for a while there were plans for a chair in Domestic Economy at Sydney University). As a mother she might support 'birth control'. In one of the women's magazines now being published she might read 'new ideas'. (*New Idea* was the name of the best selling of these magazines.)

She might congratulate herself on the Married Women's Property Acts, passed in the last decades of the 19th century, in which women were given virtually the same property rights as men, or on the beginnings of divorce law reform and reform in the provisions for the guardianship of children. As a middle-class woman, she might now also congratulate herself on the opportunities that, after a fight, had been gained by women in university education (even if Greek and Latin texts were expurgated to make them decent for female eyes and even if the dean of the Sydney Medical School had said he marked women medical students 20 per cent harder than men). If she came from a family of lower income she might at least welcome the way in which new kinds of jobs – teaching and nursing in particular – gave women a chance to rise in the world.

She might even have been a 'suffragist', one of those who had campaigned for women's votes as a member of the Womanhood Suffrage League or the Women's Christian Temperance Union – organising petitions, handing out leaflets, marching, supporting deputations, preparing questionnaires for male candidates at election time. If this was so, she might have had yearnings for other kinds of reform. If she was a temperance advocate she might have seen the vote as 'a weapon of protection for their homes from the liquor trade'; if she was a supporter of 'women's self reliance' she might have hoped to move on from the suffrage to the appointment of kindergartens and children's

The Dawn *(right), a feminist monthly magazine, was founded by Louisa Lawson, poet Henry Lawson's mother, and survived for 17 years.* The New Idea *(below), the first of the commercially successful women's magazines, was launched in 1902.*

Modern woman: Catherine Helen Spence

The Grand Old Woman of Australia was how Catherine Helen Spence was described on her death in 1910 at the age of 84. Writer, reformer and preacher, she had more than earned the title. Her novel, *Clara Morison: A Tale of the South Australian Goldfields*, was the first published about Australia by a woman (although initially in 1854 it appeared anonymously as did her second book in 1856). In 1880 she published *The Laws we Live Under*, the first social studies textbook to be used in Australian schools. Spence was Australia's first female political candidate, standing unsuccessfully for the Federal Convention in 1897.

By the time she was in her fifties, although she still wrote fiction, Spence had become preoccupied with political activism. She enthusiastically promoted democratic electoral reform and wrote about it extensively, claiming later that it had been the major interest of her life. In the 1890s her oratory was a feature of public meetings in support of her campaign for proportional voting.

Catherine Spence was a keen supporter of education for girls and votes for women, and she helped pioneer a foster parent plan for orphaned children, herself fostering three orphaned families. Having become an accomplished public speaker she frequently preached at services conducted by the Unitarian Christian Church, and in 1893 she went to the Chicago World Fair to address conferences on voting, tax, peace and women's issues.

courts, the early closing of shops, the end of 'sweating', control of prostitution, the widening of chances for careers for young women or even equal pay; if she was a pacifist she might have been hoping for an end to conscription and war.

As a suffragist she could enjoy the feeling that a great victory had been won against the prejudices of those who had warned of the dangers of women 'meddling in politics' – with their arguments that women were too soft-hearted to make hard-headed decisions and might let socialism slip in through the back door . . . or that they would naturally become mere echoes of their husbands . . . and that in any case women lacked 'the creative faculty'. ('Where is the woman Raphael, Shakespeare or Beethoven?' . . . 'Wherever there is the demand for originating power, whether to contrive a mangle or to write an epic poem, then the man has and always will take precedence of the woman.') Above all it had to be remembered that 'a woman's highest duty and privilege was to be a wife and mother'.

Any suffragist who saw in the shape of past victories the shape of victories to come, was to be disappointed. Attempts to form specifically women's political organisations failed, and when women's organisations were formed within the political parties, they supported the interests of the parties more than those of women. Just as males' getting the vote did not necessarily mean continuing social advance, so it was with women. In fact a backlash began, as if women, having gained their victory, now had to be put back into place. The fact that annual birth rates had dropped by something like a third was seen as 'race suicide', and, although the typical family still consisted of four children and a third of women had families of seven or more, the decline in births was seen as a wickedness resulting from 'the emancipation of women'. Royal Commissions were held into the falling birth rate. The moral delinquency of selfish women in not having more children was presented as one of the greatest and most threatening scandals of the age.

At home, women were seen as morally delinquent; they were seen as morally depraved because they preferred to work in factories, shops or offices rather than as domestic servants. (At the beginning of the 20th century more than half of the working women now worked outside domestic service, yet it was still believed that 'the very best thing for girls is domestic work'.) One of the theories used to explain the fallen birth rate was that factory work lowered the

Women at work: *the commercial success of many small manufacturing enterprises depended partly on the low wages paid to women factory workers like those in the bookbinding room of the New South Wales Government Printery (below).*

Teaching was one of the most acceptable professional careers for women. Like nursing, it was seen as a 'caring' vocation. Students at the Sydney Institute of Education at a science class (above).

capacity of women to bear children. Yet the profitability of shops, factories and offices depended partly on females because, in one of the greatest of the inequalities of the modern age, the wages of women tended to be only half those of men. Even in the schools, where women made up almost half the teachers, they received little more than half the male wage. In factories, for some of the best-paying work – the work that was described as 'skilled' – women were excluded. There were scarcely any forms of apprenticeship open to them, and even in work where apprenticeship was not available to keep women out, the better-paid work tended to be graded as 'man's work' and only the lower grades were seen as 'woman's work'. Yet despite these deliberate exclusions, the argument could still be put that women were paid less because they were worth less on the free market: 'Surely women's work is subject to the ordinary conditions of supply and demand like any other commodity, and if it is less well paid than that of men it is because it is not worth so much.'

For those who stayed at home and could not afford domestic help, housework itself could be a hard day's work: the morning of washing day was spent in a steam-filled laundry and the afternoon bent over flat irons heated on a fuel stove; kitchens were always hot from the cooking fires; cleaning was a matter of back-breaking scrubbing, sweeping, dusting and polishing, cleaning out the fireplaces and sometimes carpet-beating. In homes where not enough money was coming in, women would go out as charwomen or washerwomen. Women with children but no husbands were not seen as demanding any special consideration: they would have to work harder and make do with less.

What was seen as one of the most progressive features of Australia as a 'social laboratory' was the determination by a court in 1907 of what was described as 'the family wage' or 'the basic wage' or 'the living wage'. The judge determined that every male should be paid enough to keep himself, a wife and three children in a condition of frugal comfort estimated by current human standards. This was greeted by one of the labour newspapers as beginning 'a new epoch in human society', but while income support was, in general, a progressive measure, it was not noted that while the new 'family wage' would go to all men, with or without families to support, it would not go to any woman, not even a woman who was a family's sole breadwinner.

An idealised Australian family: *Family Group*, by *Charles Hill (right) is a romantic view of family life, although there is one realistic note – the mother has had seven children. Other than that, she has little in common with the mother of seven children in an isolated town (below right).*

The suffragists: *the largest feminist movement in Australia was that of the suffragists, who demanded votes for women. They frequently marched to Parliament House to wait on members of the Legislative Council (far left). Most of the Press derided feminists (left).*

Girls train to be women in a cookery class at Redfern West State School, Sydney (below).

The class question

Another modern trend – the revelations of socialism – had now come to Australia, if only to the chosen few who could look forward to a great turning over of things in which the just would be raised up and the wicked would be cast down.

An Australian Socialist League was formed and in Sydney, on Sundays after an afternoon's spruiking in the Domain, its members would meet in their upstairs club rooms in a building in George Street and feel that they had some connection with the Second Workers' International: on some Sunday nights they would listen to lectures on the inevitability of socialism and argue about whether its liberations would come by peaceful means, or whether the powerful would fight back and there would be revolution; on other Sunday nights they might listen to a lecture on idealist philosophy or coin collecting. Throughout Australia several groups like this, numbering perhaps 2000 people in all, would debate the form of human liberation so passionately that their main arguments were with each other.

Socialism did not, however, have much of a base in the growing trade union movement. It remained generally true that 'the word "socialism", which appeals to many European reformers by its philosophic and general nature, repels and disturbs Australian workers by its very comprehensiveness'. One of them, asked to summarise his program, replied, 'My programme? Ten Bob a Day!'. One of the most eloquent of the trade union publicists said, 'Socialism is just being mates.' Even those, such as W.M. Hughes, who had a stronger belief than that, were likely to see socialism (as in Germany, the Social Democrats also saw it, at that time) as something that 'would grow and develop at its own pace and in its own way, just as manhood came to a boy'. When complete collectivism arrived, it would appear the most ordinary, natural and inevitable thing in the world. Its growth would have been 'so gradual as to almost escape attention'. But for a season, a form of revolutionary belief did show some growth in Australia. It was not a belief in political revolution, but in revolutionary syndicalism. Its origin was not Britain or Europe, but the United States. Most of the socialist literature in Australia at the time was printed in Chicago. International Workers of the World (IWW) clubs began to form: they brought from the secular revivalism, jailings, bashings and lynchings

occupation	income £
salaried general manager of a bank	3500
doctors (higher ranking)	3000
managers	750–1500
other doctors	600–1000
solicitors	500–800
self-employed shopkeepers	300–400
clerks	150–300
artisans	150–200
shop assistants	125–200
butchers, bakers	100–150
unskilled workers	90–120

What they earned: *the approximate yearly incomes of middle-class Melbourne in the 1880s (above).*

Strike bound: *the Great Maritime Strike of 1890 produced one of the most memorable quotes of the Australian working-class movement when Colonel Tom Price, with Mounted Rifle Corps officers at the ready, said on the eve of a demonstration, 'Fire low and lay them out!' (above left). On the actual day of the demonstration, however, there was no firing.*

A year after the Great Maritime Strike came the Great Shearers Strike of 1891. An illustration from the Queenslander *shows the shearers in military training, preparing themselves to meet the enemy (left).*

of industrial disputes in the United States the syndicalist belief that the apocalypse that would herald the arrival of socialism was the general strike. While waiting faithfully in Newcastle for this event, one's duty was to disrupt things as best one could. There were bitter quarrels within the IWW clubs as to how this disruption should occur, and between the IWW clubs and the rest of the union movement as to whether it should occur at all. There was a great deal more debate than action, but in some unions, the miners' in particular, these new promptings produced an intensity of concern that went beyond immediate material advantage.

It was the coal miners, in 1888, who, without meaning to, precipitated a new kind of strike – one which the newspapers presented as a national crisis and one in which the government intervened, and this new kind of strike made some of the rhetoric of the syndicalists seem more credible. The newspapers sent special reporters to the coal fields and the government an artillery unit with 70 men, seven officers and a field gun. Sixteen strike leaders were arrested. When the miners tried another strike in 1896 their failure was again abject. Another ten years passed before they recovered the conditions of 1888; then in 1909, when

Lockouts: *Broken Hill remained the scene of some of the most bitter strikes. The mines were picketed during lockouts (above), which often lasted for months at a time.*

OCCUPATION	% OF WORK FORCE	1857	% OF WORK FORCE	1901
professional	4	8 987	7	35 221
domestic	10	22 818	12	66 815
commercial	10	21 722	15	79 018
transport and communication	6	13 166	6	31 516
industrial	17	39 675	27	146 233
primary producers:				
•mining	36	82 428	6	31 447
•agricultural and pastoral	16	37 010	24	126 840
•other	—	—	1	6 860
independent means	2	1 923	2	10 066
total		227 729		534 016

How Victoria worked:
Victoria was the most industrialised of the colonies in the latter half of the 19th century. The main employers remained agriculture, mining and industry (left).

The Worker's illustrator used Art Nouveau techniques to show Australia's shame at the suppression in 1912 of the Brisbane Tramways Strike (below).

Striking in style: *the Hunter Valley coal fields were another of the large strike centres. When the miners left their pit towns and set up camp at Lake Macquarie, the coal owners realised they might be in for a long struggle. A miner's wife cooks breakfast at Lake Macquarie during the 1909 miners strike (above).*

they called a general coal strike, one of the most bitter known, the government came out singlemindedly against them, even passing specific laws to jail them. Miners were led off in handcuffs, their leader chained in leg irons. (But at the next elections this action helped defeat the government, and the new government released the miners.)

Although in the 1880s when 'the loyal toast' was proposed at trade union dinners, the talk was likely to be of strikes as 'relics of a bygone age' in the new spirit of cooperation, and although, rather than a syndicalist revolution, the preoccupations of most union leaders were a 'living wage', a universal eight-hour day (with a Saturday half-holiday) and preference to unionists, the new techniques of government intervention against union action had led even some of the more peaceful unions into disaster – most notably in the maritime strike of 1890, which involved a range of unions in the three eastern colonies. In each capital city special constables of militia took arms; in Newcastle the mines were shut down and guarded by troops; in Melbourne an officer ordered 'Fire low and lay them out!' (the order was not followed); in Sydney 36 mounted troopers charged a crowd of 10 000 protesters; the

Queensland Parliament passed a severe Peace Preservation Act to give itself more power. After two months of sensation, the strikes collapsed, and so did some of the smaller unions. When the shearers struck in 1891 in Queensland, they formed into camps of as many as a thousand and did military drill under the Eureka flag. (The Eureka legend could now be interpreted as part of the 'working-class struggle'.) In camps nearby there were government artillery, militia and armed police. There was talk of revolution and civil war.

A new attitude developed: strikers were 'a closely knit band of criminals', 'a force of bandits'. They also had their supporters. They would be able to rally up to 50 000 at

Images of the working man: *it was a time when artists had special styles with which to suggest the dignity of labour. Projecting this idea was one of the principal aims of Tom Roberts when he painted his nationalist work* Shearing the Rams *(below). The* Queensland Worker, *a weekly paper, could be relied upon to provide regular reminders of class division (below right) for the entertainment of its readers.*

their meetings; long processions marched through the streets; the Chief Justice of Victoria, in sympathy, paid £50 to a strike fund and Henry Lawson, like Paterson a myth–making poet, wrote them a poem, 'Freedom on the Wallaby':

> But Freedom's on the Wallaby
> She'll knock the tyrants silly.
> She's going to light another fire
> And boil another billy.
> We'll make the tyrants feel the sting
> Of those that they would throttle;
> They needn't say the fault is ours
> If blood should stain the wattle.

As it turned out, no blood stained the wattle. By the end of it all, much of the union movement had collapsed, but it was reconstituted, and by 1914 it had multiplied five times. Except for the 1890s depression (and even then, for those who kept their jobs, real wages rose) the chronic scarcity of labour had given manual workers both status and prosperity. By 1900 the demand for labour was as high as ever and of a total population of nearly 3 750 000 only 30 000

form of interpreting the news to wage earners. A sense of belonging to a 'working class', different from the rest of society, became characteristic of many individual wage earners, and in some suburbs and towns it approached a group ethos. Not all – not even most – city manual workers owned their own houses. While by 1910 about half the houses in Australia were owned by their occupiers, a ratio that was probably at that time the highest in the world, in the capital cities only a little more than a third of houses were occupier-owned. In the cities most manual workers still crowded into the old inner zones of rented houses, now dilapidated and out of fashion. Part of the rinds of the inner cities of Melbourne and Sydney were now decaying: the slapped-up terraces – inadequately drained, rat-infested, damp, unhealthy, crumbled into slums. Those who lived there were seen by the suburbs as roughnecks, but by themselves as the only true Australians, working class.

The strongest sense of a beleaguered working class, self-defined, suspicious and sometimes heroic in style, existed in those partly closed communities in which most householders shared a common occupation. Of these the communities around the city docks, and above all, the mining

Photographers could also be intent on conveying the quiet dignity of the working man, as in this photograph of station hands playing cards (right).

were out of work. Two-thirds of trades had gained the eight-hour day. In the rhetoric of some trade unions both capital and labour were again assumed to be marching together towards a common goal. The union movement was commended by the Catholic Archbishop of Sydney. Although, within the apparent success of the trade unions was concealed the fact that the unions were, among other things, a way of keeping women in their place (which was at half the wage rates of men) and of upholding a race hatred so virulent that it could portray non-Europeans as a greater threat than bosses to trade unionists, the Australian trade unions were often seen as among the world's most advanced. In the last three decades of the 19th century, more than a hundred labour newspapers were founded. Some didn't last long; some became national organs. Some of the most significant were those that, in some regions, were the main

communities – especially in the coal fields north and south of Sydney, and at Broken Hill – were the most clearly delineated. It was among them that there was the strongest continuing trade union militancy. At Broken Hill in particular there could be a feeling of endless, heroic struggle. At times mounted troopers were on patrol and the police marched through the streets with fixed bayonets; there were boycotts, effigy-burnings, pickets and even dynamitings, yet when a British labour leader came to Broken Hill he was asked not to talk about socialism.

But trade unions in Australia were marked by the peculiarities of economic life in Australia. Mining was strong, and the mining unions were militant, but there was virtually no heavy industry and only a weak manufacturing industry. The rural unions were strong but, after the failure of the 1890s, not militant: many members of the rural

The rise of the employés

unions were smallholders as well as part-time workers, and it was in the country that home ownership was strong. Visitors could marvel at an Australia where it was estimated that one out of every four male adults was the possessor of some property, compared with about one in 11 in Britain.

The 'petty suburban proprietor ... who sat on his veranda on sunny Sunday mornings', could even be seen as hoping for a peaceful end to industrial disputes. His small, iron-framed, time-payment piano attested to his respectability, and it was hard for him not to see some order in existence. A Royal Commission had said: 'It is frankly admitted that a great many disputes originate in ignorance, in mutual misunderstandings, in unfounded suspicions, in exaggerated claims, and that very much is gained if all these disturbing accessories can be got rid of, and the controversy can be narrowed to its simple issues.' New South Wales, later followed by the others, took over the New Zealand system of compulsory arbitration by quasi-legal bodies in industrial disputes. It was becoming clear that here was another area in which Australia would show the world: it would become the country where the social discord of industrial disputes would disappear.

Not all of those who worked for wages saw themselves as 'workers', and certainly not as members of 'the working class'.

After the modern idea of 'the worker' had been clarified in Australia during the 1890s, one of the central drives in the lives of many Australians was to distinguish themselves from 'the workers'. The French word *employé* (soon translated into English as 'employee') did this rather neatly: it was accurate, in the sense that it admitted that one drew wages (or, preferably, a 'salary') but it could also infer that one did not work with one's hands. The distinction between those who

Office life: *in office life the divisions between males and females were well worked out. They might work in the same room (bottom left), but while the men would do less routine work, the women would get on with the typing. The relation between male and female is shown in a 1907 advertisement for the dictaphone (bottom right). By 1905, when these commuters were photographed at Circular Quay, Sydney (below) the Australian capitals had an 'office life' that led to people coming in and out of town by train, bus, tram or ferry.*

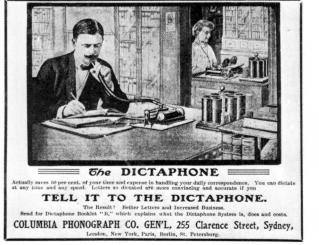

The DICTAPHONE

Actually saves 50 per cent. of your time and expense in handling your daily correspondence. You can dictate at any time and any speed. Letters so dictated are more convincing and accurate if you

TELL IT TO THE DICTAPHONE.

The Result? Better Letters and Increased Business.
Send for Dictaphone Booklet "B," which explains what the Dictaphone System is, does and costs.

COLUMBIA PHONOGRAPH CO. GEN'L, 255 Clarence Street, Sydney,
London, New York, Paris, Berlin, St. Petersburg.

worked with their hands and those who didn't was becoming one of the great divisions of humankind.

It was when 'office life' developed as an idea, with telephones and typewriters adding to its pace, and its projection of modernity and expansion adding to its size, that the idea of 'the employee' became useful. The 'brighter' members of a family, those who were a bit better at school than the others, might look for clerical jobs in the pastoral houses and importing firms, the shipping and trading firms, the friendly societies and insurance offices, or in the 'business offices' of the new department stores. Others settled for becoming 'sales assistants' in the large stores. At the same time the civil service in each colony had been reformed (and renamed 'the public service' to show that it was different). Offering permanence of tenure, pensions and guaranteed incremental rises in salary, and with low standard entrance examinations, it offered the children of the not-so-well-off a safe respectability as 'government officers', and became, it was said, 'an attractive haven of mediocrity'. The Post and Telegraph offices provided a satisfyingly graded series of positions; the Railways Departments, Australia's biggest employers of labour (their now independent Commissioners treated like lords in their ornate offices and lavish special trains), offered clerical jobs and officers' postings; so did the other semi-independent government-owned businesses now being formed.

For some, to become a schoolteacher was to arrive, since teachers, although low in prestige when related to the older professions, tended to rate somewhat higher than shop assistants, clerks, and railway or postal officers. To enter a bank could be better. Even the rich had to maintain polite relations with their bank managers.

Within this division between those who 'worked with their hands' and those who, more politely, didn't, there was another division – between males and females. In the offices, what were declared to be the more skilled jobs went to men; the positions of typist, telephonist, stenographer and receptionist were seen as work fit for women. In the department stores, some types of goods were seen as appropriately sold by men, some by women. In the schools, most of the best positions were simply not available to women. In the government departments, single or widowed women might work as telephonists or typists or counter clerks, but they could not rise any higher, and there were no positions for married women. Nevertheless there was now in Australia a new social type – 'the business girl', admired by some, seen by others as a threat to the social order.

To those who chose office work as a career, there were Public Service examinations, Institute of Bankers examinations, Teachers Admission examinations. But there were no government high schools to prepare students for them. By the beginning of the century, the United States had 7200 State high schools; Australia had only five, all in New South Wales. There were arrangements here and there for minor forms of secondary education, but a Victorian Royal Commission reported that the government education departments, tied to imitations of the English system, 'had been quite stationary'. Not even government teachers were properly educated. Under the 'pupil teacher' system, 14-year-olds were apprenticed to headmasters; they would do a full day's teaching and after hours pick up a

little more education; most received no further training.

Prompted by the need to provide an education system for the new 'employees' and 'government officers', Royal Commissions were set up and then revealed the hollowness of the Education Department's optimistic annual reports; officials were sent to Europe and the United States and after they returned with their reports the Education Departments set up high schools and junior high schools in each capital city. They were considered an expensive item, restricted to 'those fitted by intelligence'; there were not many of them, and their curricula were quickly shaped to fit the entrance requirements of the universities, although most of those who went to them could not afford to go to the universities. Those who could not attain the high schools were channelled off for a few years into commercial, technical, agricultural or domestic science schools, as befitted their mental station or the financial situation of their parents.

A minimum standard of secondary education had been improvised to meet the demands of a new society, with new ways of making a living. But to many of those employees who went off in trains or trams to office desks, the new standard meant little more than a ration of clerk's virtue.

The telephone exchange was also recognised as one of the accepted forms of 'women's work' (above).

The Railways Departments were Australia's biggest employers of labour. The Station Master at Flinders Street, Melbourne (right).

The suburbanites

In the new century, after a Polynesian boy had gone body surfing at Manly beach in Sydney, surfing developed so rapidly that property values in some beach suburbs trebled.

As the habit spread around other parts of the 19 000 kilometres of coastline, shooting the breakers became 'an institution as important to Australia as standing armies, established churches, music halls and sturdy beggars are in older civilisations'. Almost as important as the ability to surf was the need to acquire a suntan: on the beach 'the white man represents the pariah class, despised by all'. After a portable reel rescue line had been invented at Bondi and a military-style rescue and resuscitation drill developed, surf life-saving clubs were formed and the life-savers became 'the Samurai, the oligarchs, the elite . . . a gladiator class, envied by all the men, adored by all the women'.

The near-nakedness of the beach was seen as a reshuffle of values, with the new elite those who were best at browning their bodies and shooting the breakers. Most of Australia's heroes were the great champions of swimming, tennis, cycling, boxing, foot racing, football and, above all, cricket,

a game followed so keenly that when there was a Test Match in England crowds stood outside the newspaper offices at night waiting for each cable that gave progress reports on the day's play. Sport could be seen as a necessary training for 'a conquering race' (since it was known that sportsmen would 'acquit themselves just as gallantly on the battlefield as on the cricket ground'). It could also be seen as the great definer of the nation (therefore defining Australia as male, since it was for its 'manliness' that sport was most praised). In this, the democracy of the beach and of sport (part of 'a genuine Democracy, the people really wanting what it wishes to get') was one of the causes of the self-congratulation on how fortunate manual workers were assumed to be in Australia.

The novelty of this new sense of achievement became so great that a French visitor said (in the habit of the time, he saw the typical Australian as a male):

In Manly Beach, Summer is Here, *Ethel Carrick Fox captured, in a French painting style, the atmosphere of an Australian beach in 1913. The first surf carnival had been held at Manly the year before.*

If the forward march, for the working class, consists of attaining the exact level of the bourgeoisie, the manual worker of Australia has raised himself as high as possible. He has, in effect, placed himself in the category of the 'respectable people' and has assured himself of the prestige of outward appearance, so useful everywhere, but more powerful in British Countries than in the rest of the world. The Australian worker has become a 'gentleman'. He dresses himself after his work, he is housed, and he behaves like a person of good society ... More and more one can observe the external difference between the worker and the bourgeois diminishing except during working hours.

In this, the idea that the typical Australian was now 'the suburbanite' had become essential. Earlier, the development of savings banks and building societies had helped those who had enough money to put deposits on their own homes; now the provision of lower-priced 'workmen's tickets' could mean that even some of those who could not afford their own homes could now at least afford to live out of the city. When a new railway station was built and nearby estates were subdivided, a shopping street would form along the railway line; footpaths would be cleared, gas and water pipes laid, schools and churches built; a telephone exchange installed, a volunteer fire brigade and a volunteer ambulance started; a new municipal council incorporated. Schools of arts went up (no longer 'palladiums of nationality', but lending libraries for light books with billiard rooms and halls for hire) and the municipal councils quickly founded sports ovals and bowling greens; there were many public tennis courts and even a number of suburban racecourses. There were beaches to go to and, as *cinematographie* spread, there was 'Saturday night at the flicks'. Above all, for many, there were the front and back gardens, now made more grand by grass lawns, made possible by the hand lawn mower, the articulation of water to the suburbs and the garden hose; and within them, befitting a modern age, the flower beds were now more likely to contain annuals rather than perennials. Australia was entering the age of the iceland poppy and the sweet pea.

Women Lifesavers, painted in 1910 (below), is probably the first depiction of the subject. In their neck-to-knee costumes the women are demonstrating the line and reel method introduced in 1906.

Suburban snapshots: *cameras were beginning to appear in the suburbs, and the photograph album was becoming a family institution. A suburban family pose in their Sunday best (below left). Back gardens could be replete with pets – dogs and cats and rabbits (below right). Dad does the gardening (below).*

There were mixed suburbs with office workers, small businessmen and manual workers all together (families might sometimes contain examples of all three) but there were some suburbs in which manual workers predominated and some – the suburbs of the rich and well-to-do – on which manual workers might never set eyes. Despite the aspirations towards 'classlessness' the capital cities were now dividing on class lines. The rich had already moved out of town to group together in new bastions of richness, their former houses becoming lodging-houses or being knocked down and replaced by shops or offices. Now some employees and government officers, together with small businessmen, gathered in new suburbs that they saw as better than those where manual workers predominated. In these new suburbs a new vogue produced a romantic profusion of the Queen Anne style in which the flourishing redness of bare brick was a confident assertion of taste and respectability. Joined in this purpose, the newly introduced terracotta Marseilles tiles were shown off to the uttermost in contorted roofs; even the iron roofs of weatherboard houses were painted red to imitate tiles. Leadlight windows and flowery decorations (gumnuts, sheep, kangaroos) of a

debased Art Nouveau then added further romantic novelties. Wire baskets of ferns hung on verandas; 'sleep-outs' were added. At the side of the house there might be a fernery, called a 'bush house'.

With the spreading of the gas cooker it was now becoming more frequent for kitchens to move not only from the lean-tos which had housed open fires but also from the partitioned-off sections of back verandas, which had become kitchens with the development of the fuel range: when there stood in one corner of a kitchen a gas cooker (even if painted black and done out with ornate mouldings so that it would, reassuringly, still look like a fuel stove) the kitchen was becoming regularly accepted as a room in the house itself. With their status elevated, kitchens were likely to have linoleum on the floor, making them easier to keep clean, and wide windows letting in light and air, with wire screens keeping out the flies. With the new idea that cookery was part of 'domestic science', there was likely to be in a kitchen the new recipe books and the new books of household hints that were replacing inherited wisdom.

On the shelves of the new kitchens were likely to be some of the most potent symbols of the modern age – the brand

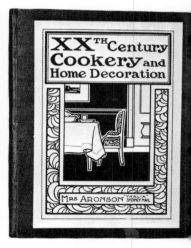

With a new century, there could seem to be a need for new cookery books. XXth Century Cookery and Home Decoration *(below) was published in 1900.*

WRIGHT'S PATENT
"EUREKA" GAS COOKER

The 'latest thing' was to replace a fuel stove with a gas cooker (above).

Advertising: *with the great development of packaged goods, a new character was being given to pantry shelves. White Wings became one of the many new 'household names' (above left).*

Advertisers were becoming concerned with giving a special personality to tobacco brands; 'Capstan' was one of the most popular (left). The advertiser was not ready to show the woman actually smoking, but the suggestion was there.

names on the packets of the various kinds of foodstuffs that were being made in the new factories. Cheese and butter were being mass-produced and the new cold stores and refrigerated vans were centralising the distribution of perishable foods: even fish could arrive more or less fresh in country towns. Production of flour was being centralised in a few city flour mills; new bakery factories were turning out white bread (for long a luxury only for the well-to-do), biscuits and cakes. Advertisements, as well as offering easy cures for diabetes, nervous depression, biliousness, asthma, neuralgia, flat busts, tuberculosis, bad backs, indigestion, thickening blood, thinning hair and all other known causes for human anxiety, could now also offer the reassurance of familiar household names: Rosella Tomato Sauce, Old Gold Chocolates, Sunlight Soap and White Wings Flour.

At the evening rush hour workers crowded into buses, trams and trains, homing to their suburbs. The boarding house districts were still crowded, and so were the slums (Sydney's most famous slum, The Rocks, was devastated at the beginning of the new century by bubonic plague); but now those who lived in or near the city by choice rather than

necessity were likely to be the 'bohemians' who, when they could afford it, might dine at places with names such as Café Bohemia, Paris House or Trocadero, and thereby distinguish themselves from the despised 'suburbanites'.

Apart from the bohemians, the central parts of the cities were becoming respectable; the prostitutes were being cleared out of the hotel bars; there were even moves to ban barmaids. Vaudeville still flourished in the cities; so did musical comedies such as *Floradora* or *The Merry Widow* (although what was left of serious drama retreated to 'the little theatres'); *cinematographie* had proved more than a 'craze'. But other than this, the cities were becoming quieter at night: they no longer seemed such a centre of things.

It was not only the bohemians who noticed the growing 'puritanical reserve' of many of the suburbanite manual workers – their Sabbatarianism, their abstention from alcohol, their polite avoidance of certain subjects or words in conversation. It was strange to visitors that a manual worker should be 'a petty suburban proprietor', and repellent that it could seem that 'the people are ... all of them gambling profit-makers, keen on realising the Individualist ideas of the lower middle class of 1840–70'.

Determinedly cheerful: Ethel Turner

'Oh I am so happy. All life seems rose-coloured, fame seems to be coming to me and money too. I *will* make such good use of the money.' So the 22-year-old Ethel Turner wrote in her diary in 1894, after she had received an enthusiastic letter from her publisher about her first novel, *Seven Little Australians*, which had just been published in England. The book was to sell hundreds of thousands of copies, be translated into foreign languages and later have stage, screen and television versions made of it. Ethel Turner's characters were recognised as 'real people', and although she was later to be seen as a children's author, in the 1890s she was regarded as being in the first rank of Australian writers.

At the age of seven Ethel Turner came to Australia from England with her twice-widowed mother, who later remarried. Ethel was one of the first pupils at Sydney Girls' High School when it opened in 1884, and edited a school magazine called *The Iris*. When she left school she and her sister Lilian launched a monthly magazine called *The Parthenon*, and Ethel began a career that, as well as journalism, was to see more than 40 books produced by 1928. However, the death of Ethel's daughter, Jean Curlewis Charlton, in 1930 from tuberculosis, was a tragic blow, and she wrote no more books although she often talked of doing so.

Ethel Turner's books reflected the preoccupations of the middle-class suburbia to which she belonged. But although much of her writing was bland, Ethel Turner possessed a talent for observing social trends allied with a sympathy for human emotions.

Wowsers: *it was a time when the wowsers, the colonial killjoys, seemed to dominate city life. Children were sometimes brought into a 'local option poll', intended to close down hotels (above).*

Increasingly, at night much of the central city was deserted. Scarcely any eating houses were open. A few restaurants, however, catered for some of the well-off and the bohemians. One of these was the Restaurant de Paris in Melbourne (above).

Although strong ties with Britain remained, an increasing national sentiment accompanied dedicated colonial imperialism; a dual loyalty – both to Empire and to Australia – was taught in government schools. Australian contingents still assisted in British Empire wars – in South Africa and China – but the majority of adults were now native-born, and they had begun to believe that all things Australian were best: the scenery, the animals and birds, the sport, mateship and, above all, 'the bush'. But these spoils were for white Australians, who took pride in the homogeneity of their nation, with no effective concern for the Aborigines.

The New Imperialism

With huge new systems of self-justifying belief, the great powers of Europe had expressed their modernity by moving into the age of the New Imperialism, and this now became a motivating factor in the Australian colonies as had earlier the age of Improvement.

Each of what were considered the four main world civilisations – Slav, Teutonic, Latin and Anglo-Saxon – was

supporting tales of adventure and derring-do; its cult of blood saw war as 'a link in God's world', a cleansing 'bath of steel', regenerating national character. In the shadows of glory there was gloom: if there were waverings, all might be lost. Old hatreds between nations swelled into fears for the whole world. Writers made reputations by discovering 'the American peril', 'the yellow peril', 'the black peril'.

The British exceeded the others both in the heights of their boasting and the depths of their gloom. Arrogant ideas that went back to the 17th century were adapted as part of the new imperial propaganda, but at the same time there were greater fears of decline: Britains's industrial power was

The English painter William Strutt spent only 12 years in Australia, but when he returned to Britain some of his largest and best-known paintings were on Australian subjects. They attempted to give Australia a present and a past that fitted the imperial imagination. His own imperial imagination reached its height in Sentinels of Empire *(left), painted in 1901.*

England was still 'Home' to many Australians, and although only the rich could afford to travel to England, there could be a sense of nostalgia in the sight of a liner leaving for England. Charles Conder caught the mood in Departure of the SS Orient, Circular Quay *(above right).*

Not only Empire Day, but all the imperial anniversaries were celebrated in Australia. Right, Trafalgar Day in Sydney, 1906.

seen by its followers as uniquely able (because of its God-given power) to save humanity by spreading Christian ideals and an equitable world order. University teachers, writers and journalists preached the good news of this messianic force; propaganda organisations, monuments and exhibitions gave testament to it. Its cult of service demanded hard, dutiful work so that an elect nation could take up the civilising burden; its cult of power justified possession as nine points of God's law; its pride in itself was evident in everything from grandiose buildings to strutting about in uniforms; its cult of the heroic made saints of contemporary colonial conquerors and ransacked history for

being challenged; Ireland was threatening unity; rival imperialisms were beginning to confront British supremacy in the cult of naval power. When Victoria celebrated her diamond jubilee in 1897 it was said that 'no sovereign since the fall of Rome could muster subjects from so many and such distant countries all over the world', but it was also the occasion of Kipling's 'Recessional': the far-flung battle lines might waver, then disappear. Dreams of a Greater Britain were revived, in which 'colonial imperialism based on a confident nationalism' would come to the aid of the mother country, to make it seem safer and bigger in a federal world structure based on the certainties of 'the British race'.

In Australia, mainly in Victoria, the Imperial Federation League had enjoyed a season ten years before. Its strongest advocates were well-to-do businessmen, squatters, officers of the colonial militia, Church of England bishops, professors – in short the club men, the Government House sets. It had propounded as Australia's true inspiration the sanctity of the Royal Family and of the British aristocracy, the destiny of the Anglo-Saxons, the power of the Royal Navy, the bonds of blood, trade and sentiment, and the excitements of knighthoods, orders, medals, flags and promotions on the field. The *Australian Naval and Military Gazette* had been renamed *Young Australia* and had issued regular calls to a duty that could only have been satisfied by the union of 500 million people, most of them not Anglo-Saxons. There were no branches of the Imperial Federation League in New South Wales, and elsewhere only a limited number of people supported it; but as the movement disintegrated its individual excesses spread, so that imperialistic rhetoric became an essential part of Australian public life in the 1890s; sometimes its dominating part.

Melbourne put up statues to both General Gordon and the eight-hour day; trade union banquets began with the

loyal toast. 'The fleets of a great empire are ready to assist us, ' said a Premier in Queensland. 'The British tie gives us a standing in the world,' said a Premier of New South Wales, 'which is illumined by all the glory of the fatherland, and which carries in its very fibre the heroic greatness of our race.' The Reverend W.H. Fitchett, author of such works as *Deeds that Won the Empire*, with 750 000 copies of his books sold, became one of the Empire's best sellers. A regular school examination question was: 'How would you answer a boy from a foreign country if he were to ask you why you are proud to belong to the British Empire?' In 1905, Empire Day was instituted as a holy day for schools, with stirring imperial oratory, flapping of Union Jacks, marches, imperial songs, brass bands and free bags of boiled lollies. (But the British were keeping a sceptical eye on colonial imperialism. 'The only good way of dealing with the local authorities is to firmly refuse to permit them to have any say as to the disposition or management of the squadron,' the English admiral commanding the Australian naval station wrote to the First Lord of the Admiralty in London. 'They understand firmness: they do not understand concession, which they always take to be weakness.')

A dual loyalty was taught in the Government schools; there was a narrow 'patriotism which is concerned solely with the country in which we live', but there was also 'that wider patriotism which embraces the whole empire'. At least a quarter of the songs taught in schools were on British patriotic themes. To teach Australians 'pride of race' it was necessary to go back to *Wulf the Saxon Boy Who Helped to Make England*, then learn the other exemplary tales of 'the great men of our race'. Britain, 'the leading nation in the world', mother country of an Empire on which the sun never set, having put its own house in order after the Civil War, 'sought and found a great work ready to her hand which she alone could accomplish': the bringing of civilisation to the 'inferior races', who were 'only children'. Britain was able to accomplish this great work through the expression of the British Christian virtues of which the Victoria Cross became a profound symbol. In an Empire built on the adventures and noble deeds of a race of clean-living heroes, the 'race' had reached its finest hour in General Gordon, 'the Christian soldier'.

The Catholic schools learnt their history differently, with martyrs instead of heroes, and if heroism was taught it was

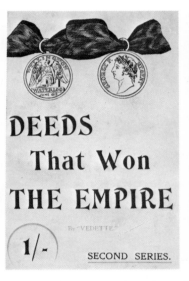

Careers were to be made out of the Empire – writing about it, or painting scenes from its history, or composing music. One of the most successful of these careers was made by William Henry Fitchett, a Methodist clergyman and headmaster for 46 years of the Methodist Ladies' College at Hawthorn in Melbourne. Fitchett wrote a series of books about the Empire, with titles such as Deeds that Won the Empire *(above left) and also edited patriotic magazines like* The Australasian Review of Reviews *(above).*

Australia would be there: *it was becoming established that wherever Britain needed help in its fighting, it was Australia's duty to be there.* Sons of the Blood, *a 1900 patriotic painting about the Boer War, celebrated the Empire's support for the Mother Country in the hour of need (above right). In the same year, three of the colonial governments sent contingents to China to help the British and other imperial powers suppress the Boxer Uprising. Members of the New South Wales Contingent were photographed in Peking (right).*

more that of St Thomas More against the 'cruel tyrant Henry VIII' or of Mary Queen of Scots against Elizabeth. When the Boer War presented an opportunity for Australians to enter the great adventure of empire-building, Cardinal Moran was one of the few public men who questioned the idea of volunteers 'expected to go to every place where a British war might happen to be carried on'.

In 1900, with an uprising in China against European control of so many activities in the declining Manchu Empire, three of the colonial governments combined to send off two warships and a small contingent to assist the Europeans put down the insurrection. But it was in South Africa, in the Boer War, that those Australians who most cared for the Empire (on this occasion, most of them middle class) showed their eagerness to go to a 'place where a British war might happen to be carried on', although others showed their opposition. After 16 175 Australian men and 16 314 horses had served in the Boer War, Australians could feel they had entered history. In 'a war to uphold the British prestige all over the world', Australia had undertaken a responsibility that 'would develop national self-respect, and the respect of the authorities in London'.

Now that a majority of adults were native-born, Australians were again beginning to develop theories about who they were. The most significant national sentiment was the simple belief that Australia was best. Best at scenery. Best at animals. Best at sport.

Banquets were held at which it was boasted that all the food and drink were Australian. Distinctive Australian clothing styles were detected. In praising Australian social reform, patriotism knew no limit: 'It is here in Australia that human society will develop itself, and that the yet unanswered riddles of the Sphinx will be finally solved.' There had been an anxiety that 'the good old Anglo-Saxon stock' would lose its stamina in the Australian climate unless there were continuing infusions from 'Home', but now some could hope that 'the Anglo-Australian stock' was 'a new strain', even better than the old. Australian success in sport and in wars seemed to have demonstrated that.

But beyond being *best*, what *were* the Australians? What was most widely acceptable as a way of defining them was to use as motifs for Australian-ness certain favoured animals

Being Australian: *one of the ways in which Australian-ness was declared was in the many Australian animals and plants in decorative motifs: a patriotic sofa (left) with inlays of a number of Australian woods including red cedar, silky oak, kauri, white ash, and black bean; a silver gilt enamelled brooch with waratah motifs (far left); a silver gilt enamelled box decorated with hand-painted Grevillea (far left below); a glass tumbler engraved with flannel flowers (centre below); and waratah design for wallpaper (below).*

and flowers. The sound of bellbirds was written into Australian music. Armchairs were carved in the shape of lyrebirds. The emu became an heraldic emblem and its eggs were mounted on silver, or turned into vases, jugs, goblets or inkwells. Koalas, kangaroos, kookaburras, goannas possums and platypuses provided many advertising brand names. Christmas bells appeared on enamelled belt buckles; Sturt's desert peas appeared on earthenware vases and the Banksia bush on silver-gilt wine tankards; the waratah was portrayed in wrought iron, on doilies, on tiles, jardinières and coal boxes and in stained glass leadlights; flannel flowers decorated enamelled pencil cases, glass tumblers and bone china.

There was a patriotism about Australian woods; eclectic displays of worthy Australian timbers decorated with patriotic themes were inlaid in chairs, tables and sofas; a mulga wood boomerang might be decorated with a silver gilt display of waratah. The cult of the wattle as a true expression of the golden openness of the Australian character became so great that an anthem was composed to 'the lovely, glorious wattle' and Wattle Day Leagues were formed; New South Wales schools made Wattle Day a holy day; there was

talk of instituting an Australian 'Order of the Wattle Blossom'. Increasingly, above all other symbols of Australianness, soared the eucalypt: the gumtree could become as stout as an English oak or as slender as a Japanese willow; sometimes it twisted with the exuberance of a baroque nude; at other times it leaned across a painting as the epitome of Australian casualness and informality. It was accepted as the emblem of the strength of character of the Australian people. When the artist Norman Lindsay idealised the koala into the cartoon character of 'Billy Bluegum', in bringing together one of the most revered examples of native fauna with the most revered example of native flora he provided a symbol that was profoundly moving to the Australian imagination.

But, beyond symbols of animals and flowers, birds and trees, the usual sources for national definition were not very helpful. For their high moments politicians now preferred the language of the New Imperialism, and for workaday speeches they stayed with the language of Improvement. Even the optimism of Improvement did not seem to have touched the few historians who had emerged: they had no theories of Australian uniqueness. In the new history texts there was no record of the struggles for land reform, for

Patriotic tree: *of all the Australian plants, the one most frequently and successfully used to symbolise Australia was still the eucalypt, the gumtree. Above, an Arthur Streeton gum from his painting* Near Heidelberg, *dated 1890, dominates the landscape.*

A citified Australia: *magazines such as* Melbourne Punch *and* The Bulletin *were very conscious that Australia was largely a metropolitan society. For a brief period, some painters also tried to give a sense of Australian cities. W. Blamire Young painted* The Smokey End of Melbourne *(above) in 1911.*

instance, or the agitation for the democratisation of parliaments, or of the peculiarities of Australian 'governmentalism'. What was seen as best about Australia was that it had 'tamed the wilderness' and adopted British institutions. Such intellectual leadership as there was came from the Press, which provided 'almost entirely for the conscious culture of the whole Antipodean community', and served what at that time may have been the highest rate of newspaper readership in the world. Most Press proprietors were themselves journalists and mostly liberals; they were usually concerned with Australian-ness only to the extent that it moved towards their liberal ideals.

Perhaps the best-performed attempt at self-description was provided by a form of Impressionism that came from a series of painting camps and spread its influence: its very spontaneity and unpretentiousness seemed to suit its subjects. One of its special characteristics was to catch the colours of certain parts of Australia, in pursuit of what one Sydney writer described as Verlaine's 'cult of faded things' – 'delicate purples, delicious greys and dull, dreary olives and ochres' in contrast to 'English ideals of glaring green, or staring red and orange'. This Impressionism was wide-ranging in subject, looking to both city and countryside, and as the most substantial body of good work at that time it provided an artistic acceptance of Australian life at a level not previously achieved.

The uniqueness that dismayed many commentators was that Australia seemed to have become the world's most town-dwelling society. With Sydney, Melbourne and Adelaide containing about half the population of the areas they governed, these three cities seemed 'huge cancers whose ramifications of disease spread far into national life'. With a lack of knowledge of economics that would have done justice to Cicero, from whom he seemed to have got his ideas, one Sydney writer saw the city-dwellers as 'non-productive inhabitants . . . carried on the back of some struggling farmer or miner or stock-raiser'. 'The civilisation in the Australian cities is not new,' said another, 'but an old, hoary-headed, decrepit European civilisation, which appears half the world over to be tottering to its grave. Any stranger can see in Sydney the luxury and refinement and vice of the old world gnawing at the heart of the new.' To one, the only hope was that 'devotion to sport and athletics' might save Australia from the effects of towniness.

MARRIAGE.

A cuddly Australia: *illustrators also found symbols for Australia by giving Australian animals human characteristics and building stories around them. Perhaps the most successful was the artist Norman Lindsay's invention of the koala character, 'Billy Bluegum' (above).*

Frederick McCubbin, who painted Backyard, King Street, Melbourne, With Seated Girl *in 1886 (right) and Arthur Streeton, who painted* Railway Station, Redfern *in 1893 (above right) also looked at aspects of 'citified Australia'.*

Out of this grew the habit for some writers and cartoonists to use the larrikin, along with his 'donah' (girlfriend) as the symbol of city, and, for some, Australian life. Ballads and short stories were written about the larrikins and their donahs; they were put into plays and vaudeville and drawn in cartoons; and when Australians made moving pictures they appeared in those. At times larrikins were symbols of violence and low life but they were often softened as comics, even sentimentalists, and their donahs could become agents of civilisation, tempting them to the perils of the suburbs. These views of the typical Australian were to reach their peak in the vernacular verse of C.J. Dennis's best seller, *The Songs of the Sentimental Bloke*.

Writers, journalists, painters and illustrators chose to find little other than the larrikin that was distinctively Australian in the metropolitan life that, from first hand, was all that most of them knew. Yet they had to find something. The proportion of writers and artists had greatly increased in the cities, in Sydney in particular, where they provided the backbone of the bohemian life of cafés, bookshops and studios, and to make a living they had to find something that was distinctively Australian. Like some of their more

modest predecessors, they turned to 'the bush'. 'It is not in our cities and townships that the Australian attains pure consciousness of his nationality.' 'The one powerful and unique national type produced in Australia is . . . the Bushman.' As part of a more general movement throughout the English-speaking world in which the work of men like Rudyard Kipling, Robert Service and Bret Harte became best sellers, ballads were developed as a commercial art form and most were about the bush. The ballads of A.B. Paterson sold better than any Australian books had sold in the colonies before. They put forward an heroic and adventurous view of Australia that seemed more exciting than city life: Australians were men – tall, lean, suntanned, self-reliant yet comradely, tough yet sentimental. Just at the time when writers and artists in the United States were making money by telling Americans they were cowboys, Australians were being told they were bushmen.

The Sydney magazine *The Bulletin* was quick to do well out of this new commercial fashion: it took up the new vogue and became its chief vehicle, combining bush ballads with bush short stories, the short story being another commercial art form of the time. Usually stylised into

The books of the balladist and short story writer Henry Lawson (above) did not sell so well as those of Banjo Paterson, Steele Rudd, or C.J. Dennis, but by reputation he was coming to be seen as the authentic voice of the Australian bush – at the very time when his life was being dragged down by poverty, drunkenness and nervous collapse.

A country girl: Mary Grant Bruce

For generations of Australian girls, life in the Australian bush was as depicted in Mary Grant Bruce's Billabong books, a series of novels about a rich grazing family. Although other books and stories by Mary Grant Bruce presented a less idealised version of the bush, at Billabong harmony and happiness prevailed in the certainties of a secure environment with its cooks and housemaids, stockmen and gardeners.

Mary Grant Bruce was born at Sale in Victoria in 1878. Her father was a public servant who had married into a landed family, which gave her much of the background for the Billabong books. At 20, having won the Melbourne Shakespeare Society's annual essay prize three years before, she left her parent's home in Gippsland and went to Melbourne to earn her living as a journalist on a weekly magazine, *The Leader*, which also published her short stories and serials. It was as a serial that *A Little Bush Maid*, the first of the Billabong books, appeared from 1905 to 1907.

Mary Grant Bruce produced nearly 40 books, the last published in 1942; sales of her books were more than two million.

By the time she was 34 she had saved enough money for her fare to England. In Ireland she met a distant cousin, Major George Evans Bruce, whom she married in 1914. They had two sons, and after the death of the younger one, they spent 12 years in Europe before returning to Australia to settle their surviving son on the land. After her husband died in 1948 (ten years before her own death) Mary Grant Bruce returned to England, where she lived comfortably on income from her books.

melodrama or farce with surprise endings, and kept very short because *The Bulletin* didn't have much room, its artificially contrived bush short stories helped sales. The new painters also began to be most admired for their treatment of the bush: in their paintings they came to concentrate on country landscapes, rural pursuits, and heroes from the past, such as bushrangers. They usually made their humans laconic, in the bush manner. The first full-length feature movie made in Australia was on the Kelly gang.

There were other modes. A school called 'the nationalists' celebrated their Australian-ness in late Victorian verse: fashionably pretty poetry was written; as evidence of their cosmopolitanism, both a poet and a painter peopled Australian landscapes with fauns and satyrs; a university poet discovered French symbolism. But the concentration on either larrikins or bush workers was the principal characteristic of *The Bulletin*, and *The Bulletin*, although its appeal was limited to a minority, was the only publication with a national sale and the 'one really talented and original outcome of the Australian Press'. For better or worse, it was distinctive, and at least the short stories it published by Henry Lawson reached high quality as, in a concentration of genius, Lawson turned to advantage the extraordinary limitations of *The Bulletin* style of writing.

It was in these stories, and in other writing, that theories of Australian-ness were developed, attempting to cast up images of a national type found on the other side of the range. The typical Australian was an outback male –

sardonic, stoic, sceptical, laconically brave. 'Sullen and sombre-souled' (characteristics blamed both on the climate and on excessive tea-drinking), he held so deeply to his freedom that if faced by patronage he might simply not recognise it although, 'biliously and satanically proud', if he saw it for what it was he would take violent offence. He could enterprisingly make something out of nothing; he was recklessly generous and a compulsive gambler: he might 'grinningly throw away his life for a trifle'. It was only as the occasional drover's wife or squatter's daughter (and that very occasionally) that the typical Australian might also be a woman.

For those who were radical, to the cult of the bushman a new history had to be added. The Eureka incident seemed to provide it. Just as Englishmen had struggled for their freedom against Charles I (as taught in schools), so Australia had 'set her teeth in the face of the British lion' at Eureka. It seemed an affront to the spirit of the age that so much of Australia's freedom and prosperity had not been earned by the shedding of blood; the diggers' blood was used retrospectively for that purpose. The Eureka Stockade, it was declared, 'led to government of the people'. For most,

The first Australian colour comic strip was 'Jim and Jam, Bushrangers Bold', which appeared in The Comic Australian *in 1911 (above).*

The Tasmanian scenic stamps, issued between 1899 and 1912, were the first Australian stamps to depict scenery and the first to be used for tourist advertising (above). The stamps were based on photographs taken by the founder of the Tasmanian Tourist Association.

the convicts seemed so remotely improbable that memory of them was suppressed; but a few turned the convicts into radicals, re-inventing them as sturdy Scottish crofters, Irish rebels, English Chartists and 'offenders against the brutal game laws', 'the best of stock for the breeding of a new nation'. But, as it turned out, by locating the typical Australia in the bush, the radicals were defining Australia as a primitive rural society that knew its place in the general British view of things and could leave the more ambitious forms of human endeavour to the British.

Even the social philosophy of bush society – 'mateship' – was probably little more than English lower-class fraternity expressed in local metaphors. But its demand for equality, its irreverence for values other than its own, was turned by some of the new cultural nationalists into a unique prescription for a new society. This was something that Australia could show to the world, a new sense of brotherhood and equality between mates. It was still a submerged attitude, alien to the kind of leaders in politics and journalism who preferred the Australian version of Improvement, and distasteful to the Anglophile imperialists, but it received confident expression in some of the trade unions and although there was no place for women in it (or perhaps because of that) it seemed to find some echo in the hearts of many Australians. This submerged feeling was probably the strongest form of nationalism that Australians had, even if it was a nationalism that lived as a minority and discriminatory movement. That there might be something to it could come out most clearly in an openness of manner that demanded at least the forms of equality even when denied the substance. 'This is a true republic,' said Francis Adams, 'the truest, as I take it, in the world. In England the average man feels that he is an inferior. In America that he is a superior; in Australia he feels that he is an equal.'

The petty suburban proprietors could sit on their verandas on a Sunday morning and take some pride in belonging to the land of the wattle and Billy Bluegum – although their knowledge of native plants and animals might come largely from advertising symbols and Art Nouveau suburban household decorations – and entertain themselves with the works of those who saw them either as slum larrikins or laconic dwellers in the bush.

The typical Australian: *the most commercially successful presentations of a national character were of the Australian as bushman. Tom Roberts's* Bailed Up *was seen as one expression of what it was like to be 'truly Australian'. Even the bushrangers were shown as matey and laconic (above left). In Charles Conder's* Under a Southern Sun *(above), the typical Australian is a pioneer. Not all the Australian painters were nationalists. Max Meldrum drew inspiration from European realism for* Family Group *(left).*

When there were none of Britain's colonial wars to which expeditions could be sent, sport seemed the most important instrument of Australian foreign policy.

Australian swimmers won world fame in England, and Australian cyclists became track stars in the United States; to the international cricket matches were added international football matches; the world heavyweight championship fought in Sydney in 1908 brought a gate that was a world record; Australia won the Davis Cup in 1908 and retained it till 1912. Perhaps it was true that 'the only names of Australians at all familiar to the general run of Englishmen are those of cricketers, rowers and prize fighters', but ordinary Australians would not have seen anything wrong with that. When expeditions were sent to the Antarctic this was an extension of the idea of a touring team; after the Australian opera singer Nellie Melba made her world reputation she was greeted on her many returns with the enthusiasm due to a sporting event.

From 1888, the anniversary of Phillip's landing was celebrated as a national holiday; a few more anthems,

including 'Advance Australia Fair', were written; Henry Parkes announced that he was going to re-name New South Wales 'Australia'; but there was little expression of political nationalism in its most significant form: the desire to cast off the bonds of Empire and establish an Australian republic. The more usual attitude was self-congratulatory on the moral advantages of belonging to the British Empire. It was only within this context that outspokenness in relations with Britain was applauded: this was a matter of the Australians and the English being British together. When the Victorian political leader Alfred Deakin spoke up in London at an Imperial Conference he became a national hero: on his return he was greeted by addresses of congratulation at every train stop between Adelaide and Melbourne. He was hailed as the first of the native-born to perform at the centre

Those who were creating a past for Australia still gave pride of place to 'the explorers', who were seen as discovering Australia. Of these, the most esteemed had become Captain James Cook. A statue of him was erected in Sydney, and in 1900 the painter Emanuel Phillips Fox was commissioned to paint The Landing of Captain Cook at Botany Bay.

of the world; but it may have been more his criticism of British government policy than the applause these criticisms generated in London that made his journey a success to Australian voters.

On this occasion, as on others, dissatisfaction with Britain was politically expressed as a concern lest 'when our domestic policy runs counter to England's imperial policy, Australian interests will go to the wall'. The English were seen as too concerned with their own affairs in dealing with Asiatic powers, and their policy in the southwest Pacific seemed perfidious. Moderates wanted the British to keep the other world powers out of the southwest Pacific; enthusiasts wanted the British to take over whatever islands were left, holding them for Australia's later acquisition. Famous as a liberal spokesman, Deakin said, 'We intend to be masters of the Pacific by and by.'

But although politicians and Press were usually pro-British and sometimes slavishly so, there was a wide undercurrent of contempt for the Old Country, particularly among the town manual workers and in the bush. Britain could seem a snobbish society of title worship, class distinctions and privilege, of oppressive injustice to the poor, of dowdy 'dust-covered customs', a stagnant nation compared with liberal, confident and progressive Australia, where 'the intellect of the people is freer, stronger and more original than in the age-old states of Europe'.

This undercurrent broke only rarely to the surface. A Republican Union, made up of 'the debating-society, hard-reading crowd', had formed in 1887 in Sydney in opposition to the Imperial Federation League. In the same year republicans had twice defeated attempts in Sydney Town Hall to pass a loyal resolution congratulating Queen Victoria on her jubilee – the resolution was passed at the third meeting only after its opponents were excluded. In 1888, when the Republican Union was replaced by the Republican League, branches were extended to Melbourne and Adelaide; there were calls to Australia to achieve greatness by following the United States. But republicanism was taken up by hardly any politicians or trade unionists; in the Press *The Bulletin* was its only significant supporter, and its republicanism was one of the most important reasons for that magazine's widespread unpopularity.

Where influential Australians seemed most ready to assert Australian independence was in its whiteness. 'Australia for

Winners: *one of the ways in which Australians could take pride in themselves was in Australian success stories – whether of a prima donna like Nellie Melba, sporting heroes like Frank Beaurepaire and Albert Griffiths, or an explorer like Douglas Mawson. By 1903 Melba (above) was one of the world's most famous prima donnas. Frank Beaurepaire (left) became the first of Australia's swimming heroes when at the age of 17 he travelled steerage to Europe to swim in the Olympic Games. He came second in the 400 metres and then beat the champion in a number of races in Europe. In 1907, with other Australian scientists, Douglas Mawson made his first visit to Antarctica as part of a party that located the South Magnetic Pole. In the Australasian Antarctic Expedition of 1911–14 (above left) he behaved so heroically that he was knighted.*

Albert Griffiths, 'Young Griffo', was the first of Australia's boxing heroes (above). After beating the lightweight champion of the world in 1890 at the age of 19, he embarked on a boxing career in the United States. 'Griffo' was illiterate; he was a drunkard and he never trained; he won his first 114 fights, then was defeated in a world championship fight – in which the Australians believed he was the true winner, defeated only by American trickery. After that, his career collapsed; but he remained a hero.

the Australians – the cheap Chinaman, the cheap nigger and the cheap European pauper to be absolutely excluded' was an idea accepted and proclaimed by politicians, Press and trade union leaders alike. A Labor writer noted for his utopianism could say that he would rather see his daughter 'dead in her coffin than kissing [a black man] on the mouth or nursing a little coffee-coloured brat that she was mother to'. A Chinese could be lampooned in the Press as 'Ah Filth' – 'not morally, physically or intellectually fit to sit down in the same continent with Europeans'. Along with the arbitration system, old age pensions and so forth, one of the tokens of Australian progress was that 'never before in any known period' had there been a continent of 'a people almost wholly of the one race and one language'. A cultivated literary critic, A.G. Stephens of *The Bulletin*, could write, 'Next in importance to the preservation of national life is the preservation of the race, the purification of the national blood ... living on the border of Asia, we are always exposed to the danger of Asiatic incursions, and it is certain that the establishment of Asiatic settlements, or of a European breed, will tend to degrade and destroy the whole breed.' Common sense (a mixture of opposition to cheap labour and of British racism) suggested that the almost complete exclusion of non-Anglo-Saxons was one of the greatest achievements in 'a land that is Freedom's from shore to shore'.

There were a few who thought otherwise. One wrote: 'England has become what she is by a fusion of races. Australia will become great by a fusion and mingling of races ... East and West will join hands. The unequalled metaphysical power of the Hindoo, the unswerving steadiness of the Chinese, the singular artistic faculty of the Japanese, will be joined by the idealism of the French, the philosophy of the German and the practical sagacity of the Anglo-Saxon.' But to most influential Australians such a statement would seem as demented as an attack on the early closing of shops.

White Australia: *of all the methods by which different kinds of Australians tried to project their ideas of what it meant to be an Australian, the idea of Australia's whiteness may have been the most appealing (below and far below). By restricting coloured immigration, the standard of living and the employment prospects of white Australians would remain safe.*

Anyone for tennis: Norman Brookes

When Norman Brookes married Mabel Emmerton at St Paul's Cathedral in Melbourne in 1911, troopers rode beside the wedding car (which was decorated with tennis rackets linked by garlands and white ribbons) and crowds were packed along the wedding route. Yet only a few years before, Australians had such scant interest in the new game of tennis that when he went to Wimbledon in 1905 Norman Brookes had to pay his own fare. Even when he and his New Zealand partner Anthony Wilding won the Davis Cup for Australasia, two years later, the event received little coverage. Few Australians had heard of the Davis Cup.

Norman Brookes was born in 1877, the year before the Melbourne Cricket Ground laid an asphalt tennis court, an act which can be seen as marking the beginning of tennis in Australia. Spare in build and reserved in manner, he belonged to a well-to-do family and had the means to indulge his enthusiasm for ball games – he was also an Australian state and national golf champion. The interest in tennis grew when the newspapers discovered that the Challenge Round for the Davis Cup in 1908 would be in Melbourne, a week after the Melbourne Cup. Brookes and his New Zealand partner again won for Australasia – and again in 1910, 1911 and 1914. Brookes had become a hero, and tennis had become a great Australian game.

"OUTSIDE, SIR! OUTSIDE!"

Mrs. Australia (to John Chinaman). "I've had quite enough of you! 'No Admittance',—not even 'On Business'!"

In 1891 a National Convention decided to found a 'Commonwealth of Australia'. After some years of discussion, referendums were held in all the colonies, and on New Year's Day 1901, Australia was officially proclaimed a federation, with each of the colonies now a State. There was no national capital city and there was little agreement on what the new government was supposed to do. Rival political groups emerged – Protectionist, Free Trade and Labor and the one issue upon which they were all agreed was the proclamation of a White Australia policy. In other fields, parties seemed to struggle with each other for the right to carry out the same liberal program. Then beginning with a Labor election victory in 1910, it began to appear that Australia might be the first country in which Labor became the usual governing party.

Coming together

'Whilst Victoria during the last thirty years had produced a host of able public men, New South Wales had brought to the front few men above the intellectual standard of the parish vestry men,' said David Syme. 'Amongst Victorians there were thousands of the very scum and filth of all mankind,' replied a New South Wales knight.

Old enmities continued. Borne up by their own ebullience in the 1880s, Victorians often urged union of the colonies; but New South Wales, with the belief that it was the only true Australia, didn't care. Then in 1889 Henry Parkes, perhaps because it was the only policy left to suit his

Royal occasion: *the opening of the first Commonwealth Parliament in Melbourne's Exhibition Hall by Queen Victoria's grandson in May 1901, painted by Tom Roberts, was more of a royal than a democratic occasion.*

political advantage, perhaps because he was old and afraid that fame might still escape him, made a speech in a town near the border of New South Wales and Queensland calling for 'a great national government for all Australia'. The politicians couldn't ignore this call. The next year the governments of all the colonies sent representatives to Melbourne and for seven days they discussed what to do about it. Out of this, in the following year, came a National Convention of delegations from the Australian colonies and New Zealand. After meeting for 38 days in Sydney they decided to found a Commonwealth of Australia.

The new Commonwealth would need a new constitution: one was drafted in ten days. The determination of existing governments not to vote themselves out of existence, regional economic interests, and the example of North America, all demanded a federal system. The envies of all the colonies demanded that the Federal Government be weak, with only certain defined powers, and that all other powers should remain with the colonies. The fears of the smaller colonies demanded that the Federal upper house represent each colony equally, the smallest having as many representatives as the largest. The example of the United

States suggested that the lower house be called the House of Representatives, the upper house the Senate, and that the colonies be known as States. For a day or so the question was raised of a separation of executive and legislature; the idea was too strange to consider.

The Convention debated the first draft of the constitution. Then the drafting sub-committee of four went off in a government steam yacht and after two days came back with the final draft. The Victorian and South Australian parliaments adopted it with no enthusiasm; none of the other colonies considered it. Federation seemed important mainly to politicians, and they had lost interest.

In 1894 another New South Wales Premier, also finding political advantage in the idea of federation, suggested a conference of colonial Premiers. A year later the Premiers met and agreed to submit Bills for elections to another National Convention. New Zealand had lost interest, and two more years passed before four of the Australian colonies got around to agreeing to hold the elections. Another year passed before the elections were held. Absorbed in its own concern about a possible split between north and south, Queensland abstained; in Western Australia the old order

Federation: *there was little nationalist, liberal or democratic fervour surrounding the Federal Conventions that drafted the Australian Constitution. The cover of the menu for the Convention's Sydney banquet (above) conveys this conservative attitude: the three symbols that dominate it are a statue of Governor Phillip, an image of Queen Victoria, and the shields of the colonial Governments.*

A speech by Henry Parkes precipitated an Australasian Federation Conference in 1890, and with his look of a prophet Parkes dominated the official photograph (above left).

When the other colonies had finally recorded majorities for Federation, there was a campaign to persuade Western Australian voters to join (left).

was trying to preserve itself against the new men on the gold fields, so rather than risk an election, its Parliament appointed delegates. In New South Wales the decision of Cardinal Moran to stand for the Convention created such bitter interest that a Protestant ticket was returned; but in the other three colonies only half the usual number of voters turned out. Newspapers attacked this apparent indifference.

Nevertheless the cause of federation was now clothed by slightly more than the interests of a small group of prominent colonial politicians. Federation Leagues formed, taking liveliest shape in border districts where intercolonial tariffs were a most obvious nuisance; there were agitated references to the need for common policies on defence and immigration; some economic interests believed they would gain from federation; others attacked it because they saw themselves as losing. A diffuse rhetoric developed in which common bonds were sealed: with a new century approaching, it seemed an appropriate time to come of age. One politician said, 'We shall create a glorious nation and meat will be cheaper.'

The elected delegates to the National Convention met for 32 days in Adelaide, for 22 days in Sydney, then for another 55 days in Melbourne, making enough speeches to fill 5000 pages. Differences between large and small colonies, between protectionists and free traders, between Victoria and New South Wales and between liberals, radicals and conservatives, came together in a set of compromises which the drafting committee finally turned into a revised constitution that was still neither democratic (it had no declaration that the government was elected by the people), nor liberal (it had no Bill of Rights or any civil liberties provisions) and certainly not nationalist, since it placed the executive power in Australia in vice-regal hands. The following year it was to be presented in a referendum to the voters of the four colonies that had accepted the idea of federation. (Western Australia had joined Queensland in staying out.)

Apart from sealing bonds and coming of age, appeals for support were mainly to economic self-interest: outback voters saw federation as an attack on metropolitan interest, some city interests saw a great new tide of profitable commerce. Opposition also came from economic self-interest in groups who saw their economic advantages threatened; they were joined by many of the Labor Leagues, who

Australia's birthday: *as the capital of the oldest colony, Sydney did the honours on 1 January 1901, the day the Commonwealth of Australia was proclaimed. The official invitation showed the ship of state carrying maidens bearing the coats of arms of the colonies, now known as 'States' (right). The central part of the ceremony was the taking of the oath by the first Governor General, the Earl of Hopetoun (above).*

opposed what they saw as a conservatively undemocratic constitution and by a few conservatives who feared what they saw as a dangerously democratic constitution. The Press was divided. Clerics intervened. Brass bands and campaign songs were added to the oratory of public meetings. This all aroused sufficient interest for the proportion of voters to rise to nearly half of those eligible.

New South Wales did not register the required majority. In 1899 there was another conference of Premiers: New South Wales was given somewhat better terms and agreed to a second referendum; this time Queensland joined in. A majority voted Yes, and at the last moment the Western Australian Government was forced into union by secessionist threats from its new gold fields. There was to be a new nation, brought into being by 42.9 per cent of all electors.

Early on New Year's Day in 1901, when the official proclamation of a Commonwealth of Australia was to be made, between half a million and three-quarters of a million people came into the city that had grown on the site Governor Phillip had chosen as a penal colony 113 years before. Some had New Year's Eve hangovers, but the proportion of hangovers was less than among the thousand or so who had stood among the red gums at the beginning of this whole enterprise to listen to the three volleys of musket fire and the Governor's proclamation that convicts found in the women's tents at night would be shot.

Almost 30 committees had met to plan the celebrations. Triumphal arches – including one made of coal, one of wool, and one of wheat – attested to material gain. Of the banners that stretched across the poles and wires of the new electric tram system some looked forward ('One people one destiny'), some back ('The crimson thread of kinship'). In the eight-kilometre-long procession there was much that proclaimed the New Imperialism; detachments of Imperial forces – Life Guards, Hussars, Sikhs, Gurkhas – marched along with the colonial troops. There was also much that proclaimed the old Improvement: no other new nation had given such a part of its celebratory procession to trade unions and friendly societies; even the eight-hour day banner was paraded, borne aloft behind the Railways Band. But there was little that proclaimed the new minority dreams of nationalism – except perhaps the shearers marching at the head of the trade union part of the procession and the 30 bush workers riding on horses behind them, sustaining a belief in rural virtue beneath the wires of the city's electric trams. Colonial governmentalism was celebrated in the dozens of carriages of top-hatted dignitaries. Old religious divisions were celebrated by the absence of the Catholics from the procession. Snubbed by a Protestant-controlled management committee on whether a Catholic cardinal should take precedence over an Anglican archbishop, the Catholics had withdrawn, although in a compromise the procession had stopped outside St Mary's Cathedral to hear 4000 Catholic children sing 'God save the Queen' and a specially composed Federal Hymn. Thirty thousand designs had been entered in the contest for an Australian flag: the winning design – white stars on a blue ensign – was curiously similar to the flag of the Anti-Transportation League of 50 years before, which had sometimes accompanied radical threats of a republican nationhood. But convicts and republics were both forgotten. It was an English earl who was sworn in as Governor General. The guns thundered. There were fireworks, dinners, picnics.

Four months later an English royal prince in an English admiral's uniform stood on the flower-decorated dais of the Exhibition Building in Melbourne and proclaimed the

Less respect: Audrey Lady Tennyson

Audrey Lady Tennyson, wife of Hallam, Lord Tennyson, Governor of South Australia from 1899 to 1902 and Australian Governor General from 1902 until 1904, wrote long letters to her mother at the time of Federation. The letters are a unique view of society behind the discreet barrier that separated colonial Government Houses from the rest of the country.

One of the important issues about Federation discussed in the Government Houses was not whether it was desirable for Australians but whether it would mean a cut in the status or salaries of State Governors. When Federation came, for Lady Tennyson it took second place to mourning for the death of Queen Victoria.

This automatically limited festivities for the opening of the first Parliament in Melbourne in May. For six months the Government House sets wore the black clothes that were always in the wardrobe, ready for the required lengthy mourning periods.

Lady Tennyson faithfully described her visit to Melbourne for the opening of Parliament: 'The first afternoon I, with some of the party, went to the Town Hall at the invitation of the Mayoress to see a procession of Stockmen. I was at the window with the Mayoress, Mrs Gillot, whose husband was knighted next day, and her importance and bliss over her position and her attempt at grandeur and absolute good nature with it all, and her conversation with some girl friends made me nearly explode with internal laughter. Lady Clarke told me that a day or two before she had said to her, "Well, Mrs Gillot, what shall you do when you present the bouquet to the Duchess on her arrival in Melbourne. Shall you make a very low curtsey?" "Oh *no* Lady Clarke, curtseys to Royalties are quite out of fashion now. I shall certainly not curtsey." "Well, Mrs Gillot," said Lady Clarke, "I hope you will forgive my saying but I assure you everybody curtseys to Royalties. I think you really ought to make a curtsey." "Oh dear no – you are quite mistaken, Lady Clarke. Curtseys are quite a thing of the past – nobody who *knows* makes a curtsey." '

But there was not much internal laughter when Lady Tennyson presented prizes at Scotch College, Melbourne, and 'Miss Clarke, the Governor's daughter, gave away the sports prizes which was very funny and quite wrong, as no woman is supposed to take a prominent part at anything if I am present, or a man, if H. is present. But things get more and more slack in the State.'

The New Protection

opening of the first National Parliament. At the concert that night Madame Melba sang a hymn to Australia and one English visitor noted that the new Cabinet Ministers had forgotten to bow when they passed the prince.

By this time the society of the black Australians had been destroyed everywhere except in a few areas where white Australians had not yet seized land to make money out of it. Although still 'blackfellows' to most, in official language they had become 'Aborigines', a coolly scientific-sounding name, as if, like the platypus or the koala, they were one of the country's zoological freaks. A new pattern for their treatment was being set. Pioneered by Queensland, and adopted by the two other States where numbers were still significant, it provided for descendants of the first Australians to be drafted into reserves or into institutions, at the will of 'protectors', most of whom were policemen. They could be forced to stay on the reserves if not lawfully employed: they could be lawfully employed only by permission of the 'protectors'. There were no provisions for appeal. A race that was assumed to be dying was, as far as possible, being got out of sight.

Now that the colonies had come together as States in a Federation a new, 'national' politics would have to be created, suggesting meanings, some of them divisive, and throwing up performers of a new kind.

By the 1890s something approaching party politics was already emerging (although not on a national scale) as various groups would find themselves concerned with the same rallies, manifestoes, lobby groups and debating clubs: with one party formed, enough of their scattered opponents would coalesce to form another. In some colonies the reason for existence of the parties was a conflict on tariff policy; in others it was a matter of a 'continuous ministry party' versus those who could not achieve office; there were other divisions. As this system spread, the words frequently used, in imitation of the English political vocabulary, were 'Liberal' and 'Conservative'.

When another English name was added – that of 'Labour' – a three-party system emerged. The trade unions had been putting individual representatives into parliament, with local Labour Electoral Leagues running

The federation of the colonies meant nothing to the first Australians. This photograph (above) was labelled 'Aboriginal murderer'.

Looking for a flag: *more than 30 000 designs were submitted to the contest, announced in 1901, for an Australian flag (above and top). The new Australian flag was flown for the first time in September 1901.*

candidates financed mainly by union levies, and with the onset of the party system the Labour Leagues joined together. In 1891, with a solid voting base in the new working-class suburbs and miner's settlements, the New South Wales Labour Electoral Leagues won 35 seats; in 1893 the Australian Labour Federation in Queensland won 15 seats, and the United Labour Party in South Australia eight. In several cases union leaders came out of jail and went almost directly into parliament. In December 1899 there was, in Queensland, the 'first Labour Government in the world' – a six-day ministry that survived for only four hours in parliament but had enjoyed the chance of having a quick look at the government files.

It was, however, the liberal forces of Improvement that dominated politics, and the Labour Parties were defined very largely by their relation to the politics of liberalism. It was only in Queensland, where Labour became the official opposition, that Labour seemed likely to displace middle-class liberalism as the main dynamic in politics. The New South Wales party acted as a 'corner party' prepared to bargain with governments. The Victorian party was a junior supporter of the Liberals; in South Australia relations

leading politician from each colony, to set up the few new government departments. Those chosen as ministers happened, in varying degrees, to be Protectionists. Through this accident, the Cabinet decided it also led a political party, but there were no national party programs or national party organisations: each State fought the first Federal election according to its ordinary political groupings and the parliament it elected was a collection of regional parties, making sense back in the States, but having to be forced into new coherence in the Commonwealth Parliament. The names they used were 'Protectionist', 'Free Trade' and 'Labour', but the meaning of these names could differ from one State to the other.

With no party having an absolute majority, those calling themselves the Protectionist Party became the Government, those calling themselves the Free Trade Party became the Opposition, and those brought together by the Labour Leagues sat in the corner giving general hints of support for the Government. Although the apparent division was on the issue of protection, this issue was not significantly debated for some years, and then in new terms. In fact, in its three years' existence practically nothing new came out

Australia's first two Prime Ministers: Edmund Barton (left) who was replaced by Alfred Deakin (right) in 1903. It was Deakin who set most of the pace in Australian politics until 1910 with a general program of liberal reform.

One of the first acts of the first Parliament was to implement a White Australia immigration policy. It did this by allowing the Government the right to give an immigrant a dictation test in any language. Hence the cartoon in The Australasian Review of Reviews *(above right).*

were so friendly that a joint Labour-Liberal coalition held office for four years; in Western Australia, although in a minority in parliament, the Labour Party held office for a year without distinctive policies; in New Zealand the Liberal Party held such a monopoly of the spirit of colonial governmentalism that Labour was absorbed into it.

The first Australian Federal Cabinet met on the afternoon of the Commonwealth's proclamation – between the procession and the fireworks – in a room lent by the Government of New South Wales. It had been put together arbitrarily (until there was an election) with at least one

of the first Parliament; in the elections that followed almost half the voters showed their lack of interest by not voting.

There was no national capital; with no agreement about where to build the new capital, the Federal Parliament was housed in Victoria's Parliament House. There was not much agreement about the new Government's functions, beyond taking over the colonies' customs houses, post offices, and some odds and ends – some expected it to do little more than this. It was recognised that each of the States should be represented in cabinet, and that no policy could discriminate against one of the States. Although there was an 'External Affairs Department', it was accepted that foreign policy was imperial, and the prerogative of the government in London. Australian foreign policy consisted of Australia making representations to London – through the Governor General. Irish brogues, Scottish burrs and English dialects were common among the new Federal members: of the six most significant men in the Labour Party, four had been born in the British Isles. In defence of the name 'Commonwealth', some had even argued that the word was apt to the new Federation's position as it suggested something less than complete sovereignty. Australia had now gained a seventh government, but whether the world had gained another nation was not clear.

Something had to demonstrate why all this trouble had been taken. The gesture was found in the proclamation of the White Australia policy. Apart from the continued use in Queensland of indentured black islanders (a problem disposed of with only a little difficulty by trading a sugar bounty for their exclusion), there was no urgent objective reason for making this first Parliament's only important Act a measure restricting immigration – at about 30 000, the Chinese were little more than one per cent of Australia's population – but it was a measure acceptable to practically everyone, and a subject on which newly elected Parliamentarians could attempt to outdo each other in oratorical assertions of national manhood and character.

With no other expression of common idealism available, Australian nationhood was confirmed in the self-evident truth that social and economic progress lay in racial purity. Students, tourists and businessmen from India and Japan were to be allowed into Australia for up to five years, but so far as permanent settlement was concerned, all 'the tinted races' were to be excluded. The only political division was whether to restrict immigration with the maximum offensiveness, or with some form of politeness; the British urged politeness, and partly out of regard for British feeling the restriction chosen was that any immigrant could be set a dictation test 'in a prescribed language'. The Labour Party had wanted a direct prohibition of 'any person who is an aboriginal native of Asia or Africa'.

The second Parliament began a period of six years of party confusion, with six different Governments forming from various combinations of support between the parties. It was described as a Parliament of 'the three elevens' until the Protectionists split into two groups, making four elevens.

In the 1906 election George Reid (above), leader of the Free Trade Party, tried to fight the election on the basis of Labour's socialism. On this occasion, with Deakin maintaining a liberal stance, the tactic did not work.

It was a time of nation-building, with some new creation every year. The search for a site for a national capital was proceeding. A party of Senators travelled to Bega as part of their quest for a site (above right). The illustrator Low caricatured the three judges of the first High Court, appointed in 1903 (right).

But political confusion had been no enemy of the previous Improvement, nor was it in these six years; parties seemed to struggle with each other for the right to carry out much the same policy. This was the policy of Australian liberalism and much of it was the policy of Alfred Deakin, the leader of the progressive Protectionist Party, who was becoming the first national figure to articulate political aims for Australians. It was almost as if Deakin had invented the whole thing and without him they wouldn't know what to do. He could be confident that even in the periods in which he was not Prime Minister his policies would continue.

Colonial governmentalism was at last given a clothing of ideology; it was a method of 'employing the machinery of the State to cope with the very great injustices which at present beset our social system'. It was George Reid, the leader of the more conservative of the four parties, who said, 'Even in the field of social economics, Australia can win victories and set examples which will teach the rest of the world.' But it was Deakin who remained master of a rhetoric in which there were to be economic justice, equal laws and opportunities for all, healthy lives, honest toil, fair wages, fair hours, fair prices, fair conditions of employment, and State mediation to end social conflict.

In the States, faith in a more rational Australia was now being seen in the schools. The tyranny of the inspectors had been replaced by the lesser tyranny of external examinations; teachers' colleges were being established; kindergarten methods were spreading in infants' schools; compulsory school attendance was at last becoming effective. Syllabuses had been revised according to new attitudes which were part of a shift in emphasis occurring in many parts of the world: education was seen to have a moral aim in which it was hoped that the new types of teaching in literature, history and science might overcome some of the failure of humans to live according to their ideals. But it now seemed from the Commonwealth that the greatest progress would come. The Victorian system of tariff protection became Commonwealth policy; there were experiments with trust-busting and anti-dumping legislation; a Commonwealth Literary Fund was set up to give pensions to old authors; the Commonwealth adopted from New South Wales models for compulsory arbitration in industrial disputes and old age and invalid pensions.

But it was Deakin's sponsorship of a policy of New Protection, in which manufacturers would be protected from foreign competition only if they paid 'fair and reasonable' wages and working conditions, that seemed the greatest novelty. As orator of the New Protection, Deakin offered Australians a civilised growth through a well-planned manufacturing industry, fostered by a scientific, carefully adjusted program of protection and based on the indisputable knowledge of capable independent experts who, as well as aiding manufacturing growth, would assist the further development of agriculture and even throw light on the mysteries of unemployment. When the basic wage was set in 1907, a great ideal seemed to be satisfied.

The New Protection was disallowed by the newly established High Court, but it remained a distinctively Australian ideal for the rest of the decade – the first distinctively expressed ideology to have come from the complexities of Australian politics. At last Australia could feel that it had a political approach of its own.

Its meaning widened beyond economic justice to a general approach of safeguarding Australians from the evils of the world. As well as being safeguarded from poverty and distress, internal tension, competition of imported goods made by 'the underpaid labour, the serf labour, the prison labour of foreign lands where less happy conditions prevail', and (by the White Australian Policy) from racial discord and sweated labour, they were also to be safeguarded from military threats in the world outside Australia where now, to possible dangers from France, Germany or Russia, there was added what was beginning to seem a threat from Japan. The Japanese victory in the Russo-Japanese War was at first seen as 'the inspiration of nationalist enthusiasm in a just cause' (New South Wales had not built a fort in Sydney Harbour to protect itself from the Russian Pacific Squadron for nothing), but later it was feared that 'the yellow man has taught the white man a lesson that Australians can neglect only at their peril'. The Labour Party fought the 1906 election in terms of the yellow peril, but even more to the point was the British naval scare: would German rearmament rival the Royal Navy? Subscription lists were started in newspapers to buy Britain

There was great interest in Australia in the Russo-Japanese war of 1905. The Sydney Mail, *in its 29 March issue, gave a lavish spread to the Japanese case and gave equal space in its next issue to the Russians. The* Mail *ran photographs of the first Russian POWs and the Japanese soldiers who had captured them (above).*

All of the Australian Press gave space to the visit of the United States Pacific Fleet ('the Great White Fleet') in 1908. Its visit drew the greatest crowds Sydney and Melbourne had ever known. The Sydney Mail ran special issues (right).

a dreadnought. While Canada, South Africa and New Zealand ('One Sea, one Empire, one Navy') remained content with things as they were, Australia ruffled the British by successfully demanding a navy of its own: a national ideal was to be fulfilled when in 1913 the battle cruiser *Australia* and the light cruisers *Sydney* and *Melbourne* sailed into Sydney Harbour.

Australia was equally seeking novelty in its policy for land defence. By the middle of the decade the idea that there should be a compulsorily raised citizen army was prevailing: National Defence Leagues were formed, and by 1908 the Labour Party had adopted compulsory military training as official policy. Only a few conservatives opposed this apparently progressive idea. With a combined system of school cadet corps and compulsory militia training for young men, Australia became the first English-speaking country to introduce conscription in peacetime. The event was hailed as showing Australia as in the van of progress. 'A citizen soldiery inspired by patriotism', 'the boldest stride yet taken in any English-speaking country towards national land defence', seemed to reject old world militarism in favour of democratic progress.

> The Labour parties were unique in that they did not grow out of socialist organisations but were the exclusive creations of the trade unions.

Socialist organisations formed after the Labour parties. The most that many Labour men knew of socialism was from American popularisations, in particular Laurence Granlund's *Co-operative Commonwealth*, which tried to digest Continental socialism in a form 'Anglo-Saxon in its dislike of all extravagances': it defined socialism as 'the extension of the functions of government'. The American Edward Bellamy's utopian novel, *Looking Backward*, was perhaps the widest influence, so that the book that could mean most in the Labour parties was one that dreamed of the love and cooperation that might prevail by the year 2000. Labour's fostering of love and cooperation by the extension of colonial governmentalism was sometimes challenged in its idealism by the single-tax simplicities of the American Henry George. 'The two great schools of economic thought,' said one Labour leader, 'are the single tax and the socialist schools.' The dreaminess of Labour idealism was matched by an eclecticism that came both from the

Cardinal Moran, the Catholic Archbishop of Sydney (above), used his influence in the Labour Party in the 1890s to remove direct declarations of socialism from the party's platform. After this, he gave the party a clean bill of political health.

By 1910 there was a Federal Labor Government in Melbourne, headed by Andrew Fisher (above right). Sitting on Fisher's right, in the centre row, is William Morris Hughes, Attorney General in the cabinet. Some of the trade unions were concerned about the promotion of their interests by the new Labor Government (right).

"THE WORKER THINKS."
MAY DAY, 1910.

prevailing liberal mood and from the desire to attract political support from small farmers and small businessmen.

By 1897 a plan calling for socialisation was nailed into the New South Wales Labour platform, mainly because of the work of a group of young socialists; but the strong opposition of Cardinal Moran, Archbishop of Sydney, helped break it. Later it was pulled out. Just as unique as the trade union origin of the Labour parties was the way they were becoming a vehicle for Catholic integration. Although a significant number of Catholics were still Irish-born and the Irish still dominated among the bishops and priests, Cardinal Moran, although Irish-born himself, wished Catholics to share an Australian patriotism. In the centenary year of 1888 he had managed to have all six colonial Governors at a ceremony marking the beginning of the completion of St Mary's Cathedral; he had urged the formation of an Irish Rifle Corps in the colonial militia; when Pope Leo XIII had issued his encyclical *rerum novarum* on workers' rights in 1891, the Cardinal had given a public lecture on its significance, sitting beside representatives of all the political parties. He had declared the various organisations of Improvement, from friendly societies to trade unions, free of Continental liberalism and socialism, and he had extended the same benefaction to all political parties. But in the new century, integration came to mean in particular a movement into the Labor Party (which now spelt itself without the 'u', to show its modernity). Through their usually low place on the economic scale, Catholics were joining Labor parties anyway; to this was added the impulse that came from attempts by minority militant Protestant and Loyal Orange Lodge factions to use the other parties against Catholics. The Catholic newspapers urged Catholics to support the Labor parties, and by 1910 as many as half the members of these parties in eastern Australia may have been Catholics.

Despite Labor's moderation in action and despite its Catholic support, the rhetoric of some Labor leaders ('socialism in our time') and the kind of resolutions passed at conferences of the Labor parties ('war on the wealthy') provided enough material for the political leader George

Reid to raise for a while the cry of the 'socialist tiger' and rename his party the 'Anti-Socialist Party'; but this was not so effective in discrediting the Labor Party as the appeals to anti-Catholic prejudices that his party was also promoting. However, the Employers' Federation began to support candidates who 'expressed a determination to protect the rights of private enterprise and oppose socialistic legislation'.

The words 'labour' and 'monopoly' were much used; the world seemed more complex, with new threats occurring in what politics were supposed to be about. Among the liberals, still commanding the political centre and most of the political power, some opposed labour more than they opposed monopoly; others opposed monopoly, but argued that monopoly should be broken up, whereas the Labor Party believed that it should be taken over by the State. It was an argument without conclusion, since monopoly was neither broken up nor taken over (nor, for that matter, greatly existed), but it was a diversion that was beginning to replace the earlier political divisions between Free Trade and Protection. It was pursued with equal passion.

The result was that the centre – the very basis of Improvement – began to disperse, and with it the new

The Commonwealth did not begin issuing its own stamps until 1913. The kangaroo design (above) was derided by almost all the Press, but there was better reception of the kookaburra (top).

Currency: *one of the early reforms of the new Labor Government was to set up a Commonwealth Bank and to introduce an Australian national currency. Before this, the private banks had printed their own bank notes. Conservatives derided the new Australian notes as 'Fishers' Flimsies' (left and above left), naming them after Prime Minister Andrew Fisher. The back of the ten shilling note (left) had a view of Victoria's Goulburn Weir.*

three-party system. With Labor more evidently in the field, and more tightly organised, the maintenance of the liberals as popular radical parties of Improvement was becoming impossible. From 1907 there was a tendency for the two non-Labor parties to 'fuse' into a group that for old time's sake called itself the Liberal Party. A generation of political enemies had united as one party, opposed to Labor. Now there were to be two parties. Founded on a non-party system, sustained during a three-party system, with a pervading concern for progress as its sustaining power, the Australian age of Improvement had reached a situation in which it no longer had a party of liberalism.

Within the Labor Party there were strains from penetration by the Catholics and from the struggle for control by the trade unions. Tensions were developing between the parliamentarians and the oligarchic State Labor machines, which insisted that they had the only true revelation of the needs of the mass of the people. In New South Wales an 'Industrial Section' was formed to run a union ticket – settled by private balloting between the unions beforehand – to obtain complete control of the New South Wales Labor

Executive. And the Catholics, now seeing themselves as 'fighting in a corner', threatened by secular education and the evils of Freemasonry ('a huge tumour growing upon the life and blood of the whole country'), mixed marriages, corrupted reading matter, divorce laws and the 'race suicide' of birth control, turned to blackmail. A Catholic Federation was formed in Victoria, later spreading to other States, with a membership of 100 000 within two years. It tried to build up electoral registration of Catholics, sent questionnaires to election candidates, encouraged Catholics to join the Labor Party, and then threatened to withdraw its support. The Victorian Labor Party called its bluff and denounced it. After expulsions and walkouts, a Catholic Workers' Association was formed, aiming at more organised penetration. 'The work before the Catholic Laborites is to capture the Labor machine,' said the Melbourne Catholic newspaper, the *Advocate*.

And Labor's political and economic opponents were organising against it. Employers' organisations were becoming stronger and tougher, and the Liberal parties, declaring themselves anti-socialist and opposed to 'bureaucratic tyranny', moved more to the right: the

Nation building: *the beginning of the transcontinental railway from South Australia to Western Australia was attacked by some as extravagance and hailed by others as an example of national vision. The survey teams travelled by camel, horse and bicycle (left).*

A federal capital: *the Governor General trots across the Canberra plain for the ceremony of naming the national capital in 1913 (below). Penleigh Boyd painted the Canberra site in 1912 (below left).*

previous general agreement on progress and reform had departed. In the States the upper houses became intractable opponents of even minor reforms and the Commonwealth constitution was proving as conservative as its Labor opponents had feared it would; two attempts at amendment by referendums failed.

Nevertheless, it seemed to be the time when Labor's hour had come. By 1910 there was a Federal Labor Government in Melbourne and State Labor Governments in Sydney and Adelaide; in 1911 Labor came to office in Perth; in 1914 in Hobart; in 1915 in Brisbane. The spirit of colonial governmentalism prospered in plans to set up State brickworks, State sawmills, State iron foundries, State metal quarries, State concrete works, State butchers' shops, State bakeries, State coal mines, State banks. The old political liberalism took new life in plans to abolish the Legislative Councils and State Governors, and to give greater influence to the people by referendum. Labor could also seem a nationalist party: it began building a transcontinental railway, it established an Australian currency and a uniform postage; it presided over with enthusiasm what could seem to be democratically organised armed services; it

announced a worldwide competition for a national capital to be built at Canberra. The winning plan, submitted by an American, Walter Burley Griffin, proposed to serve Australian self-definition by making Canberra a kind of super-Versailles in the modern style of a follower of Frank Lloyd Wright. And the old Improvement seemed to take on new meanings when Labor instituted workers' compensation for government employees, union preference, invalid pensions, maternity allowances, a land tax and a Commonwealth Bank, and extended old age pensions. There were plans for nationalising the health services, formulating new industrial laws, further reforming education and breaking up the business monopolies and the large landed estates.

In Europe, while some might agree with the Russian revolutionary Lenin that the Australian Labor Parties were merely 'bourgeois liberal parties' in disguise, to other Europeans they could seem to be made up of 'realistic democratic socialists' whose country was to be the first in the world in which government would be controlled by social democrats – because the Australian labour movement was 'the most advanced in the world'.

Labor reformer: Andrew Fisher

Born into a poor mining family in Scotland in 1862, from the age of ten Andrew Fisher worked in the mines to help support his family. At 23, ambitious to better himself, and urged by his family, he decided to emigrate to Queensland.

Settling finally in Gympie, he was active in union, Masonic, church and other community activities, and by the end of 1891 he was president of the Gympie Workers' Political Organisation, the local branch of the new Labor Party. As a Labor candidate he topped the poll for Gympie in the 1893 election for the Queensland Legislative Assembly. His first experience as a minister was in the Dawson Labour Government in 1899, claimed to be the first Labour government in the world, but which lasted only six days. Fisher was elected to the new Federal Parliament in 1901, and was made Minister for Trade and Customs in the first Federal Labour Government in 1904; he was now in a position to introduce some of the reforms he believed in. Elected Federal Labor leader in 1907, he presided both as Prime Minister and Leader of the Opposition over the making of Labor into a party the electorate could see as competent, stable and trustworthy. The election he won in 1910 gave Australia a three-year period of reform unmatched until the 1940s. In 1914 Fisher made the famous pledge of Australian support for Britain to the last man and the last shilling. But unlike W.M. Hughes, who succeeded him as Prime Minister in 1915, Fisher was not a warmonger, and he was privately opposed to conscription.

The Fisher Labor Government's victory in bringing in legislation for child allowances was lauded by The Worker *(below), which also urged its readers to vote 'yes' in a referendum to give the Government power to smash trusts (far below).*

OCTOBER 10. 1912

IN THE SPRING OF NINETEEN-TWELVE.
THE NEW AUSTRALIAN: "Hooray! Someone's raised the CHANCE of living."

Crush the Serpent, Australia!

At the height of the development boom in Australia, expressways could seem one of the most important forms of human development.

Part three
The age of Development
1914 to 1980s

After the bloodshed of World War I, much of the idealism in the Australian imagination died. Instead of remaining 'an exemplar to the old lands' in liberal reform, Australia seemed given over only to the materialism of 'national development'. But that was to change, too, as materialism, at least for some, was accompanied by new ideals.

13. Blood sacrifice: 1914 to 1919

When World War I came, Australians could imagine that through bloodshed and sacrifice they had at last become a nation. The idea was born of the Australian as 'the Anzac' and as 'the Digger' and the celebration of Australian-ness on Anzac Day. But the war also split the Labor Party and bitterly divided Australian society, with both class and religious divisions whose hatreds and distrusts were to last for many years after the war had ended.

When news came in 1914 of a new crisis in Europe, Australians were almost unanimous in their desire to be part of it.

Labor and Liberal leaders tried to outdo each other in offering Australia's last man and last shilling. In the streets crowds sang traditional songs such as 'Rule Britannia', 'Soldiers of the King', and 'Sons of the Sea', and Archbishop Kelly said 'Whether our schools are treated fairly or not, we will do our duty'. In a challenge even more exciting than a cricket test, or the Boer War, Australia would send off an Australian Imperial Force of 20 000 men. A new song was written – 'Australia Will Be There'.

Volunteers were measured for size and assessed for health. The biggest and healthiest were chosen and collected at

emergency camps in racecourses. They were clothed in uniforms of pure Australian wool, shaded by slouch hats bearing a badge of the rising sun, given overseas pay of six shillings a day (which, said King George V, was too much for a soldier), then sent through the streets so that everyone could have a look at them. In October off they went in 28 transports, along with ten transports of New Zealanders, in the biggest military expedition ever to have sailed across the world, many times larger than the expedition that had founded New South Wales.

Rumours of spies began to spread; there were stories of lights flashing signals out to sea, of hostile aeroplanes and submarines. Other expeditions for the Australian Imperial Force were recruited – apparently the war was going to last longer than expected. They completed their training in

TWO BEAUTIFUL HUN HOMES AT NEUTRAL BAY.

WHERE GERMAN WOOLBUYERS ARE LIVING IN LUXURY.

"Enoshima," Burroway-street, Neutral Bay, the beautiful home of P. Schlesinger, the German woolbuyer.

"Marengo," Bertha-street, Neutral Bay, where L. Bersch, another German woolbuyer ,lives in luxury and ease.

When the first recruits marched off, there was little understanding of the tragedy and bloodshed to come. Australian soldiers march to the wharf (right) in August 1914, on their way to capture the German colony in New Guinea.

There were many German spy scares and Germans were rounded up and interned. Later, most of the German place names in Australia were replaced by English names. The ultra-patriotic Mirror *(left) specialised in attacks on 'Huns'.*

Arrows indicate the main Allied thrusts against the Turks in the Middle East (below).

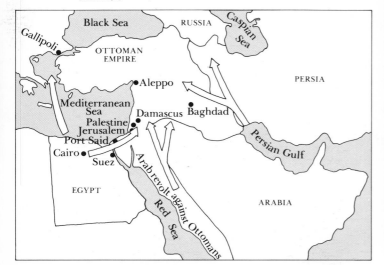

Egypt, at a tented camp near the Pyramids, to which the first expedition had been unexpectedly diverted because training camps in England were already overfull. The word 'Anzac' was used to describe the Australian and New Zealand troops.

On 29 April the Prime Minister made a brief announcement that on the previous Sunday, Australians had landed on the Gallipoli Peninsula. That was all that was announced, except for a message of congratulation from the Colonial Secretary. The next day congratulations came from the First Lord of the Admiralty and King George. What were the congratulations about? On 3 May the first of the long lists of casualties was released, but there were still no details of what had caused them.

Then on 8 May a dispatch from an English war correspondent was published describing the Anzacs' landing in terms so full of praise that they touched deep into Australians' longings and uncertainties and brought forward at once the belief that from this sacrifice of its youth Australia had been tested as a nation and had proved its worth. On the day of the dispatch the Melbourne *Argus*

announced that Australia had 'in one moment stepped into the worldwide arena in the full stature of great manhood'. This brave, bloody adventure had given Australia 'a place among the nations'. 'On the anvil of Gallipoli was hammered out the fabric of what is destined to be our most enduring national tradition.' The Anzacs had made 'a new Australia'. Nationhood had come too easily; now the gladiators and martyrs were to die to make it real.

The Anzacs fought on, mainly in the mine tunnels and by sniping in the less than eight square kilometres of dust and furze they had seized from the Turks after a second great attack had failed in August, leaving the bodies of Turk and Anzac four or five deep. The bacteria of dysentery and diarrhoea was in their food; water was scarce; they clothed themselves in bits of uniforms, wearing what they liked, many half-naked. They rested, with shrapnel bursting above them, in the gullies that fell down from behind the trenches, sometimes less than a kilometre from the centre of the front line; they swam from the beach they had named after themselves.

Squashed together in common distress, they had found in each other the comradeship of adversity. Life showed them

Creation of the Anzac legend: *in the few months they were at Gallipoli, the 'Aussies' became (with the New Zealanders) the 'Anzacs'. They had created a new legend so quickly that the first anniversary of their landing was celebrated in all the Australian States and in London as 'Anzac Day', with special commemorative issues of newspapers and magazines, such as that of* The Sydney Mail *(below). Australian soldiers at Gallipoli were forbidden to carry cameras, but there was much illegal photography. A soldier's 'snap' of the support area behind the forward trenches (right) and a 'snap' by another soldier (below right) record trench life.*

two meanings: common fellowship and readiness for death. English literary men admired their brown bodies and turned them into classical heroes, but what they most admired in themselves was that they had 'learned to accept a lost throw courageously'. From the honour and bravery of this failed adventure, in one of those mysteries in which people decide who they are, many Australians began to find simple shadows of themselves, telling them what they thought they were, or ought to be. The experience went so deep that in 1916, only one year later, there were ceremonies in all States marking the first anniversary of 'Anzac Day', and in London it was celebrated in Westminster Abbey by King George and Queen Mary.

The Anzacs had left as silently as they had arrived, creeping away with guile; the Turks knew that they had gone only when an attack found the Anzacs' trenches empty, with nothing between Turk and sea except a couple of hundred metres' walk. With the Anzacs temporarily out of the casualty lists, the Labor Party Prime Minister, the once-socialist W.M. Hughes, now had his season, showing that Australia could 'be there' in the rhetoric of war (in

which he proved one of the most eloquent in the world) as well as on the battlefield. On a visit to Britain he joined the 'Wake Up England' campaign with immense vigour. In city halls and guildhalls, over formal luncheons and dinners and in ceremonies giving him the freedom of cities or honorary degrees he assured the British that although the war had 'plunged civilisation into an inferno, which had saturated the earth with blood', it had nevertheless welded the scattered nations of the Empire into one united people, full of the valour of their ancient race and now providentially purged of dross and purified by the spirit of self-sacrifice. This campaign of Hughes's made such a noise that he was praised in the French newspapers ('he represents the real views of England') and attacked in the German newspapers ('the darling of the imperialists and jingo agitators'). Australians read reports of the fuss he was kicking up in the Old Country with such amazed pride that on his return he was greeted by enormous mobs at Perth and Adelaide shouting 'Hullo, Billy', and on the train trip from Adelaide to Melbourne crowds gathered at every station to cheer him and sing 'God Save the King' and 'Home, Sweet Home'. His speeches were compared with those of great orators

The Western Front: *one of the many new phrases to come into the language was 'the Western Front', the long line of barbed wire and trenches stretching across France. In the first Australian action on the Western Front, at Fromelles (above left) the 5th Australian Division in one night lost more than 5000 men. In the newspapers the*

long casualty list was becoming commonplace, and one of the normal forms of photography was now of the wounded coming home. The first blinded man, carrying sticks, returns to Sydney (above right).

among the ancient Greeks; a scholar translated one of them into Greek and published it in the journal of the Melbourne Classical Association.

It was again the turn of the Anzacs to die to help the birth of the nation. At first, when they were shipped to the Western Front, the going seemed quiet and things well organised, far removed from the debilitating improvisations of Gallipoli. But an argument was going on at British General Headquarters that would soon throw a division of Anzacs into a disastrous night's battle. It seemed obvious enough to the British generals that a feinting attack south of Lille would be a clever move. Fingers pointed on maps at a bump in the line near Fromelles beside which was lettered 'sugar loaf salient' ... one general thought this was the place to attack ... others didn't ... then they let him have the 5th Australian Division to test his hypothesis.

The Anzacs went over the top late one afternoon to fight their way through the third line of German trenches. Scattered groups broke out, leaving butchered comrades, but there was no 'third line' – only muddy ditches. In the dark they tried to dig the third line, but the Germans were behind them, attacking. Ammunition was running out. All

they could do was to charge through the Germans back to their old trenches. By breakfast time the next morning the Division had lost 5533 men. For several months it was to remain out of action.

Three other Australian Divisions were now fighting. With 100 000 British casualties already from the first two stages of his plan to 'roll up' the German line on the Somme, General Haig was now organising 'a third great blow'. More fingers pointed; the name of the 1st Australian Division was lettered on the map opposite the village of Pozières. The village was already mere mounds of rubble and shreds of trees, British corpses hanging on barbed wire, when the Australians attacked it and seized its mud. When the Germans realised that it was the only success achieved in the third great blow, they concentrated their artillery on it, obliterating even the mounds of rubble. The 1st Division lost 5285 men. When the 2nd Division relieved it they were ordered to throw themselves at a crest that was drawn on the maps. They seized it at night and lost 6846 men. By the time the 4th Division had relieved the 3rd, British pencils were again pointing at some lettering on the maps. The 4th Division charged to this new stretch of mud and lost 4649

A war for women: *one of the important roles women played in the war was as material in the propaganda posters. Very few of the posters did not appeal in some way to Australian men to protect their wives, mothers, sweethearts, daughters or sisters. Mothers and children could be represented as pathetic victims, left homeless and desolate (left), or defiant (below left). Some posters showed 'the Hun' in Australia itself, despoiling Australian women, portrayed with grotesque and savage detail by the artist Norman Lindsay (right).*

The Director-General of Recruiting, Victoria Barracks, Melbourne

men. One after the other, the three divisions were patched up and sent back to the attack. They fought for seven weeks – 19 attacks, 16 at night. On two kilometres of this disastrous crest they lost 23 000 men.

In Australia there was a heightened sense of being, with pride in the Aussies' part in the inexplicable drama being fought in Europe, and terror that such distant events could pull so many sons, husbands and lovers away from their homes and turn them into 'the boys' at the front. Ceremonies of sacrifice were now established for the making of an Aussie: one of 'the boys' would come home one night and blurt out his decision to enlist; he would have a 'send-off' with piano-playing, songs and dancing; after he left with his ship a photograph of him in his uniform decorated with his regimental colours would go up on a drawing-room table, a modest altar of hope. If he were gassed, or wounded, his next of kin would be told by telegram. If he were killed, a clergyman was sent.

At home, at times, it could seem to be a war being fought for the sake of women. In the recruiting posters and the great recruiting rallies it was mothers, wives, sweethearts or sisters for whom, as well as God, King and Country, men were being called on to lay down their lives. ('Any right-minded woman would rather be a mother or sister of a dead hero than of a living shirker.') Even a large part of the small pacifist movement consisted of women – a Women's Peace Army had been formed in July 1915, with a regular magazine, *The Woman Voter*, that was censored regularly and sometimes banned – and when women pacifists made their calls for peace, they did it as sweethearts, wives, sisters or mothers. Their most successful campaign song (so successful that the Government declared it illegal) was 'I Didn't Raise My Son To Be A Soldier'.

In Britain, many women went into the factories, but Australia was not a great industrial country: when women were wanted, it was mainly in the commercial world, as 'business girls'. The real women's work was to run the canteens, visit wounded soldiers, sell buttons on button days, rattle collection boxes on collection days, organise fêtes, bake cakes, put together 'comfort parcels' – and, above all, *knit*. Australian women knitted 1 354 328 pairs of socks for the Comforts Fund during the war. The 'new woman' was going out of fashion: replacing her was 'the flapper', but 'the flapper' was seen as a silly young thing.

There was little doubt – least of all among the Protestants – that God was on the Empire's side. Britain was again obeying Heaven's command: the war was a cleansing war summoned by divine will to restore self-righteousness to the countries of the Empire. Protestant clergymen called on Australians to fight God's cause at home, as well as at the Front, by abstaining from gambling and desecration of the Sabbath, by abandoning sport ('War and Football are rivals') and giving up drinking, or at least drinking after six o'clock, the time decided on in the new hotel early closing legislation. 'In the name of liberty,' said one Anglican bishop, 'I say we want to free our country from the German menace and I say that is going to be done far more quickly by closing the bars at six o'clock.'

Above all, the New Imperialism was proclaimed, with its gloomy satisfaction in blood-letting. ('As gold is tried by fire so nations are punished by suffering.') But war was also the greatest of the Australian sporting events; the Aussies were not only better fighters than the 'poms' but bigger, cleaner and more handsome, and all military failures were the fault of stuck-up British generals. The Aussies stuck by their mates, their sardonic wit sustaining them in facing death; on leave they were larrikins; on duty they were disciplined only when it mattered, showing remarkable initiative and readiness to 'give it a go'. And they were not only game but democratic, a people's army that, to the disgust of the British generals, did not even shoot its deserters.

The democracy of Australians was now about to be tested in an extraordinary manner, and at home. Universal Service Leagues were already demanding conscription; so was Archbishop Kelly; and when the British provided figures of necessary reinforcements (later found to be 'enormously in excess of the need') Hughes defied the Labor Party (which soon split) and put the matter to a national referendum, perhaps the first occasion in history when, at the height of a war, a people was asked to vote on the extent of its own sacrifice. Even the soldiers were to vote, as Division by Division they returned to their rest areas.

Feminist and pacifist: Vida Goldstein

Vida Goldstein was born in 1869, the year that pioneer feminist Harriet Dugdale wrote what is believed to be the first letter published in Australia (to the Melbourne *Argus*) demanding full citizenship rights for women. On her father's side Vida Goldstein had a Jewish-Polish-Irish background; her feminist mother was the daughter of a Scottish-born squatter. Vida's public career began in 1890 when she helped her mother collect signatures for a huge Woman's Suffrage petition.

By the turn of the century, the witty and capable Vida had become the leader of the Victorian women's movement; in 1902 she was elected secretary of the International Women's Suffrage Conference in the United States. She was five times a candidate for the Australian national parliament: for the Senate in 1903, 1910 and 1917, and for the House of Representatives in 1913 and 1914. In spite of refusing to ally herself with any political party and standing as an Independent, although never elected, she polled well, except in 1917 when she lost her deposit, a humiliation attributed to her pacifist stance.

Vida Goldstein was chairman of the Peace Alliance, and in 1915 formed the Women's Peace Army to fight conscription. In 1919 she accepted an invitation to represent Australian women at the Women's Peace Conference in Zurich. Although she continued to lobby governments for social improvements, Vida did not remain a prominent public figure. However, she became increasingly involved in the Christian Science movement and continued to write about internationalism and disarmament. She died in 1949, at the beginning of the Cold War.

Hughes knew he would win. How could the orator who had heard such loud applause in so many halls in Britain not prevail with his righteous eloquence? True, there had been agitation against universal military service in Australia before the war, when an anti-conscriptionist Australian Freedom League had formed, and it had claimed 55 000 members . . . But that was before the war. 'Germany has long coveted this grand and rich continent,' Hughes warned, 'and if she wins she will certainly claim it as an important part of her spoils. If Britain falls, in Australia there will not be warfare, but massacre. We will be like sheep before the Butcher.' Posters went up that showed 'the Hun', in his spiked helmet, killing Australians in their own back yards. Hughes spent 40 days and nights moving from one cheering crowd to the next, preparing for his victory. The campaign exploded with excess against Irish rebels ('Sinn Feiners'), against German agents who had been secreted into Australia and, above all, against the anarchists of the International Workers of the World (IWW). In Sydney, where five big city fires were believed to have been caused by IWW arsonists, 12 members of the IWW were jailed. Just before polling day a newspaper placard warned,

'IWW ASSASSINS WANT YOU TO VOTE NO'. On polling day a manifesto appeared urging a 'Yes' vote – it was signed by 13 of the 14 political leaders in Australia. (Only the Queensland Labor Premier did not sign.)

Against Hughes the only organised opposition seemed to come from the women pacifists, and from what was left of the labour movement after most of its leaders had deserted it. The labour movement used the scare language it knew best – an appeal to the White Australia Policy. ('This lonely outpost of the white man's civilisation will be deprived of its scanty garrison and left open to cheap Asiatics, reduced to the social and economic level of Paraguay or some other barbarian country.') The Women's Peace Army appealed to a mother's love for her son. The most famous campaign leaflet on the 'No' side (banned in some States and handed out illegally), featured a poem, 'The Blood Vote', which began:

> Why is your face so white, Mother?
> Why do you choke for breath?
> O I have dreamt in the night, my son,
> That I doomed a man to death.

Working-class distrust of authority, along with a

The first conscription referendum: *on the home front, the bitter divisions that were to mark the war began with the first referendum on conscription, in 1916. The single most famous of all the uses of women in wartime propaganda came with the 'Blood Vote' leaflet (above), put out in 1916. Prime Minister 'Billy' Hughes speaks at a conscription rally (above right). The Sydney Mail (far right) provided its rundown on the case for and against, posing a woman against the German kaiser. It was only when the Catholic Archbishop Daniel Mannix of Melbourne (right) spoke against conscription in 1916 that the 'No' side gained a significant public supporter.*

disproportionate part of the women's vote and the self-concern of farmers who were doing well out of the war and did not want their labour conscripted, meant that the referendum was lost. But its defeat was seen not as a protest against the war, but as an affirmation that the war was to be fought in the Australian manner. 'Fight for freedom's cause in freedom's way' was a principal 'No' slogan. When the Labor Party split caused it to lose office in the Commonwealth, New South Wales and South Australia, the 'Nationalist Parties' that were formed out of a combination of the Labor conscriptionists and the Liberal Parties proclaimed themselves the 'win-the-war party'. Since the Federal Nationalists looked the more warlike of the two parties, they got back with a bigger majority in the election that followed the referendum. Nation-making now demanded more blood.

After the butchery of Pozières, the Aussies had spent a gloomy autumn. Absence without leave increased: men began to disappear just before a battle. Heavy rains brought mud so thick that it might take up to ten hours with five or six relays of stretcher-bearers to bring the wounded back to casualty clearing stations. Some wounded asked to be shot. Haig's attempt to 'roll up' the German line petered out in mere reflex actions, and as winter came the Aussies became as concerned with mud and lice, rain and frostbite as with the bullets, bombs, shells and phosgene gas of 'the Hun'.

The new year brought cold bright weather, with mud and water frozen hard and covered with snow. The Anzacs were now working out a new name for themselves – 'the Diggers'. At Bullecourt the Diggers lay on snow-covered banks waiting for tanks that did not arrive . . . they charged barbed wire that the artillery had only half cut . . . their sense of irony increased. By May the first 16 mutinies broke out in the French Army; the Russians were already in revolt. The Diggers were again thrown forward at Bullecourt, seizing and holding a narrow foothold deep in German ground, tactically useless, but keeping attention from the French. Bullecourt cost them 10 000 casualties.

Now Haig had a new strategy – the 'step by step' approach in which, with a proper coordination of infantry and artillery, one bit of land would be seized and consolidated, then there would be an advance on another.

The battles of Ypres: *one of the most ghastly of all the battles on the Western Front, the battle of Ypres in Belgium brought the Australians 55 000 casualties. Australian artillery move into action at Ypres (left). Walking wounded, straggling back after one of the battles of Ypres, pass wounded men on stretchers (below).*

Maps of the Western Front (left) appeared almost daily in the newspapers.

The new great blow would come from the battered Belgian town of Ypres; the morale of the Germans would collapse; the cavalry would charge through gaps in the line; the Germans would be driven from the Belgian coast. But it rained for days before the offensive, turning the battlefield back to mud. The new strategy demanded dry weather. The offensive started in the wet.

When the weather again grew fine the Diggers found that the new strategy worked. Two of their Divisions attacked side by side, in a single line, following a great barrage. Advance one kilometre. Pause for half an hour. Advance 500 metres. Pause for two hours. Another 200 metres. The plan worked perfectly: there were 5000 casualties. It worked again: 5500 casualties. In October four Anzac Divisions fought side by side in a single line, to seize a ridge: 8200 casualties. Then the rain came back. Diggers pushed forward in Divisions, but only fragments of them reached objectives, then they fell back. In five weeks five Divisions suffered 38 000 casualties.

As winter came again, after 55 000 casualties, despite reinforcements and the return of patched-up men, the Diggers were 18 000 short. At home, recruiting became more and more frenetic. In posters God was asked to 'bless dear Daddy who is fighting the Hun and send him HELP'. In Melbourne the Anglican bishops declared that 'the forces of the Allies are being used by God to vindicate the rights of the weak'. Forty-two German place names were changed: in South Australia, Hamburg became Haig; in New South Wales, German Creek became Empire Vale; in Victoria, Mount Bismarck became Mount Kitchener. Modern novelties were used: recruiting handbills wrapped around parcels, recruiting films, recruiting slogans hanging from box kites. Recruiting drives were held in the cities every day, with brass bands and long lines of speakers. At dances wounded soldiers appealed for volunteers and there were recruiting speeches at the beaches. Huge footprints were painted on city footpaths leading to recruiting depots, riderless horses rode past recruiting platforms and volunteers were called to fill the empty saddles.

The feelings of class difference that had been only hinted at in the referendum campaign came out in what seemed, for a time, as if it might become the greatest of confrontations between capital and labour – a general strike. Feelings of hatred and revenge pervaded Australia.

War correspondent: C.E.W. Bean

In September 1914, when the Australian Government decided to appoint an Official War Correspondent to the Australian Imperial Force (AIF), it decided to ask the journalists themselves to recommend the person they wanted. The Australian Journalists' Association held a ballot. The runner-up was Keith Murdoch, of the Melbourne *Herald*, who later became the head of Australia's first large newspaper chain. The winner was Charles Bean, an Australian-born but English-educated journalist on *The*

Sydney Morning Herald, who had an heroic vision of the Australian bush and the men who lived in it.

It was at Anzac Cove that Bean was able to project his love of the bush image of Australia into the symbol of the 'Digger'; he devoted the rest of his life to maintaining this myth. As war correspondent, armed with telescope, notebook and camera, he insisted on obtaining frontline experience, seeking all the time, at continuing physical risk, a first-hand account. On the Western Front he was present at every engagement of the AIF. A few months after the evacuation, he published *The Anzac Book*, to commemorate the Diggers of Gallipoli. At his insistence the Australian Government appointed its own war photographers and more official war artists than it would otherwise have done. It was also at Bean's insistence that the Government established a War Records Section, and kept relics for a War Museum.

In 1919 Bean was appointed Official War Historian and began work on the official war history, writing six volumes of it himself, compiling another volume of photographs, and editing the other five volumes. The central part of this history was Bean's own six volumes, which he regarded as a 'memorial' to the ordinary Australian soldier. During the 1920s, largely at his inspiration, the War Museum took shape as the Australian War Memorial, now a national shrine.

Recruiting drives: *as the casualties grew higher, the recruiting campaigns grew more desperate. Norman Lindsay's poster 'A Terrible Record' (right) was one of the most fearsome 'anti-Hun' posters of the war. Compared with this, German propaganda was mild. In a cartoon from a German paper (far right) Australian Prime Minister Hughes is shown as saying: 'We Australians will slaughter half the German people and Mr Wilson (the United States president) has kindly undertaken to slaughter the other half.'*

The dispute had begun in railway workshops in Sydney as a protest against what seemed to be 'American speeding-up methods' but the details did not matter: both sides were looking for a fight. Often against the advice of their union leaders, workers 'went out' in an expression of desperation – railwaymen, tramwaymen, miners, wharf labourers, coal lumpers, seamen, warehousemen, slaughtermen, electrical tradesmen, workers in the sugar and liquor trades. Gas and electricity were rationed; transport was cut; food distribution was limited. The Government attacked the strikers as 'tools of anarchists, revolutionaries, Sinn Feiners, German agents and every disloyal section of Australia' and 'National scabs and blacklegs, reckless wreckers of all the aspirations and ideals that the workers have for years been fighting for.' Camps for volunteer strikebreakers were set up; the government commandeered lorries, carts, motor vehicles and colliers; Women's Loyal Service Bureaus were established for female strikebreakers; farmers hastened to the city to help defeat the strikes. For their part, the strikers' orators maintained that 'all kings, bosses and parliamentarians were parasites fattening on the backs of the workers' and that 'in the greatest fight for liberty

Australia has ever known' they were fighting 'a tyranny worse than that of Kaiser or Tsar'.

After almost 12 weeks the unions were broken. With nowhere else to go, the unions swung to the Left: ambitions developed more strongly towards an accumulation of working-class strength into 'One Big Union', and even for a socialist society in which Parliament would be replaced by a Supreme Economic Council, elected directly by 'the producers'. Several years later the Labor Party bowed in the direction of the new union militancy by adding the word 'socialism' to its official objectives – it was almost alone among the world's labour parties in not already having done so – but this was mainly an adjustment in rhetoric: the word 'socialism' was not added to the party's immediate program.

Class hatred was followed by sectarian hatred – for most of November and December in a second conscription

The great strike: *during the great strike of 1917, Hughes, contrary to his earlier attitudes to strikes, was deliberately provocative. Strikers' wives marched on Parliament House, Sydney (below) after a mass rally in the Domain (far below).*

When Direct Action, *the newspaper of the syndicalist and anti-war International Workers of the World, published this anti-war cartoon (above), its publisher was jailed. At one of the protest meetings that followed his sentencing, one of the IWW orators shouted: 'For every day Barker is in jail, it will cost the capitalists £10 000.' When what seemed to be acts of arson followed these words, 12 of the most prominent members of the IWW were arrested and jailed, and the organisation was broken.*

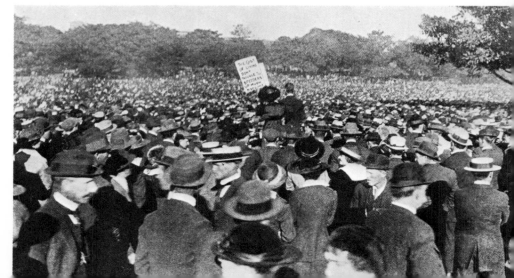

referendum in which the Catholic Archbishop Daniel Mannix, of Melbourne, now ferocious and provocative, became to his opponents the most notorious spokesman for 'No'. 'He has,' said Hughes in a message to the troops, 'preached sedition in and out of season.' To the Protestant middle class the Catholics could seem as great a threat as revolutionaries. 'Romanism,' one speaker said, 'stands confessed as the irreconcilable foe of democracy.' The move to Irish self rule ('Fenianism') was 'another form of treachery to Empire and to our faith'. The referendum was again lost, this time with a wider margin, but the hatreds it had stirred, like those of 'the great strike', became part of the memory of a whole generation. The secret armies that were to be formed in the 1920s would be organised as much against 'Sinn Feiners' as against Bolsheviks.

The despair that had spread at home now seemed to spread to the Western Front. In 1918, as the Allied political leaders and military commanders squabbled about what they would do next, or whether they should just wait for the Americans to do it for them, the Germans moved 35 Divisions from the Russian Front, and with this extra strength smashed at the Allied Line, trying to push the British up against the English Channel and destroy them. The Diggers found themselves advancing through an Allied retreat, past deserters, stragglers, looters.

At home some questioning of the assumptions of the war were beginning to show in the Labor movement. In an atmosphere in which the war was seen as a war of benefit to the rich, a relatively easy assumption in Australia where 70 per cent of its cost was carried by loan money rather than taxation, some Labor Councils were becoming restless. In June the Federal Conference of the Labor Party passed a motion favouring a negotiated peace and attached conditions to continued support for recruiting. However, the war was still seen as a great cause even by most of the anti-conscriptionist political leaders of the already split Labor Party: to save a second split a ballot was called for November. But although it was a time when articulate opposition to the war was growing in other countries, there was still not much articulate opposition to it in Australia – apart from the Women's Peace Army and ambiguities from some Irish clerics – except in the trade unions. Although the ordinary people were confident of the achievements of the Diggers, even this expression of national pride was doubted by some more conservative Anglophiles as a kind of disloyal expression of superiority over the Old Country.

There was new occasion for Australians to feel proud in the two Anzac Cavalry Divisions fighting in Palestine (one of which had carried out a three-kilometre charge through shrapnel and machine-gun fire against the Turks at Beersheba with nothing to wave at the enemy but bayonets). An Australian general commanded all the Allied cavalry that broke out into the valley of the River Jordan. In this dry, grim desolation, epidemics plagued the Australians, but they were riding on to Damascus and towards the fall of the Turkish Empire. On the Western Front when an Australian general – John Monash, son of Polish-Jewish immigrants – was given command of the Australian Divisions, the Diggers felt safer with their own general between them and the British. They admired the thoroughness with which this citizen soldier, in civil life an engineer, gave a new kind of care to planning the

coordination of tanks, aeroplanes and infantry. His first set attack made a big enough mark to earn an immediate visit from the French Premier, Georges Clemenceau. The Diggers boasted that the British command took over Monash's methods; they even speculated that he might take over the whole British command.

Then it was over. Of a population of less than five million more than 400 000 had volunteered to fight on the other side of the world. Of those who took the field almost one in two was wounded and one in five was killed. There was hardly a family group that had not feared the knock of the telegraph boy or the clergyman. There was supposed to have been some reason for it all. The Empire was safe . . . the war had been fought to end war . . . but the deeper feeling was that the Diggers had 'established the name of our country amongst the foremost of all brave nations'. By their fighting it was believed they had decided what Australians were.

The name of the country now demanded further establishment. Although Hughes's Cabinet thought it an unnecessary impertinence that Australia should have a seat

Myth making: *in sketches, and in paintings by the official war artists, Australians had now been given new heroes, myths and legends. The illustrators tended to show 'the Digger' as a larrikin: 'Trooper Bluegum, the Jester at the court of Mars' (above) and 'Overdoing it altogether' while attempting to impress a young lady (right).*

of its own at the Peace Conference, Hughes successfully kicked up a fuss in support of the Canadian demand for separate representation, and his face was to be there among the others, in the official painting of the signing of the Peace Treaty at Versailles. As 137 different ships on 176 separate voyages brought the Diggers home, Hughes fought the peace settlement single-handed.

He secured the cooperation of President Wilson in discarding a Japanese move that a declaration of race equality should be put into the preamble of the Covenant of the proposed League of Nations. And he became enough of a nuisance for a 'C' class mandate to be invented ('a 999 years lease') to satisfy him that the Australian control under the League of Nations of the former German colony in New Guinea would be given a special freedom. Hughes added the last of the claims to nationhood when he announced on his return to Australia that it was by having recognition at the Peace Conference that 'Australia became a nation'.

What kind of a nation? The human qualities apotheosised by the Diggers in their desperate comradeship found only a small place in the new official rhetoric; the old, confident boasts of the Improvers had gone. The best that Hughes

could think of when he returned was that Australians had volunteered to die 'to maintain those ideals which we have nailed to the very topmost of our flagpole – White Australia, and those other aspirations of this young Democracy'. What the other aspirations were was not stated. Corpses rotted in the fields of France and Belgium and in the deserts of Palestine, and maimed men began to draw their pensions at a time when Australians were losing official direction about what their aspirations were to be.

War without its horror: *few of the official paintings showed any of the horrors of a war in which Australia suffered a high percentage of battle casualties (below). The Light Horse could be presented as the most typical of the 'Diggers'. George Lambert's* A Sergeant of the Light Horse *(below left) became a famous war painting. The wounded were treated with dignity (below centre) in George Coates's* Arrival of First Australian Wounded From Gallipoli at Wandsworth Hospital, London, 1942. *Some of the paintings, like H. Septimus Power's* Following Through Near Harbonnières, 9 August 1918, *showed war as romantic (below right). The most famous of all was George Lambert's* The Landing at Anzac *(above right).*

POPULATION	ENLISTED	KILLED AND DIED FROM WOUNDS	WOUNDED	TOTAL CASUALTIES	PERCENTAGE OF TROOPS IN FIELD TO POPULATION	PERCENTAGE OF BATTLE CASUALTIES TO TROOPS IN FIELD
4 875 325	331 781	59 342	152 171	211 513	6.8	64.8

The Returned Men became influential members of society after the war, in a society moving out to the new suburbs with detached houses, neat gardens and time payment as Australia became the first 'suburban nation'. With the drive for respectability came 'wowserism' with its attacks on hotel hours and gambling as well as birth control, modern art and lipstick. Australia was becoming a politically more conservative society: Improvement was coming to mean less emphasis on social reform, more emphasis on national development. When the New York and London money markets collapsed in 1929, Australia's whole financial system appeared to disintegrate.

The Returned Men

Now that the dead Diggers had to be commemorated, there was not a town or a suburb that did not set up a wayside shrine. In churches, lamps of remembrance were installed, often in special soldiers' chapels, and in almost every institution rolls were set up with the Diggers' names in gold. Large temples were dedicated to their honour in capital cities, and the national war museum became a sacred place of national self-definition. Worship of the Diggers had become a dominant cult.

A Repatriation Department, with six State branches, 800 local committees and its own hospitals and artificial limb factories, served the disabled with treatment and a quarter of a million pensions. 'Repat' became a sanctuary not only for the immediately disabled but for many of those who later fell by the way: prayers for solace were offered to it in the form of claims that illnesses had been caused, however remotely, by the war. Money was available for 'Returned Men' to buy houses, and just as Roman legionaries claimed

Three of the most potent symbols of the Australia of the 1920s and 1930s: a badge of the Returned Sailors and Soldiers Imperial League of Australia ('the RSL') (right); a sprig of rosemary (above) for wearing on Anzac Day; and a set of service medals (above).

The South Window in the Hall of Memory of the Australian War Memorial in Canberra (left) celebrated the 'resource', 'candour', 'devotion', 'curiosity' and 'independence' of the Australians with stained glass representations of soldiers, a sailor and a nurse.

Anzac Day, between the wars, continued to be celebrated with pomp and ceremony. The Sydney Mail featured a front-page photograph of the service in the Domain in 1931 (right). By the 1930s the surf life-savers were seen as carrying on the tradition of the Diggers (far right).

land when they gave up fighting, Returned Men could gain farms (half of which, in the Australian manner, thereupon failed). Preference in employment to Returned Men was accepted as such a sacred necessity in the Commonwealth Public Service that the regular recruiting of juniors ceased until 1933: the Returned Men got almost all the public service jobs. The only other main form of entry was to be taken on as a messenger boy and try to work a way up.

Reflecting the class and religious divisions of the conscription referendums and 'the great strike', some of the most bitter of the Returned Men saw themselves as a national reserve that might be called upon in any emergency that might be caused by the Sinn Feiners or the Bolsheviks. Sir Brudenell White, the Army Chief of Staff, called a secret conference of State police officials in 1919 to make plans for using loyal Returned Men in any revolutionary situation that arose in Australia. In 1923, at a time when he had become Chairman of the Commonwealth Public Service Board, he organised a secret paramilitary force, code-named 'the White Guard', to be ready, if the time came. On some occasions Returned Men took things into their own hands, most notably in March 1919 in 'the Red Flag riots' in Brisbane when on two successive nights Returned Men rioted in protest against a trade union march in which some of the marchers carried red flags (an action forbidden under the War Precautions Act against which they were protesting). Thirteen of the trade unionists were sentenced to six months' jail for carrying red flags.

On the whole, the Returned Men were more interested in 'Repat' and in celebrations of the spirit of Anzac than in riots. The Returned Soldiers and Sailors Imperial League of Australia (the 'RSL') developed an influence greater than that of the veterans' organisations in most other countries. Its representatives sat on each of the main boards in 'Repat', deciding to whom these secular monasteries would dispense alms; the sacred rites of Anzac Day were in their control; and RSL officials were a lobby all politicians respected. Although attempts to form a soldiers' party ('above politics') failed, even in the more orthodox parties, especially in the country, the RSL mystique could be significant. Between strangers, the combination of an RSL badge and a Masonic handshake could make a weighty greeting.

Outside the Labor Party, the sacrifice of the fallen Diggers became more sacred than the White Australia Policy and partly replaced it as an ideal appealed to in speech-making. In 1929 a strongly RSL government in New South Wales banned the novel *All Quiet on the Western Front*. In 1930 the RSL called for 'the prohibition of war books which defame the soldiers of the Empire' and sought to arrange 'that all war books should be censored by the official war historian before being admitted to the Commonwealth'. War had become a mystery that to many was greater than the Christian faith – and the RSL was its prophet. As the 1940s approached, when many Returned Men met each other they had nothing to talk of except their war service. Even when they were with those who had not been to the war, almost any conversational opening might remind them of an incident at Bullecourt or Pozières, Beersheba or Fromelles.

In Anzac Day, with the RSL as its custodian, Australia at last had a national day – a day marking 'the irresistible entry of Australia among the nations of the world . . . sanctified by the lives of those who made the great sacrifice', 'essential as a crystallising point in the evolution of a national pride and consciousness'. Anzac Day became Australia's secular Easter: in the morning, sacrifice was honoured in marches and religious services (with Catholics breaking off after the march to go to their own church rather than join the others in a common mourning); in the

The SYDNEY MAIL

Wednesday, April 29, 1931.

The Anzac Service in the Sydney Domain

The first suburban nation

evening the resurrection of the nation was declared at drunken suppers. Apart from New Zealand, Australia was probably the only modern nation to celebrate its nationhood by recalling with solemnity and pride an overseas military expedition. What was celebrated was the purifying flame of war, mateship, the fortitude of sacrifice – and, by inference, a man's world, in which only volunteer male soldiers could seem true Australians.

As the Returned Men 'began to get on a bit', another male definition of Australia developed (at least in the surfing States) in the Surf Lifesaving Clubs, an Australian invention, with their own techniques, and their own rituals and ceremonies. These culminated every summer in the 'surf carnivals' in which clubs competed with each other in unique Australian skills and in which the highlight was a march past of tough, strong and deeply suntanned young males bearing flags and dressed in uniformed swimming costumes as they stamped across the beach to a background of military marches. They were all volunteers: seen as the finest young men of their generation, they became known, in speech-making, as 'the bronzed Anzacs'. They appeared on posters, symbolising Australia.

With the spread of the motorbus, suburbs began to sprawl further into the bushland away from railway lines, and when the 'California bungalow' was adopted as the most commonly desired middle-class Australian residence, houses were spaced further apart. The six capital cities, which held half the total population, uniquely suburbanised, covered a greater area for their population than any other city in the world.

In the new streets of dark purple brick bungalows, 'set low and close to the ground as a fortress', in which the veranda was often reduced to a porch with the roof humped over it, the suburban Australians were realising by regular instalments some parts of their ideal of what life was about. It was not an ideal all could afford – overall only a little over half of Australia's houses were owned, or being paid off, by the people who lived in them, and in Sydney a majority of houses were still rented. But for most Australians outside the rural areas (by 1939 two-thirds of the population) 'a home of one's own' set in its garden seemed

Having a good time: *one of the favourite uses of the camera was to record leisure pursuits, so that they could take their place in the family album: when suburbanites went for a 'spin' in a motor car, they were likely to line up to be 'snapped' in front of one of the cars that took them there (left); two women golfers practise on a country town golf course in the 1920s (below); a bush picnic (below left).*

Not everyone lived in a suburban house. Sali Herman's Near the Docks *(above), painted in 1949, attempted to give a sympathetic European feel to what suburban Australians saw as slums.*

Keeping it new: *in the 1930s the word 'modern' got one more meaning – as a description of a new style of architecture as epitomised in the 'California bungalow' style (right). To householders with enough money, 'modern' could mean the all-electric kitchen (below). To those without much money, 'modern' could mean building a house in the new material, 'fibro' (below right).*

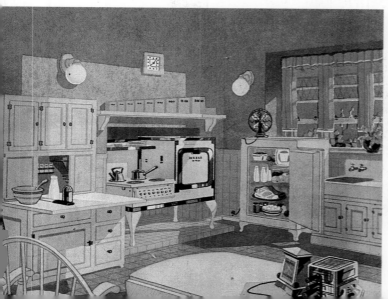

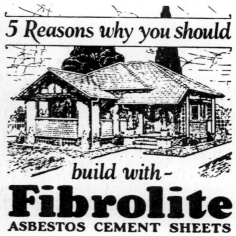

5 Reasons why you should

build with –

Fibrolite
ASBESTOS CEMENT SHEETS

to represent the end of that searching for dignity and independence that had failed in so many rural land reform schemes, and that had first driven many of the 'bloody Emigrants' from the industrialised cities of the British Isles.

Australians were suburban in ways as complex as their history. There were many displays of respectability, but the drive to respectability had been endemic since the first convict got his ticket of leave. At the same time suburbanites could still see Australians as larrikins, sometimes approvingly, sometimes not. Some saw their fellow countrymen as lazy boozers, some as Bible-banging wowsers. The ideas of mateship, articulated in the 1890s, were maintained in the unions and in another way in the RSL, even if not usually expressed in suburban streets.

At the same time the individualistic self-assertion of the 18th century was still there, as old as the Emancipists and the early traders. Often it was a view of the Australian as a gambler that gave a suburbanite a feeling of national distinctiveness, even if he himself didn't gamble. Three large lotteries flourished (two Government-run) and the racehorse was seen as 'the one great symbol of events that carried one outside the deadly round of daily toil'; and the complex network of illegal starting price bookmakers that accompanied it gave a small sense of authority-snubbing and adventurousness. The enormously successful comic strip, *Ginger Meggs*, provided one of the symbols of Australia: out in the streets there were 'the fellers' and with them in his weekly adventures 'Ginge', the boy hero, needed the cheeky, sardonic spirit to survive; but Ginge's adventures almost always began at home and usually ended at home, and at home it was the respectable common sense of his mother that prevailed.

The march of progress: *many Australians were poor in the 1920s and 1930s, but consumer advertising could give an impression of permanent progress: Electrolux 'the embodiment of modernism' (below), and a warehouse offering 'suites' of furniture (below right).*

Sometimes, if they 'wagged it' from school, Ginge and the fellers would go fishing: good fishing was never far away from most suburbs. Many ran alongside the water. Others were near stretches of bush. There was a craze for hiking, access to sport continued to increase (the number of golf courses quadrupled), surfing became even more popular and summertime sunburn even more fashionable. For their holidays suburbanites dreamed of camping in the bush or roughing it in a coastal weekender. To those who had a motorcar (rising to more than one family in ten), or knew someone who did, a 'spin' to a stretch of nearby bush, and a lunch of lamb chops grilled over a fire and washed down by tea was a reminder of what it was like to be an Australian.

Suburbanites accepted the collective restraints of modern metropolitan life more than most of the other people who were congregating in cities. In the various ways in which people rub up against each other in cities, Australians were usually self-restrained and orderly without an outwardly imposed discipline. If naively, D.H. Lawrence wondered at how 'they ran their city very well ... There seemed to be no policemen, and no authority, the whole thing went by itself, loose and easy, without any bossing'. 'Our street' had become the unit they belonged to, and in their streets they combined helpfulness when it was really necessary with a care not to destroy the sense of independence they gained from their privacy. They seemed born to suburbanism, as often, by now, they were. Sometimes 'their aggressive familiarity' startled visitors, but usually it was only when rights or dignity were threatened that some became touchy. When this happened they could be devastatingly sarcastic. However, an inner violence was more usually tamed into sardonic wit, or in 'chiacking', a kind of chaffing that threatened offence without meaning it, like the fighting games of animals. Their openness of manner was seen by foreign visitors as a freedom from servility, a humbling of the mighty in which taxi drivers preferred passengers to sit next to them in the front seat as a token of equality.

Lawrence noted 'that air of owning the city which belongs to a good Australian'. That the people should walk around their city as if they owned it seemed remarkable.

As Spanish Mission style was added to California Bungalow, and then as architectural styles fragmented into a new diversity, even the competitiveness in style of suburban houses seemed to affirm the dignity of those who lived in them. Contempt was felt for the dull uniformity of the old streets of terraces close to the city, jammed wall to wall, all monotonously the same, without proper gardens to spend the weekends working in. Whatever their condition, these were 'the slums', and they should all be pulled down. When the Swiss-born painter Sali Herman began painting some of the inner-city terraces of Sydney, presenting them with the eye of a European, his work was dismissed as 'slumscapes' . . . 'spiritless and depressing'. The new blocks of flats that were being built were seen as a threat to family life and an affront to Christian civilisation. The 'brick bungalow' became such a symbol of the new age that many councils in Sydney and Melbourne forbade the building of houses in any other material: those who could rise to only weatherboard, or the new 'fibro' (about a quarter of new buildings), had to go somewhere else to build.

For those who could afford time payment, comfort and self-content could be found in selling off old furniture and buying a 'breakfast-room suite', a 'dining-room suite', a 'lounge suite', a 'bedroom suite', all of a piece, matching and 'modern'. For those with less money there was at least the prospect of one day moving from linoleum as a floor covering to carpet. In families with enough credit, the kitchen table began to go, being replaced with pine 'work tops' and with it went the old kitchen dresser, replaced by the smart, new 'kitchen cabinet'. In modern-minded families the idea of the kitchen as a family centre could seem a symbol of poverty, or of the old days. By the 1930s there was talk of 'streamlining' kitchens, with built-in cupboards, and work tops and sinks of stainless steel.

Most Australians had not yet acquired the bathe-daily habit (although soap advertisements urged them to do so), but bathrooms were also being 'streamlined', with white tiles, built-in baths and the replacement of the old chip heaters with gas. In kitchens, beside the gas or electric cookers in white enamel, there were beginning to sprout shiny electric toasters, electric hot-water jugs and electric irons. ('Be Modern – Think Electrically.') In laundries, wood-burning coppers began to be replaced by gas. Brooms were replaced by carpet-sweepers, carpet-sweepers by vacuum cleaners. The consumption of gas doubled; the consumption of electricity went up five times. In Melbourne and Sydney the railways were electrified. Just as exhibitions held in the late 19th century showed new machines like the lawn mower and the sewing machine, the Electrical and Radio Exhibitions of the 1930s provided new forms of liberation. By the mid-1930s even buildings were being 'streamlined', in plain, horizontal bands of concrete or brick, and plate glass. When confident façades of chromium-plated steel and shiny black glass were put up to hide Victorian façades in the cities there seemed no end to the prospects of modernity.

The mode for private lives placed new limitations on the diversions of suburbanites. Hotels ceased to be general meeting-places. Because of licence reductions, half of them

ceased to exist and, in the three States that kept the six o'clock closing time imposed during the war, 'all around the bar a heaving mass of men elbowing, pushing, trampling on each other's feet' shouted orders for enough beer to fill their bellies in the 'six o'clock swill'. In Sydney, a small fashionable café society developed around two nightclubs and a hotel within a few minutes walk from each other ('night after night the same two hundred dance, laugh and gossip'); a bohemian life was maintained at King's Cross; four or five speakeasies bribed their way into survival and sold alcohol after 6 pm; but otherwise nightlife disappeared. In the other cities there was no sign of it. Hardly any city restaurants stayed open at night, and those that did were forbidden to serve drink; diners-out could bring their own bottles but they had to empty them by a specified hour. The police raided hotels and restaurants to make sure they were keeping the law, or they were bribed not to do so. Towards the end of the 1930s Sydney could seem more sophisticated than the other capitals because it now had coffee shops.

After the arrival of the talkies only three 'live' theatres survived in Melbourne and only one in each of the other capital cities, and they contented themselves mainly with

Middle-class socialist: Jessie Street

Lots of energy and enthusiasm, a private income, access to the politically powerful, a social conscience, and a tendency to authoritarianism made Jessie Street one of the most important figures in the Australian women's movement between the wars.

Jessie attended a progressive school in England, took an Arts degree at Sydney University, married a lawyer and had four children. With domestic help, Jessie Street was able to devote herself to many outside interests. On her travels she had observed militant British suffragism, and in New York had helped in the rehabilitation of 'fallen women'. In 1929 she welded various Australian women's organisations into the United Association of Women and was elected its first president.

In the anti-feminist climate of the Great Depression the association spoke forcefully against women being removed from the work force to make way for men, and it questioned political candidates about their feminist views. It campaigned for social and economic equality for women and against sexual exploitation.

Jessie Street was radical in her feminism but conservative on other political matters, until in 1938 she went to the Soviet Union where she was impressed by the position of women. She returned a convinced socialist. But her politicisation caused a split in the Australian women's movement. There were many women who felt uneasy with left-wing politics and, especially in the Cold War atmosphere of the late 1940s, with a feminist leader who when standing as a Labor candidate in a conservative electorate, could be put down with the crude slogan: 'Jessie Street, the Road to Moscow'.

revivals of the musical comedy successes of earlier decades. With reproduction marble statues, reproduction oil paintings, reproduction chandeliers, reproduction coats of arms and reproduction antique furniture, the most ambitious of the new city picture palaces provided much of what was available in the visual as well as the performing arts. (In the latter category as well as 'the pictures' there were full orchestras, stage shows and Wurlitzer organs.)

Joining the picture palaces as spectacles of wonder were the palaces of the department stores, the largest of them owned by families that bore the reputation of princes and, like princes, provided some of the communal gossip of a city. They were large mail order houses as well as city shops, and some of their 'buyers' were among the most travelled of Australians. The department stores bore aristocratic façades and carried impressive slogans ('The House of Distinction' ... 'While I Live I'll Grow' ... 'The Model Store'). They set taste with art exhibitions, put on Christmas pantomimes and other entertainments, and their restaurants were among the few places in the city that offered more than fish and chips or meat pie and tomato sauce; when the department stores added the new idea of

cafeterias, the design of these was likely to be 'streamlined'. Most visitors to the cities were suburban women, in for a day's shopping, or visitors to the picture palaces: the cities (seen by some as 'too Americanised') were principal diffusers of new ways of living.

For many, keeping their gardens neat and their houses in running order became their chief diversion. In gardens it was the era of the hedge, usually privet, running along the front and sometimes down the sides, either straight-lined or battlemented, as a prime symbol of privacy. It was also the era of the rose. Whole gardens could be made up of lawn and beds of roses – tea roses with names like 'Shot Silk' or 'Crimson Glory' or 'Red Radiance' in the centre, with a border of clumps of polyanthus rose around them for variety. In winter a garden of bare rose bushes could show that one was a responsible, serious-minded gardener.

For those who liked reading, popular magazines were developed; newspapers produced bolder display, more pictures, shorter paragraphs, readers' contests and comic strips; and novels could be borrowed from small private lending libraries in suburban shops, or from the schools of arts (whose old ideals were so forgotten that people

wondered at their funny name). Even by 1930 there were only eight municipal libraries in Sydney.

It was the radio that now dominated home entertainment. It was an unnecessary exertion to wind up a gramophone or pedal a pianola. By the end of the 1930s there were more than a million radio sets, and 130 broadcasting stations; some of the best-known Australian performers on the radio were as famous as Hollywood film stars – in particular the rapid-fire, 'Americanised' Jack Davey, comedian, compere, quizmaster, crooner, who, from his opening greeting of 'Hi-ho, everybody', seemed to bounce off the microphone straight into people's houses, reassuring them with modernity and good fellowship. At breakfast time the radio saw grown-ups off to work and children off to school; it entertained housewives during the day; quarter-hour serials such as 'Flash Gordon' and 'K7 – Secret Agent' poured in from the United States, and 12 Australian companies produced local ones – 'Mrs 'Arris and Mrs 'Iggs', 'The Search for the Golden Boomerang'. Soap manufacturers were among the greatest culture-patrons of the age: the Colgate Unit was dominant among the networks; the most prestigious commercial radio drama came from the Lux

A few painters at last moved from the predominantly male and bush themes to portray women in the suburbs. In Woman at a Washtub *(right), Niel Gren showed the kind of laundry that existed in almost all houses between the wars, although in some of them a gas copper would replace a fuel copper. In* Breakfast Piece *(above), Herbert Badham gives a late 1930s impression of middle-class existence.*

The kitchen: *in many households the kitchen was still an important family living room. The photographer Max Dupain captured the mood of a 'modern' middle-class kitchen (left), but to many Australians the kitchen of the Meggs family (below left), in the enormously popular 'Ginger Meggs' comic strip, was more like the real thing.*

Modern entertainment: *the 'movies' (which then became the 'talkies') and the 'wireless' (which then became 'radio') were the two main forms of family entertainment. Film magazines (far left above) were usually on sale at the cinemas as well as newsagents. Jack Davey (far left below) the radio comedy, quiz and singing star, became Australia's single most widely known entertainer in the 1930s and 1940s.*

Radio Theatre ... young hopefuls put their trust in 'The Amateur Hour', sponsored by Lever. Radio brought a new 'reality' into life with 'actuality, on-the-spot broadcasts', even when, as in the case of the broadcasts of test matches in England in the 1930s the impression of 'actuality' was faked ingeniously. Politicians began to use it in elections. The advertising jingles and slogans provided part of a city's culture. The commercial 'I Like Aeroplane Jelly' became a national song.

A general sense of belonging was to be found on the beaches, at spectator sports, and at the suburban picture shows. For some there were the churches and their socials; for the young there were the local dancing 'hops' or a night at the city 'palais' – and, towards the end of the 1930s, local hamburger shops and milk bars. Since in the suburban shopping centres everything shut down at six o'clock, the packed suburban cinemas (the 'picture shows') were the main opportunity for the people from a suburb to gather together and look at each other; this was the only kind of night out most of them knew. 'Dining out' was almost unknown, except for the rich, or the bohemians: in the suburbs, with no restaurants, it was not possible. Other

Motherhood was also being modernised. A regular visit to the baby clinic was becoming one of the essentials of sound motherhood.

than the cinemas, the suburbs provided no sense of community, not even good shops. All the good shops were in the city. Although millions of pounds of loan money now went into public works, in the cities it was even difficult to keep the water and sewerage pipes up with suburban development. New lines of criticism of Australians appeared: 'Sydney is not so much a city as an agglomeration of small municipalities grouped around a semi-Americanised core and the real estate offices of a score of professional boosters.' Suburbanites were fragmented by 'stereo-typed forces ... conveyor-belt systems'.

There were still lively feminist movements. An Australian Federation of Women Voters was formed in 1921, which made many submissions to government departments and approaches to ministers; a United Association of Women was formed in 1929, which gave regular radio broadcasts on feminist issues, sent questionnaires to members of

parliament, lobbied politicians, issued pamphlets and called public meetings; and a Council for Action on Equal Pay was formed in 1937, which saw itself as an important part of the labour movement. But most suburban women knew little or nothing of these. What addressed them as women were the women's magazines and 'women's pages' and 'social pages' of the newspapers, and these simply told women to go on being sweethearts, mothers and wives. When a women's news-magazine, *The Australian Women's Weekly*, was launched in 1933 (price twopence) this seemed, for a season, to have something extra to say – with articles on women's rights (on the front page of the first issue it carried a report 'EQUAL SOCIAL RIGHTS FOR SEXES') and women's careers ('No longer tied to the home, the daughters of today have the world at their feet'). Then it settled down and made its main business telling women how to be sweethearts, mothers and wives. It was a time when motherhood had become 'scientific': baby clinics were extending, and they had a message of time-tabling babies, so that their feeding hours and their bowel movements would be regular; babies were to be weighed and measured to make sure they were normal; and they were not to suck dummies, or their thumbs. ('To avoid thumb-sucking, teach the child to place his hands together and pillow his face on them.') Special baby foods were now on sale.

Diet had also become scientific. Salads were added to menus (apart from casseroles, they were the main dish added to recipe books between the wars) and vitamins had been discovered. For a season in the 1920s, Flinders Street Railway Station bore the advertising sign:

> Spark up! Get on the good health route,
> Each day take home some citrus fruit.

Fruit juice stalls spread through the cities; health food kiosks were opened (fresh fruit, dried fruits, nuts); new health foods were introduced – peanut butter, Marmite and an Australian invention, Vegemite. There was a new cult of belief in the goodness of milk, expressed not only in a love of milk itself (fresh, condensed or powdered, or, in the 1930s, available in 'milk shakes' or 'malted milks' in the new milk bars), but in 'dairy milk' chocolate, in the new processed cheeses (Kraft cheese came to Australia in the 1920s), cocoa, special brand-name milk drinks such as Bournvita and Milo, and in ice cream – called, by the largest ice cream company, 'the health food of a nation'. Milk was also to be used on the new 'breakfast cereals' (Kelloggs also came to Australia in the 1920s). In the thirties there was a concern with 'roughage', seen as good for the constipation that had previously been one of the great anxieties of the patent medicine ads. When Kelloggs invented All-Bran, a high roughage product, it was possible to combine with the goodness of milk the daily elimination, by natural means, of bodily evils.

It was the woman's role to continue to express herself in the neatness and taste of 'the home', which in extreme cases could become a sacred place, unspoiled by use. But now, especially for women with middle-class tastes, it was also the woman's role to do this with an eye to modernity in its many forms – in furniture, diet, domestic equipment, child-rearing, house design, husband-pleasing. Meanwhile, men lorded it over most leisure pursuits. The shrivelling of opportunities for men and women to enjoy themselves together in public seemed sometimes to shrivel their other relations with each other. The Meggs comic strip household was dominated by Ginger's mother, and Ginger's father was presented as a tolerated guest. Some of the men continued the aggressive assertions of maleness of a society in which there had once been several times more men than women. But behind the displays of masculinity there sometimes seemed compensating anxieties. A fearful holding-back would drain affection.

Some families lived in almost complete isolation from everyone else; for others their only home entertainment was within extended family groups, usually on a Sunday (in their best clothes). Those who did not have cars and lived in suburbs distant from each other might have to make three or four transport changes before they got there, and then go through it all again on the way home. Some kept up wider fields of home entertainment (some of the poor and some of the rich most successfully). Women developed the rituals of afternoon tea (dainty sandwiches and many varieties of sponge cake) into a complex art – but for most, if privacy and removal from a sense of community other than that of family and close friends was what they wanted, they had it.

Even if, like any other success, the development of the suburbs had its disappointments, part of what Australians had most desired from the Improvement had now been obtained. What was unexpected was that, in its public expression, the sense of Improvement had suddenly died.

From being a pioneer country in social and political reform, Australia had become backward. The only reform in social welfare introduced in the 1920s was a system of child endowment brought in by a Labor Government in New South Wales. The only reform introduced in the 1930s was a free hospital scheme introduced by a Labor Government in Queensland. Even the British, not an advanced nation in social security, had medical benefits, widows' pensions and unemployment insurance schemes: Australia had no national provision for any of these. In 1928, after five years of Royal Commissions, special committees and reports, a Nationalist Government had proposed a compulsory contributory scheme of national insurance with all employees paying one shilling a week each and employers contributing equally. It came to nothing. Ten years later, another non-Labor Government proposed a similar scheme, with a medical benefits system. This also came to nothing. In 1937 there were Commonwealth-State discussions on unemployment insurance. These came to nothing.

Australia's history was defeating it. The friendly societies, themselves expressions of Improvement, attacked the schemes as destroying the spirit of independence and thrift. Used to the idea of the Government as a provider, which went back to the convict period, employers attacked national insurance as too costly, and the Labor Party attacked it because it didn't appear to be 'free'. Still retaining the nobbishness of the early days, the doctors rejected the panel system as an assault on their dignity.

The drive for political reform also petered out. The preferential system of voting was introduced in five States and the Commonwealth (with Tasmania preferring the proportional system), and voting was made compulsory, first for the Queensland Parliament and then for the others, but that was all. There was rigging of the electoral system in some States and in all of them the upper houses remained stockades of the old nobbishness; but only Queensland got rid of its upper house, and Labor governments were among the worst electoral riggers. The 19th century liberal and radical programs for political reform had nothing much left over for 20th-century Australia, and there seemed to be no new ideas coming from Britain: the one new idea that *had* emerged in Britain – to take away most of the powers of an upper house – seemed too difficult to carry out in Australia.

As part of the general puritanism of the English-speaking nations at that time, there was a triumphant impetus to the old drive to respectability. As well as the halving of the number of hotel licences, the restrictions on trading hours, the prohibitions on serving drinks with meals, on off-course betting and on almost any organised Sunday activity, there were attacks on birth control (the size of families had

'The wowser and the wowser's wife', by Norman Lindsay, sums up the feeling that Australia was being stifled by Puritanism.

halved), living in flats, swimming trunks for men, smoking, twin beds, trousers for women, the depravity of modern art, the wearing of lipstick. Even spectator sport was attacked as undermining the nation's morals. From ignoring literary censorship (up to 1928 only three literary books had been banned, although 120 seditious works, mostly Bolshevik, were impounded), the Commonwealth Government, applauded by church bodies, women's clubs and the RSL, launched a campaign to protect the values of 'the patriotic family man'. By the mid-1930s, 5000 books had been banned as 'filth'. Film censorship was instituted. There were exhortations that sport was not to be enjoyed: it was to be pursued as a national duty.

That people should want to live in cities seemed even more evil than it had in the 1890s, and as country life declined in economic importance, praise for it became more anxious. The third of the few special-issue postage stamps that were released in that period commemorated Charles Sturt, the explorer. The wool industry was given special honour: history books presented it with an earlier and more consistent importance than it had, and John Macarthur, as an early wool grower, was turned into one of Australia's principal heroes, giving him a greater significance in the development of fine wool than he merited (while his wife, Elizabeth, also a pioneer in fine wool production, was given no credit at all). Another of the special-issue postage stamps commemorated Macarthur. Australia was said to ride 'on the sheep's back' and a statue was raised to the Peppin merino ram, progenitor of a large proportion of Australia's flocks. At the time of the annual sheep shows, distraction could be found from life's disappointments by looking at the photographs in the newspapers of the champion rams, their necks garlanded with prize ribbons. If Australians wanted to admire themselves they could look at pictures of rams.

The most admired landscape paintings were still of undulating plains of yellow grass, scattered with gumtrees, leading to blue hills in the distance – idealisations of the grazing country that was seen as the only true Australia. It was so idealised that export of the film *The Breaking of the Drought* was banned by the Commonwealth Government in 1920 because it showed these landscapes desolated by drought. Yet although wool was important as an export item, contributing 38 per cent of total exports from 1935 to 1939, it had lost its late 19th century pre-eminence.

There was no hope for the cities in the 'society' that coagulated at the top of them: it was much the same as the Black Hat society of the 1840s, with gentlemen's clubs as its most important meeting-places, the Legislative Councils as its unique political expression, the fee-paying schools as its main training grounds, and the Government Houses as its principal sources of honour. The squatters and such 'ancient nobility' that each State could muster dominated the clubs, along with leading doctors, lawyers, professors, financiers and merchants, while a blackball awaited retailers, Catholics, Jews and others who were not 'the right type'.

From being radical or liberal, the Press became mainly conservative, although parts of it, most notably the Sydney *Daily Telegraph* in the late 1930s, gave expression to a contemporary philosophy of Improvement. In the *Telegraph's* view, having overthrown the 'stodgy bumbledom' that gave Australia a bad name overseas, Australia would rise again with progressive developments such as airmail services, a mature film industry, light wines in cafés, appreciation of modern arts and uniform railway gauges. Dress would be reformed, slums would be abolished, music concerts would be provided for children, science

The tyranny of the bush: *although Australia was already one of the most suburban societies on earth, the idea continued that it was mainly a nation of the bush. One of the first special stamp issues, in 1934 (above), continued the cult of John Macarthur, presented as 'founder' of the wool industry. The contributions of others, including his wife, were not known to most people. Elioth Gruner's* Murrumbidgee Ranges, Canberra 1934 *(left) typifies the popular presentation of Australia as a land of grazing properties with yellow grass, eucalypts and blue hills in the distance.*

would be cultivated. There would be liberalisation of shop-trading hours, tuberculin testing for cows, rent control, and better treatment of the Aborigines. Examinations and homework would be abolished; tariffs would be lowered; betting would be legalised. There would be sponsorship of the arts and the removal of restrictions on wearing swimming trunks on beaches.

Within politics the once more-or-less prevailing agreement on the values of Improvement withered now that Australians had achieved their version of the two-party system political theorists had demanded since the 1850s. Although the Nationalists inherited some of the liberalism of men like Deakin, they didn't do much with it, becoming more cohesively and openly a party of special business interest, in reaction to the special trade union interest of the Labor Party. The Nationalists were not even in control of

their own finances. Independent groups did their fund-raising for them, making much of the Nationalists as an 'insurance against Bolshevism', a belief for which some sustenance had been provided when a small Communist Party was formed in 1922, mainly out of trade union leaders, and later set up within the unions a 'Militant Minority' movement that sometimes prompted anti-leadership militancy. Through its overwhelmingly trade unionist nature, it also sometimes influenced factions within the Labor parties; it attacked all the institutions of Improvement as weapons against the workers. In reply, the Nationalists denounced the 'small minority of foreign extremists who have managed to capture the trades union movement'. An Australian Council of Trade Unions was formed in 1927, but it was far from being 'One Big Union': it took years to achieve a significant presence.

At the end of the 1920s, Australia, for its population, was losing more working hours in strikes than almost any other country. The greatest sense of threat had occurred when the Victorian Police went on strike in 1923; the centre of the city was in the control of looters until Returned Men volunteers intervened, summoned by appeals at the city cinemas. But there was also violence (and even more talk of violence) in Sydney during the timber workers' strike and the waterfront strike when the Commonwealth Government tried to deport two union leaders (the High Court stopped this) and then introduced coercive legislation that almost destroyed the union. Direct government intervention in big strikes, initiated in the late 1880s, had become routine and the governments usually won. In the 1928–29 coal fields lockout (exports of coal had collapsed), the New South Wales Government secured a victory at Rothbury that shocked Australians – police opened fire and launched baton charges, one man was killed (if accidentally) and nine were wounded.

'Working-class consciousness' in occupational groups such as the coal miners and the wharf labourers was growing strong enough to be an irritant, and in mining towns, especially Broken Hill and Wonthaggi, unions could provide civic leadership; but usually attempts at union militancy had few results other than provoking successful government retaliation and a further weakening of Improvement. The Nationalists denounced the big strikes as foretastes of Bolshevik revolution and warned voters against putting Labor into power in the Commonwealth Parliament lest the 'red raggers', through their influence in the Labor Party, gain control of Australia. In such political melodrama there was no place for a belief in social progress.

In some States it was the Labor parties, not the Nationalists, who came to seem the natural governing party. In Queensland, where Labor governed from 1916 to 1929, and then returned to power for what was to be 25 more years, its attitude seemed 'more moderate, more positive and apparently more attractive than that of the opposition'. With 20 years' office in 23 years, Labor developed a similar reputation in Western Australia; in Tasmania, after five years' government in the 1920s, it reassumed government in 1934 and stayed in power for 35 years. Such support for Labor seemed to indicate a continuing hope among voters for social progress, but the State Labor governments did not achieve much. They were hampered by the nobs in the Legislative Councils and by the puzzles of a Federal system; but in any case, whatever their practice, much of their precepts made up a doctrine for situations that did not exist. The Labor parties had discarded most of their doctrines without finding anything to replace them. Prompted by trade union pressure, they still instituted a reform now and again, but often their aim was simply to look more normal than their opponents. With agreement on social values gone, they were now the parties of progress; but they did not progress and their opponents were no longer prompting them to Improvement. In some Labor parties more than half the members were Catholics; this produced much heady plotting and counter-plotting, but it did not induce Improvement.

When A.W. Jose wrote his *Short History of Australia* in 1889, he could not find any flourish with which to end it, but in the 1909 edition he had decided what destiny had in mind for Australia. 'To this point, then,' he said, 'the course of Australian history has led us – that we hold a whole continent of valuable land, using it very imperfectly, but free for the moment from outside interference. This free moment we must use, if we want to retain our hold; we

must use it to take seriously in hand the developing of the country's natural resources by cultivating its richer soils, irrigating its drier, exploiting the fisheries along its coast, opening up and thoroughly working the mines hidden below its surface . . . To do this methodically, scientifically, is Australia's task for the future.'

After the Great War the idea of 'Improvement' in Australia narrowed down to that of economic 'development'. Public expression of the belief that Australia would show the world how to live was replaced by the philosophy of the real estate speculator. Australians were told in the 1919 election, 'You are all shareholders in the great company of Australia Unlimited, the greatest firm in the world'; in the 1928 election the Prime Minister said he was 'the managing director of the greatest company in Australia, the Commonwealth Government, and its duty is to develop Australia'. In Tasmania, where Labor was to hold power longer than almost anywhere else in the world, progress became, primarily, a matter of hydroelectricity programs: Tasmania was proclaimed as the 'all-electric island'. The boasters could still speak of an Australia of a hundred million people or more (all white), but there was

The industrial bitterness of the 1920s reached its climax in December 1929, in the tragedy at Rothbury, in the Hunter Valley, when police fired on miners, killing one and wounding nine.

It was an age of 'Populate or Perish', caricatured in this drawing of a woman in fear of a 'baby plague', rather than the more traditional 'mice plague'.

no longer any special reason for people to be there, beyond their own survival. Australia was 'Unlimited', but it had ceased to be a place in which there was bold talk of social changes; optimism narrowed to a belief in economic activity.

Much of this economic activity was not carried out for rational economic reasons. A prime motive was the belief that Australia must 'populate, or perish' ('We must populate this country or we shall never be able to hold it.'), which could mean that any economic scheme could be good so long as it increased the population. But to this was added the moral reasoning that it was wicked to control such 'vast resources' (by which was meant 'natural resources') and not develop them. There could be self-interest in this also: if Australians did not develop their resources, since they would have no moral right to them, someone else would come and take them away. There was also a simple belief in development as something that was good in itself: Australia was 'capable of almost indefinite expansion', not least of all because Australia was 'a continent for a nation and a nation for a continent'.

As it happened, much of the 'development' was not only economically irrational; even by its own standards it was

also a failure. The professedly expansionist idea of 'men, money and markets' was the great slogan of the 1920s, but of the 500 000 British immigrants hoped for in ten years, only half arrived – and unemployment ran at eight per cent over the decade; of the £225 million raised in the London money market much was wasted; new markets were obtained, but only by a high cost in subsidies or special concessions. The word 'development' had assumed great emotive content, but it was 'development' without consideration of cost. The basic weakness was that the 'vast resources' of Australia were all seen as 'natural resources', and rural development was seen as the only basis for progress. What was to be unlimited was Australian farming. Governments, still seeing themselves as the prime innovators, assisted immigration, paid for closer land settlement schemes for immigrants and Returned Men, subsidised farmers with bounties and marketing schemes and built huge irrigation systems and other public works. But by 1928, half the money advanced to rural settlers throughout Australia had been written off.

Some irrigation schemes had been instituted in a remarkably carefree spirit: the Hume Weir, for example,

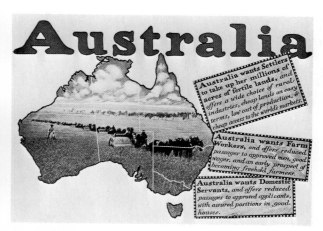

'Development': *as this advertising material in England shows, the emphasis on Australian 'development' was on the land, not on manufacturing industry. Posters were placed at agricultural shows in England to attract British immigrants to Australia (above). The female immigrants the Australian Government wanted were domestic servants (above far left) and the males were bush workers (above centre).*

As a hero of war, John Monash was famous as leader of the Australians on the Western Front. In peace, as Chairman of the State Electricity Commission in Victoria he became Victoria's principal hero of 'development'. Monash uses a dictaphone in the studio of a radio station (left).

was partly built before thought was given as to how it was to be used. Even where irrigation schemes seemed to be making a return on the money outlayed on irrigation works, the return could diminish or disappear when the cost of other public works was added. When the birds that had eaten grasshoppers' eggs on the plains found food in irrigation channels, grasshopper plagues threatened the wheat.

The farmers themselves were now well organised; the wheat farmers in particular. As in the United States and Canada, the rise of wheat farming had produced new groups of discontent. Governments set up bulk handling facilities for wheat, and Government research developed new strains, but the wheat farmers wanted that place of honour in the nation they had begun to imagine in the late 19th century, combining with small graziers and the dairy

farmers to promote the idea that the small settlers of rugged independence and integrity ennobled the whole land. To most Australians it was still unbelievable that small farmers should receive respect – but small settlers took themselves seriously enough to promote Country Parties (sometimes with an RSL flavour added) that in four Federal Parliaments became an important part of the political system. In these four parliaments Australia was back to a three-party system, but this time the alliances were not those of progress, but of who could capture 'the country vote'.

Even the history of Australia as a mineral-exporting country was neglected in favour of dreams of farming expansion. Although there was some promotion of oil searches, surveys of mineral resources were ignored. In 1938 it was declared that Australia's reserves of iron ore were so limited that export of iron ore would be banned. Ironically, it was in the 1920s that the trend of investment moved clearly in favour of the cities. At the very time when governments gave renewed emphasis to rural areas, Australia was moving towards becoming a manufacturing power – without anyone noticing.

Developing the waterworks: *from 1857 to 1940, 40 dams, weirs and reservoirs were constructed around Australia, mainly in South Australia, Victoria and New South Wales. Irrigation schemes were authorised in Renmark (SA) and Mildura (Vic) in 1887, Leeton and Yanco (NSW) in 1906, Harvey (WA) in 1916, and Theodore (Qld) in 1923.*

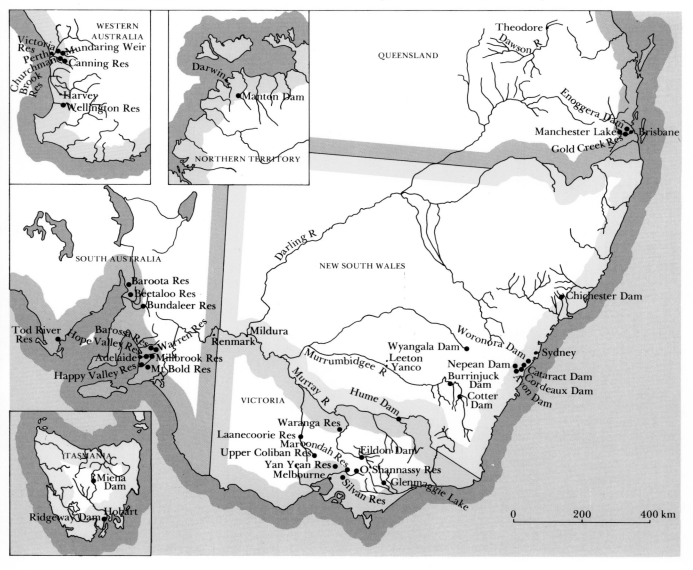

When the Australians were organising themselves for the Great War, the Governor General had written home, half-patronising, half-admiring, that 'happy-go-lucky methods' were typical of 'this people'. There was 'a grasp of realities, an astuteness and energy' in them: 'extremely adaptable, they quickly seize on every device that suggests itself for accomplishing desirable ends'.

This happy-go-lucky but practicable adaptability was shown in a wartime expansion of manufacturing which by 1921 saw New South Wales, now the leading industrial State, with nearly a third of its workers engaged in manufacturing industry. The most marked advance was in heavy industry and the metal trades, where New South Wales was pre-eminent – even more so when a second steel plant was built, this time at Port Kembla. The war had broken the remote control by German cartels of much of the Australian minerals industry, and Australian-owned smelting and refining plants had been strengthened. After

the war the BHP, protected from imports (and, after it bought the Port Kembla plant, from domestic competition), was, in the 1930s, to produce the world's cheapest steel.

In the 1920s manufacturing expanded by about a third, in the next decade perhaps by 40 per cent, but compared with the rest of the economy, manufacturing remained relatively weak in Australia. Australia had many of the advantages of industrialism without itself really being an industrialised society. There was a concentration in New South Wales, and in any case the uniform success in heavy industry was not accompanied by equally uniform success in making consumer goods. For instance, although motor vehicle assembly and the production of motor bodies and tyres was well under way in the 1920s, no Australian-designed car was being manufactured by the end of the 1930s. Such initiative as there was had come from the Government's offering a bounty and proposing, as a form of protection, to put the assembly of foreign cars under licence; but none of the proposals submitted to it was economic.

There were difficulties. In the 1920s (although not in the 1930s) wages were as much as 50 per cent, even 100 per cent, higher than in Britain, and working hours were less,

A cigar-smoking Essington Lewis is interviewed by visiting American journalists in August 1940 outside the Newcastle Steelworks, which he established for BHP in 1915.

Industrial dictator: Essington Lewis

One of the most important and powerful Australian industrialists was a blunt, demanding and authoritarian man. Essington Lewis presided over the development of Australia's steel industry in the period in which it became one of the most competitive in the world; after a visit in 1934 to Japan and Europe, seeing the need to prepare for a world war, he made plans for Australia to build aircraft and ships and manufacture munitions.

Essington Lewis was born in Burra, South Australia, in 1881, of country pioneering stock. His father, John Lewis, became a rich property owner and ironically (in hindsight) named his son Essington after the failed settlement on the Gulf of Carpentaria; apparently the name had been chosen because John Lewis liked it and the tough connotations of a deserted tropical Australian harbour. The young Essington was caught between his love of life on the land and his desire for further education. In 1905, having studied mining engineering at the South Australian School of Mines, he joined the Broken Hill Proprietary Company as a miner at five shillings a day, to get practical experience. Ten years later he was

chosen to establish BHP's iron and steel industry at Newcastle, and he was to orchestrate the takeovers that by 1935 had given BHP a monopoly in Australian steel.

On his frequent long train trips around eastern Australia to oversee company business, Lewis would read reports and study the small notebooks into which he crammed an enormous amount of information. He was BHP's managing director or chief general manager from 1926 to 1950, continuing to hold the job after he accepted a position in Menzies' War Cabinet in 1940. As Director-General of Munitions, Lewis had powers so sweeping that the position was described as 'the most responsible ever allocated to an Australian', and as that of an 'industrial dictator'.

When Lewis retired as Chairman of BHP in 1952, although remaining Deputy Chairman and a Director of Subsidiaries, he went back to his first love, the land, spending more time at Landscape, his country property, occasionally reading the works of Henry Lawson or Banjo Paterson or riding his horse. It was at Landscape, when Essington Lewis was 80, that his horse slipped on steep, rough ground. Horse and rider fell together, and the strong man died instantly.

producing high internal costs. The population, not reaching seven million until 1940, was small, and with Australia so far away from 'world markets' this small population seemed the only market. Manufacturers, both Australian and those foreigners, mostly British, who had been persuaded to set up in Australia, fell back on the Government; a Tariff Board had been set up in 1921 to recommend protective duties, and while higher protection encouraged efficiency in some cases – the BHP was the most notable – in others it simply supported high prices.

While this period saw investment in manufacturing becoming significant (if mainly in New South Wales), most factories apart from the heavy industries were still short of capital. The banks were the main regulators of capital, and bankers were very conservative. The Commonwealth Bank, although its board was government-appointed, was given an independent status by the Nationalists and, if anything, it turned out to be even more conservative than the private banks. The whole financial machine was still partly that of a farmers' and merchants' society, and while governments were still big investors they in fact distorted investment by putting so much money into uneconomic rural programs –

sometimes, in the case of the Nationalists, to the irritation of some of their own supporters. An Australian Industries Protection League and a campaign journal, the *Australasian Manufacturer*, were set up to harass governments, but what they wanted most was protection of their own weaknesses. In manufacturing, there was scarcely any understanding of technological innovation and, apart from the half-hearted attempts to foster an Australian-designed motorcar and a native motor industry, governments showed practically no effective interest in developing manufacturing technology. Since Australia was a country where private enterprise was increasingly dependent on government backing, this meant that in manufacturing it remained very largely in a state of babyhood, depending on other societies to do the thinking.

Two great distractions helped take attention away from this lack of effective manufacturing 'development'. One was the enormous delight Australians took in the growth of aviation. At a time when there were scarcely any special issues of stamps, three of the first eight special issues were devoted to aviation, one of them to Kingsford Smith, seen as the greatest of 'the aviators' who, along with sporting stars, made up Australia's heroes. They were a modern

W.J. Smith (nicknamed both 'Knockout' Smith and 'Gunboat' Smith) was one of the few enterprising industrialists of the period (above). He started life as an apprentice glass-blower and, through a series of brutal mergers, ended his career as managing director of Australian Consolidated Industries, which, among other things, virtually monopolised the glass-making industry in Australia. He was, however, more a tough company manipulator and improviser than an industrial innovator.

The cult of 'the aviators': *the aviators, like Charles Kingsford Smith (above right), were among Australia's greatest heroes. The fact that they were using a modern vehicle, the aeroplane, could give Australia a more modern look than its manufacturing industry merited. When the Australian Government in 1919 offered £10 000 prize money for the first Australian flight from England to Australia, Ross and Keith Smith, two brothers who had served as pilots during the war, and two sergeant-mechanics, covered the route in 27 days 20 hours. Above, Ross Smith receives a hero's welcome.*

The myth of 'the Bridge': *Australians saw Sydney Harbour Bridge as an example of how Australia was becoming a modern industrial society, although in fact Australian manufacturing was still weak. The Bridge became a popular gimmick for advertisers (right), where the Bridge traffic is in chaos and 'Minties' are called for. It was also a popular subject for artists. Grace Cossington Smith painted* The Bridge in Curve *(far right) in 1931.*

version of the 'explorers' Australians were taught at school to revere as the greatest of Australians. Along with the opening of airmail services, the bravery and dash of the aviators appeared to associate Australia with a technological progress towards which, in fact, it was not making any contribution. (A small Commonwealth Air Corporation was, however, set up in the late 1930s – by the Government.) The other great distraction from the weakness. of Australian manufacturing (also meriting a special stamp issue) came with the opening of the Sydney Harbour Bridge – an event reported 'as it happened' by a national network of 40 wireless stations. The bridge, largely the product of British engineers, was projected as one of the wonders of the world ('Across Sydney Harbour has been thrown the greatest bridge of the age.'), and as a result of it, Sydney was declared to be 'a New York in miniature'.

In so far as it was industrialising, Australia was doing so without developing some of the social characteristics of an industrial society: it was sufficiently like the innovative industrial societies in other countries to be able to take over their innovations into a high-cost system protected by tariffs, but this occurred so relatively easily that it did not

throw up strongly all the new institutions and types of people usually produced by industrialisation.

Technical education, although more prominent, went prominently backwards. As modern industry's increasing diversification made the apprenticeship system even less efficient than it had been, it was the apprenticeship system that became the main basis of technical training in Australia. In 1934 a Royal Commission reported on the 'shocking inadequacies of the entire system' of technical education; in 1939 another Royal Commission said that most efforts were 'half-hearted and belated'. There were no courses in management or marketing or schools in industrial design, or any indication that the making of business decisions might require training of any kind. And although non-Labor parties seemed to put as much trust in government intervention as the Labor Party, no special attention was given to the recruiting of government officials. Until 1933 there was no provision for admission of graduates, although some State public services instituted small cadet schemes. The Commonwealth Treasury was run by accountants, and when things went wrong the Government had to appoint a committee of university

economists to see what had happened because it had no economists of its own.

Australia was still failing to provide a wide educated class with a confident sense of its own importance. Expenditure on education was less than in the United States, Britain, Canada and New Zealand. By the end of the 1930s, when the United States was planning that all children between 14 and 18 should be at secondary schools, in Australia the proportion was less than a quarter; in Queensland it had dropped from 17 per cent in 1921 to 13 per cent in 1939. In the schools and universities between 1920 and 1940 there were hardly any curriculum or even textbook changes. In 1935 a United States expert reported that Australian libraries lagged behind those of most civilised countries; at an international New Educational Fellowship Conference in Canberra in 1937 most of the visiting speakers attacked Australia's backwardness.

There was an extra difficulty: Australia was industrialising at a time when British enterprise had run down. The lack of interest in vocational education was British, the very amateurishness of some Australian decision-makers was British (if without a classical education, and sometimes tempered by more astuteness, energy and adaptability). Although some Australian leaders knew of the importance of science in German industry and of the importance of education for businessmen in the United States, they could not impose these ideas on a British-derived education system in which honour was given to uselessness. Among the decision-makers, Nationalist or Labor, business boss or union boss, education was so little considered that not even its uselessness was honoured; that education could be useful seemed even more ridiculous.

There was a slow but important development as 500 committees with 5000 members set about the long task of

The CSIR achieved a scientific breakthrough in the late 1920s with the Cactoblastis *moth, which destroyed prickly pear (top). Hundreds of square kilometres were cleared in a few months (above).*

coordinating industrial standards, looking for what was best in current practice. In 1939 a National Standards Laboratory was established; chemists, engineers and physicists' institutes were formed; there was sufficient specialisation in radio research at Amalgamated Wireless Australasia (AWA) and at Sydney University (where it led to the establishment of a secret radio-physics laboratory) for a Radio Research Board to be set up; but with very few exceptions (AWA was one of them) there was no serious research in private firms. Even the steel industry sponsored little private research. The pattern of Australian industry was that in foreign-owned firms the parent company told the Australian company what to do, and Australian-owned firms bought ideas from other countries.

The post-graduate schools of science and technology were weak, so, in the manner of colonial governmentalism, a government research body, the Council for Scientific and Industrial Research, set up in 1926 despite opposition from the universities, became the dominant force in Australian scientific research. To 'progress with the times', Australia needed 'the most modern and efficient scientific methods'. The CSIR rented some rooms in Melbourne and began a program that was to provide a thorough research base for Australian farming. It achieved one early success – popular enough to get into the newspapers – in destroying the prickly pear, which had infested about 25 million hectares, in some cases smothering whole districts. Tests had revealed that the caterpillars of the *Cactoblastis* moth from Argentina and South Brazil would do the job; by 1930, 3000 million of their eggs had been distributed with such effectiveness that hundreds of square kilometres of prickly pear could be destroyed in a few months. In 1929 CSIR set up a Soils Division, beginning a long study of the fragility of Australia's greatest 'natural resource' – the soil itself. In the 1930s, partly because of publicity given on the newsreels to the United States 'dustbowls', some Australians were beginning to speak of 'soil erosion'. The CSIR was a model of a rational concern for Improvement: its general research provided a better basis for expanding rural industries and opening out opportunities for new ones, such as timber growing for paper manufacture. But apart from the establishment of an Aeronautics Division, its concern was almost completely with farming.

A class of businessmen now demanded all the esteem of industrial innovators. But in fact they were not innovators, although sometimes they were improvisers. Rhetoric about the importance of 'private enterprise' was strong, but the ideas behind the enterprise were of foreign origin and its practice usually by virtue of government support and protection. Sometimes the very stridency of these claims seemed an expression of the half-realised anxieties of people who claimed a status they had not earned, and which, by and large, would not be given by the ordinary people, who, if they were going to bestow it on anybody, still preferred to bestow status on doctors, squatters and other nobs. In a nation in which the styles of industrial activity were rapidly becoming significant, the pretences of 'enterprise' spread through significant parts of Australian society, perhaps helping to spread an atmosphere of derivativeness and second-ratedness.

At first when two Australian loans failed in London early in 1929, this appeared merely a matter for the banks, but by the year's end, stock market values in the United States had fallen by £26 billion and the world's economy seemed stricken by plague.

Australia was so quickly and drastically infected (wool prices dropped by half and the London money market had collapsed) that its whole financial system appeared about to die from this new and mysterious rottenness. For several months, with a Treasury Department run by book-keepers, the Commonwealth Government didn't know what to do. Then it put together a 'tariff wall', which blocked half Australia's imports and started a 'grow-more-wheat campaign'; this was followed by a disastrous fall in the price of wheat. The exchange rate was devalued – not by the Government, but by a private bank. The crisis extended to government budgets and for several months the New South Wales Government defaulted, with the Commonwealth paying its debts. Then in May 1931, governments agreed, in the 'Premiers' Plan', to cut salaries and pensions by 20 per cent (except old age pensions which went down 12.5 per cent) and to increase taxes and reduce interest rates. After two years Australian governments had a policy for what was now known as 'the Depression'; but by then unemployment was up to 27 per cent. By 1933 nearly a third of breadwinners were out of work.

For many, life went on much as usual: for those who wanted it, among the rich there was still 'the social whirl' and most middle-class and lower-middle-class people simply had to make do with less – lose a servant perhaps if they were well-off enough to have one, or do without hired help, or cut out the telephone and a few other extras, or, at the worst, take a job that was beneath them. Some working-class people were actually better off. However, even for the lucky there was the question of how long their luck would last. (Expectations were low: the birth rate dropped.) For the unlucky, they were unemployed in a country that had no scheme for unemployment pensions. Many families had furniture seized by debt collectors. Others were evicted by rent collectors. If they couldn't find somewhere to live with relatives, the men might 'hit the track' as swaggies; families might be reduced to living in humpies of scrap timber and galvanised iron in one of the 'happy valleys' on the outskirts of the cities (which then became objects of interest for more fortunate families who were going for a weekend 'spin' in their motorcars).

Apart from tripe, and occasionally mutton, meat might almost disappear from family meals: it was a time for treacle and bread and dripping. Women patched, darned and re-made clothes for those who were still looking for work or for children going to school; they turned sugar bags into aprons or towels and flour bags into underwear; domestic improvements were made with strips of hessian. There was some relief work, but not for everyone, and it offered only one or two days work a week for those who could get it. Most of the unemployed were reduced to handouts – they queued up for the dole or 'susso' (sustenance) food vouchers, sometimes food itself, sometimes old clothes or clothes left over from the Great War. For unemployed women, apart from a few short-lived sewing centres or jam-making centres, there was no relief work, and for most of them not even the dole. In Victoria, the Minister for Sustenance said there was no justification for giving 'susso' to women so long as domestic service (at any wage, under any conditions) was available anywhere in Victoria.

There were unemployed mass meetings and mass marches and anti-eviction picketings; on a few occasions of desperation the dole itself was declared black and dole offices were picketed, but these could be dismissed as the work of 'red raggers' (as, in fact, they sometimes were, since it was the Communists who formed and led the Unemployed Workers' Movement.) In Broken Hill or Wonthaggi a whole town could show responsibility towards the unemployed: at Wonthaggi in 1934 most of the town went communal during a long strike, and enjoyed a famous victory. But usually there seemed nothing ordinary people could do – beyond voting against governments. They did this with pleasure, as, one by one, each of the country's seven governments was thrown out of office. Whether the governments were Labor or Nationalist did not matter: if they were in, they should be thrown out. In Canberra the

Economic manager: Sir Otto Niemeyer

Otto Niemeyer, financial expert from the Bank of England, could not have imagined the notoriety he would achieve by coming to Australia in 1930, at the invitation of the Scullin Labor Government, to advise on the management of the Great Depression. According to his bitter opponent, New South Wales Labor leader Jack Lang, Niemeyer believed that 'Australians were enjoying a champagne income standard of living on a small beer income'.

While most politicians meekly accepted Niemeyer's advice on lowering costs and paying overseas debts, Jack Lang believed that Sir Otto's remedies were worse than the economic depression they were intended to cure. To Lang, interest repayments on overseas loans at such a time would only make near-financial chaos worse.

On 22 September 1930, after the New South Wales conservative government had resigned, Jack Lang delivered a fiery election policy speech, and later wrote: 'If London proposed to make Repudiation the issue, then I intended to make Sir Otto Niemeyer my political chopping block. He had asked for it. He had butted into our domestic affairs. So the fight became centred around the Niemeyer Mission almost exclusively. It was almost as if Sir Otto was himself standing for election. The people of this State were to vote for or against his programme. It was a ... unique position for a Director of the Bank of England to find himself in.'

Lang won the election, only to be dismissed from office two years later. Sir Otto returned to England and later carried out similar economic missions in Greece, Egypt, Argentina, India and China. In Australian memories of the Depression he became as much a symbol of British arrogance as bodyline bowling.

Labor Party had come to government just before the Wall Street crash. Baffled by its own ignorance, divided by personal factionalism and idealogical differences and blocked by a hostile Senate and a hostile Commonwealth Bank, it split into three parts and then lost an election so disastrously that it again seemed a naturally defeated party. As in Britain, what seemed to be 'the workers' party' had, at a time when the workers needed it, let them down.

It was a time of hopeful slogans ... 'Grow More Wheat' ... 'Share The Burden' ... 'Balanced Budgets And More Employment'. There was a battle of plans: some were concerned, above all, with maintaining the confidence of London financiers; some with spreading the burden more evenly; some with providing large public works programs; some with cutting wages and balancing budgets. The Theodore Plan, named after the Federal Treasurer, urged a mild deficit expansion; the Lang Plan, named after the New South Wales Labor Premier, urged default; the Premiers' Plan decided on deflation. Appeals were made to wartime memories ('Let the whole world know that the heart of Australia is sound, that her people possess the same fighting spirit in peace as they showed in war'), and to the love of

cricket ('The greatest Test Match of them all – to be won').

To some, it seemed a time to end ordinary politics. For the Communists, this would come with the revolution; for the followers of 'Social Credit' it would come with a simple reform of the credit system. On the right, new groups were forming (the All for Australia League, the Soldiers and Citizens' Party, the Emergency Committee of South Australia, the Sane Democracy League, the Liberation League, the Citizens' Federation), and among some of them there was a desire to do away with 'sectional' party politics and replace them either with all-party governments or with governments of businessmen and others who were 'above party', or by closing down parliaments altogether and setting up a National Council, or even a dictator. (One group wanted John Monash as dictator.) There was some talk of the inevitability of fascism. Right-wing revolution threatened New South Wales when Jack Lang attacked the 'Shylocks of London' and tried to turn the depression and his concern for maintaining his own strength in the Labor Party into a great drama of his own righteousness. A 'New Guard' formed to put out 'the bushfire of Langism' – a secret paramilitary organisation claiming 100 000 members,

A great divide: *the Great Depression of the 1930s marked one of the periods of open division in Australian society, exemplified in a 1932 cartoon (below). A huge minority lived in, or near, destitution: the worst that could happen to those who had jobs was that they were worse off; some, including wage earners, were comparatively better off. Both the realities of rural poverty and the indomitable spirit of the poor are expressed in this 'snap' of a country family lined up outside the makeshift shack into which harsh circumstances had forced them (right).*

led mainly by ex-officers with support mostly from angry and frightened middle-class and lower-middle-class men, organised in zones, divisions and localities, each with its own commander, with orders ready for mobilisation. Plans were made by cliques of Returned Men and others in country towns to set up provisional governments for three secessionist States, which would proclaim rebellion when coded telegrams came from Sydney. As it turned out, although fighting the national Government with a second default and seizing documents and funds to keep things going, Lang went when the Governor dismissed him.

The Theodore Plan (whether it was Theodore's own work is debated) was one of the few constructive ideas put up by a member of government anywhere in the world at the time, but both Left and Right moved in to destroy it. Appeals to sacrifice were preferred. When a newly formed 'United Australia Party' took over from Labor (the Nationalists under another name, but with Joe Lyons, one of the men who had split from Labor, as leader) it proclaimed those principles of 'sound finance' that the banks had forced on it. Remembering the disgrace of the Australian bank crashes of the 1890s, and terrified of the German kind of financial disintegration if the politicians took over, the banks pressed only for policies of debt servicing. In a time of despair, when people gathered in city halls to keep up their spirits with community singing, when as many as a hundred thousand could attend a protest meeting, and when the world was so absorbed in its own misery that it had no time to remember Australia, the idea of paying interest on debts seemed something to cling to. To some it was a test of 'Australia's good name', in which the fate of the unemployed represented their individual sacrifice, as, earlier, had the deaths of the Diggers. There was a great deal of self-congratulation by those concerned that the Premiers' Plan had balanced the budgets. Men had not lost their jobs in vain: Australia's reputation was again good in the city of London.

It seemed obvious that cuts in wages and other costs would help the farmers, in whose hands Australia's future still lay, and when the world prices of farm products again went up, prosperity would be found around that elusive corner which was now the subject of so many jokes. But although governments looked to the farms for recovery, as they had looked to them for development, recovery came

Protest: *the favourite form of presentation of the unemployed was as passive victims of unavoidable fate, as in this Tasmanian photograph of a Depression family (left). When there were protests, they were likely to be presented as threats. A protest march in Adelaide (above) was described as a 'riot', and police on horses and motor bicycles 'dispersed' the 'rioters'.*

Some of the most publicised victims of the Depression were men who 'hit the track' as swaggies (far left). It was sometimes forgotten that women suffered as much, and coped as well, as men. Household chores and child-raising were done under miserable conditions, and in the case of this woman in a slum outside Sydney (left), done with dignity.

earliest, strongest and quickest from the factories; a trend not noticed by governments, or at least not commented on. It was expanded manufacturing production, stimulated by the rise in protection, by the restriction of imports and by cuts in domestic costs, which put people back into work.

Despite whatever moves that were made towards a sense of national unity, the Depression heightened the politics of envy. Western Australia saw the Depression as a plot from the East and voted for secession. South Australia developed a State nationalism, with plans for attracting enough industry to bring its population of 600 000 up to Queensland's million. Tasmania hoped by re-afforestation and hydroelectric plants to at least keep its quarter of a million population from drifting to the mainland. Victoria, with less than two million people, envied New South Wales its two and three-quarter million. Melbourne, which now saw itself as 'the most British' of the cities, attacked the 'Americanisation' of Sydney. But in both States there was a mood of such dispirited caution that even envy could not arouse hope for any sense in constructive policies. Even as the rates of unemployment began to fall to the 1920s' level, shock and uncertainty remained. For many, the Depression

had been as critical an experience as the Great War and, although no granite monuments went up to it, it remained a despondent memory in unions and Labor parties and in many individual hearts. Frightened of their budgets, governments kept silent on questions of hospitals, schools, slum clearance, city transport and social security; although manufacturing was expanding, politicians and writers, traditionally bound to see Australian expansionism as a rural matter, ceased to speak of Australia's future. Immigration had stopped. There were forecasts of a decline in population. A book, *The Myth of the Open Spaces*, helped some Australians to see themselves as a nation that must necessarily remain small forever, a country hemmed in by difficulties and limitations, in which nothing very new could be done.

Despair: *the mood of despair that came with the Great Depression continued to be represented in painting, as in Yosi Bergner's* Pumpkins *(right) and Vic O'Connor's* The Dispossessed *(below right), both painted in 1942 when the economy had received a boost from Australia's involvement in the war.*

Conflict: *the bitterness of political division during the Great Depression is exemplified in the opposing personalities of, on the one hand, J.T. Lang (right), Labor Premier of New South Wales and here caricatured by George Finey, seen as a near-bolshevik by his opponents, and dismissed in 1932 by New South Wales Governor Sir Philip Game; and on the other hand Eric Campbell (below), a Sydney businessman who organised a secret army, the New Guard, against Lang, and was seen as a Fascist by his opponents.*

Among the Left, there could also be positive expressions of hope. Noel Counihan sketched Workers Demonstrate Against War *in 1933 (below), signing it 'Cunningham' so that he could still claim the dole.*

15. Tuning in to Britain: 1919 to 1939

The ties of Empire were strengthened deliberately by the British after the war: there were visits from three royal princes. Australia's role was to support the mother country's industrial might with a farming policy; manufactures could be imported from Britain; there was a policy of 'Imperial Defence'. Australia remained a provincial society, but among some there was a yearning for greater maturity and sophistication. Foreign theatre and ballet companies toured, and the ABC established concert orchestras in each State capital. Canberra, the Federal capital, was built although the States reaffirmed their own importance with a series of pageants to honour the start of white settlement. Aborigines played a minor part in these celebrations – they remained an oppressed race, suffering under inhumane restrictions.

The creed of the Black Hats

The Governor General had written in 1917 that he feared Australia might develop 'a weakening of a sense of dependence in the Mother Country'. As part of a concern that Australia and Canada should stay loyally dependent, the Prince of Wales was sent to both countries as soon as possible after the return of their troops.

The Prince stayed in Australia for six weeks, visiting 110 towns: in Melbourne there developed such a craze to touch him that he had to take a week off to recover. In Sydney he let people meet him by walking past him, for two and a half hours, 12 abreast. His great themes were those of war, empire and loyalty. In speech after speech he told those who had come to see him that he would report their loyalty back to his father. His speeches reached an emotional climax in a feudal pledge: 'As Australia stands by the Empire, so will the Empire stand by Australia.'

The rhetoric of Empire was even greater than that of White Australia and the Anzac spirit. In fact the simple stoicism of Anzac Day and its democratic nationalism that turned the ideal Australian into the Digger, with much the same characteristics as the earlier bushman, became weakened by its forms of ceremony. What came to seem most Australian about it were the drinking and chiacking that took place when the formal rituals were over. In the ceremony itself, the Protestant and British God of 'Onward Christian Soldiers' took over so that Australia's national day became partly imperialist. It was true that many Australians still distrusted 'the poms' – and when the English developed bodyline bowling as a cricket tactic, with the ball bowled not at the wicket but at the batsman's body, the perfidy of the poms was there for all to see. But except for occasional outbreaks from the Labor Party, it was the creed of the Black Hats that usually prevailed in public rhetoric and ceremonies. There was even a literal concern with Black Hats: a criticism of Lang and other Labor men was that on formal occasions they refused to wear top hats.

Englishmen were still appointed archbishops and headmasters; Stanley Bruce, the Nationalist Prime Minister of the 1920s, had been educated in England, had gone to the bar in England and had taken his wartime commission in an English regiment. Loosely connected groups of Anglophiles were sustained both by a self-interested belief that Australia's prosperity depended on Britain and its very existence on the British Navy, and by a mystical belief that the ideals of the late 19th-century British version of the New Imperialism represented the greatest degree of civilisation known to man. They commanded most of the high places of national aspiration. At times their fellow countrymen appeared barbarians who must be kept pledged to the distant imperial metropolis. Against the alleged thinness of Australian life (its lack of depth and 'history') and the assumed mediocrity of Australians were set the challenges of sacred words … the Throne, the British heritage, the Mother of Parliaments, the Bank of England.

Royal occasions: *three British princes visited Australia between the two wars – the Prince of Wales was the first, in 1920, to maintain 'the bonds of loyalty sealed in blood' during the Great War.*

There were affronted outbursts when it became known that the Commonwealth Labor Government wanted an Australian as Governor General, and it was only after Prime Minister Scullin threatened King George V with an election or a referendum that Scullin won. Two royal dukes toured Australia, one in 1927 and one in 1934 (along with the English Poet Laureate and the band of the Grenadier Guards). Canada abolished British honours in 1935, but only the Labor Party opposed them in Australia. In 1920 a Labor member was expelled from the Federal Parliament because he criticised British policy in Ireland; some book censorship was directed against works that blasphemed the Empire. At the founding of the colony in 1788, Phillip and his officers drank two toasts – one to the King and one to the colony's success; at the luncheon celebrating the building of Canberra there was no toast to Australia – the one toast (in fruit cup) was to the British King.

Only the British (in the 'Empire Settlement Scheme') were sought as immigrants, although the Italians and Yugoslavs who came in unsought were more suited to the ideals of closer settlement, since they actually wanted to be peasants. In the north Queensland cane fields and in some irrigation districts in the southern States, Italians were the principal successful settlers, but their success – more widespread when Italian immigration to the United States was restricted – stirred a sense of threat and envy. In 1934, at Kalgoorlie in Western Australia, miners looted Italian and Yugoslav shops and clubs and burned down 50 houses, then for three days conducted a 'dago hunt'.

Even the 'Yanks' were criticised – for taking so long to get into the war, for being bad soldiers, for rejecting the League of Nations, for causing the Depression. 'Americanisation' was attacked, but the United States' promise of independence to the Philippines was also attacked – as a Yankee desertion of the West Pacific.

Labor had had enough of a world whose wars and depressions brought party splits, but the Nationalists and then the United Australia Party (UAP) that replaced them put their trust in the idea of 'Empire defence'. This belief was fostered by the 1923 Imperial Conference decision to build a naval base at Singapore for Pacific defence, a belief that still survived when the base was finished in 1939, although it was a base without a fleet. The Department of the Chief of the General Staff of the Australian Army was

Once a Labor Premier in Tasmania, then a defector from the Federal Labor Government because he found it too radical, 'Joe' Lyons was Prime Minister of Australia for most of the 1930s at a period of great conservatism. He took to wearing a 'black hat' (left) as if he were born to it.

Official Introductions on the Wharf at Port Melbourne

The Duke of York visited in 1927, to open the first Parliament held in Canberra (top), and the Duke of Gloucester came in 1934, to attend the bicentenary celebration of the 'founding' of white settlement in Victoria (above).

Stanley Melbourne Bruce was the most British-looking of all Australian prime ministers. His whole economic policy was one of fitting Australia into the Empire's economic framework. From a patrician Melbourne merchant family, he was educated at Cambridge, and during the Great War he served in an English regiment. Bruce poses, in 1923, in front of his Rolls Royce (above).

called 'Australian Section, Imperial General Staff'. At the end of the 1930s, British officers were at the head of the Australian Army, Navy and Air Force. The Irish Free State and Canada set up independent diplomatic services, but Australia did not even adopt the Statute of Westminster, which offered it independent status, until 1942. The Nationalists and the UAP believed that Britain should consult Australia on matters of foreign policy but mainly because, as Bruce said in the 1920s, 'We have to try to ensure that there shall be an Empire foreign policy.'

The United Australia Party's slogan was 'All for Australia and the Empire', and when Joe Lyons, its leader, fought his first election, he added a contemporaneous touch with another slogan – 'Tune in to Britain'. As well as being a partner in 'Empire defence', Australia was part of 'the Empire as an economic unit'. The overriding concern for meeting overseas debt payments during the Depression at the cost of so much extra unemployment had come from a sense of loyalty to London: most of the world's other debtor countries had suspended debt payments or reduced them and then negotiated a moratorium, but the Australian Government had invited a governor of the Bank of England to come to Australia and tell it what to do. In the 1920s, when the Queensland Labor Government put up the rents of government grazing land, the London money market boycotted a new Queensland loan. The Queensland Government campaigned against the 'absentee capitalists' and 'money lords of London', then gave in. London loan money resumed – a quarter per cent higher in interest. The whole Empire Settlement Scheme idea that had prompted the 'development' fiascoes of the 1920s was British, formalised in a special Imperial Conference in 1921: if the Empire were to be an economic unit, 'a redistribution of the white population of the Empire' should be made from its heart to its periphery, where it could produce raw materials for the Mother Country. The policy of 'men, money and markets' meant that Australia should encourage the emigration of surplus British population to Australia, where they could be placed on farms developed on money borrowed in London and produce raw materials to send back to Britain. The whole emphasis on rural development and the lack of concern for manufacturing was part of a larger plan for economic development in which Australia's role was to support Britain's industrial might with a farming policy. Australia did not need to develop a strong, independent manufacturing industry. Why develop manufactures when they could be imported from Britain?

The most extraordinary expression of Australia's 'loyalty' came with the 1935 trade diversion policy when, after representations from British commercial interests in Australia, the Commonwealth Government prohibited the import of certain goods outside the British Empire except under licence. Imports from the United States and Japan were restricted in the hope that this would benefit British manufacturers. Japan was Australia's second-best customer for wool, and cheap Japanese imports were to Australia's benefit; but imports from Japan were against British commercial interests, Japan having replaced Britain as Australia's largest supplier of textiles. So, in response to the British textile lobby, Australia risked its own exports by imposing heavy duties on Japanese textiles. The United States administration was merely bemused, but the Japanese at once banned the import of Australian wool and wheat. Having lost one of their best customers, the Australians gave in. However, the incident had frightened the Japanese, and when they resumed purchases from Australia it was at a smaller rate. They increased their research into synthetic substitutes for wool.

More royal occasions: *as well as the arrival in Australia of royal princes, there were great events in London – jubilees, births, deaths, marriages and a coronation – to be celebrated in the Australian Press and on the radio. And when there weren't any special occasions there were 'royal personalities' to read about.* The Australian Women's Weekly, *founded in 1933, celebrated King George V's Silver Jubilee in 1935 with a portrait of his wife, Queen Mary (left).*

Princess Elizabeth

In 1937 the Weekly, *having discovered that nothing sold better than a cover featuring a royal person, ran a special cover story on Princess Elizabeth, 'the girl who would be Queen' (above).*

THE AUSTRALIAN
WOMEN'S WEEKLY

MOTHER *of* EMPIRE

Although there was now no Deakin or Hughes to give meaning to political action, Australians did not lack national heroes or a sense of achievement. Olympic swimmers and Wimbledon tennis players were seen as carrying on the work of the Diggers in putting Australia on the map.

When 'Boy' Charlton won the 1500 metres gold medal at the 1924 Olympics, one newspaper proclaimed BOY CHARLTON'S FEAT AMAZES THE WHOLE WORLD. The aviators, in their desperate flights across oceans and continents, competing for prizes or sponsored by governments or businessmen, sometimes finding death, sometimes tens of thousands of cheering people, seemed as great as sporting stars. Of the two greatest Australians – the cricketer Don Bradman ('Our Don') and the racehorse Phar Lap – Bradman was the symbol of equality of opportunity, the boy from the bush whose effigy stood in Madame Tussaud's, and Phar Lap was a symbol of Australian gameness; when he died his heart was put on display in Canberra so that people could see how big it was.

In school histories Australia was a place notable for being 'discovered' and for the fortitude of those who explored it. But other than the explorers, there was little in their history of which young Australians were taught to be proud. The Government schools saw the real basis of Australian liberty in Magna Carta, Simon de Montfort's Parliament, the English Civil War, the Great Rebellion of 1688, and other victories by English oligarchs. Young Australians learnt nothing of their country's history as a pioneer in social and political reform, nor any history of social struggle, nor any distinctive views of themselves as Australians, except as explorers or fighting men.

But while the ethos of mateship was not in school texts, the idea of the Australian as larrikin still had commercial success. In the vaudeville chain of the Tivoli theatres, comics such as the team of Stiffy and Mo, or George Wallace, maintained a larrikin humour that gained an extra edge because it was seen as vulgar by suburbanites. A new publication, *Smith's Weekly*, based much of its success on the idea of the Digger as larrikin. And there was still commercial appeal in the idea of 'the bush'. In book publishing, most of the best-selling lines were in

Heroes: *as well as the Diggers, seen as collective heroes, and the aviators, seen as great individualists, Australians chose sporting stars for their heroes. The swimmer Andrew ('Boy') Charlton (below), first of the post-war sporting stars, gained headlines in 1924 when, at the age of 16, at a contest in Sydney, he beat the world champion and equalled the record for 440 yards, and five days later beat him in the 220 yards. Charlton then went on to win a gold medal at that year's Olympics.*

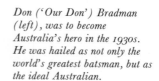

Don ('Our Don') Bradman (left), was to become Australia's hero in the 1930s. He was hailed as not only the world's greatest batsman, but as the ideal Australian.

One of the most popular 1930s heroes was the racehorse Phar Lap (below), whose mysterious death in America was to give him a permanent place in Australian sporting history.

'outbackery' (a 1920s writer complained of 'the absence of publishers interested in anything but bushranger yarns, south-sea romances, or studies of flying foxes').

Australian-made movies had titles like *The Man from Kangaroo*, *A Girl of the Bush*, *The Hayseeds* or *Orphan of the Wilderness* ('Gloriously Refreshing Romance Amid the Grandeur of Australia's Great Outdoors'), which showed the typical Australian as engaged in the taming of nature – a view that matched Australian export policy. In that way in which images of the world can support economic interests (whether this is consciously planned or not) the ideal of Australia as 'the bush' was exactly the kind of view that matched Empire economic policy. One of the most virulent supporters of bush painting said that the great landscapes of Australian grazing country pointed 'to the way in which life should be lived in Australia, with the maximum of flocks and the minimum of factories'. (He then added, 'If we so choose we can yet be the elect of the world, the last of the pastoralists, the thoroughbred Aryans in all their nobility.')

In painting, the Impressionist rebels of the 1890s had all become reactionary; two became knights. Modern painting could be rejected as 'elaborate and pretentious bosh'... 'the work of perverts'. As to the bush itself ... most Australians, being suburbanites, saw it only on holidays or on 'chop picnics'. When 'hiking' came to Australia it was naturalised as 'bushwalking', and accompanied at times by some small amount of interest in the bush itself. But apart from the national parks, in the setting up of which, along with the United States, Australia was a pioneer, 'the bush' was, in economic terms, simply an impediment to economic expansion, and even the national parks were mainly picnic areas. It was only in Tasmania, where the Government set up a Scenery Preservation Board, that the bush, as wilderness, was seen as being worthy of being preserved.

The novel *Such is Life*, by Joseph Furphy ('temper democratic; bias offensively Australian'), although published in 1903, did not come into its own until the 1930s, by which time it was an inspiration to new novelists (as many of them women as men) trying to give an idea of what it might be like to be an Australian, a concern at that time largely confined to novelists. One of the woman novelists said, 'My work has been, I think, knowing the Australian people and interpreting them to themselves.' But the Australian people these novelists interpreted were not

ME PAL 'E TROTS 'ER UP AN' DOES THE TOFF 'E ALLUS WUS A BLOKE FER SHOWIN' OFF. "THIS 'ERE'S DOREEN," 'E SEZ. — "THIS 'ERE'S THE KID." — I DIPS ME LID —

Australian 'movies': *although Australian film makers between the wars also attempted films with international themes, two of the great stand-bys for the film makers were to present Australians as a people of the bush, or as larrikins.* The Sentimental Bloke, *based on the best selling book, was twice made into a movie (above). There was another successful remake of a silent movie in* The Hayseeds *(right), which was a crude play on old themes. An 'on location' shoot by Ken G. Hall for* Orphan of the Wilderness *in 1935 (above right) shows Hall successfully bringing Hollywood approaches to the bush.*

The tradition of the Australian as larrikin was carried on between the wars most convincingly by Smith's Weekly, *a paper especially aimed at 'the Returned Men'. Stan Cross was a prolific cartoonist for* Smith's Weekly. *His drawing captioned 'For gorsake, stop laughing: this is serious!' (left) became a famous joke. Some humour was racist (above left): 'Now did you strike him in the face, or vice versa?' 'In der face boss. I bin kick him in der vice versa afterwards!'*

usually suburbanite – if they did live in suburbs they were unhappy about it – and mateship was still seen as the Australian creed. When he was safely dead, Henry Lawson, given a State Funeral, became 'National Poet': a statue went up to him in Sydney's Domain. Mateship might now sometimes be intellectualised into an Improver's liberal humanism, but with its belief in human goodness now rendered impotent by scepticism about the possibility of successful action.(Some of the greatest opportunities for goodness were seen in the accommodations of the unsuccessful to their lack of success.) A composer sought a vocabulary of Australian sounds in bird cries and the other noises of the bush, and in the late 1930s the 'Jindyworobaks', an Adelaide-centred group, sought Australian-ness from the Aborigines, writing poetry that adopted Aboriginal words and explored Aboriginal legends.

On the Left the Eureka Stockade was still a pivotal point, particularly to Marxists; perhaps because, through an error in translation, they thought Marx had written about it. Some saw the unions and the Labor Party as the main, or the only, agents of progress in Australia's history: as part of this purpose the 1890s shearers' strikes were given a special significance, and political history was interpreted so as to turn the Improvers into agents of reaction. Some Melbourne intellectuals began to believe that they were the repository of an Australian democratic traditon that had flowered in the 1890s.

In Sydney a countervailing cosmopolitanism decried as provincial all that was traditionally 'Australian' and claimed for itself a unique international excellence. Christopher Brennan, a Sydney professor, was described as 'the only genuine *symboliste* poet in the English language'. Around the artist Norman Lindsay in the 1920s gathered a number of people who proclaimed a renaissance of world culture in Sydney with artists who had 'gay hearts and the courage of their desires'; and around the Philosophy Professor John Anderson in the 1930s was a group that saw Sydney University as the only significant centre of philosophy in the world. (Even Jack Lang was pronounced by his Sydney followers to be 'greater than Lenin'.)

There were strong desires for greater 'maturity' and 'sophistication'. The long tradition of commercially successful tours by foreign opera companies that had made opera an intermittent part of Australian entertainment

Given a State funeral after his death in 1922, Henry Lawson was also quickly given the status of 'national poet'. Eight years later, a memorial sculpture went up in Sydney's Hyde Park (below).

ended in commercial failure early in the 1930s. There were, however, four successful tours of foreign ballet companies in the second half of the 1930s, and ballet replaced opera as a reminder of European culture (and two of the ballet stars stayed in Australia and set up their own schools, and then their own companies). In drama, however, apart from the struggling little theatres, all that was offered in ten years was a season of Noel Coward plays and a tour by Sybil Thorndike. It was only the government-sponsored Australian Broadcasting Commission that ran to Australian drama. About half its serials and plays were Australian; its drama department sifted through a thousand contributed Australian plays a year. At the same time it was not narrowly Australian. The other half of its production was likely to feature anything from Sophocles to W.H. Auden: over three winter seasons it put on every play that Shakespeare wrote (cut down to 90-minute versions). The ABC also set itself up as a large concert agency, establishing orchestras in each State capital, and launching 'celebrity concerts' with imported conductors and performers.

In painting, when the field was dominated by bush landscapes, it was women painters more than men who tried to introduce modern painting to Australia. The great showdown came in 1937 when the conservative politician R.G. Menzies helped establish an Australian Academy of Art that was seen as a citadel of traditionalism; the anti-traditionalists counter-attacked in 1938, with the formation of a Contemporary Art Society, whose first exhibition was opened by Justice H.V. Evatt, of the High Court and earlier a Labor politician. In 1939 a fine collection of post-impressionist painting toured Australia.

By the end of the 1930s the Sydney poets Kenneth Slessor and R.D. FitzGerald were seen as a literary establishment, and poets who wished to contest their position were grouped around university student magazines in Sydney and Adelaide. Several specialist academic journals were

'Modern Art': *if sometimes timidly, and despite much surrounding ill will, some Australian painters, many of them women, were beginning to seek new painting styles (right). To guardians of morality, however, 'modernism' in painting could seen an un-Australian perversion.*

himself seen by his disciples as one of the great artists of the times; Scottish-born Sydney University Philosophy Professor John Anderson (above) was seen by his followers, 'the Andersonians', as the principal philosopher of the age; novelist Christina Stead (above left) spent most of her working life away from Australia, living in Spain, Paris, Belgium, England and Switzerland and the United States. There were others who saw themselves, one way or the other, as refugees from a prevailing atmosphere of oppressive philistinism in Australia.

Escaping the philistines: *there were other views of Australia between the wars than that of 'the bush'. Artist and writer Norman Lindsay (above) saw Australia as one of the few safe places in a world of declining culture and was*

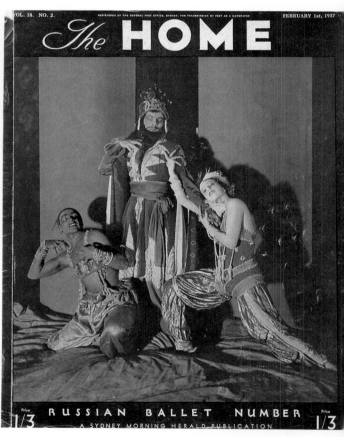

Colonel de Basil's Russian Ballet Troupe (above) toured Australia in 1937. Ballet in Australia was given impetus by the visiting Russian ballet and dance troupes.

In Watermelon *(top), painted in 1930, Margaret Preston showed a 'modern' use of colour. Grace Crowley developed an interest in abstractionist techniques, apparent in* Woman (Annunciation), *1936 (left). In* Arrested phrase from Beethoven's Ninth Symphony in red major *(above), painted in 1935, Roy de Maistre expressed his theory that paintings could symbolise sounds.*

237

established; a few books on Australian history appeared, although on the whole, the study of anything about Australia, other than its physical characteristics, was seen at the universities as too thin to be given consideration. The ABC 'Talks' Department gave some veneer of popular intellectual culture – if within a range inhibited by in-house timidities and concern about government pressure – and an annual Political Science Summer School gave some small, beleaguered scope for those who saw themselves as having an intelligent interest in politics. Campaigns continued for the admission of graduates to the Commonwealth Public Service, and in 1938 provision was made for ten per cent of recruits to be graduates (a decision criticised by some Sydney philosophers as an assault on the honorific uselessness of knowledge).

Two internationally minded groups became important in intellectual life, although neither could be described as cosmopolitan. In the second half of the 1930s, as part of the general Popular Front strategy, the Communists began to influence a number of unions, by 1940 almost dominating the Australian Council of Trade Unions. In a war of concealed party tickets and expulsions, they tried to penetrate the Labor Party, for a short while actually dominating the New South Wales branch. They also set up 'fronts' with some influence on intellectual life, the peace movement, and some church groups. On the other side, a Catholic lay movement had developed. Beginning in University Campion Societies, it started as anti-capitalist ('the greatest force in spreading communism at the present time is the failure of capitalism'), and when the monthly *Catholic Worker* (rising to 55 000 sales) was started in

Melbourne it, too, was at first concerned with social issues: the decline of the birth rate, the virtues of family and rural life, the evils of capitalism and State control. Similarly, when a National Secretariat of Catholic Action was set up in 1937 it was concerned with social issues.

But the Spanish Civil War and the Popular Front were causing a change in direction. In 1938 small informal Catholic-dominated groups began to conspire against Communist conspiracies in the unions, and in both Sydney and Melbourne open campaigns against the Communists had begun, especially in the universities, where the campaigns were noted more for enthusiasm than for accuracy of aim. Both Communists and Catholics were opponents of Improvement, and with the apparent failure of liberalism in both the Depression and in the League of Nations it became not uncommon for such intellectuals as there were to feel that they must choose between the Communists or the Catholics: 'Only [these] two organisations in Australia grasped the total situation as a crisis in liberalism.'

The bohemian groups of the 1920s frequented a few coffee shops and wine bars, a few Chinese and European restaurants, and a few clubs, and fabricated a sense of a separate community where the search was for 'the party to end all parties'. When Brennan was sacked from Sydney University, 'usually very dirty, smelling like a stale brewery', bumming drinks in pubs, memory of him became a symbol for those who saw themselves as outside their society. In this atmosphere of dispossession all politicians and businessmen could seem crooks, and the whole society

Australian art: Margaret Preston

Margaret Preston was the first major Australian painter to come to terms with the patterns and colours of the Australian landscape. Sometimes dismissed by contemporary critics as a 'mere flower painter', her exploration of Australian-ness was given texture and richness by her interest in oriental art and her practise of modern-ist techniques in painting, woodcut and pottery, as well as her traditional academic training.

She was born Margaret Rose McPherson in Adelaide in 1875

and studied in Sydney, Melbourne and Adelaide until 1904, when she went to Europe for three years. Painting as Rose McPherson, she supported herself by teaching until she left Australia again in 1912 to spend seven years in Europe. At the beginning of World War I she took pottery lessons in London so that she could help teach soldiers invalided from the Front. On her return to Australia she married a well-to-do businessman, William George Preston, who was to be a supportive husband until her death in 1963, allowing her to paint without financial worry.

They travelled extensively in outback Australia in search of Aboriginal art, through the Pacific Islands, to Africa, Japan and the Middle East. She was 81 when she made her last overseas journey, to India. A lively redhead with great intellectual en-thusiasm for confronting aesthetic problems ('the mind must rule the eye'), she became increasingly interested in the search for a uniquely Australian form that would take into account the mac-hine as well as the wildflower. Her native flowers, landscapes and still lifes were not intended merely as decorative description but as intellectual exploration. She was a member of the Society of Artists, the Australian Art Association and the Contemporary Group in Sydney.

Margaret Preston had definite views about being Australian. During World War II, appalled by bureaucratic actions, she corresponded (with a characteristic lack of punctuation) with fellow nationalists: 'We are firstly Australians and after that British. I mean no ill-will to our forefathers but I insist on being alive and not a relic . . . I think Australia has gone mad . . . It seems no one is pro-Australian its a matter of treason against Old England anyway I'm going on painting only Australian subjects and you stick to your Australian poetry – if its a hanging matter, well it just must be . . .'

worthless – 'the shop-window dummies of standardised neatness, the nitwits of patent leather hair, the good-timers with a repetitive gramophone record of slang for the brain, the gigolos of jazz, the shaven gorillas of the old-school ties'. The suburbanites were betrayers of the nation.

While intellectuals in the 1890s tried to find things in Australia that made it the best country in the world, their successors in the 1930s sought evidence that it was the worst. The word 'suburbia' was used as a term of contempt. Australian society was 'jerry-built' like a speculator-builder's house. There was no real nation, no sense of mission except for 'the platitudinous rhetoric of the Millions Club'. The censorship system was seen as one that 'neither the English nor American people would tolerate'. In Melbourne the Book Censorship League, formed in 1934, became a gathering point for some who saw the shoddy in Australian public life. Some of the best Australian novelists were believed to be the expatriates who had sought a more sympathetic climate to warm their talents. Canberra, declared 'open' in 1927 and intended to be a symbol of national aspiration, was seen as 'a city of eight million trees and not a single idea', 'the bush capital', a white elephant.

Educated persons began to blame the mass of the Australian people for their predicament. Those who accepted the values of the Black Hat society were contemptuous of the 'mediocrity' of their fellow countrymen, rather than of themselves. A people 'whose attention is divided between beauty competitions, the racing and betting news, and the latest of inane revues' were seen as 'a fraternal but rather drab company of one-class passengers'. Even some who rejected the standards of Black Hattedness might also blame the people, even democracy, for their sense of exclusion.

Following a pattern set by Lord Bryce in his *Modern Democracies*, they detected in the ordinary Australians a destructive jealousy so great that 'exasperation' was dominant in the public life of Australia. 'Where other distinctions are absent, and a few years can lift a man from nothing to affluence, differences in wealth are emphasised and resented ... the more because they often seem ... due to no special merit in the possessor.' Ignoring the long history of Australian nobbishness and overdoing the 'classlessness' of Australians, they blamed the destructive jealousy of the people for the weakness of intellectual life, rather than the dominance of Black Hat values and the weaknesses of educational institutions. Overestimating Australia's democracy and egalitarianism, they could believe that 'in Australia nobody is supposed to rule, and nobody does rule ... The proletariat appoints men to administer the law, not to rule.' By such arguments it could seem that the weaknesses of Australian administrative and intellectual leadership were not those of the administrators and intellectuals, but of the people.

To some, D. H. Lawrence was seen as the true interpreter of Australia:

This is the most democratic place I have *ever* been in. And the more I see of democracy the more I dislike it. It just keeps everything down to the mere vulgar level of wages and prices, electric light and water closets, and nothing else. You *never* knew anything so nothing, *Nichts, Nullus, Nients*, as the life here ... They are healthy, and to my thinking almost imbecile ... Yet they are very trustful and kind and quite competent in their jobs.

A special set of stamps was issued in 1927 to mark the opening of Canberra as the national capital, but what could mean more to Australians in a celebratory mood were the stamp issues in 1935 to mark the 20th anniversary of the Anzac landing and, in the same year, the stamp issues celebrating King George V's silver jubilee, an event marked by newspaper supplements and promotions.

To the people of Victoria, South Australia and New South Wales, however, the stamp issues that could mean most were those commemorating the founding (or, in Victoria's case, what purported to be the founding) of their colonies. In 1934 Victoria celebrated what it decided was its 'founding' – the first seizure of land from the Aborigines in 1834 – by inviting to Australia a royal duke and by organising an air race from London to Melbourne. On the celebratory day itself the royal duke arrived at Portland in a British warship, where he watched an 'historical pageant' which played a re-enactment of the landing of the Henty family there a hundred years before. It began with Aborigines preparing meals as they readied themselves for the hunt, then when the Henty party landed, muskets at the ready, the Aborigines ran away: the re-enactment of the unloading of livestock and chattels proceeded unembarrassed by Aborigines, and proceedings closed with a children's chorus singing 'Land of Hope and Glory'.

In Adelaide, in 1936, six warships anchored off Glenelg and 'while Aborigines approached cautiously to watch the

---

Aboriginal activist: William Ferguson

William Ferguson was one of the pioneers of the modern Aboriginal protest movement. The son of a Scottish boundary rider and an Aboriginal housemaid, he was born in rural New South Wales in 1882. By the age of 14 he was working in shearing sheds, later becoming a shed organiser for the Australian Workers' Union and active in local Labor Party politics. In the 1920s Ferguson became politically motivated to fight for Aboriginal rights against humiliating restrictions. He launched the Aboriginal Progressive Association in Dubbo in 1937, and his election to the Aboriginal Welfare Board in 1943 saw his concern extended to Aboriginal Reserves.

Inspired by the United Nations Declaration of Human Rights, in 1949 he stood for Federal Parliament with a policy of civil rights for all people, but he collapsed after his final speech and died a month later from heart disease. He had polled 388 votes.

In 1938 Ferguson had supported enthusiastically the idea of the 150th anniversary of European settlement in Australia being presented as a Day of Mourning. (The original idea has been credited to the Aboriginal activist William Cooper, who in 1932, aged 62, organised a petition to King George asking for better conditions and parliamentary representation for Aborigines. The Federal Government declined on constitutional grounds to forward the petition.) A week before 26 January 1938, a pamphlet, *Aborigines Claim Citizenship Rights*, seen as the first documentary statement by Aborigines of their view of Australian history, was published; Ferguson was co-author. The pamphlet opened with: 'This festival of 150 years' so called "progress" in Australia commemorates also 150 years of misery and degradation imposed upon the original native inhabitants by the white invaders of this country.'

scene' the landing of a hundred years before was re-enacted, followed by a procession to the Glenelg Oval, where the proclamation of the colony was read under a replica of 'the Old Gum Tree'. Proceedings closed with a singing of 'God Save the King' and 'Song of Australia' (which had become South Australia's official song).

In Sydney in 1938, around the setting for the landing pageant were anchored warships from France, Italy, the Netherlands and New Zealand. This re-enactment for the 150th anniversary of the landing began with an Aboriginal corroboree, but when the first boat landed 'marines with fixed bayonets leapt ashore and drove the blacks back'. After the actor playing Governor Phillip proclaimed the founding of the colony through the public address system the actors playing the landing party joined a three-kilometre procession that gave a school textbook view of Australian history, ending with floats celebrating 'The Conquest of the Air' and 'The Future of Australia'. At the end of the day there was a gala night at the showground, at which proceedings concluded when the Australian musical comedy star Gladys Moncrieff, swathed in the Union Jack, sang 'Land of Hope and Glory'.

The organisers of the Sydney pageant had not intended it to appear that the Aborigines were being driven away, merely that they should be reduced to the role of interested spectators, but the newspapers reported the marines as 'putting the blacks to flight'. The incident represented a new state of tension regarding the Aborigines. On the one hand there was beginning to be some recognition of their culture; but on the other hand they were still being treated as outcasts.

The development of anthropology – with a chair established at Sydney University in 1925 and a journal, *Oceania*, in 1930 – provided some encouragement of the view that Aborigines were also human beings, although, to the most prejudiced, if the 'Abos' were to be seen to have any humanity at all, it was in inverse relationship to 'the proportion of Aboriginal blood in their veins'. At one end of the scale were 'full bloods', still regarded as members of a dying race; at the other end were 'octoroons', only one-eighth Aboriginal in descent, for whom there was some hope. In 1937, when the Commonwealth and State administrators of Aborigines held their first conference, it still seemed obvious that the full bloods were dying out, but

Celebrations: *the three greatest civic celebrations of the 1930s were in commemoration of white occupation of three sections of Australia – of the hundredth year of occupation of Victoria (top left), and South Australia (top right), and 150 years of occupation of New South Wales (above). An Aboriginal featured in only the Victorian stamp, and then merely as a symbol of the primitive, accentuating European progress.*

Images: *some painters were becoming troubled about how they should present Aborigines. In* Thomas Foster *(right), painted in 1934, Percy Leason tried simple realism. In* The Music Lesson *(centre right), painted in 1904, Sydney Long tried to give an Aboriginal woman dignity by presenting her in an end-of-the-century painting style. But the best-known representation of Aborigines in the 1930s was in the advertisement for Pelaco shirts (far right).*

it was conceded to 'the natives of Aboriginal origin, but not of the full blood' that their destiny lay 'in absorption by the people of the Commonwealth'. 'Abos' were likely to be seen as human by modern painters who were aware of the influences of African and Oceanic artefacts on modern art: the bark painting came to be particularly admired and by the 1930s Aboriginal motifs had been adopted in pottery and textiles – one coffee shop had curtains that showed the influence of bark paintings. The novel that won the New South Wales Sesqui-Centenary literary prize was Xavier Herbert's *Capricornia*, a saga of the Northern Territory that placed the cruel treatment of the blacks as part of his disordered and surreal world. In 1939 the Commonwealth Minister even promised 'the ordinary rights of citizenship' to Aborigines, but he warned that for this to happen 'one must not think in terms of years but of generations'.

The realities were that Aborigines were still an oppressed race; in fact, with a new round of 'protection' legislation in the 1930s, control over them increased. They did not have freedom of movement or freedom of association; there were special restrictions on their rights to marry and on their sexual relations; control of their property could be taken

from them; they were denied the right to vote; they were forbidden alcohol; their right to work was restricted; so was their right to carry guns, or even to own dogs. Girls could be forcibly taken from their mothers and sent to institutions where they might learn to be 'good wives to the class of white man they are likely to marry'; in the cattle industry in the north, half of them received only their keep, with no wages, and those who did receive wages were paid much less than white people. In some States, if white parents objected to their presence they could be excluded from State schools; they could be excluded from many amenities in country towns, from hairdressers' salons to swimming pools. In 1928, after Northern Territory Aborigines had killed one white and wounded another, a retaliation party shot 32 Aborigines; this was found to have been 'justified' by a court of inquiry.

It had now become traditional for humanitarian organisations to protest from time to time against what was happening to the Aborigines; in 1911 an Association for the Protection of Native Races had been formed and it would usually lead the protests. But in the 1930s a new form of protest developed – from the Aborigines themselves. They

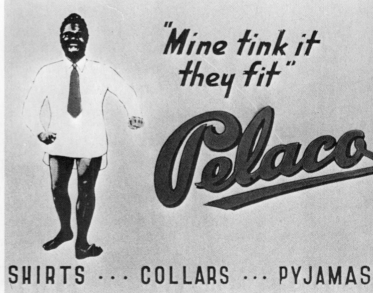

had been 'protesting' since 1788 in their own way: what was novel was that they were now beginning to develop white forms of protest. Beginning in the 1920s, Aboriginal associations held meetings, arranged deputations and, on one occasion, petitioned King George. In 1938 the Aborigines Progressive Association decided to declare a Day of Mourning on the day of the Sesqui-Centenary celebrations in Sydney, in which it held its own meeting, to which only Aborigines were invited.

Its manifesto 'Aborigines Claim Citizenship Rights' began: 'This festival of 150 years of so-called "progress" in Australia commemorated also 150 years of misery and degradation imposed upon the original native inhabitants by the white invaders of this country.' Only one newspaper reporter attended the meeting.

Not like last time

'Unhappy-looking men in long greatcoats, generally carrying an attaché case and in a hurry' were by 1938 being seen in King's Cross and elsewhere. They were the 'reffos', the first of the 5000 refugees from the new European totalitarianism whom the Commonwealth Government had decided to let into Australia.

In 1938, 274 German and Austrian citizens living in Sydney boarded a German freighter, sailed outside the three-mile limit, voted by 272 to two for union between Germany and Austria, then came back for dinner. In a country which commemorated its nationhood by celebrating a military defeat, the question 'Will there be another war?' came naturally enough with each new threat – the Japanese invasion of Manchuria, the rise of Hitler, the Italian invasion of Ethiopia, the Spanish Civil War, the Japanese invasion of China, the German seizure of Austria. This was the familiar world of Anzac Day. But there were not the same responses in the country's leadership.

In the UAP only Hughes spoke the language of the Diggers. Others saw Communism as a greater threat than Nazism; a few defended Hitler as a man putting his house in order. Most tuned in to Britain, listening to the static. Where Britain went they went. When the Munich Agreement was announced Lyons called for a day of thanksgiving. The UAP still spoke of Empire defence, and brought it into the 1937 election to confound Labor's lack of policy, but the Australian army's equipment was still mainly what the Diggers had brought home in 1919.

Many members of the Labor Party saw the causes of war in trade rivalries and the conspiracies of armament kings: in this view, war with Nazi Germany would be merely a fight between rival camps of capitalists looking for world markets. Others attacked 'scaremongers': Japan would never be aggressive; the seizure of Austria was an expression of the self-determination of peoples. Within the union movement the Catholics and Communists were fighting on foreign policy: to have chosen one side or the other would have split the Labor Party.

The Communists had now broadened their approach with a 'united front' policy: they and those who followed them stirred the unions sufficiently for the Australian Council of Trade Unions' conference (which had opposed

Victor O'Connor's The Refugees *paid tribute to the victims of Nazi persecution at a time when Australia had already accepted a few thousand 'reffos' from various European countries that had been devastated by the war.*

The Age, 4 September 1939, headlines the outbreak of war with Germany. Australia followed Britain's declaration.

sanctions against Mussolini in 1935) to support collective security against Hitler in 1937, although the rearmament that could make sense of collective security was still seen as a plot of the arms kings. In the summer of 1938–39 a two-month strike at Port Kembla against the export of pig iron to Japan failed in its immediate purpose, but it expanded the horizon of threat. The Labor Party remained inactive: many of its Catholic members supported Mussolini and Franco and saw Hitler as a bulwark against Communism. 'Absolute isolation, strict neutrality' and withdrawal from the League of Nations was proclaimed as Jack Lang's foreign policy when New South Wales faction-fighting led him to seek right-wing support against the Communists.

But there were two promptings to new policy, one from the UAP, one from Labor. The UAP was taking up, if in fear, the idea of Australia as a Pacific power that earlier had been taken up in boastful confidence. At the 1937 Imperial Conference, Lyons had suggested a Pacific Non-Aggression Pact. With no diplomatic service, he became his own envoy, approaching the ambassadors of a number of Pacific powers while he was in London. The Russians, the Chinese and the French said they were interested; the Japanese were hostile, the United States indifferent, the British cool. A small External Affairs Department was re-established in 1935; goodwill missions were sent to countries in Asia; in 1939 it was decided to establish legations in Tokyo and Washington. When R.G. Menzies became Prime Minister he said, 'We will never realise our destiny as a nation until we realise that we are one of the Pacific Powers.' Of course Australia would not act as 'a completely separate power' but as 'an integral part of the British Empire'; though 'what Great Britain calls the Far East is to us the near north'.

The Labor Party was deprived by its divisions of any opportunity of defining a foreign policy, but for the same reason it was able to put up a more original approach to military planning than 'Empire defence'. Labor urged a strong air and naval defence force to replace a 'defence' policy that depended on a base in Singapore which in wartime the British could never adequately service.

'Great Britain has declared war ... and, as a result, Australia is also at war.' To the old Diggers it seemed just like last time, except that it was now the turn of their sons to show what Australia was made of. They had already shown some of this when after the German occupation of Prague a recruiting campaign for the militia attracted 70 000 volunteers in three months. But last time the Japanese had been allies. Now doubts about what it might really mean to be a Pacific power penetrated the Government. It took almost a fortnight to decide to raise a special military force of 20 000 men (instead of 'the last man and the last shilling', in the first week of war Menzies proclaimed 'business as usual') and then it was left open whether the force would stay in Australia. It took until November, and then perhaps only after prompting from New Zealand, to take the risk of deciding to send this new 6th Division to the Middle East and most of the Australian Navy to the Mediterranean. It was to take another four months to decide to send anyone else.

Early in the new year, trains ran through the suburbs of Sydney and some of the 6th Division embarked on four converted luxury liners on their way to the Middle East. Many had known or feared that this was why they had grown to manhood. But it was not to be like the last time.

The early recruiting posters (above) were of a there-is-a-job-to-do kind that appealed to emotion.

One of The Australian Women's Weekly's early war covers (left). The Weekly was seen as playing a significant part in boosting wartime morale.

16. The orphans of the Pacific: 1940s

In 1939, fewer men seemed prepared to answer the call to defend the Empire than had rushed to join 'the Great Adventure' in 1914. An incompetent public service, staffed mainly by Returned Men over 40 and former messenger boys, hampered government attempts to organise the war effort. Japanese attacks in the Pacific, reaching to Darwin, brought the war to the home front, and suddenly the United States was providing the alliance in which Britain had failed. From an emergency war program developed an influential class of manufacturers and a complex national administration that became, to some, part of a more general hope for an intellectual breakthrough.

Convoys sailed off across the Indian Ocean, soldiers posed for their photographs in front of the Sphinx, but, after two years, volunteers were only 188 000 out of a population of seven million, compared with 307 000 from a nation of only five million in what was now spoken of as 'the first war'. For many, the reality of the war was mainly newsreel images.

It was 12 months before Australian soldiers saw action, and when it came it was confusing. Victory over the Italians was clear in the two months' push into Libya – the newsreels showed men wrapped against the desert cold advancing in the dawn light on shattered white buildings, but a month later the Germans pushed everyone back. Within a few months, towns never before heard of had become names for both victory and defeat. By then Australians and New Zealanders were in Greece; they arrived on 3 April 1940 and were given the name 'Anzac Corps' on 12 April; seven days later they were defeated. All except 2000 prisoners scrambled out, some to Cyprus where, a week after the Germans had infiltrated their positions with paratroopers,

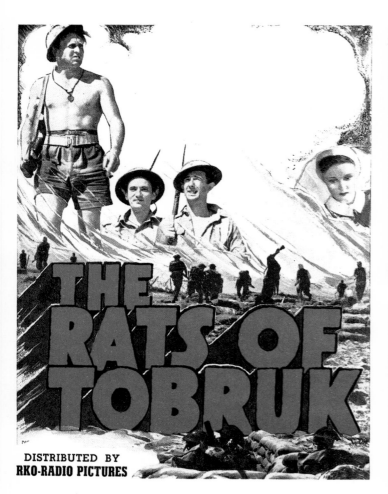

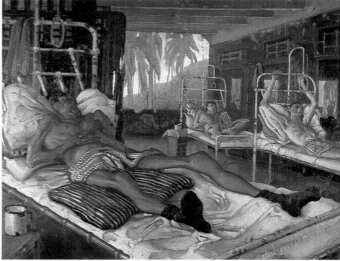

The siege of Tobruk by the Germans provided the only legendary episode in the Australian fighting in North Africa and the Middle East – legendary enough to mean that only three years after the siege of Tobruk was over, The Rats of Tobruk *came out as a film (above).*

244

they again evacuated; this time 3000 prisoners were taken. There was some sense of betrayal; then after only a fortnight's action in Syria against the Vichy French, victorious Australians, like their fathers before them, were marching through the streets of Damascus. It was the 242-day siege of Tobruk that seemed most familiar. Trapped in the German advance, with an Australian general in command of the allied garrison, Tobruk held the attention of the newsreels with an extraordinary story of unlikely survival.

Although imperialist, or perhaps because they were, the UAP Government had failed to arouse the open fervour expected of Australians in wartime. Most Australians were concerned about the war, if more sceptically than before, but they were not prepared to make a fuss, and the Government's belief in Empire loyalty could make an appeal to national feelings seem 'disloyal'. Seeing the war primarily in terms of defending the Empire in the Middle East, with Singapore as Australia's inner defence, the Government even adopted a subdued approach to Japan's proclamation of a 'Greater East Asia' policy, despite its earlier uncertainties about sending troops away from

Australia. It asked Churchill for a fleet in Singapore – as a kind of naval metaphor, he dispatched two ships – and itself sent a division to Malaya; but Malaya seemed an exotic kind of place for Australians to be. One question asked was whether Australians were psychologically suited to such garrison duties.

In the early months the incompetence of the public service had been of the greatest assistance in sustaining the dilatoriness of the Government. With a public service staffed mainly by Returned Men over the age of 45, along with promoted messenger boys, it took four months even to make a decision to manufacture new field guns to replace the guns of 1914–18. It was only when a number of businessmen and graduates were pushed into departments that decisions began to flow. When the UAP Government went to the polls in 1940 it almost lost the election. In 1941 it collapsed from its own sense of inadequacy. Labor took over. The imperial call had come, but the UAP had failed to make a political success of answering it.

Troops in Australian army camps woke on 8 December 1941 to discover that Japanese aircraft had bombed the United States naval base at Pearl Harbor and blown up

Disaster: *the fall of Singapore in 1942 produced a brief revulsion against the British among many Australians. Decades of loyalty to Britain had not produced the reward that was intended. In Singapore itself, in Changi camp, and in other Japanese camps elsewhere in Asia, there were 20 000 Australian prisoners, a third of whom were to die in captivity. Murray Griffin's* Hospital *(left) shows Australians in the Changi camp hospital in 1943, and (below left) preparing food in* Frying Rice Cakes, Changi 1942.

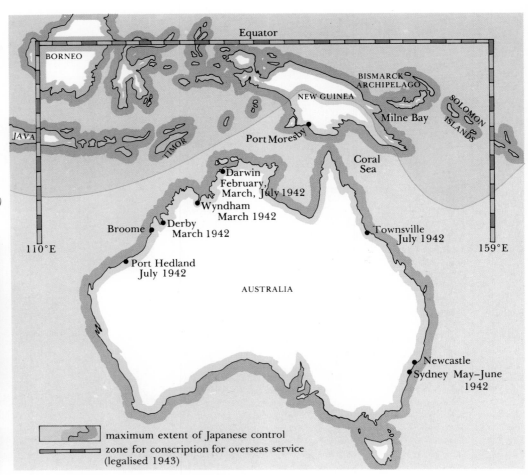

Only four days after the fall of Singapore, the Japanese made the first of 64 raids on Darwin. On the first day, fire fighters behind an asbestos shield watch an oil storage tank burn (above).

The Japanese threat: *by 1942 the Japanese controlled Malaya, Indonesia, Timor and part of New Guinea. Although they were defeated in the Battle of the Coral Sea in May 1942, the Japanese continued to bomb northern Australian cities, and even launched submarine attacks on Sydney and Newcastle.*

much of the US Pacific fleet. By nightfall many of the troops were moving to improvised battle stations here and there on the 19 000-kilometre coastline. At dawn they stood to, facing sand and sea. The Japanese invaded Malaya and the Philippines; after two days they sank Churchill's two warships and seized Guam: a fortnight later Hong Kong surrendered; five days more and the Americans evacuated Manila; another two weeks and Australian soldiers were fighting to defend the approaches to Singapore; a fortnight after that they withdrew to the island of Singapore; a week later the Japanese attacked. A week later Singapore fell, and into the smoke and flame of its quick destruction went the whole edifice of Empire defence. With a loss in prisoners of war proportionate to 100 000 British or 300 000 Americans, to Australians the disasters of Singapore could seem one of the greatest military defeats of the 20th century. All the newspapers beat the drums that signalled, in effect, the failure of Empire: 'There have been few more serious miscalculations in all British history' ... 'The results continue to be tragedy after tragedy, based on blunder after blunder.' The Prince of Wales had sworn in 1920 that, as Australia stood by the Empire, so the Empire would stand

by Australia. This had not proved to be true: there was talk of 'guilty men', and, among some, of British chicanery.

Surprise air raids on Darwin left blazing oil tanks, sunken ships, broken buildings: the Australian Chief of Staff warned that a Japanese invasion in the north might be expected early in April and an attack on the east coast in May. In Japan, General Tojo mocked Australia as 'the orphan of the Pacific, helplessly expecting Japan's attack'. Guerilla groups formed; there were suggestions for squads of blacktrackers and there was talk on both the Right and the Left of a 'people's army'. Some harbourside flats in Sydney emptied. Barbed wire and sandbags went up on its beaches. Signboards were pulled down, small boats impounded; 80 000 cattle were overlanded from the north to the south so that the Japanese couldn't eat them. There were plans for a scorched earth policy. Government departments moved their archives to safe places.

Two of the volunteer Divisions were brought back from the Middle East, and another 114 000 men were conscripted to add to the 132 000 already drafted into the militia, but there was a soreness about both the dispersal of forces home from Empire defence and the inadequate equipment and

Peculiarly Australian: Chips Rafferty

Born John Goffage, in 1909, Chips Rafferty had been a drover, an opal miner, a cane cutter and a deck hand, and had worked in a wine cellar before he became an actor. In *Forty Thousand Horsemen*, made in 1940, Rafferty, tall and lanky, with a slightly nasal voice and a gruff irreverence for authority, began to be seen as a prototype Australian. The film, about Australian soldiers in the Sinai Desert in World War I, was presented as 'a message of inspiration for a new generation of soldiers'. The film's famous light horse charge had been filmed before the outbreak of war, on 1 February 1938, in the sandhills at Cronulla in New South Wales, using a cavalry division that had been brought together for the sesqui-centenary celebrations, and which could spare only a day for filming.

Chips Rafferty starred in two other famous Australian war films: *The Rats of Tobruk*, made in 1944 and intended as a tribute to the Australian fighting spirit shown at the siege of Tobruk in 1941; and *The Overlanders*, made in 1946, about a gigantic cattle drive across northern Australia in 1942, intended to deny a possible Japanese invasion easy access to food supplies.

Several of Rafferty's other films had story lines based on enduring Australian themes: *Eureka Stockade*, made in 1949, in which he played Peter Lalor and was seen as miscast; *Bitter Springs*, made in 1950, about early relationships between Aborigines and white settlers; *They're A Weird Mob*, made in 1966, about immigrants' puzzles with Australian ways; and *Wake in Fright*, made in 1971, which underlined the clash between urban and rural values.

training of the home forces. The home army had only half the trucks and a sixth of the anti-aircraft guns it needed, only 18 tanks, only six days' supply of anti-tank ammunition. Some of the men who went to battle stations in December had had no weapon training. In theory the air forces had 32 squadrons, but their main equipment was trainers, and they were drastically under-crewed. It was decided that planes and men for 60 squadrons were needed.

Lines were drawn on maps. Not maps of France or the Middle East this time, but maps of Australia. The Newcastle-Sydney-Port Kembla area was to be held, and if possible, the 1600-kilometre stretch from Melbourne to Brisbane; there would be garrisons in Darwin, Port Moresby and a few other places. There was a certain amount of hope when General Douglas Macarthur arrived in March from the Philippines to be appointed Supreme Commander in April, and by June Australia had assembled, with varying degrees of equipment and training, almost half a million men in uniform, to which the United States added another 88 000. The Department of Information instructed the radio stations to play a new patriotic song, with the refrain, 'We're all together now, as we never were before,

ON'T FIGHT...DON'T WORK...DON'T LEND!

Thankyou!

Invasion?: *in the first threat of invasion of Australia since 1788, Australia itself was seen as a fortress. There was a lively circulation of anti-Japanese posters (above). Instruction booklets were sold on guerilla warfare (right), and there was talk of a 'people's army'. In May 1942, three Japanese submarines entered Sydney Harbour; a torpedo fired at USS Chicago hit a Sydney ferry converted into a barracks ship and killed 19 men (below left).*

THE AUSTRALIAN GUERRILLA
BOOK I

SHOOT TO KILL

by Ion. L. Idriess.

Ships were sunk in the Japanese bomb raids on Darwin, captured by Arthur Murch in his painting Wreck of the Neptuna, Darwin 1943 *(above left).*

The Aussies and Yanks, sure we're gonna win this war.' But by then Japanese submarines were sinking ships on the Australian east coast and had seized most of New Guinea. What was left of New Guinea was seen as the last stronghold from which to fight 'the battle for Australia'.

Credibility was first given to the possibility that this battle might succeed when in the Coral Sea in May a United States naval force that had two Australian cruisers attached to it turned back a Japanese fleet moving to invade Port Moresby as part of a general plan to seize New Guinea, New Caledonia, Fiji and Samoa, isolate Australia and New Zealand from these bases, and attack key points in both countries to frighten them out of the war. The American repulse of this Japanese invasion force provided instant and enormous sustenance to Australians. They had lost Singapore, but gained the United States Navy.

In July, the Japanese seized Gona and Buna, pushed on to Kokoda, and threatened Port Moresby. In August, they attacked again, at Milne Bay, on New Guinea's extreme eastern tip, seeking its airstrips as a base for their endgame. They landed among Milne Bay's sago and mangrove swamps, but after a week's confused fighting in relentless rain, each side lacking maps and blundering into the other, the Australians won. It was the first land defeat the Japanese had known. Field Marshal William Slim was later to say, 'It was the Australian soldiers who first broke the spell of the invincibility of the Japanese army.'

On the newsreels the mud and rain of the Battle of the Owen Stanley Ranges now placed it alongside Tobruk as a continuing cinema story. Two small armies confronted each other, both weakened by malaria, strung out in the slush of tracks that cut a path through sweltering jungle. The Australians conquered the mountains and gorges, then the flat swampy country, then took their two bases back from the Japanese. It was 1943. Who would win the war still remained to be seen, but the feeling had begun that Australia was no longer in immediate danger. It was again part of something bigger. It no longer had to fight for itself, but for an ally.

Despite what had seemed a direct threat to Australia's survival, there had not been much appeal to national sentiment. Australians wanted to save themselves, but there was little speech-making about what they were supposed to be saving. In one of his first war speeches, staying with the prevailing fashion, John Curtin had said, 'We shall hold this country ... as a citadel for the British-speaking race', as if Australians were holding their nation for King George. There was shock when he came out more realistically: 'Without any inhibition of any kind I make it quite clear that Australia looks to America, free of any pangs as to our traditional links or kinship with the United Kingdom.' The habit of wars being an occasion for imperial rhetoric was so strong that this speech (privately denounced by Churchill as 'flaunted round the world by our enemies') was treated as a stab in the back for Britain. The Archbishop of Brisbane said, 'The most audacious piece of Fifth Column activity hitherto seen in this country has been the effort to belittle Britain's part in the war'. Other changes, such as having more Australian commentators on Australian radio and attempts to make 'Advance Australia Fair' the national song, were seen as further blows to Australia's patriotism.

What summed up the laconic wartime faith of Australians was a sentence in a union newspaper: 'It is not in the Australian make-up to squib a fight.' But this was not the language of speech-making. Soldiers could still call each other 'mate' or 'Dig', as if they were their fathers, but this time within the army there was no sense of building a nation. The division between volunteers and conscripts caused much bitterness – there were two armies, not one – and there was not much pride in the despairing scramble to throw brigades into New Guinea, or in the lonely fear of fighting in some of the world's most difficult country, with malaria, dysentery and typhus greater killers than the enemy. As the war settled into shapes of possible victory, the Americans sailed north after prestige, leaving the Australians with the humble, debilitating, dangerous and strategically unnecessary role of mopping up leftover Japanese. The Australian war machine was now working so vigorously that it became overheated: soldiers began to be released from munition-making and fighting to maintain Australia as a supply base for the Americans; but the Australian Government wished to keep men fighting, so that Australia might have a voice at the Peace Conference.

This time it was in the arena of world politics that the war and its aftermath gave intimations of nationhood. Dr H.V. ('Bert') Evatt, now returned to politics and become the External Affairs Minister, threw himself with a showman's enthusiasm into creating the drama of an independent Australian foreign policy. He issued a warning to the great powers that Australia might be small in the world but it was big in the Southwest Pacific: to make this sound real, Australia entered into its first independent treaty. All it could find was New Zealand, but Evatt discovered a bigger stage in the San Francisco Conference of 1945, called to settle the constitution of the United Nations. He appointed himself champion of the smaller powers, fought hard against big power domination, and achieved some reforms and a wide personal reputation.

With a rough-and-ready drive, and with the single-minded impatience of an ambitious entrepreneur, he threw up around him a bigger, if disordered, External Affairs Department to carry out his 'bustling diplomacy'. Australia now had 15 diplomatic missions; it was one of the four nations on the Allied Commission in defeated Japan (where it represented Britain and India): an Australian

commanded the British Commonwealth Occupation Forces; Evatt became chairman of the United Nations General Assembly. Menzies attacked 'the utter independence of Australian thought and action – which, for seven million people in a small island continent is more pretentious than sensible – as if no special British relation assisted at all', and Evatt's Australian style was derided as 'a sort of larrikin strain in Australian foreign policy, a disposition to throw stones at the street lights just because they are bright'. But Evatt was driven by the adventurous ambition of making Australia one of the consciences of humankind, determined on a fair go among nations, 'in the forefront of the councils of the world', with a policy on everything.

Although there were no Australian diplomatic missions in Southeast Asia, there was a feeling of concern for an area where European colonialists, knocked over by the Japanese, were trying to put themselves back into place; there were attacks on 'outmoded, reactionary and feudal forms of government' and hopes for 'a harmonious association of democratic states in the Southeast Asian area'. When the Dutch began to try to put down the revolt of the Indonesian nationalists (describing it as a 'police action') Australia brought the conflict before the Security Council, and Indonesia appointed Australia as its representative on the three-man Committee of Good Offices. With the second 'police action' Australia moved on the UN for the expulsion of the Dutch, and when Indonesia entered the UN it chose Australia as one of its two sponsors, and saw Australia as one of its greatest friends.

But Australia did not feel big enough to face the future. 'Asian countries will undoubtedly be looking at us,' said Ben Chifley, who succeeded Curtin as Prime Minister, 'and there will be increasing pressure for an outlet for their populations.' Unless Australia quickly got more people these Asians might come and take its empty spaces. To fill them up, Australia could not be too fussy: for the first time in its history, it now had to buy immigrants who weren't British. At first there was a hope that 'for every foreign migrant there will be ten people from the United Kingdom'. But the British were harder to get than that. The Government turned to the International Refugee Organisation and contracted to give large numbers of 'displaced persons' free passages. As 170 000 Poles, 'Balts', Russians, Ukrainians, Hungarians and others from

New Guinea: *the first land defeat suffered by the Japanese was inflicted by two Australian infantry brigades at Milne Bay in August 1942. A wounded Australian is led to an aid post by a Papuan in the Buna area (far left). An Australian company headquarters, 40 metres from the Japanese (left). An Australian soldier destroys a Japanese 'pillbox' (below left).*

The American 'invasion': *by the end of 1944 there were half a million United States troops in the southwest Pacific. General MacArthur and Prime Minister John Curtin in Canberra in 1942 (below). United States troops at lunch in Melbourne (below right). Ray Hodgkinson painted United States servicemen relaxing (right):* One Sunday Afternoon, Townsville 1942.

the refugee camps came to Australia, these 'DPs' began to outmatch the British immigrants. Immigration agreements were signed with other countries; assisted Italians, Germans and Dutch joined the DPs; the target of 70 000 a year for immigration went up to 150 000.

Many of the immigrants were tied for two years to working where they were sent, and this gave the Government a chance to send them to jobs Australians didn't want; but in a country which had always hated its immigrants there were fears of new outbursts of prejudice and hostility. The name 'New Australian' was invented to reassure Australians that even 'Balts' and Italians were fellow creatures, but for safety's sake the Immigration Department set up an Assimilation Branch in the hope that as quickly as possible these foreigners could be made to look like Australians. However, the immigrants' labour broke bottlenecks in steel production, housing, public works, transport. Things began to move again. There were again hopes that if it could be 'developed', Australia might again be Unlimited.

This hope was nowhere stronger than among the businessmen who during the war had gone into the

departments and improvised an armaments industry. Because of the confident strength of the BHP and its associates, along with several other monopolies or near-monopolies, there had been enough engineering and management tradition for remarkable examples of wartime resourcefulness. The manufacture of the 4000 component parts of the first field gun was farmed out in two days, and the gun was being produced within seven months. The British had said it would take two years. Optical glass was manufactured against British warnings that the task was beyond Australia and against a boycott by the British manufacturers. An aircraft industry that produced 3500 aircraft of nine different types was thrown up. Destroyers, corvettes, frigates, merchant ships and 33 643 small craft came from Australia's shipyards. The BHP developed 140 specialist steels. Machine tools, not made on any scale before, were produced in great number and variety. Improvised technical training mass-produced tens of thousands of skilled tradesmen. There was not much of a science base to most of this, nor much technological invention – it was mainly a case of getting the instructions and having a go – but there were inventive modifications.

POPULATION	ENLISTED MEN	ENLISTED WOMEN	OVERSEAS SERVICE	KILLED	WOUNDED	TAKEN PRISONER
7 176 312	926 900	94 000	550 000	30 508	58 351	30 560

National effort: *in World War II almost one in seven Australians was in uniform. However, casualties were not so great as in World War I.*

The Labor Government's External Affairs Minister, Dr H.V. ('Bert') Evatt, believed that Australia should engage in an active and, to some extent, independent diplomacy. At the San Francisco Conference to establish the United Nations (left) the Australian delegation was one of the most active.

The Labor Government was determined to increase Australia's population and agreed to accept 'displaced persons' and other continental Europeans (below). To avoid the use of insulting terms, Labor's Immigration Minister suggested the phrase 'New Australians'.

Women at war: *World War II was to be a much more active war for Australian women than the first, with participation in the armed services (above right), although there was still some appeal to traditional ideals of femininity. Ponds Face Cream appealed to women's patriotism by urging them to make themselves adorable 'for him' (right).*

With this further onrush of industrialisation and the broadening of experience in the production of capital equipment, when the war was finished an impressive number of buildings, skills and machines went off into private manufacturing; but an equally important product of the crash war program was the development, for the first time, of an influential class of manufacturers – emergent businessmen who saw themselves as 'the real life-savers that Australia always needed', and who had 'got into the habit of relying on their own resources on practically all occasions . . . accustomed to making decisions all round'. They now saw themselves as the backbone of the long-delayed development of Australia as a manufacturing country: but Australia was still a country without industrial research, without management skills, and without a sophisticated banking community.

The improvisation of an Australian industrial effort had also made it a 'different war from last time' for women. In the first war, women had become, if anything, more womanly, in the sense that, in relation to the great dramas of the age, they were being defined not in themselves, but merely in relation to the boys in uniform – as mothers,

wives, sweethearts, sisters. This time, some women were themselves in uniform (although paid only two-thirds the male rate for equal work) and, at least over the time when it seemed possible that Australia might be invaded, women could also see themselves, potentially, in a frontline – instead of knitting socks they could dig air-raid trenches; with 'the American invasion', those who befriended United States servicemen were able to experience a sense of change available only to men in the first war. And this time a much greater number of women went to work in factories – a minority of them into men's work women had not been allowed to do before, where, although they were expected to go back home after the war, as a result of the interventions of a special Womens Employment Board set up by the Government, they were being paid up to 90 per cent of men's wages or, in some cases, as much as men (thereby building up a challenge for the future). However, those who went into traditional 'women's work' were paid scarcely more than half the male rate, a wage so low that a shortage developed, forcing the Government's significantly named 'Manpower Control' to draft women into factories, where they were made to work as cheap labour. (Finally, the

Ideas of 'women's work' were affected by the war. A 65-year-old Adelaide woman digs an air-raid trench in her back garden (centre above). Factory work, including work in munitions factories (above), was one of women's significant economic contributions during the war. Running single-parent homes (with fathers in the services) and fighting the black market were also 'women's work' during the war. A cartoon in The Bulletin *(left) captures the desperation of both.*

Government overrode both the employers and the Arbitration Court and increased those women's wages – but only to 75 per cent of male rates.)

Although there were many humiliations for women in this, the first time in Australia's history when the State encouraged women to work in some field other than domestic service, it was also a time of raised ambitions. But *The Australian Women's Weekly* and its advertisers worked to remind women of where their true ambitions should still lie – that whatever they were doing during the war it was still their first task to remain 'feminine'. 'She's doing a job of national importance,' said a Pond's Face Cream ad in the *Weekly*, 'but she doesn't forget the importance of looking lovely for *him*.'

The war had also given Australia its first complex national administration, parts of which also saw themselves as the backbone of national development. The number of departments had nearly doubled, the number of employees had trebled, and new powers had come to the Commonwealth: a virtual monopoly of income tax had been gained from a High Court decision and full powers over social services from a referendum. All except one

civilian department gained new heads during the war – several in their 30s, one aged only 32, others in their 40s; the Public Service had become younger and much more ambitious in its sense of what it could do.

Some of the university-educated people who had pushed themselves into the departments stayed after the war and within them a smaller group, 'the planners', showed the same talents as the businessmen for hard work, devotion and improvisation, the same self-belief and resourcefulness, the same confidence that they could do anything without thinking about it very deeply. Attacked as 'long-hairs', they acquired special strength in the Post-War Reconstruction Department and as 'the Chifley men' – a group of advisers who surrounded Ben Chifley. At their most cohesive, this devoted group saw themselves as the agents of a social revolution based on the joint ideas of rationality and welfare; they represented another attempt to bring Australia into a state of Improvement through colonial governmentalism. With a stronger momentum and a more definitive sense of purpose than their Labor Party patrons, they became the principal initiators of policy. No field of endeavour seemed outside their talents: Government

Digger, mark II: *new stereotypes of 'the Digger' were presented by the war artists. Some, as in William Dargie's* Corporal Jim Gordon VC, Syria 1941 *(above left), were recognisable sons of their World War I fathers, but new styles of painting could produce new moods, evident in Sali Herman's* Back Home *(above right), painted in 1945.*

Australian agony: *the opimism that had marked almost all Australian painting was now gone, and so were many of the older themes. The disasters of depression and war and the stimulus of new styles had brought new themes of alienation and menace. In her study* Lovers *(top right), painted in 1956, Joy Hester went beyond romance to see love as unsettling and claustrophobic. Albert Tucker's* Victory Girls *(right), painted in 1943, portrayed wartime Melbourne as a city of evil, hostility and crude, alienated sex.*

Australia as desert: *perceptions of Australian landscapes now changed. It was no longer the gumtree and the rolling paddocks of the grazing properties that could seem typical of Australia, but its deserts. Russell Drysdale was the first to project new views of the desert. His first deserts were strong, red and cruel:* Desert Landscape *(far right above) showed a slightly softer desert, with a little more mercy. Sidney Nolan was the first of the new painters to gain significant recognition 'overseas' (although not until the 1950s). Paintings such as* Pretty Polly Mine *(far right) were seen as symptomatic of the Australian character.*

support for the arts, higher education, town and regional planning were on their list along with economic growth, full employment, immigration and social welfare. An Englishman was brought out to advise on the setting up of a national theatre.

When the bustle subsided, one of the significant changes that remained from the excitements of adventurous improvising carried out under the name of planning was that Australians regained some of the position in social welfare of which they had earlier been so unexpectedly deprived, although they were still to be behind most of the other prosperous countries. A comprehensive social security program emerged, based on 'non-contributory' methods. In a five-year battle, doctors sabotaged a proposed free medical scheme, but there were now widows' pensions, unemployment and sickness pensions, pharmaceutical, hospital and funeral benefits, an employment service, a housing scheme.

Colonial governmentalism produced bodies to control the stevedoring and coal industries and the marketing of farm products; it nationalised international telecommunications and the Australian overseas airline QANTAS, and it set up

a government-owned internal airline, a shipping line, a whaling industry and an aluminium industry. The idea that humankind might be saved by public works and irrigation projects reached its apotheosis in the Snowy River Scheme, one of the largest engineering works in the world, declared by Chifley to be 'the greatest single project in our history. It is a plan for the whole nation.' It was more than an economic plan: it was a claim to Australian greatness. One of Chifley's most significant advisers said, 'In a very real sense public works contribute to a fullness in the national life by adding a sense of achievement and consciousness of growth to the life of the individual.'

It was now hoped, as had happened at the very beginning of New South Wales, that it might be the Government that controlled initiative in almost everything. The hopes of the planners reached their highest points in the last six months of 1944 when they were drafting a White Paper on full employment. A product of both the politicians' bitter memories of the Depression and the planners' ideals of rational conduct, the White Paper was to provide the theoretical basis for all future achievement. Its first draft was ready by December 1944; its seventh draft

Economist and humanitarian: H.C. Coombs

At the outbreak of World War II Herbert Cole (Nugget) Coombs, a young Treasury economist in Canberra, was a pacifist, but the threat of Japanese invasion affected his attitude: 'I found that the territorial instinct was after all strongly developed and out-weighed my pacifist convictions.' He was considering enlisting in the services when Prime Minister John Curtin appointed him Director of Rationing.

Coombs had less than two months to establish how rationing should work, what commodities were to be rationed, what quantities would be available and on what principles they should be distributed. He was to have a long public service career: Director General of Post-War Reconstruction; a principal author of the 1945 White Paper on the Economy; Governor of the Common-wealth Bank and Chairman of the Reserve Bank. His wider interests gained him the positions of Chancellor of the Australian National University and Chairman of the Council for Aboriginal Affairs and the Australian Council for the Arts.

He was a respected advisor to eight prime ministers, from Curtin to Whitlam. The latent dilemma in his role as planner-bureaucrat and concerned individual is expressed in a memory of his 1946 tour of Japan: 'The ultimate destructiveness was of course Hiroshima. I became convinced that no human being could per-sonally commit such horrors, it is only when we create institutions to which we subordinate our personal wills and at whose orders we silence the voice of conscience and personal responsibility that such things become possible.'

reached Cabinet in April 1945; by the time the politicians had finished with it, it had been re-written enough for some planners to think about going back to their universities; but it was nevertheless seen as a 'unique and historic prospectus'. Chifley declared in the 1949 election, 'So far as it can humanly contrive, never again will dole queues be seen in this country.'

By then there had been defeat for an attempt by referendum to gain the Commonwealth all the powers it needed for controlling all the activities it wanted to control. Two more limited attempts were then also defeated, but the spirit of the White Paper remained: with initiatives coming from the Government, Australia would expand and develop through industrialisation and immigration so that there would be jobs for everyone and fair shares for all. The belief in economic growth was so great that Labor's plans were not really for a welfare state, but for a society of high economic growth: from this would come jobs, and jobs were the true basis of human happiness and prosperity.

'The planners' were part of a more general hope for an intellectual breakthrough. New painters in Melbourne wanted to apply to Australian complacency 'incessant waves of shock'. Some of them abandoned the naturalistic style for a version of the German expressionist movement around the time of World War I, in which what mattered was not that painters should 'convey' reality, but, by the way they painted, show their relation to existence. Painters in both Sydney and Melbourne had returned to the landscape as a symbol for Australia and the human spirit – but the landscapes they found were not the conventional hopeful grasslands of the sheep country but the red deserts of the arid interior. In the Adelaide-Melbourne magazine *Angry Penguins* there was a sense of literary and intellectual apocalypse; in the Brisbane-Melbourne magazine *Meanjin Papers* old democratic voices took new literary forms. As part of the revulsion against the savagery of the Depression, the drabness that followed it, and the near-disasters of the war, for a while the Labor Party had the aura of social change: it had won by such a landslide in the 1943 election that the already disintegrating UAP was smothered, and a new party, the Liberal Party, had to be formed out of its wreckage. New horizons seemed to break out; there were new senses of the possible. New men were seen as relevant for new occasions.

But things could also get back to seeming the same. 'I am a refugee from Australian culture,' said Albert Tucker, one of the new Melbourne painters, when he left Australia in 1947. Some of the planners did go back to the universities. Despite the noise, a dullness fell over focal points of political struggle. Chifley called for a 'golden age' but people could not find out which way he was looking. In a period of shortages and shoddiness, they wanted not distant goals of 'national development', for which austerely puritan sacrifices were said to be necessary, but something to go on with after the shortages and shoddiness of an economy debauched by war. (The economists derided this as 'the milk-bar economy'.) Political debate sank into trench warfare: from prepared positions increasingly intense barrages on both sides concealed a lack of movement. Newspapers engaged in 'constant propaganda to show that all politicians are knaves and fools, all Government enterprises hopelessly inefficient, all civil servants bumbling idiots tied up in their own red tape'. When Chifley abruptly decided to try to nationalise the banks he was cartooned alongside Hitler and Mussolini as one of the 'National Socialist leaders of the 20th Century'. From these crudities Chifley retreated to the over-simplifications of his planners. The businessmen who had shared much of the experience of the planners and had much the same improvising adventurous spirit began to retreat to the other side, joining the more conservative financial and professional interests who had been there all the time. In a situation in which there was on both sides an impatience with complexity and a brutalising of debate, and in which the Government seemed to be running out of ideas anyway, Labor was defeated by the new Liberal Party in the 1949 elections. But to many it seemed obvious that Labor would be out of office only long enough to fix itself up and come back fighting again. The 1940s had seemed Labor's decade and, as it had seemed before World War I, Labor could appear to be the natural ruling party.

To this time of bitter dispute when men could see all light on one side and all darkness on the other (anti-planners sneering at the planners' 'road to serfdom', planners sneering at the 'freedom to starve') melodrama was added by the Australian Communists who saw themselves in a world in which total victory was near. They had made spectacular advances in the trade union movement, on some occasions, in their righteousness rigging ballots, smearing, threatening violence; and in 1945, with some help from non-Communist supports, they gained dominance of the Australian Council of Trade Unions (ACTU).

With 60 per cent of its caucus Catholics, the Labor Party counter-organised. 'Industrial Groups' were formed in the unions to fight the Communists, taking strength from earlier anti-Communist organisations including a 'Catholic Social Studies Movement' known to its followers as 'the Movement', which had already gained practice in getting the numbers at union meetings. In an atmosphere hot and sticky with suspicion of the intrigues of the 'Commos' or of 'Catholic Action', Labor fought back, recapturing some key unions and the ACTU; the Government jailed two Communist leaders for sedition and set up a security service to find out what the Communists were doing.

Giddy with their general world success, the Communists, who had earlier spoken of 'a peaceful path to socialism' and had offered cooperation with the Labor Party, now denounced it as 'just as anti-Labor as Hitler and Mussolini and Japanese imperialists' and proclaimed (in its own language) that the time had come for the party to 'show its face', and take over the leadership of the labour movement. As a step in this improbable adventure the party threw its support behind a miners' strike that, its leaders hoped, would be an exemplary struggle against a 'reformist' Labor Government: the Communist Party would demonstrate what true militancy looked like. In retaliation, Chifley's Government raided the Communist Party headquarters and froze the funds of the Communist unions; when union officials took money out of their banks, seven were jailed. More than 500 000 were thrown out of work. Train and tram services were severely cut. Electricity was rationed. Gas was down to an hour's supply a day. At this stage Chifley put soldiers in to work the mines. The strike

collapsed. For the workers, there had been another betrayal of the revolution.

No Australian Government had ever launched such attacks on the Communist Party, but the Liberal Party denounced the Government for being soft on Communism and campaigned for a complete ban on the party. Communist armies were in seven European countries. A Communist army was winning in China. Communists were leading the guerilla war against the British in Malaya and the nationalist war against the French in Indo-China. In 1948 an opinion survey in ten countries showed that it was Australians who had the highest expectancy of another world war. The orphan of the Pacific looked to its turbulent north from which only a few years ago had come invasion fleets, armies, bombers, submarines.

The Cold War: *during the war, friendship for the Soviet Union as an ally had grown so great that even* The Australian Women's Weekly *pictured a benign Stalin on its cover in 1945 (far below). But by the crucial election year of 1949, the Cold War had begun, and although the Chifley Government had proven to be determinedly anti-communist, it lost the election (below).*

The post-war increase in home-ownership and the steady maintenance of full employment turned Australia into what could seem a nation of city-dwelling 'little capitalists' — eager consumers of hire-purchase goods and proud owners of Australia's own car, the Holden. In the long post-war boom, with its partial affluence for many (if not for the poor) there was growing euphoria; one sign of this was an optimistic belief in youth. Euphoria increased even more with the minerals boom, although most of the early mining expansion was carried out by foreign firms for export overseas. The collapse of the boom, at a time of world economic downturn, created a previously unthought-of combination: high inflation with high unemployment. Australia turned inwards, and the sacking of the Whitlam Labor Government in 1975 confirmed the belief for many that the country was uniquely conservative.

From back yard to barbecue

The first post-war aim of thousands of young Australians was to join their parents and grandparents in 'owning their own homes'. Building costs had risen twice as high as other living costs, labour was scarce, slapdash and expensive, and materials were in short supply, so many young people, in a return to an 1850s form of individualism, built their own houses.

They would live in a garage for two or three years, and in their spare time construct a house alongside it, doing all the work themselves, or having some of it done by paid labour but supervising it without a contractor. For a while, half the new houses were built by owner-builders. To cheer up houses that costs had kept down to essentials, their owners looked to cans of paint, turning from the 1930s gentility of cream to the brightness of the paint cards of suburban shops. With fireplaces gone, 'feature walls' were created to keep some memory of centredness. But, although romantic in their use of colour, house owners also dreamed of rationality: their urges to human perfectibility turned to the 'dream kitchen' where careful planning of cupboards, space, work benches, cooker, refrigerator, stainless-steel sink and easily cleaned surfaces, would provide a more efficient basis for life. As part of this, the small hatches that connected cooking and eating areas were abandoned, and replaced by 'breakfast bars'. But neither housewives nor their children were always rational enough to use dream kitchens according to instructions. Among those with money, hopes then moved to 'open plan' houses.

Under the thousands of suburban roofs where both romance and reason were proving inadequate, there was still scepticism about the availability of money and jobs, and a balance-of-payments recession in 1952 had a familiar ring. Then things picked up, and from about the mid-1950s, despite occasional dips, the belief began that all this might last. The new generation had no doubts. That dream of becoming 'a nation of little capitalists' that had alarmed a

Changing places: *among middle-class people who sought some of the pleasures of inner-city dwelling there was an increasing tendency to move to the inner city. What had been regarded as slums in Melbourne's Carlton, or Sydney's Paddington (left), or in North Adelaide, were now seen as sophisticated dwelling places. Many immigrants from continental Europe also bought houses in the inner city. The expanding frontier was on the ever-widening outskirts of the cities, sometimes in expansive colonial or ranch-style houses, sometimes in very simple houses in new suburbs with few social amenities (above).*

Labor cabinet minister in the 1940s was now being realised. The number of Australians who owned or were paying off or were planning to pay off their own homes rose in not much more than a decade from less than half to something approaching three quarters of all occupiers of dwelling places, and some of the greatest aggregations of home ownership were in working-class suburbs – in the newly subdivided areas on the outskirts of the cities.

With flat-dwelling acceptable because flats could now be owned by their occupants, there followed a boom in residential towers and smaller blocks of flats. There were experiments in medium density housing. The older examples of this – the now dilapidated terraces ringing the central city areas – were restored and painted light colours by 'migrants' and by middle-class people looking for urban living. By the late 1960s almost one in five households in the Sydney metropolitan areas lived in flats; in some districts they constituted 75 to 100 per cent of all new building. To this extent the first suburban nation was again becoming citified. And the recognition of Australia as a nation where most people lived in large cities had now spread from statements in a few books in the early 1960s to Government spending programs: with pipes, wires and concrete there was an attempt to make up deficiencies caused by earlier refusals to accept the nation's predominantly urban nature. By the beginning of the 1970s, when people at universities were beginning to speak of 'urban studies' and playwrights and fiction writers were writing about city people, Labor politicians had begun to put their hopes on a 'metropolitan strategy' that would attract the votes of home owners; by the 1980s 'the mortgage belt' was seen as a decisive factor in all elections. By then it could seem political suicide not to give overriding priority to the interests of home owners, and

they had indeed become 'little capitalists' in the sense that during the long property boom they would often discuss over their family teas the capital gains that came with the increases in the value of their houses. To many, or most, working-class people, where they lived could matter more than where they worked. The number of Australians who were to tell public opinions pollsters they saw themselves as 'middle class' was to rise to 55 per cent, with only 35 per cent seeing themselves as 'working class'. Even a quarter of the most poorly off manual workers were to classify themselves as middle class. In the minds of its own people, Australia was to become what could look like the most 'middle-class' society in the world.

By the mid-1950s the use of hire purchase had become even more confident. A slogan in one of the State elections in the 1940s of 'A refrigerator in every home' had almost been realised ten years later. Some new form of cooking was always offering Improvement ... the pressure cooker (with its promise of ease and greater 'goodness') followed by the electric frypan ('no fuss') ... finally, the microwave oven ('an ultimate in convenience'). 'No home was complete' without an increasingly large number of electric miracle workers – the mixer, the pop-up toaster, the floor polisher, the coffee percolator, the blender and others. Just as refrigerators ended up in almost every kitchen, there was to be an electric washing machine in almost every home; for the less well-off there were electric dishwashers to look forward to and electric air conditioners; by the 1980s one in ten houses was to have a swimming pool. Women were becoming skilled equipment managers and purchase officers. Earlier, saving, hard work and frugality had seemed necessary for economic growth: now what was essential to keep money moving was indulgence and high spending. In

Gadgetry: *one of the greatest symbols of Improvement continued to be the advertisements for household electrical equipment, from the mixer in the 1950s to the microwave oven in the 1980s.*

their role as the principal shoppers, women were performing a profoundly important economic function and a great deal of money was paid on market research to analyse their hopes and fears so that advertising and merchandising might flatter them, divert them, or touch on their anxieties.

Already a great home-owning democracy, with an average of one car per family at the beginning of the 1960s and an average of two at the end of that decade, Australia by the 1970s was to become the world's third greatest car-owning democracy: there were as many cars in Australia as in the whole Soviet Union. In all its ramifications, the motor industry was providing about a seventh of Australia's jobs, and it had revolutionised both the appearance of the cities (where the use of public transport dropped by half) and the lives of almost all of the people who lived in them. The launching of 'Australia's Own Car', the Holden, in 1948, at a ceremony in which an orchestra played a Brahms waltz in A flat as the ivory-coloured first model slowly revolved on a stage covered in black velvet, was, economically, socially and spiritually, a much more important event than the opening of the Snowy River Scheme; the Redex reliability trials of the 1950s had much

of the appeal of the great air races of the 1930s; even after the Holden lost its extraordinary command of half the market, each year's new model was given a greater display than all but the most important of the royal births. The construction of 'service stations' changed the character of many of the main city roads; some of these roads – many of them beflagged or decorated with gaudy signs – with their service stations and their motor showrooms, used-car yards, spare parts dealers, tyre suppliers, tow-away trucks, auto-electricians, transmission specialists, could seem devoted to a festival of the motor car. For a period, when 'freeways' were in vogue, there were plans to destroy large parts of the cities so that people could get to work five minutes earlier. In some houses two, or even three-car garages were built, in others at least a 'carport'. A new type of building, 'the parking station', was designed. Buildings were cleared and replaced with great stretches of asphalt to use as carparks.

Motels and caravan parks extended holiday choices along the coastlines; collapsible furniture, portable barbecues and 'Esky' cold boxes made picnics almost like a meal at home; drive-in theatres, drive-in bottle shops and supermarkets with carparks were then followed by whole new suburban

The car revolution: *some of the great changes in the way Australians earned and spent their money came from the continuing growth of the motor vehicle industry. As its height, motor vehicle manufacture, in its ramifications, became Australia's biggest manufacturing industry (above). In its early days, the Holden was patriotically seen as 'Australia's own car' (right). As more and more families bought cars, picnics in the bush became a popular weekend pastime (above right), complete with 'Esky' and barbecue. The new 'shopping centres' (far right) were another of the changes in life style brought by cars.*

THE BEAUTIFUL HOLDEN – AUSTRALIA'S OWN CAR

HOLDEN
Australia's Own Car

shopping complexes, with their 'malls' and 'courts', and sometimes even their own fountains and theatres, giving some of that sense of community and importance to the suburbs that previously they had lacked. And the car manufacturers themselves provided as great a sense of Improvement as the makers of kitchen goods, by offering new revelations of the possible – in automatic transmission, air conditioning, disc brakes, front-wheel drive, power steering, stereo tape recorders, self-adjusting brakes, radial tyres and other marvels. The transport revolution also helped develop the new habits of 'convenience foods': freezer trailers delivered to supermarkets throughout the country quick-frozen peas, beans and potato chips, quick-frozen fish, cakes, pies, or for that matter quick-frozen spaghetti bolognese, chicken maryland, beef stroganoff or lamb's fry and bacon and above all, quick-frozen poultry. Shoppers placed packages of quick-frozen food in their supermarket trolleys, unloaded it into their cars, then, when they got home, packed it into their freezers.

Takeaway foods also developed; the first Colonel Sanders was established in 1968 and the first McDonalds and Pizza Hut in 1970; they were followed by takeaway Chinese food, takeaway Lebanese food, and a range of other supplements to the fish and chips that had earlier been all that could be taken away. The concern for health foods that had begun in the 1920s and 1930s was still there, but now people didn't have to squeeze oranges: orange juice came in plastic containers. Vogel's Bread arrived in Australia, with its mixed grain offering a more sincere kind of bread.

The hopes that had looked to feature walls and dream kitchens turned to 'outdoor living'. Paved terraces spread across lawns, sometimes shaded by pergolas or umbrellas. (A play was written satirising suburban bad taste called *The Multi-Coloured Umbrella*.) Garden furniture, in imitation wrought iron or timber painted either white or 'natural', became good selling lines in the shops, along with barbecues and barbecue equipment. The idea of the 'patio' began to express a new sense of progress and a wider sense of relaxation in suburban life. The use of gardening as a self-discipline began to be abandoned. Back yards lost their rows of vegetables and their hen runs and were simplified to make a more casual setting. Electric lawn mowers whisked away grass, and circular metal hoists where clothes were hung when they came out of electric washing machines were erected as monuments honouring both progress and Australian ingenuity, although by the 1980s these in turn were replaced in something like four out of ten households by tumble clothes driers. With gardens no longer done up in their Sunday best, easy-going native trees and shrubs began to appear. Names like 'Melaleuca' and 'Grevillea' could replace names like 'Crimson Glory' or 'Iceland Poppy'. Most sincere and natural of all the new gardens were those that were carefully planted to look like 'natural' bush.

In this more relaxed style, even some of the certitudes of spectator sport weakened: there was less concern with moral fibre. Worship of surf life-savers declined, sales of surfboards went up: the young 'surfie' who just surfed for pleasure and not to save lives was seen as a symbol of a new hedonism. Skiing, sailing and other sports were partly democratised, as tennis and golf had been for an earlier generation.

Delight in winning became naked and unashamed, especially in the 1960s, a decade of sporting miracles:

Australians won most of the Davis Cup seasons, beat England in all the cricket test series, won Olympic gold medals and broke world records in swimming and athletics, produced two world champions in boxing, one in car racing and one in squash, itself a game that suggested a new, more sophisticated Australia. By the end of the 1960s Australians were so debauched by victory that they lost interest in the Davis Cup, and in one of the test series some of them wanted England to win, for a change.

In the 1970s all the old nationalist fervour and moral fibre seemed fatally threatened when the television stations turned sport into commercialised telecast entertainment. In a ceremony in which the handing over of the sponsor's cheque became the climax of honour, sponsors' logos were more flamboyantly obvious than political symbols in a one-party state. Six or more cameras followed the main action. Well-placed microphones gave intimacy. Hand-held cameras gave actuality. There were close-ups, long shots, slow motion replays. Now larger than life, sport became an experience that could be adequately experienced only on television. When cricket was commercialised and one-day matches were invented, there was a sense of great moral

The back yard: *slowly, the 'back yard' became the 'back garden'. The old clotheslines and clothes props disappeared. The barbecue was installed. Native trees were planted. In some houses, the patio was built. One of the first changes came with the electric motor mower.*

crisis in an age of change. But the old faith was still
there: Australia won the America's Cup in 1983, and the
enthusiasm was as great as when Trickett had beaten the
British at sculling in 1876. It was again said that Australia
had come of age.

Now families met around veneered television cabinets
rather than around bakelite radio consoles. Transitorised
into 'the trannie', radio became personalised; stations
created distinctive 'images' to help people determine who
they were, providing meaning like the music track of a film
that never ended, or through talk and talkback bringing the
reassurance of the human voice. Television was the
group experience, offering in one week more drama than, in
some civilisations, was available in a lifetime (and, along
with the quizzes and chat shows and the variety shows,
offering a world that was largely dominated by middle-class
Anglo-Saxon males). The news became part of this drama,
projecting simple stories of familiar heroes and villains,
along with the unknown victims of life's immutable forces,
in a world that, when it wasn't Australian, was usually
British or American. Throughout the 1960s, as a result of
their unsatisfactory performances on television, there was a

The sporting revolution: *there were many changes to the face
of sport. Women became more visible in sport. Dawn Fraser, Sandra
Morgan, Lorraine Crapp and Alva Colquhuon (top) after winning
the 4 x 110 yards freestyle relay at Cardiff, Wales, in 1958. The
introduction of World Series Cricket in the summer of 1977 brought
commercialism to the game (top right). The arrival of the 'surfies' in
the 1950s gave a different emphasis to the beach scene (right). With
the winning of the America's Cup in 1983 (above), Australians again
believed they had demonstrated their superior nationality through sport.*

concern with the inadequacies of politicians' 'images': then, in both State and national politics, parties began to provide politicians who seemed adequate television personalities.

As part of the general moving away from the idea that self-denial was necessary for respectability, enforced puritanism broke up and things returned to what had once been normal: it was possible now for men and women to publicly enjoy themselves together. Formal dressing relaxed: men could wear long hair; women could wear trousers. Sabbatarianism was relaxed almost to vanishing point; off-course betting became legal; in a few places casinos were allowed; drinking was again 'mixed' at hotels and hotel trading hours went back to what they used to be, with night entertainment in many of the hotels, just like the old days; restaurants again served liquor; there was more drinking at home; wine-drinking (once commonly seen as degenerately un-Australian) became more common, especially after the development of sweetish white wines for unaccustomed drinkers. This prompted one of the wonders of Australian technology: the 'wine cask' with its collapsible plastic bag.

Eating places proliferated not only in the cities, but throughout the suburbs and country towns. For whole classes of people 'eating-out' became sufficiently commonplace for the newspapers and magazines to devote space to columns about wine and food; the monopoly of an Australian version of English cooking disintegrated, to be replaced by a variety of 'continental' and 'Asian' cuisines. In the mining town of Broken Hill, the Workers Club offered 'Bouyabaise' and 'Fillet Mygnon Richelieu', the Kokoda Room of the RSL Club offered Chicken Chow Mein, Chicken Hungarian, Chicken Chasseur, and there was a choice of spaghettis at the Capri Espresso.

A 40-hour working week was made statutory in 1948; later provisions extended paid holidays and sick leave and made long service leave a compulsory charge on employers. The holiday business (and the length of holidays) expanded and a new city – the Gold Coast, south of Brisbane – and

Having a good time: *the development of the poker machine clubs in New South Wales in the 1960s became one of the symbols of the times (below). When The Australian Women's Weekly began its 'Women's Weekly World Discovery Tours' in 1966 (far below) it presented new opportunities for travel for ordinary people.*

The television revolution: *with the spread of television the functions of radio and films were redefined. Television became Australians' principal storyteller, bringing many changes in social life – from new styles in politics to new styles in sport. A young Graham Kennedy faces the beginning of his television career (top). The ratings success of 'The Dismissal' (above) in 1983, a dramatisation of the last days of the Whitlam Government, was seen as marking a higher than usual degree of audience sophistication.*

a number of towns grew up in dedication to the pleasures of holidays and the comforts of retirement. In 1966 *The Australian Women's Weekly* began its 'World Discovery Tours'. In New South Wales poker machines were made legal and in the suburban centres and country towns big clubs, belonging to the ordinary people and designed like United States resort hotels, were financed out of their profits. The biggest, £3 million of it, had eight bars, squash courts, indoor bowls, billiards, gymnasia, sauna baths, 200 'pokies', and 20 000 members.

Still walking around their cities as if they owned them, the deeds of their houses held by their savings banks, insurance companies or building societies, and their barbecues in their back yards, many ordinary Australians could imagine they were moving towards fulfilment of that dream of dignity of the common man first manifested by the Emancipists and Natives and then by the mutual societies of the Emigrants. They held much of their achievement to be in their access to material things and to the privileges of leisure, but they also cultivated an openness of manner and a cult of informality that, its aggressiveness now less evident, had in it some

seeking towards a common humanity, even if its rituals could conceal or even frustrate differences between individuals. Remarkably similar in some ways to early descriptions of the Currency Lads and Lasses, it was, for better or worse, the Australian style.

With Australians' length of experience of high urbanisation, their long concern with social cohesion and their established moderation in the use of social violence, the cities remained remarkably stable at a time when cities in other countries were seen as symbols of disorder, or even doom. Australians could be violent in their individual relations – the larrikin was still in many of them – but except for the destruction of Aboriginal society and the wars that were fought outside Australia, their history had been relatively peaceful. Social disturbances were so rare compared with the violence embedded in almost every other country's memory that some history writers, affronted by such abnormality, tried to make these incidents larger than they were, while others, unable to recognise such open conflict as there was in Australian society, made them insignificant, or did not even see them.

As ever, the suburbs were under attack: 'Behold the man

Suburban nightmare: *John Brack's* Collins Street, 5 pm *(left), painted in 1956, with its image of conformist commuters, became one of Australian intellectuals' favourite symbols of the despair of the suburbs.*

Suburban dream: *the television series 'The Sullivans' projected an image, both favourable and realistic, of a suburban family (left); it became the most successful suburban series ever produced in Australia, and appealed in many other countries.*

– the Australian man of today – on Sunday mornings in the suburbs, when the high-decibel drone of the motor mower is calling the faithful to worship. A block of land, a brick veneer, and a motor mower beside him in the wilderness.' But among intellectuals the suburbanites had also now found a few defenders, notably the Adelaide historian Hugh Stretton, who did not quarrel with the ideals of suburbanism ('It reconciles access with work and city with private, adaptable, self-expressive living space at home') but with the failure, because of bad planning, to carry many of its ideals into practice. It was, for instance, not sufficient to have convenience foods, if travelling to and from work was becoming more and more inconvenient. And in fiction, in drama, and in television serials as well, it was now at least being recognised that so many Australians were suburban. 'The Sullivans', one of the most commercially successful Australian serials, raised suburbanism to almost mythic qualities and in 'Sandy Stone' and 'Edna Everage', the actor Barry Humphries created two suburban characters whom audiences turned into folk figures. For the first time in Australia's history a female prototype had been created of Australians, even if it was a man dressed as a woman.

Dame Edna Everage with son Oscar

Brilliant eccentric: Barry Humphries

It is ironic that Australia's best known woman is really a man satirising, sometimes lovingly, sometimes cruelly, the pretensions and aspirations of Australian suburbia.

Dame Edna Everage started life as an improvised party act in Melbourne in the 1950s, the invention of a brilliant, eccentric prankster-student. Barry Humphries was born in 1934 and educated at Melbourne Grammar School. He became a noted actor and author, putting on his own one-man shows and appearing in musicals in England and the United States as well as Australia. Dame Edna, with her awesome vitality and equally awesome belief in herself, was as recognisably (and controversially) a national type as the Anzac and the surf life-saver. She was one of several Humphries' creations, ranging from Sandy Stone, 'a decent humdrum little old man of the suburbs' to Bazza Mackenzie, the 'typical' Australian abroad.

By the 1970s Humphries was caricaturing recognisable types in business, 'the Yartz', the trendy Left and the world of skiing and tourism. Reactions against him developed, but his audiences loved him, laughing happily as he pilloried one of their number. Exchanges with the audience were a Humphries trademark; as was the maniacal tossing of gladioli into the auditorium at the end of a show, accompanied by the audience singing a Humphries song that satirised themselves.

Before the war, young people were still thought of, in the manner that had grown up in the new industrial societies, as 'adolescents' – in-between people, neither children nor adults, usually with pimples and problems, who were passing through a period of trial before they became proper people. But as the 1940s moved into the 1950s they became 'teenagers', no longer on trial, but a threat, or the world's main hope (or both at once).

Their existence received a significant recognition when in 1959 *The Australian Women's Weekly* launched a new supplement, *Teenagers' Weekly*. Early teenagers were the 'bobby soxers' who screamed their delight after the war whenever they heard a new recording of Frank Sinatra's or one of the other new brand of singers and, when they were at a dance hall, jitterbugged and jived. The satisfactions to be found in this way of being a teenager were realised in the 1950s with the 'Big Shows' in which idolised singers came to Australia and their fans screamed so loudly that at times scarcely a note could be heard. A new language began to develop with special teenage meanings, and with derogatory terms for those who were 'square', and, in particular, for the 'oldies' and the 'wrinklies'.

By then another element had been added to the 'scene' – rock and roll. With this, the element of threat could be more defined, partly in the raucousness of the new music and the rowdiness at the suburban halls where it was played, and partly in what could seem the depravity of Elvis Presley and the menace of the long-haired 'bodgies', in their leather jackets and tight-fitting black slacks, and their 'widgies', the young females whom they treated as group possessions. Rock began to become domesticated, however, when Australia produced its first rock star in Johnny O'Keefe who, although trade-named 'the Wild One', was nevertheless 'wild' with an Australian suburban reassurance.

Adolescents' clothes had merely been a sub-set of what older people wore: when the 'New Look', with its long, swinging skirts and wasp waists came in after the war, and men's double-breasted suits developed wider shoulders and an exaggerated roll, young people adopted them as evidence of modernity, but with the emphasis on 'teenagers' young people began to adopt fashions of their own. The arrival of the 'sack' and the 'shift' at the end of the 1950s began a period when the clothes of the young seemed to be setting the pace not only for themselves, but for everyone else. In the clothing trade, as elsewhere, there was much talk of a 'youth market', and the fashion whirl of the mini, the maxi, the midi, hot pants and pants suits gave the impression of a takeover by youth – accentuated even more by the spread of the T-shirt, and the popularity of jeans with their equality (tempered by connoisseurship of brand names, styling and other tests of *chic*).

By the time of what had now become 'the jeans revolution' the young, or the more sophisticated of them, had discarded words like 'square' and 'teenager', because they had now been widely adopted by the enemy, and declared themselves with new code words like 'dropout', 'groove', 'uptight' or the ubiquitous 'doing your own thing'. When the youth market extended to films, with *The*

Graduate in 1968, and *Easy Rider* in 1969, there was a further extension of the impression that youth was conquering all.

However, the sense of threat had also increased – mainly in connection with what was spoken of as 'the drug scene', with confusions between pot smokers, takers of 'hard drugs' and that majority of young people whose drug addictions remained conventional (alcohol and nicotine), but also in fears that 'the hippies' (although there were scarcely any 'hippy colonies') were a threat to society. But, as with most other aspects of what was now called the 'youth culture', hippiness could also be suitably commercialised: in clothing, temple bells, beads and other decorations, fluorescent paint, strobe lighting, incense, astrology charts.

For a period in the late 1960s and early 1970s there seemed to be a threat from the universities, as denim-clad radicals in university cafeterias spoke of how, in a sharpening of the class struggle, 'student power' must now become allied with 'worker power' to speed the revolution. Among a multiplicity of factions, a few self-appointed 'Red Guards' saw themselves as the vanguard of revolutionary change. Loud hailer oratory, a small amount of broken glass and an occasional occupation of some university inner sanctum could seem a challenge to the social order, but in business offices it was also a time when the idea had been developed of the 'junior executive' and whole firms would decide they 'must go for a younger image'.

For many, especially those of liberal inclination, youth could now seem to be leading the way. 'They are sharp, up-to-date, ambitious, image-conscious, materialist – and more

The threat from youth: *even before the advent of rock, the 'fans' at the pop music concerts were seen as symbols of youthful depravity. With rock, the figure of 'the bodgie' became a symbol of threat. The late 1960s and early 1970s were haunted by the figure of 'the hippy', a creature of affluence. With unemployment, the threat came from 'the punk'. Fans at a Frankie Laine show (below left).*

Youths dressed in 'bodgie' style queue at a city cinema (below) to see Rock Around the Clock, *the first of the rock music films, in 1956.*

The greatest of the 'hippy' festivals was the Aquarius Festival at Nimbin (far below) on the New South Wales north coast. After the festival, Nimbin became a centre for 'alternative society' settlements. The 'punk' fashions (far below left) developed from the new moods that came when full employment ended.

than anything else they are *aware*: aware of ideas, fashions, cults, overseas trends, music, business techniques, in a way very few groups of Australians have been before.' It was also said of them that they seemed greater masters than any earlier generation of the easy manner so long sought by Australians: they had found an emphasis on naturalness and on a relaxed, open style that in turn had its effect on those who were older. When the new television public affairs program 'This Day Tonight' began in 1967, its front-of-camera people were all young: it may have been the youngest public affairs program on earth. When the rock station 2JJ opened in 1975 this seemed a further expression of 'the youth revolution'. Beneath all the enthusiasm, whether from 'Red Guards' or from 'junior executives', there was the confidence of a generation that had grown up with neither war nor depression to frustrate its dreams. There had never been such material prosperity. People were now living in an age in which a miracle had occurred: there were jobs for everyone. Whether it was a whole change in society that was sought in a university 'demo' or a change in market planning at an executives' conference, change had never seemed so easy.

By the late 1950s Australia had one of the world's most industrialised farming industries and one of the smallest proportions of farm workers. CSIRO research and the fairly rapid spread of scientific findings, along with advice from State Agriculture Departments and news of labour-saving machines, had helped major farming industries to remain among the world's most efficient.

In a spectacular follow-up to the 1920s destruction of the prickly pear, the CSIRO in 1950 introduced the myxomatosis virus and soon millions of rabbits were dead. At the same time, the expansion of wartime manufacturing skills, along with the special protection given by import licences, encouraged an unparalleled expansion of investment in manufacturing. Australia was 'industrialised'.

Much of the expansion was made, however, in manufacturing by foreign firms, and almost all of it was based on foreign enterprise (of the prosperous industrial societies Australia was uniquely unable to think up new things to make or new ways to make them), but it was

With the development of the idea of a 'teenage revolution', merchandisers began to speak of a 'youth market'. Coca Cola promotions (left) led the way for many other advertisers.

In 1965 an English model, Jean Shrimpton ('the Shrimp'), was flown to Melbourne for the Cup Carnival as a public relations gimmick for a synthetic fibre company; she was to wear clothes made from their products. But the skirts she wore in her several appearances during the carnival were 8 centimetres above the knee and at once became a 'media sensation' (above). At the next year's Cup, however, many women's skirts were shorter than that, with the acceptance of the new fashion of the 'mini-skirt'.

When Sydney's Channel Ten put out a public affairs program, Telescope, in 1965, they chose Bill Peach (above) as its compere. Peach had begun his broadcasting career with the ABC 'Talks Department', and when the ABC started This Day Tonight, Peach returned to the ABC to compere it.

The sleeve of Business as Usual (left), by the Australian (and internationally successful) rock group Men At Work. One of their hit songs, 'Down Under', became the theme song for the Australia II challenge in the America's Cup.

typical of the times that this was scarcely noticed. Australians congratulated themselves on the Hills Hoist and the Victa electric lawn mower as if these were great industrial innovations; in 1983, part of the rejoicing about winning the America's Cup was that this was seen as an example of Australian skill in high technology.

This time foreign money was being put to a different use from what had happened under the 1920s policy of 'men, money and markets', or the 19th-century policy of 'spirited public works'. Governments were not borrowing foreign money and channelling it in an attempt to keep the economy predominantly rural: foreign money came in direct investment by foreign firms when they established new manufacturing plants in Australia or bought out Australian companies. The amount of manufacturing activity rose to figures that indicated a fully industrialised nation; thereafter it was the proportion of activity in tertiary industries that went up; it was becoming one of the world's highest.

Many of the most boring jobs in Australia were in manufacturing: to fill these, throughout the 1950s and 1960s there was a steady flow of immigrants. Immigrants provided, altogether, about a quarter of the work force, but for factory work they provided more than half. Some of the most boring jobs were filled by immigrant women. Overall, for women, whether immigrant or native-born, the 1960s provided as big a change in employment as had happened during the war: in ten years the proportion of women in paid employment increased by almost half. And within this change there was another: half the women in the work force were married. In a high-consumption society the 'two-income' family was becoming normal. By the 1980s only about one family in five still fitted the old ideal of an 'average family' in which a working father supported his wife and children. In two families in five, both husband and wife were working.

From the mid-1950s there began another boom (again depending predominantly on immigrants' labour): 'developers' began pulling out the hearts of the existing central city areas and rebuilding them. Height restrictions were eased and shining new prestige buildings rose above the Renaissance-palace commercial styles of an earlier age. In marble, mosaics, oiled timber, bronze sculptures and garden forecourts, self-belief flourished. Architectural

The boring jobs: *as full employment came with the long boom, the least skilled jobs tended to go to women and immigrants. The most boring jobs, such as those of factory process workers (left), were likely to go to immigrant women. Labourers on construction projects like the Snowy Mountains Scheme (below left), tended to be immigrants.*

The shopping 'mall' came to be seen as one of the new forms of Improvement. When Premier Don Dunstan opened the Rundle Street Mall in Adelaide in 1976, champagne bubbled from the fountain.

novelty spread to churches and government offices; city fountains were constructed in the new styles; the Sydney Opera House, which was to cost about $100 million because the New South Wales Government had accepted a series of sketches without enquiring whether it was feasible to construct the building, prompted other cities to put up their own temples of culture. Guesses were made that the population of the Newcastle-Sydney-Wollongong urbanising area might reach seven million by the end of the century, with five million of them in Sydney. There was talk of 'corridor growth' along the east coast of Australia, so that from Townsville to Eden there would be 'a necklace of cities'. In Sydney there were plans to pull down and replace

the whole of the Rocks area and all Woolloomooloo; in Adelaide the Metropolitan Adelaide Transport Study (MATS) of 1967 proposed to clear great swathes through Adelaide for a system of freeways.

Protest movements and changes in intellectual fashion finally halted such excesses, but development went on – in a new fashion of building to 'human scale'. No sooner had most of the old city arcades been pulled down, than new arcades were built; then human aspiration settled on the pedestrian mall as one of the new symbols of Improvement.

For the early part of this period the old rhetoric about national development revived, still with the idea that there was no price too high to pay to bring natural resources into production. Closer settlement schemes continued, governments still scattered public works around the countryside with the traditional disregard for economic considerations, and subsidies to farmers became greater. To the idea that it was immoral to leave natural resources unused was added the idea that it was dangerous – some other country might come and take them. In the late 1950s and early 1960s a 'develop the north' movement became popular since the north was the part that was closest to other countries. But, as time went on and markets became less certain, belief in rural expansion declined. Money spent on farming and rural areas became defensive: rural public work projects degenerated into isolated attempts to maintain country votes; rural subsidies (despite beliefs to the contrary) were much less than in many other prosperous nations; by 1970 closer settlement schemes had been abandoned and with the new slogan of 'get big or get out' there were plans to get small farmers off the land. The idea of decentralisation went into a new form: the building

Redevelopment: *plans were made for pulling down large sections of the cities and redeveloping them as high-rise projects. In Sydney in the early 1970s, there were plans for destroying and rebuilding both Woolloomooloo (left) and the Rocks (below left), two of the oldest remaining parts of the city, and replacing them with modern buildings. Both plans were blocked by Resident Action Groups.*

The mining boom: *the principal new finds, other than coal, during the great mineral boom (right).*

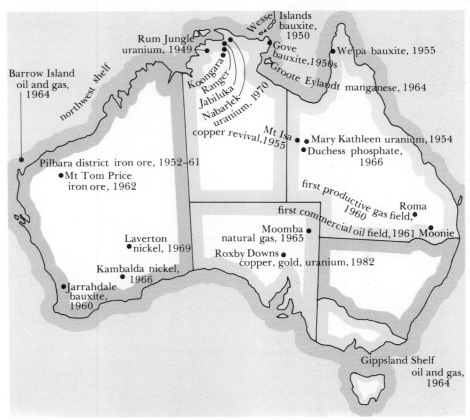

267

of new cities in the country. Plans for Monarto, in South Australia, and an extended Albury-Wodonga on the New South Wales-Victorian border had their day; then these plans also were abandoned. The old itch was still there, however: in the 1980s politicians fighting elections were still likely to promise grandiose schemes of water conservation or plans to build the Alice Springs-Darwin railway, but with less and less credibility.

With the great minerals boom that began in the 1960s 'development' now meant, above all, mining. Australians had for almost a hundred years seen sheep as their symbol of initiative and prosperity: now television documentaries of the caravans and drilling rigs of geological survey parties and the bulldozers that scooped away mountains provided new symbols of enterprise and nationhood.

The explosion of activity in iron ore became the symbol of all this new activity. Until 1960 Australia had an unimaginative approach towards iron ore exports – whatever it had it would keep. When this policy broke down survey work was stimulated. Huge new resources were found. At the same time technology was now available to bring this iron ore profitably from outback to coast, and the

up such hopes that ten years later it was still possible for a prime minister to fight an election on a new 'resources boom' (that did not, in fact, exist).

As with the 19th-century wool rushes and gold rushes, the mining boom was largely a matter of foreign money coming into Australia to arrange the exporting of Australian products to foreign markets. Almost all the early mining expansion was carried out by foreign firms with their own capital and technology: the Australian financial and business communities had proved too conservative, and when Australian firms did begin to play a part – and an expert part – in the new developments it was mainly as partners with foreign companies. This foreign domination of the minerals boom raised doubts about the capacity of Australian businessmen but they were not much expressed. The ironically titled *The Lucky Country*, a best seller of the 1960s, raised some of these doubts, but so great was the euphoria of the 1960s that the irony in the title was ignored and the phrase 'the lucky country' passed into the national vocabulary as a term of praise. The high spirits of the mining boom had obscured Australian failures to develop greater technological sophistication. It was easier to agree

Companies used television commercials to present their contributions to Australian developments. In the early 1980s, some of the most popular were the ads done for Esso by television personality Mike Willessee.

Japanese 'economic miracle' provided a customer. Railways were flung across sunburnt country; new ports sprang up on desolate coasts; 100 000-tonne iron ore carriers began to shuttle between Western Australia and Japan. With less publicity, but with equal or even greater significance, Japanese industrial expansion gave the coal industry relief from its long slump; the world's largest bauxite mine was opened in Queensland; nickel was added to the list; there was expansion in a wide range of other minerals, some of them metals whose very names had been unknown; drilling rigs spouted oil; pipes were planned to carry natural gas hundreds of kilometres to the cities. In one of the longest gambles in the 'stock exchange casinos' in Australia's long history of mining speculation, one company increased its capital in five years from £300 000 to £100 million before, in 1971, it collapsed. The whole speculative boom was collapsing with it, but the mining itself still went on, compensating for the decline in farm exports, and buoying

Industrial developer: Sir Charles Court

One of those who presided most publicly over the turning of Western Australia from a predominantly agricultural economy into a prosperous minerals producer was Charles Court, Premier from 1974 to 1982, but more significantly, Minister of Industrial Development in the booming 1960s.

To his most bitter opponents, projects such as Pilbara iron ore, Laporte mineral sands, Northwest Shelf natural gas, the alumina of the southwest and Kimberley diamond mines were scars on the countryside and threatened Aboriginal land rights. However, like the early developers of European Australia, Court saw materials as providing the financial backing for Improvement for others as well as himself.

In spite of his acknowledged wit and genial charm, Court, with his distrust of what he called the Liberal Party's 'Eastern State trendies', was considered by many to be extremely conservative. His background, however, was traditional Labor, and as a cornet player in the 1930s he was such a militant member of the Musicians' Union that the Australian Broadcasting Commission is said to have refused to negotiate with him. Court claimed his move to the Liberal Party was a result of being saturated with unionism at 'breakfast, dinner and tea as children. When there's excess in a household the younger generation goes the other way.'

with the Australian author who wrote that as a result of the mining boom Australia had been 'virtually rediscovered' ... 'It is no overstatement to say that the country that has stepped so affluently into the seventies is a New Australia.'

The prosperity of Australia in the long boom was part of a period of high hope in the world's most prosperous countries. Some of the greatest puzzles of the modern age seemed to have been solved. Jobs were seen as the principal means for gaining human dignity and welfare and so long as there was a continuance of economic growth (carefully measured by sophisticated statistical methods) there would be more and more jobs. There seemed no reason why growth should stop. Elaborate 'models' were programmed into computers to make 'fine tuning' of the economy possible. If there was slight inflation, then the economy could be slightly tuned down to create a small amount of unemployment and that would end inflation: alternately, if there was unemployment a slight tuning up could again create more jobs. An economist had worked out a graph that showed it was not possible that there could be simultaneous high unemployment and high inflation.

Apart from the majority of Australians, who were beginning to imagine that they might get more of what they had grown up to believe they wanted from life, there were the largely hidden minority, who were getting less.

These were the people, whether families, or loners living in bed-sits, whose constant concern with debt forced them to borrow from relatives, friends, welfare agencies or pawnshops; when too many bills came in at once they cut down on their eating; some suffered repossession of household goods on which they couldn't keep up the payments (in a period when the wall-to-wall carpet was spreading across the country some Australians were reduced to bare boards); some were evicted. They clothed themselves in charity cast-offs; if they had children the children were likely to be shamed by the clothes they wore, and the lack of spending money. Often the poor couldn't

More than half the aged single persons were below the poverty line. On an international scale of poverty, Australia was middling.

afford haircuts, let alone medical care, or dental treatment, or glasses. Impaired by anxiety, some collapsed into 'nervous breakdowns'. If they were old they might be left to rely on the visits of charity ladies for such human comfort as they could still find in life.

For some time not much attention was paid to the poor: with what seemed the miraculous arrival of permanent full employment the prime problem of industrial societies seemed to have been solved. The poor (if they really existed) either were poor because they were wasters or, if they were deserving poor they would just have to wait a little longer – then, with continuing economic growth, they could be attended to. Australia, once a pioneer in social welfare schemes, was now almost at the bottom of the international scale of prosperous countries in the proportion of money spent on programs for income maintenance. In the 1950s a national health scheme had at last appeared – produced by a Liberal Government as a contributory scheme, with Government subsidy – but this scheme was achieved only after almost ten years of exhausting political contest. After that, there were expansions here and there in welfare – but nothing much.

However, in the 1960s a new interest was developing in poverty. As with most new radical movements of that time, this new interest had begun in the United States – in this case, with Michael Harrington's book, *The Other Americans*, and the United States 'War on Poverty' program. It took some time to get going: the first book, *The Hidden People: Poverty in Australia*, did not appear until 1966, and the first detailed survey results did not come out until 1967. It was not until 1970, with the publication of *People in Poverty* by a Melbourne survey team, that full survey results were published. The head of the Melbourne team was then given a Government commission to survey poverty in Australia. In his first main report he declared that ten per cent of Australians were 'very poor' (below the poverty line) and another seven to eight per cent were 'rather poor' (less than 20 per cent over the poverty line).

Those most likely to be poverty-stricken were the old and families without fathers: more than half of single aged persons and more than a third of married aged persons were below the 'poverty line'; so were about half of families without fathers. More than a third of sickness or invalid pensioners were living in poverty; so were a quarter of the

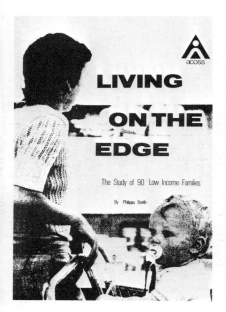

The discovery of poverty: *for much of the long boom, not much attention was paid to poverty in Australia, and when interest in poverty did begin, it was at first inspired by new approaches being taken in the United States. After that, books began to come out (far left above and below). Many of the inner-city terrace houses were in slum districts (above and left). But the Aborigines suffered the most; a child scavenges in an inner-city street in Redfern, Sydney, (centre above) after a fight with police.*

unemployed and a quarter of people in large families; about a fifth of single women and families without mothers were also living in poverty. Of all groups, the Aborigines were the most dispossessed: they did not live as long as other Australians; they suffered a wider range of diseases; Aboriginal infants were three times as likely to die as other Australian infants; about a quarter of all 15-year-old Aborigines had had no schooling; they were 13 times as likely to be in prison as non-Aborigines; and about a third to a half of the Aboriginal work force was unemployed. About half the city Aborigines were classified as 'very poor'. In rural areas the position was worse.

In international scales of poverty (whatever they meant), Australia came through as middling – worse than 'welfare states' such as the Scandinavian countries and the Federal German Republic, but better than some other countries, including the United States, Canada and France. By the time of the poverty inquiry the Whitlam Government, a reform Labor Government, was in power and there had been increasing talk about 'equality'. New programs and new initiatives were being prepared on the assumption that with ever-expanding growth, progress could be bought in spending programs. A reform Liberal Prime Minister who had held office briefly had already said that 'tax revenues, though not the only part, are *the essential part* of social progress'. Whitlam's first Treasurer had announced, as if it were a relatively simple matter, that what was required in government was to 'achieve general welfare through full employment without inflation'.

Then the boom ended. The words 'stagflation' and 'slumpflation' had already begun to appear in overseas journals that came to Australia: these words had been coined to describe an almost unbelievable situation in which in most of the prosperous societies there was both inflation *and* unemployment. It was the inflation that came first in

Australia: 4.9 per cent in 1970, 7.2 per cent in 1971 ... then inflation increased under the Whitlam Government and was joined by unemployment. Without this extension into Australia of the beginnings of the world's most significant economic crisis since the 1930s Depression, the Whitlam Government might have proceeded with its reform program without much fuss. But the times were out of joint.

Many (perhaps a majority of) Australians blamed Whitlam himself for what was in fact a general condition in most of the prosperous industrial societies. But many also blamed the unemployed. There rapidly developed the myth of 'the dole bludger', the belief that unemployment was the fault of the unemployed themselves, helped on by headlines in newspapers such as 'SEX ON THE DOLE CHEAT DISCOVERED: Lovers Living on Island Paradise', or 'LUXURY LIFE ON THE DOLE: Two homes, a car and private pool'. Other theories followed. There was talk of consumer-led recoveries and resources-led recoveries, of recovery through price-income accords or recoveries by greater reliance on market forces.

But there was not much conviction in any of them. The secrets of obtaining human dignity and welfare through economic growth seemed to have been lost.

Dole queues: *when unemployment returned, old-timers compared the facilities now offered to the unemployed (below right) with the treatment that had been given the unemployed during the Great Depression; then there was no unemployment pension, and men had to suffer the indignity of lining up for food relief tickets near Circular Quay (above right) and then walking to Central Station to use them.*

'Dole bludger' news stories began to appear in the mid-1970s. Six young women, termed 'dole dollies' by The Sunday Telegraph, *were described as living comfortably on their combined unemployment benefits (left) in a rented house complete with swimming pool.*

Government from above?

When he landed in Sydney in 1836, Charles Darwin saw that the Australian colonies had made more material progress in 'scores of years' than Latin America had achieved in 'an equal number of centuries'.

Some of the greatest creative impulses in the settlement of Australia were those of the English age of Improvement: belief in material progress was part of Australia's nature. Although not usually innovating material change, Australia could not help accepting it, and adjusting to it. Something that had been set going did not stop. Steam engines were built; so were radio telescopes.

A belief in general human progress was also part of the age of Improvement. This 'fragment' of one of the conflicting attitudes of British society was also lodged early in Australia, and although at the start it was very weak, it grew with the Emigrants and some of the Emancipists. Otherwise born with little faith, the colonists, if they were to believe anything, could believe in human betterment. At first, in a convict colony, many found betterment in access to respectability. It became one of Australia's greatest secular faiths, given material form in the 'manly independence' of a 'home of one's own', and this was later extended to an obsession with not only having a home, but owning it. There could also be a sense of Improvement in the manners of equality in relations between persons (thereby softening the realities of inequality) and in access to what used to be the leisure pursuits of the rich. There were continuing proclamations that betterment could be found in education (although the education programs themselves were usually paltry). With the end of the 19th

century and into the 20th century there came aspirations from those who now saw themselves as 'the workers' that in some way they might provide the creative element in society; but this was only a minority faith, and it could offend respectability.

When at the end of the 19th century, Australia at last produced painters, writers and orators who could suggest what Australians might be, there was an expressed belief that betterment was to be found in distinctive human styles and relations. But since this belief was given flesh in the bush hero and then in the soldier hero it was not accessible to suburbanites except during bush picnics and wars, and it seemed inaccessible to women. In any case, the Black Hats took over Anzac Day and partly turned it to other purposes. There was another possibility for betterment. With the beginnings of parliamentary democracy there had been hopes that if the people sought conspicuous virtue, it would be by Acts of Parliament. In the confusion of parliamentary factions of self-seeking men, Australia, by the standards of the age, soon became one of the world's most progressive countries, with leaders of all political groups congratulating themselves on Australian leadership and ideals, although (with sceptical wisdom) enthusiasm for political leaders was restricted to only a few practitioners. Then these impulses grew less. Once so remarkable for the speed with which it could put new ideas into practice that books were written about its progressiveness, Australia's governments now seemed to move so slowly that books were written about its political backwardness. By 1960 Improvement was mainly a matter of home ownership and 'national development'.

From the end of 1949 to the end of 1972 the conservative parties were in power in Canberra. At first the victory of the

The search for an 'image': *with the departure of R.G. Menzies, the ruling Liberal Party seemed to lose confidence in how to behave. The word 'image' began to appear and there was much concern with the extent to which prime ministers were 'with it'. The contrast between Harold Holt (right), Prime Minister from 1966 to 1967, and John Gorton (far right), Prime Minister from 1968 to 1971, is shown in two* Australian Women's Weekly *covers. Holt had a relaxed style, associated sometimes with informal photographs of him in a wetsuit. But even then there was a 'socialite' air about him, and when he was formally dressed he showed all the ease of a member of Melbourne's smart set. John Gorton, in contrast, was inclined to portray the casual 'dinkum Aussie', which did not seem to go down well with Australians, although later it was to be a prominent part of the appeal of Prime Minister Bob Hawke.*

The old and the new: *before the arrival of Bob Hawke, the two post-war Australian prime ministers who attracted the greatest emotions were R.G. Menzies and E.G. Whitlam. The intensity of the emotions may have been related to the way in which each symbolised attitudes to social change. Menzies presided over many social changes but in his public roles he acted as a defender of stability. His acceptance of the British honour of the Lord Wardenship of the Cinque Ports (far left) was treated by some as an honour for Australia, and by others with derision. Whitlam became prime minister after an election campaign that promised change (left), and therefore, to those who wanted change, a hero, and to those who didn't, a villain.*

Federal Liberal Party in 1949 seemed merely one of those swings of the pendulum supposed to be essential to the two-party system that Australia had tried to imitate. After its 1940s success Labor had seen itself as the 'natural government' of Australia and its defeat as merely an aberration. The theory was held that Labor was the great initiating force in Australian politics, and in the 1954 election it won slightly more than half the votes, only electoral inequalities depriving it of office. But to many Australians the Liberals could still seem a pleasant change; their victories had placed an emphasis on the pursuit of happiness through the purchase of consumer goods, and Labor's defeat was a reminder to governments that they were not God Almighty. However, the Liberals became a permanency when in 1955 the Federal Labor Party collapsed from its own contradictions. R.G. Menzies, who had helped create the Liberal Party out of the wreckage of defeat, seemed to have become Prime Minister by divine right.

The Labor Party's collapse had come from its undermining by the greatest of the Catholic conspiracies. The 'Movement' had organised Catholic cells in many parishes, forming a secret political machine to act as servicing agent to Labor's industrial groups. These tactics brought success against communists in some trade unions, but then the ambitions of the 'Movement' and some 'groupers' expanded towards political influence in the Labor Party, perhaps control of it. So great was the fear of 'Catholic Action' that this extraordinary plot was not exposed until H.V. Evatt, the Labor Party leader after Chifley's death, switched sides among the party's factions and, for his own preservation, spoke of what had been

happening. The effect of the subsequent manoeuvre was a split that produced the new Democratic Labor Party in an attempt, prompted by what was left of the Movement, to bring the Labor Party low and re-occupy it. This disarray, combined with slight electoral inequalities, inadequate leadership and a generally backward and Depression-oriented look, seemed to turn Labor into a permanent Opposition, with a mainly ceremonial role in Parliament.

Menzies also looked backwards – beyond the Depression, back to those certainties of the 1920s that had first marked Australia's political decline. In a party in which there were many RSL badges and old school ties, political leaders sometimes spoke as if loyalty to the British Empire could still be Australia's saving. The bureaucracy set up in the 1940s was still there and, although swinging from an over-adventurous spirit to an over-cautious one, it sufficiently reacted to events to save the Liberals from the more florid parts of their declared policy; but the Liberals could not fully exploit this new instrument of administration. Once so marked in its use of government for human betterment, Australia ignored new techniques of government long after

Men from the States: *there was a similar concern with 'image' among the premiers in the States. Some of them were seen as national stereotypes of images new and old. Don Dunstan (below), Premier of South Australia from 1967 to 1968 and 1970 to 1979, was the first political leader to be accepted as having an acceptable 'contemporary' touch. Joh Bjelke-Petersen (below left with members of the British and Foreign Bible Society), who first became Premier of Queensland in 1968, was to his enemies a reactionary and to his supporters a crusader. Henry Bolte (below left), Premier of Victoria from 1955 to 1972, projected the image of a simple man of the Right.*

Neville Wran (right), who became Premier of New South Wales in 1976, was considered to be the first of a new, pragmatic breed of Labor politicians. When photographed, Wran the conservationist had just completed a two-day hike in the Colo River area and announced that he would gazette it as a national park.

they had been tested in other countries. As the 1960s proceeded, much else was changing, but of all the nation's institutions, Government was one of the slowest to change. Even most of Australia's successes were not to Menzies' liking, so that the Government could not dramatise them and claim them as its own.

That spirit of liberalism that had been the lively element in Australian politics seemed to have dried away. In Australia's liberal age, for a while, before the two-party system was set up and Australian politicians could feel that they were now 'normal', the blunderings of short-term political coalitions had allowed the fairly regular introduction of novelties that made Australia seem progressive. But when the political system became more rigid there was less acceptance of change. Affronted by Labor's apparent 'socialism', the non-Labor parties had moved from the liberal-radical centre where the dynamic had previously been, and in administrative and economic values increasingly adopted capitalist-Protestant ethics of 'free enterprise' that were foreign to the Australian experience. (At least they adopted them in theory; in practice, as in the early days when trading and speculative factions of rugged adventurers had tried to unseat governors, 'free enterprise' usually meant the Government protection of special interests.) And partly because of strong Catholic influence, partly because of the contrary impulses of a continually unrealised belief in socialism (a belief without a strategy) the Labor parties also moved away from the liberal-radical impulses that had earlier seemed to be an essential part of the Australian style.

Perhaps there was another factor: while, as a fragment of the age of Improvement, Australia had naturally sought radical change, it was also a product of the earlier, and contradictory, age of Authority. Government had not begun with dreams of betterment but with the despotism of a penal settlement. Even with self-government, participatory local government was weak and in a country that was so early in developing large bureaucracies there was a vested interest in keeping things as they were. In that

way they could be quietly administered according to precedent. Government was provided from above.

It was not from the politicians but from 'the people' that the spirit of liberalism revived. Just as the crowded meetings and processions and other forms of action in the 1850s and early 1860s had been followed by so many democratic reforms, and the strikes and other actions that began in the 1890s were followed by the formation of a labour movement, so, beginning in the second half of the 1960s, there was a return to popular initiative: 'protest' again took its place as one of the democratic processes.

It was not, of course, all of the people who revived the tradition of protest. The protestors were mainly 'concerned' or 'caring' middle-class citizens or optimistic youth or radical unionists, and some of them saw themselves as socialists rather than as liberals, even if the issues they were taking up were liberal. The protests dramatised new perspectives and changed the shape of what politics seemed to be about. By traditional liberal methods ranging from the writing of books and court actions to street processions and police arrests, the protestors put on theatrical displays that could change views of what mattered. New items were forced on to the political agenda – race and ethnic equality, environmentalism, feminism, new concepts of national interest, relaxations of puritanism, new democratic modes.

In politics, whether wittingly or not, the symbol of most of these new liberal aspirations came to be the Labor leader, E.G. Whitlam, whose 'It's Time' election campaign in 1972 assumed a deep symbolic significance even for many of those who did not vote for him. Whatever it was that people imagined it was 'time' for, they could find it in Whitlam's campaign. He had become a great articulator of Improvement, greater perhaps than even he knew.

That he was dismissed from office in 1975 when the Governor General intervened in a political dispute gave Whitlam, for some, an even greater symbolic significance – either as martyr-hero, or as arch-villain. Improvement could seem to have been overthrown by Authority. To some this was an expression of Australian evil; to others, an expression of Australian virtue. To those who saw Whitlam as hero, his dismissal and subsequent defeat at the 1975 election confirmed their belief that Australia was a uniquely conservative society. Yet by 1983, the Labor Party was in power in Canberra and in most of the State Parliaments. There was again talk that Labor might be the 'natural' party in Australia.

Election posters from 1949 (below) seem dull and long-winded and lacking in visual impact in comparison with those from the 1983 Federal election campaign (below right) in which images are most important. Despite its call to 'forget personalities and look at the policies', the ALP poster prominently featured the party's chief drawcard – the personable Bob Hawke.

18. The urban sophisticates: 1950 to 1980s

With the spread of education, a 'new middle class' whose careers were based mainly on education began to develop in Australia, and its coming was accompanied by many important social transformations. There was a wave of 'permissiveness', part of a general world change in which almost all censorship and much of the old puritanism was abandoned. With a new feminist movement, also part of general change, there were many important redefinitions of the role of women – in the work force, in households, and as individuals. An environmentalist movement grew, challenging many of the conventional wisdoms of the doctrines of national development in a way that would once have been unimaginable. And, at long last, Australia began to develop a cultural awakening – in intellectual life and in the arts – that seemed one of the real signs of the long-awaited national maturity.

The new middle class

When Bob Hawke, the new Labor Party leader, won the 1983 election, one of his opening acts of political theatre was to call a 'National Economic Summit' of leaders of business, unions and government (and a few representatives of the professions, the churches and social groups).

The Summit sat in the House of Representatives chamber in Canberra, and for almost a week played live on television and radio – a remarkable show quite different from what ordinarily happens in Parliament.

There was scarcely any talk of free enterprise: what these government, business and union leaders were speaking was the language of managed capitalism, of Australia as a mixed economy in which a great deal of economic activity was influenced not by a free market but by big business, big unions and big government. In the special form of economic management that had been associated with the long boom, whether they were from government or business or unions, most of the conference speakers were using the same keywords of expertise, showing the same reverence towards the same statistics. Not only was the rhetoric different from that of parliamentary debate: even more important was the fact that it was these representatives of big business, big government and big unions rather than parliamentarians carrying out the ceremonies of Parliament who could appear to be the people who were 'running the country'.

Not present were the foreign business firms and the foreign governments that set the limits within which things were decided in Australia. But there was no doubt that the people at the Summit were those who sat in the office blocks where decisions most often seemed to be made. They were overwhelmingly male. They were overwhelmingly British or Irish descent. A majority of them had been born with some material advantages in life. And they were 'executives'. They were a new kind of person in Australia (sometimes spoken of as a member of the new middle class) whose immediate access to power was likely to come through expertise and education. For the first time in Australia (even if the children of the better-off still had better chances) education had become a general means of getting jobs with status beyond the traditional professions.

This new situation had been several decades in the making. The idea of a person whose merit was specifically based on tertiary education had its first victories in the Commonwealth Public Service in the 1940s. In the wartime improvisations of virtually creating a new Public Service,

graduates had usually proved fitter to their tasks than those who had entered the departments as Returned Men or messenger boys, and after the war an appetite for them sharpened. By the 1960s Australia's single most important organisation had developed something like a meritocratic élite. There was extra pay for university degrees, special entry for particularly promising graduates, and a recognition that second division public servants constituted a corps of top administrators, generalists able to move in

Corporate leader: Gordon Jackson

Gordon Jackson was described in the 1980s as being one of 'that new breed of businessmen with a social conscience'.

Born in 1924 in Brisbane, he was educated at the Brisbane Grammar School, and at the age of 16 joined CSR (the Colonial Sugar Refining Company as it was then known). Jackson became its chief executive in 1972 and supervised the company's expansion from a sugar milling and refining group to a more diversified organisation. Such expansion led to the sort of confrontations that were becoming familiar in the 1970s: conflict with the Aboriginal land rights movement at Noonkanbah in Western Australia, and with unionists in the 'coal miners' tax revolt' in Queensland.

Gordon Jackson's quietly spoken, reserved style promoted cooperation rather than confrontation. It may have been his reported belief that big businesses must be good corporate citizens, guided by community standards, that involved him in public life, assessing and analysing the directions of Australian society.

From 1974 to 1975 he chaired a committee to advise the Federal Government on policies for manufacturing, and in the 1980s he headed a committee enquiring into Australian aid to foreign countries. Jackson was also appointed a Director of the Reserve Bank and, with an interest in management training, was a founding chairman of the Australian Graduate School of Management and Australian representative to the Board of Governors of the Asian Institute of Management. Widely travelled, he held executive positions concerned with Japanese and German industry and commerce. In 1980, soon after being chosen Australian of the Year, he said, wistfully, he would like 'more time for fishing'.

their upward progress from one department to the other.

By then, the hope that rationality might be more methodically and expertly applied to human affairs had extended to business. The words 'management' and 'executive' became common, reaching their culmination in the phrase 'top management'. A product of large, de-personalised organisations, at the most romanticised the new 'executive' was a 'technician of general ideas' with such perfect techniques of policy-making and administration that he (almost always a 'he') was able to pass from one bureaucracy to the next applying the same general principles of behaviour. He was a man of merit whose qualifications, based on education, were believed to challenge the privileges of wealth or seniority, and he was a man of reason, whose mastery of mathematical techniques and programming brought the orderliness of science to human affairs.

In this ideal form the 'executive' was not, at first, believed to exist in Australia; in imagination he lived in the United States; or, for a few, in Japan; for even fewer, France. But some young Australians were trained in US business schools; US companies that extended into Australia

brought their organisational methods with them; and the semi-monopolist tendency in Australian-owned firms produced bureaucracies large enough to adopt some of these approaches. Gradually, special management courses were introduced into Australia. Within business firms there were long, irritating struggles, with new ways confronting old, but by the early 1980s more than two-thirds of top business executives held tertiary education qualifications; almost all had made their way to the top through a bureaucratic structure; scarcely any were 'self-made'. To the prestige of the old-fashioned boardroom with its mahogany and its leather chairs was now added the prestige of the polished natural woods and Australian paintings (whether as prints or as originals) of the 'executive suite'.

There was a proliferation of other forms of experts in the smaller, talent-based firms – advertising agents, architects, town planners, public relations agencies and so forth, along with a proliferation of lawyers, accountants and other kinds of consultants. By the 1970s the unions were also hiring graduates, at first as research officers or in other specialist jobs; but then graduates also began to move up through the bureaucratic structures of the unions to higher office.

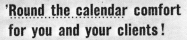

'The executive': *as the idea of the 'executive' spread, new stereotypes emerged. For a period executives were seen as wearing double-breasted suits (top centre). They were first to have air conditioners in their offices (top left). Later, one of the symbols of the executive became the slim-line attaché case (top right). It was mainly executives who travelled first class in air travel (on their expense accounts), and the airlines worked out special advertising strategies to appeal to them (above left). The 'executive office suite' (above right) became one of the important ways in which businessmen or government officials could proclaim their status. Some of the executive style spread to trade union leaders, especially the younger, university-trained people. The Victorian union leader Simon Crean (left) was seen as one of a new breed.*

Accompanying all these other changes was the growth of white-collar dominance of the work force. At the beginning of the 1960s the work force was split almost 50–50 between blue-collar and white-collar workers. By the mid-1970s almost 60 per cent of the work force was white collar.

A nation that had shown a unique lack of interest in relations between economic progress and education was now changing as it scraped together a larger education system which, although it had other professed aims, was to service this new demand. In 1939 there were only six universities with 13 000 students; by 1975 there were 18 universities and 94 Colleges of Advanced Education with, altogether, 275 000 students. In 1939 there had been little more than a hundred full high schools throughout Australia; by 1975 the number of schools had increased more than sixfold and the number of students more than tenfold. From 1955 to 1975 the number of people employed in the education industries trebled. Expenditure on education went up by almost 2000 per cent. By 1975 the growth in student numbers at the universities was nearly four per cent per year, and at the Colleges of Advanced Education 17 per cent.

What went almost unnoticed in the middle of all this activity was that to the high standards of training of engineers, doctors, dentists and other specialists had been added a high training of scientists. With one in 60 world scientific breakthroughs occurring in Australia, it was reckoned that Australia ranked tenth in the world in its contribution to world science. Photographs of Australia's biggest radio telescope appeared in tourist pamphlets; there were television documentaries on Australian research into viruses; two medical scientists shared Nobel Prizes; when the United States space program reached its most spectacular moments there were new angles on the part played by the Australian space-tracking stations. In one year alone, the CSIRO reported on activities not only in agricultural science research (in which it remained one of the world's leaders) but on a wide range of other research, from a new landing guidance system for aircraft and new treatments of copper ores to research into the leakage of

energy from microwave ovens and the improvement of fire alarms. But these attracted small attention and prompted little pride. On the whole, business firms undertook very little research and between 80 and 90 per cent of the best scientists remained in universities or government research institutions, among which the CSIRO provided a huge refuge with its 80 laboratories and research stations. It was not the displays of Australian originality in science that gained the headlines, but the luck of the mining boom (carried out, at first, by foreign initiatives). Australian businessmen were still unable to harness the creative power of Australian research. And when, in the 1980s there was talk of 'high technology', Australian attention was still fastened to the low technology of 'resources development'.

With the arrival of what was seen as a recession, growth in education abruptly stopped and something of a squeeze was put on both education spending and student numbers. But although in terms of the percentage of teenagers at education institutions Australia was still low on the international list (placed between Ireland and Greece), the increase in the education industries had already changed the look of Australian society.

The contributions of Australian scientists to world scientific research was, proportionate to population, among the best in the world. Radio astronomy was one of Australia's specialities and the radio telescope at Parkes (above) became one of the chief tourist attractions of New South Wales.

Automation began to affect the nature of work and employment prospects. It was first evident in the blue-collar work, such as the assembling and testing of 4-cylinder engines at the General Motors Holden plant (top). But by the late 1970s automation was also affecting white-collar work; the computer rooms of Channel Seven, Sydney (above).

The permissive society

In the most superficial aspect, there was the new diversity in restaurants, the 'new sophistication' in the wine and food columns and travel pages in the newspapers and magazines, the turning towards terrace houses, 'project houses', 'town houses' or city apartments, the new advertising directed towards 'executive' taste. There were also changes in the media. *The Age*, *The Bulletin* and *The Canberra Times* were all substantially changed (if in different ways) to meet new expectations. *The Australian*, *Sunday Review* (later *Nation Review*) and *The National Times* were all founded to meet a new market (if, again, in different ways).

There also developed new interpretations of Australia in which the 'technocrats', not the capitalists, were seen as the rulers. To these, radical responses affirmed new beliefs in the salvationary role of the working class of a kind that became popular amongst European intellectuals in the late 1960s. To this view, one reply that was made was that the working class, in the sense of blue-collar workers, was no longer the prevailing element among wage earners. There was another change: with the decline in manufacturing as a source of employment, partly from the greater importance of service industries and partly from the increase in factory

Australian businessmen's ability to turn research into practical effect lagged behind the output of scientists. At a time when there was talk of 'high technology', Australians found proof of their industrial innovation in the keel of the America's Cup winner, Australia II.

automation, there were proportionately fewer factory workers; yet the factory worker had been seen as typifying the whole idea of 'the workers'. The reply of some of the radicals to this was that automation might also deplete the ranks of the white-collar workers and that in any case Australia was about to see a new radicalism – from the white-collar unions.

Where it was seeing a new radicalism was from the 'new middle class' itself. It was true that most of the 'executives', professionals and other members of the 'new middle class' were conservative in approach: they were the people who could see themselves as holding the whole show together. But there was also the development of that minority group within the 'new middle class' whom their enemies dismissed as 'the left liberals' or, even worse, 'the trendies'. While radicals saw the media as conservative, conservatives saw the media as rotten with 'trendies'. Radicals attacked the education system as conservative; conservatives saw it as even more riddled with 'trendies' than the media.

The European settlement of Australia was seen by some to have been marked by unparalleled scenes of depravity and licentiousness. By others it was marked by the way it brought respectability within the grasp of previously dispossessed people.

As the 19th century progressed, and into the 20th century, Australian life became almost fully clothed in the restraints of a puritan respectability that also spread over the other English-speaking countries – at least so far as public policy went; what people did in private was another, and partly unknown, matter. In a few years in the 1960s and early 1970s, Australia's puritanism ('wowserism') became almost altogether unstuck, again following movements in the English-speaking world, not only in the restraints on drinking and betting and Sunday behaviour, but in matters of general decorum and – what most interested the liberals – in the near-abandonment of censorship.

When Australian liberalism reached its lowest ebb between the two World Wars, Government censorship was seen by the few remaining liberals as one of the extreme expressions of the essential rottenness of Australia. This sense of desperation was still there early in the 1960s. *God's Little Acre*, *Appointment in Samara*, *Catcher in the Rye* and other novels that were seen as part of normal literature studies had at last been removed from the banned list, although it still included new arrivals such as *The Ginger Man*, *Lolita* and *Borstal Boy*.

At a time when they could point to the greater liberalisations in other countries, the liberals took heart – and won. They used familiar liberal devices. Books were written exposing what were presented as the follies of censorship. Writs were issued against the Customs Department for its book seizings. There were letter-writing campaigns. Court actions were taken. Then came the traditional liberal drama of deliberate law-breakings. Copies of books whose import was banned were smuggled in and then printed in Australia. With the appointment of Don Chipp as Customs Minister at the end of the 1960s the liberals found an ally in Government. Chipp dismantled most of the book-banning by the Customs Department; Whitlam's Government dismantled most of the rest of it.

Liberals also applied their techniques to film censorship, sometimes picketing a cinema exhibiting a censored film and even distributing leaflets describing what had been cut. If films imported for film festivals were censored, the festival organisers would issue statements announcing that they had withdrawn the films altogether. At the opening night of one Australian film from which scenes had been cut, blank footage was inserted to show where the censor had made the cuts. Again Chipp moved in, and instituted a new category, the 'R' movie. Again, what he had begun was completed by the Whitlam Government. By the 1980s the debate had moved on to the question of 'X' gradings for films on video cassette recorders.

In the case of drama, what was begun by the liberals was completed by a commercial entrepreneur. When one part of *America Hurrah* was banned in Sydney in 1968, liberals got together and sponsored a free performance of the whole play. But several months later, *The Boys in the Band*, a play about homosexuals, was performed in Sydney, and survived. The king-hit against theatre censorship came the next year, however, with the performance of *Hair*, replete with forbidden words (most of which could not be heard above the noise of the rock music) and, at the end of the first act, 40 seconds of frontal nudity. Perhaps it was the great commercial success of *Hair* that gave legitimacy to nudity and forbidden words; shortly, in most States, the stage was almost as 'free' as in most other liberal-democratic societies.

'Permissiveness', as the new freedoms came to be described, now spread to television. In the form of 'irreverence' it had already arrived, with the satirical *Mavis Bramston Show* in 1964, but it was only in 1972, with the beginning of the television serial *Number 96*, that permissiveness, in the sense of sexual explicitness, seemed accepted by television. The show topped the ratings and gained part of its prestige from commercial success.

By now there were new styles of protest against censorship that were different from the older liberal approaches. They were tougher, if simpler, and so concerned with the display of forbidden words and forbidden flesh as a matter of principal that some of the older liberals were offended. Several 'underground film' groups were formed, on a United States pattern that had been set some years before, and for a while they depended largely on United States imports. There were also a few examples of 'underground' presses, the best known of which was an extension of a Sydney student newspaper that by sheer dogged repetition broke the heart of the State censorship authorities. At meetings there could develop an obsession with shouting forbidden words – both by speakers through their microphones and loud hailers and in abusive chants from an audience. The most explicit product from the above-ground press was *Nation Review*, a masterly example of how vernacular abuse could be translated into the literary language and given intellectual form.

The desire to celebrate the goodness of the natural went beyond the use of words to actions, beginning in the commercial world with 'go-go girls' who danced 'topless' in nightclubs, and in the protest world with 'streakers', who ran naked through public places. Beaches for nude bathing were set up. Even on the public beaches some women bathers went 'topless'. By this time nudity had become an acceptable feature on the stage. During the period when

The campaigns against literary censorship, which began in the 1930s, were beginning to show results by the 1960s. As well as protests, several books were produced, such as Australia's Censorship Crisis *(below). In the theatre, the big breakthrough against censorship came with the production in Sydney in 1969 of the rock musical* Hair *(above).*

New trends were coming to television. For the new and more critical middle-class audiences, the satirical 'Mavis Bramston Show' (above), starring Maggie Dence, was one of the signs that Australia was 'coming of age'. For the general public the long-running 'Number 96' (right) reached new extremes of 'explicitness'.

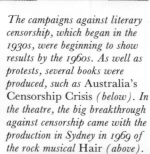

With the relaxation of censorship, some of the new Australian movies were 'SEX-ploitive'. One of the first and commercially most successful of these was The Adventures of Alvin Purple *(above).*

'The trendies': *with the 1970s the word 'trendy' entered the language, to begin with associated with new fashions, and then applied to new ideas. Don Chipp (caricatured left) was seen as an arch 'trendy'.*

there was a fashion in 'see-through' dresses, one Sunday newspaper gave a crochet pattern for a 'see-through mini' dress.

Movements developed, with varying degrees of success, for changes to the laws penalising homosexual conduct. Some met with very bitter reactions, but acceptance of the existence of homosexuality became more open as people 'came out' and declared their homosexuality to a degree previously unimaginable; there were recognised areas where the homosexuals ('the gays') met, and there was that same commercial exploitation of them that seemed to be characteristic of all forms of permissiveness. At the same time there developed, in some magazines, extremely frank sexual counselling, and in the early 1980s this was extended to radio; a career of 'sexology' developed; in most cities 'adult bookshops' were opened.

An international survey carried out in 1983 showed that something like 80 per cent of those Australians interviewed believed in God and about 50 per cent believed in life after death; these figures placed Australia ahead of Japan and France in religious belief, but remarkably behind the United States, where the figures indicated a 95 per cent

belief in God and a 70 per cent belief in life after death. Perhaps this suggests why there was not such a backlash against permissiveness in Australia as there was in the United States. Nevertheless there was a backlash.

Some of it was not on religious grounds at all, but on humanist grounds – that what were seen as the extremes of 'permissiveness' were being exploited commercially and, in particular, that, in advertising and in reading matter and films, there was actually an increase in the exploitation of the image of women. Some feminists wished to reimpose censorship. Some of the backlash was on purely religious grounds – what was being shown was evil in itself – but it was also suggested that society would disintegrate once the old puritanism had gone.

Yet if it was assumed that Australian society was not held together by Evangelical morality, but by habits such as seeing the meaning of life partly in work and partly in the acquisition of consumer goods, and in both cases in terms of pay packets, then there was not much sign of the disintegration of Australian society, unless it was in the fact that pay packets were becoming more scarce and were buying much less.

Critics: *for some of those who were discontented with things as they were, the weekly* Nation Review *(far left), with its cartoons by Michael Leunig (left) became, for a season, a sign that things might change. After a successful start, however,* Nation Review *folded for want of support.*

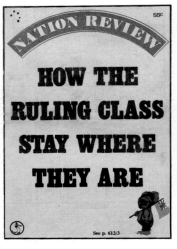

Since the 1930s the figure of the beach inspector had been a symbol of 'wowserism', as beach inspectors fought a losing battle against growing exposure. Les Tanner in The Bulletin *(above) satirised the failure of beach inspectors to ban the bikini.*

Protest and counter protest: *'protest' became a routine part of the Australian way of life. At first it was in the hands of those who were fighting for more permissive ways, such as Wendy Bacon (left), who campaigned in turn against censorship and city development and then for prisoners' rights. Then conservatives such as the Reverend Fred Nile (above) of the Festival of Light, developed techniques of counter protest.*

Women's 'liberation'

In the 1960s new feelings began to stir about the place of women in the world. Some of these new moods were connected with 'the Pill', which, when it came on the market in 1961, at once assumed a symbolic as well as a biological importance. Although it was estimated that a third of the women who began taking the pill abandoned it after two years, it was nevertheless seen as a strong symbol of female independence.

There was disapproval in the Catholic Church, where the papal encyclical of 1968 against contraception caused great internal dissensions, with some protest meetings and even some defections from the priesthood. As well as the pill there was the increase, throughout the decade, in the number of married women in the paid work force; by the end of the 1960s, when the boom still looked as if it would last forever, both employers and government were speaking of plans for child care centres. With what seemed a permanent labour shortage, to some it could now seem a patriotic duty for married women to work. A few years later, with

unemployment, some would again say it was the duty of married women – or even women generally – not to work. In 1970 a Liberal Minister for Labour was speaking of the need for women to work: nine years later one of his successors said, 'The increased number of married women working must have weakened the imperative for the traditional breadwinner to remain in, or take, employment.'

At the time when women's employment was booming, and perhaps as part of the same process, there were a number of equal pay decisions. These still left many discriminations against women, but they removed one of the most flagrant. By this time new words had floated from the United States into the Australian media and into some Australian conversations: 'sexism', 'male chauvinist', 'patriarchal society', 'sex object' and other new ways of describing things were declarations that ideas of reality should be rearranged so that women had an equal place as human beings with men. Of these words, the one that may have had the most immediate impact (whether of hope, or threat) was 'women's liberation', or 'women's lib'. The women's liberation movement had begun to declare itself in the United States towards the end of the 1960s; the first

Working women: *part of the economic basis of the new wave of feminism was the movement of women into the paid work force. In traditional white-collar jobs such as banking, automation increased career opportunities (top left), but sometimes only because jobs had been downgraded through automation. What was new was the entry of women into some of the blue-collar trades (above). With the growth of the women's movement came magazines such as* Mejane, *in 1971, followed by* Refractory Girl *in 1972, and* Girl's Own *(centre top).*

Protesting: *the women's movement produced a range of publicity forms – from books to 'demos'. The Women's Electoral Lobby produced a series of books, such as Iola Mathews'* Going Back to Work *(centre above). Women marched peacefully to celebrate International Women's Year in 1975 (top right). However, one of the most controversial forms of women's demonstrations were the Women Against Rape in War marches on Anzac Day (above).*

women's liberation groups formed in Australia in 1969 and 1970. The symbol of 'bra burning' – that women should discard the kind of clothing that accentuated them as 'sex objects' – had been part of the symbolism of the movement in the United States: the first 'bra burning' speech in Australia was made at a political rally at Sydney University in 1970. (Scarcely any bras were burned.)

The number of women's liberation groups were small, and mixed in their aims, although they were all concerned with going about things in a more democratic and participatory way than is usual in organisations, and with the kind of 'consciousness-raising' that would help women redefine the world, and themselves. Two magazines were published; conferences were held (at which the male journalists would find the main news in the fact that they were excluded); a publishing group and a film group were formed; an occasional more-or-less sympathetic program was aired on the ABC. Some special campaigns were run against existing institutions: one group put on a demonstration outside an Australian Council of Trade Unions conference; another group demonstrated against Mother's Day ('Creches – not Chrysanthemums'). Some

women began to be addressed as 'Ms'. The replacement of 'chairman' with 'chairperson' was often demanded. New word usages were sought to overcome the use of 'man' for 'human'. At public meetings, if there were no women on the platform, or not a fair proportion, women in the audience might attack the meeting as 'sexist'; at the same time if women *were* on the platform, they ran the risk of being dismissed as 'token women'. Some women discarded not only brassieres but other traditionally 'feminine' habits such as make-up (which had, in any case, among the young, gone somewhat out of fashion). All of these changes, or attempted changes, were met by enormous male derision – which, for a time, dominated media presentation of women's issues. However, as with other new movements, there was money to be made out of the new feminism. A magazine, *Cleo*, was launched, marketing itself as 'liberated but not aggressive'.

'Women's lib' was seen as politically radical and 'women's libbers' were often supporters of other radical movements. The movement received a more middle-class look with the formation in Melbourne in 1972 of the Women's Electoral Lobby (WEL). WEL formed branches in other States and gathered a thousand members. Its initial promotional technique was to present a questionnaire on women's issues to candidates in that year's Federal election. This proved a very successful manoeuvre: the results of the survey made news, and many of the candidates learned with surprise that there was such a thing as a 'women's issue'. With the Whitlam 'It's Time' election campaign, for some women it could also seem 'time' for the women's movement: women's issues became part of the Labor Party's program, although it was with more expressions of good will than actual achievement.

In 1975 – International Women's Year – there could seem more sense of betrayal than of hope, but if reformers must first redefine the world before they can change it, 1975 had a special significance: up to then, the women's movement had relied on books from outside Australia (even if one of them, *The Female Eunuch*, had been written by an Australian); in 1975 four books were published about women in Australia. They were a beginning to the long task of rewriting the study of Australian history and Australian society so that the presence of women was recognised. As the demands for new perspectives were raised, there were many sharp disputes among historians and social scientists; in the schools there were demands that textbooks should be rewritten to eliminate their endemic sexism, as well as their endemic racism; some of the media disembarrassed themselves of some of the traditional approaches to women.

If in a small way, women became slightly more visible in parliaments; a few were made judges; some became prominent in the middle reaches of the professions; a few were appointed to senior public service positions; some publicity was given to the few women who had gained executive suites in business. One of the most important gains – at least in the spreading of awareness – may have been in the anti-discrimination legislation that was passed by some of the Australian Parliaments in the 1980s. But in practice, discrimination was still entrenched in most places, and in work places in particular. There was still a disproportionately large number of men in the top

Abortion: *one of the most divisive issues in the new feminism was the abortion law. An anti-abortion protest in Melbourne's Royal Women's Hospital (above). An Abortion Law Reform Association protests in Sydney's Macquarie Street (top).*

positions (often there were no women there at all) while in the bottom jobs there was a disproportionately large number of women.

What could seem most inspiriting to those who needed encouragement (and the greater a woman's vision of what was still to be done the more she might need encouragement) was the recognition that whatever had been achieved had been achieved by the actions of women themselves – whether directly, as with female support centres, or indirectly, as with anti-discrimination legislation. There had been argument about whether earlier reforms in women's emancipation had been achieved by the actions of women themselves, or from male indifference. This time there was no doubt that the initiatives had come from 'the sisters', inheritors of a long (if at times weakened) tradition of feminism in Australia. But it was also recognised that the women's movement had been mainly middle class and that probably, at least in personal relationships, the first beneficiaries were mainly middle-class women. Although open declaration of male prejudice had been inhibited, or at least made self-conscious, there seemed no doubt that Australia was still a male-dominated society.

Even so, when the backlash came, it came partly from women, in movements of which the most prominent in the early 1980s was 'Women Who Want To Be Women'. There was a special reason for this. While the Women Who Want To Be Women expressed as a general ideal the desire to maintain some of the traditional concepts of 'femininity', their special concern was opposition to abortion. The campaigns for changes to the abortion laws were part of a wider claim to a woman's 'right to control her own body' in which the two other most important elements were a right for women to express their sexuality and a desire by women to protect themselves from rape. But while the other concerns could seem particularly offensive to some men, the belief in the right to abortion could seem particularly offensive to some women.

The abortion campaign – about to become one of the bitter divisions in Australian society – opened in Adelaide in the late 1960s when the Liberal Country League Government appointed a committee of enquiry to recommend on changes in the abortion law, with special reference to the changes that had been instituted in Britain in 1967. An Abortion Law Reform Association was formed and although it failed to gain abortion on request, it did gain a system in which an abortion could be legalised by a certificate signed by two doctors. Not long afterwards, judges in New South Wales and Victoria interpreted the law in a new way so that New South Wales and Victoria also became, as opponents described them, 'abortion states'. In 1970 a Right to Life Movement was formed in Queensland. It spread nationally, and began to fight back. At a time of single-issue politics the abortion issue divided both of the main parties. Some of the most active supporters of change were Liberals; some of the most convinced opponents were Labor MPs who were Catholics. And it was an issue that could override party preference. In New South Wales the 'anti-abortion' vote could win comfortable majorities for candidates for the upper house and become a focus for more general reactions to change.

Belief in economic growth has been a sacred faith in all modern societies. In Australia it had taken the special form of national development, a driving urge to 'utilise resources' that went beyond mere economic calculation to the belief in development at any cost.

To some Australians there could seem something inherently wasteful in water that was not being dammed, in grass that was not being nibbled, in soil that was not sustaining crops, in minerals that were not being mined, in fish that were not being netted, in trees that were not being chopped down. There could seem something inherently good in irrigation schemes, closer settlement schemes, the extension of country roads and country railway lines and, above all, in exports and in electricity-generating schemes. These all became matters of a faith that went beyond economic calculation. For decades they became the only positive expression of Australian urges to Improvement. For much of the time, Australian development worked. But when it didn't work it could lead to soil erosion and wasting of other assets, uneconomic subsidies and enormous wastes of money.

Chief judge: Elizabeth Evatt

One of the most ambitious projects of the Whitlam Government, in office from 1972 to 1975, was the Royal Commission into Human Relationships. It was established to enquire into and report on the family and the social, educational, legal and sexual aspects of male and female relationships 'so far as those matters are relevant to the powers and functions of the Australian government'. Chairman of the Commission was Justice Elizabeth Evatt, a brilliantly qualified lawyer and a member of a noted Australian legal family with strong links to the world of politics and art.

Elizabeth Evatt was born in 1933. She graduated from Sydney University, took a master's degree at Harvard University and lived and worked in England for 17 years, where she married and had two children. In 1972 Prime Minister Gough Whitlam, anxious to give Australian women a more public role, offered her the position of Deputy President of the Commonwealth Conciliation and Arbitration Commission. Acceptance meant several years of family life spread over two hemispheres. But it also gave her some experience of two increasingly important social factors: the role of the single parent and potential conflict between the careers of husbands and wives.

Although initially the enquiry into human relationships was dismissed by some as pretentious, the reactions it drew from written submissions, 'phone-ins' and from its own investigative techniques, produced a unique study of the way people live. As well as being informative for the community and its planners, it also provided Elizabeth Evatt with experience relevant to her next appointment as Chief Judge of the new Australian Family Law Court, the first woman chief judge in Australia.

The post-war period began with a fanfare of development schemes, of which the most expensive was the Snowy Mountains hydroelectricity scheme. By the 1960s the development cult was seeking its wildest dreams in the idea that Australians must 'develop the North': the actualities of northern development were more modest than the plans, but all the major plans that were carried out in the North were extravagant failures. Of these the most extravagant was the failure of the Ord River Scheme, put up by a Prime Minister at election time without any research as to what crops would grow, or who would buy them. The result was a project that cost £100 million, from which farmers could not make a profit. In one of its many ironies, at one stage of the scheme waters in the dam were breeding insects that were eating the crops watered by the dam.

There was some patriotic pride in the fact that in the 1950s Britain used Australia to test some of its nuclear weapons; by the 1960s there were dreams, for a while, of exploding nuclear devices to create new harbours along the Australian coast; plans were then made to establish a number of nuclear energy stations. By the early 1970s there was enthusiasm for uranium enrichment plants. At the end of the decade enthusiasm had shifted to gigantic schemes for aluminium processing – none of which appeared to have been adequately analysed to estimate what profit there would be in them for Australians. The excitement of the developmentalist vision was epitomised in the verses quoted by a Labor Party minister in 1975, in a speech made when he had been forced to resign from his ministry because his imagination was so inflamed with visions of petrochemical complexes, networks of oil pipelines and uranium milling plants that he had forgotten the necessity for politicians to concern themselves with politics: 'Give me men to match my mountains, give me men to match my plains, men with freedom in their vision, and creation in their brains.'

The early criticisms of 'development' were largely based on questions of a rational allocation of resources. As such, they did not interest many Australians. Criticism of unthinking 'national development' reached a wider audience with the beginnings of 'environmentalism'. Once again, the way was shown in ideas imported from the United States. Once again, it came partly in the form of new words redefining what mattered in life, of which the two most significant may have been 'environment' and

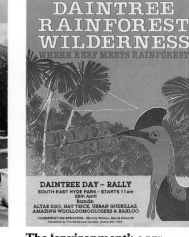

Pollution: *one of the first things to shake some of the faith in 'development' was the discovery of 'pollution' as a social crime. Newspapers began to publish photographs of days* *when pollution was particularly bad in the cities and to include details of pollution levels. Melbourne was declared to be Australia's smoggiest city (above left).*

The Snowy: *the most dramatically convincing of all of Australia's plans for national development was the Snowy Mountains Scheme. Construction workers were camped in snow during winter (above).*

The 'environment': *a new word came into popular speech – the 'environment'. With the growth of the environmentalist movement, protest methods also grew. Rallies had speakers and bands, to entertain as well as inform (above). A postcard was produced as part of a campaign against sand mining in coastal forests at Middle Head in northern New South Wales (below right).*

Projections made at the time of the Franklin River dispute showed the planned wilderness diminution (left).

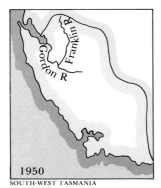

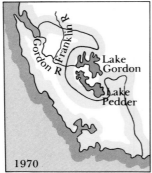

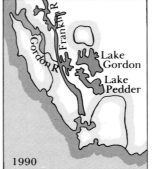

SOUTH-WEST TASMANIA

extent of wilderness area   hydro-electric development

'ecology', with its extension of 'ecological disaster', in which it was foreseen that resources would run out, water, soil and air would be poisoned and the protective layers of the earth's atmosphere might collapse. These fears had first defined themselves in political terms in a concern with 'pollution' (another word given new meaning) brought on in particular by footage on television of local ecological disasters in the United States. By the early 1970s anti-pollution legislation was being prepared in various governments; the Federal Government had set up a Department of the Environment (and also of the Aborigines and the Arts); Earth Week had been celebrated; there was talk of 'Environmental Impact Statements'.

Again, new perceptions had come through protests. Great battles had been fought. Some were won – the Little Desert in Victoria was saved; Fraser Island in Queensland; the Colong Caves in New South Wales. Others were lost – of which the most mourned was Lake Pedder in Tasmania, flooded by a hydroelectricity scheme. But protest itself had become part of the planning system. The developers now had to take protest, as well as engineering decisions, into account. Quite soon, some of the protestors themselves

moved into the Government or business bureaucracies as environmental advisers. New types of expertise developed. Centres of environmental studies were established.

Improvement was now being expressed not only in the desire to 'tame' nature; it was now also being expressed in the desire to 'preserve the environment'. As part of a more general cult of naturalness which expressed itself in craft shops, health food cafés, organic farms, natural woods, easy manners, loose clothes, there was a newly imagined Australia of 'the wilderness'. Nature had now gone beyond the conventional 'bush': it could include mud flats, deserts, mangrove swamps, sand dunes, rainforests, all previously seen as useless. When the desire for economic rationality and the desire to preserve the wilderness came together in the 'No Dams' campaign to prevent the damming of the Franklin River in the 1983 national election, there was the once unimaginable sight of politicians trying to win an election not by promising to build a dam, but by promising to prevent a dam being built.

As well as protesting to preserve the wilderness, environmentalists used posters, petitions, meetings, court

'No dams': *politicians in Australia used to begin election campaigns by promising to build a dam. In the 1983 election the Labor Party began the campaign by promising to prevent the Tasmanian Hydro Electricity Commission from building a dam on the Franklin River. Part of the 'greenies' tactics on the Franklin was to create diversions and blockades to secure television coverage (above).*

A man of principle: Jack Mundey

It was an occasion that symbolised a changing Australia when in September 1983 the Governor of New South Wales, Sir James Rowland, unveiled a plaque in the Uniting Church in Pitt Street, honouring the Irish Catholic-turned-Communist Jack Mundey. The ceremony was to celebrate the fact that during the great building boom of the 1960s and 1970s the old church had been saved from demolition because the Builders Labourers' Federation had placed a 'green ban' on it.

Then the secretary of the Federation, Jack Mundey originated the idea of green bans, motivated by the belief that people who lived in an area should have a say in the environment, and that the workers who raised the bricks and mortar had a right to influence the social decisions concerned with the work they did.

Kellys Bush in Hunters Hill on Sydney Harbour was saved. So was Centennial Park, and the Botanic Gardens fig trees. A building ban was imposed on Sydney University over a decision to limit a women's studies course; a work ban was imposed at Macquarie University until a homosexual student expelled from college was re-instated. During this turbulent period Jack Mundey was beset by faction fighting within his union, which finally led to his expulsion and a period of unemployment. But his integrity and incorruptibility remained unquestioned by his admirers who saw his election to the Council of the City of Sydney, in 1984, as a vindication.

Jack Mundey was the son of a sharefarmer on Queensland's Atherton Tablelands. But the farm boy who had had only a sketchy formal education was to become notable for his intellectual contribution to environmentalism.

actions, processions, sit-ins and other forms of protest to try to frustrate some of the city development plans. This was not just a middle-class action. One of the most effective forms of protest came when trade unions placed bans on what they saw as environmentally unsound development: when the Builders Labourers' Federation invented the telling phrase 'green ban', the story of how Australian unions were knocking back work for motives of public interest made world news. To the union actions there were added 'Resident Action Groups' (RAGs), 35 of whom in 1971 formed CRAG, the Coalition of Resident Action Groups. These groups became concerned not only with protest but with the nature of democratic activity itself: women were particularly active in them and often it was a case not of women coming to political activity through feminism but of their becoming feminists after finding new meaning for themselves in political activity.

Some of the city development protests were simply against what could increasingly seem senseless engineers' plans for building wider and straighter roads, and some of it was directed against what was seen as the destruction of existing communities. But there was another element, as new to Australia as a scepticism about the building of dams – a concern with the past. Almost everything that was old had been destroyed and even in the 1960s there were still plans for pulling down most of what was left. Now each new proposed act of destruction was likely to be contested by protest. All over Australia, State and local governments were becoming concerned with preserving at least some old buildings. Almost a hundred years after the Europeans had put together open-air folk museums by setting aside areas to which old peasant houses were moved, Australians began to assemble a few folk museums by assembling old wooden buildings. If there were none left they built some new ones.

'The timber vernacular': *with the growth of environmentalism, previously despised wooden structures in Australia became revered as part of 'the timber vernacular', and many were restored carefully (above).*

'Australian audiences heard for the first time in their lives Australian characters on stage speaking the Australian idiom of the streets.'

Words like these hailed the success of the play *The Summer of the Seventeenth Doll* in 1956 as the beginning of an Australian national theatre. In the 1950s such prophecies of artistic maturity were commonplace. 'Renaissances' were detected in all the arts apart from film-making. In fact by the 1950s the general achievement was superior in quality and much more diverse than in the 1890s, the last time Australians had begun to believe in their own artists. The tedium of some of the intervening decades was drifting away.

The first drama renaissance lasted little more than four years (it coincided, although quite independently, with outbursts of anger on the London stage), but in other arts Australia began to seem a place where things continued to happen. In the composition of music a belief developed in established Australian practitioners, to whose existence other practitioners could react; new performing groups were established, usually with public money. In writing, a new self-confidence was manifest when critics began to make out

lists, hierarchically arranged in the classroom fashion, according to guesses about how the writers' works would 'last' or how 'universal' their themes were. There were successive waves of literary movements, each leaving the literary culture more diverse; when Patrick White received the Nobel Prize in 1973, this 'overseas recognition' of an Australian novelist was seen as a general confirmation of the value of Australian writing. Some of the writers began in a modest way, to 'make news'. For people who still sought contemporary construction of reality from fiction, there was a variety of works that might suit their needs, and for those who read verse, there were possibilities for self-definition by the verse they read. In painting, acceptance of achievement was so wide that by the 1950s it was already beginning to attract the rich, and with the 1960s there was a harvest of dealers' galleries, art openings and prizes from business firms. Belief in Australian painting spread and some painters also 'made news'; offers of prints became a promotional device of newspapers and magazines. At first it was overseas praise that helped establish acceptance of Australia's new painters, and most of them went to Europe to find success: then, in the late 1960s and early 1970s they

began to come back home. And, at last, in the late 1960s there eventuated the beginnings of those government subsidies to the performing arts first urged in the 1840s, although this time the inspiration was found in Canada, not, as had been suggested in the 1840s, ancient Rome. This was accompanied by a resurrection of film-making, long-defunct in Australia, and another renaissance of the drama that, this time, survived. There was something about Whitlam's style as Prime Minister that, along with the formation of the Australia Council in 1975, increased the impression that the arts now occupied a permanent place in Australian public culture.

Now that there were many more university graduates and more belief in education, Australians interested in ideas and concepts began to speak more confidently of themselves as 'intellectuals'. From the late 1950s onwards, beginning with the magazines *Dissent*, *Prospect*, *Voice*, the *Observer* and *Nation*, new publications served the emerging intellectuals, and, more generally, the educated; some older publications changed. There was a flourishing of conferences, seminars and travel grants, and government money began to sponsor research in the universities. Professional associations were

Ray Lawler's The Summer of the Seventeenth Doll *(left) won a Playwrights' Advisory Board competition in 1955, and when it achieved commercial success, with 300 performances, it was seen as the beginning of a renaissance of drama in Australia. However, it was not until the early 1970s that Australian drama clearly became established. One indication was the success of David Williamson's plays* Don's Party *(above left) and* The Removalists, *both of which later became films.*

Creators: *Australia was going through a cultural awakening in which new names were emerging, or established names were acquiring new meanings. The Nobel Prize-winning novelist Patrick White (top left) became a public figure in some protest movements. Manning Clark (centre top), whose six-volume* A History of Australia *attained a 19th-century largeness of imagination, was seen as a secular prophet. Janet Dawson (above), a painter of lyrical abstracts and landscapes, became recognised as one of the best contemporary Australian women artists. The revival of opera in Australia became associated with Joan Sutherland (centre left). Of the writers who emerged in the 1960s the best known was Frank Moorhouse, photographed in 1972 (left) walking barefooted in his back garden.*

formed in the humanities and social sciences, and they brought out their specialist journals; other groups concerned with the arts and the intellect mustered outside the universities. Some who moved in among the old terraces of the inner cities were intellectuals; they felt more at home there than in the suburbs where they had been born. There could even be a sense of intellectual neighbourhood: words like 'Carlton' in Melbourne or 'Balmain' in Sydney could be taken to mean a particular kind of person. Young people began to find it less difficult to display their talents; starting a new publication was almost as easy as it had been in the 19th century. There was at last a new middle class of intellect and taste where intellectuals could feel they belonged (or to which they could react) even if the sense of isolation and threat could also remain.

For a time the old idea of the Australian as bushman or Digger seemed altogether overthrown. *The Summer of the Seventeenth Doll* questioned mateship; *The One Day of the Year*, a successor play, questioned the values of Anzac; the rise of the poets James McAuley and A.D. Hope as literary figures was seen as a defeat for literary nationalism (if also for literary modernism). In painting, the old bush

impressionism had disappeared, and even if some painters still sought metaphors in landscape the landscapes were now likely to be abstract, or primitive or surreal, saying something quite different from the old assurance of gumtree and grazing paddock. Some painters turned to urban scenes, finding tedium, or despair, or saw modern society in terms of mass culture, or junk, or found some comfort in its jocularities and banalities.

Even *The Bulletin* had the bush taken out of it and was modernised. The traditional naturalistic style was questioned: Patrick White's novel *The Aunt's Story* was praised because it showed that 'the Australian novel is not necessarily the dreary, dun-coloured offspring of journalistic realism'; and as soon as the first drama renaissance got going it was attacked as 'backyard realism', and a second renaissance – of anti-naturalism – was proclaimed. In novels there developed a fashion in disjointed prose. With the new writing of the late 1960s, with their little magazines and small presses, sharper and even more determinedly urban images appeared and the establishment of the beginnings of a continuing drama tradition brought to the stage something of the life of both suburbia and the inner-city

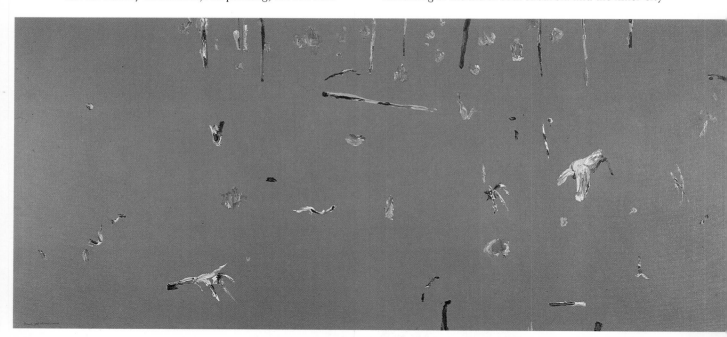

Fred Williams was obsessed, in the Australian manner, with landscapes, but on occasion he would reduce his landscapes to such sparseness that they developed some of the qualities of an abstract painting, as in Landscape *(above), painted in 1969.*

terraces. It was mainly in film and television that there was a return to the mythic themes of the bush, but even here there were also urban themes.

What could seem the frustrations of living in 'an unimportant country which has contributed little or nothing of a distinctive character to the world' had sent not only the painters abroad. Colonies of 'expatriates' of a wide variety had formed, mainly in London, and even some of those who remained in Australia could develop a mentality, similar to that of lost Russian intellectuals in a 19th-century novel or play, in which they could feel 'expatriates in their own country', looking, at first, to London and then to a more general 'Overseas', as if it were also a country.

There had been no end to dissatisfactions with Australian life. The first volume of verse published in Sydney, in 1819, had seen Australia not as part of the initial creation but as 'an afterbirth, not conceived in the Beginning'; in the 1950s A.D. Hope saw Australia as 'the last of lands, the emptiest'. Charles Harpur had written of the 'dead murky level' of the 'intellectual grossness' of his fellow countrymen; McAuley wrote of 'white Australia, as she hugely squats, above her pint-pot, fly-blown and resigned'. There was a recurrent

belief that the country was so spiritually dried out that it would crack into pieces to be picked up by Asian powers. In a wave of satire, with Australia being savaged as a uniquely barbarian land, the RSL became the most hated symbol of out-dated Australian provincialism, the paradigm enemy of the new sophisticates. Beginning with *The Australian Ugliness*, a criticism of Australian design that was seen as a general onslaught on the Australian condition, there developed a market for books making comprehensive attacks on Australia; but, with the new sophistication, self-criticism became so quickly institutionalised that some of these books were soon set as school texts.

In the manner brutally articulated by D.H. Lawrence and others in the 1920s and 1930s, the 'expatriates', whether at home or 'Overseas', had been likely to blame their predicament on the ordinary Australian people. In a sad misunderstanding of their sense of isolation, making them hate those who should not have been blamed, they attacked the 'apathy' and 'intolerance' of the common people for inadequacies of intellectual life in Australia. In the 1840s the fatal facility for making money had been seen as a corruption of the people; now it was the affluence of the

Although an 'abstract expressionist', John Olsen kept a strong sense of place and time, so that paintings such as Journey into You Beaut Country No. 1 *(right) painted in 1961, were seen among other things as being statements about the vulgar exuberance of Australians.*

Arthur Boyd's Shearers Playing for a Bride *(left) painted in 1957, was one expression of Boyd's haunting concern with the symbol of a part-Aboriginal bride that affected a number of his 1950s paintings, providing images of love and rejection, hope and disorder.*

suburbs that aroused uneasiness. Patrick White's play *The Season at Sarsparilla*, a study of suburban vacuity, was taken to be a study of the whole nation; 'Mrs Everage' was seen both as typical of Australia and unique to it.

The ordinary people were being blamed for a failure to take initiatives that were beyond the reach of the common people in any country. Sometimes the fate of disappointed intellectuals was due to a failure they could meet anywhere, but when frustration came from being Australian it was not always realised that it came from the colonial origin of the country, not from its democracy. Australia, as a country with 'no gods, no songs, no history', was seen as not worthy of art, or even investigation. Both Australian society and the learnt-off culture could seem unreal. Then, with the cutting edge of the new sophistication, it began to seem that, in yet another way, Australia had 'come of age'. Perhaps, in this field, it really had. Overall there at last seemed to be an acceptance of Australian themes as valid subject matter for art and intellectual inquiry and there was also, at last, an acceptance of diversity – there were now many ways of being an Australian. Perhaps it was the writers, artists and intellectuals (and the scientists) who had advanced furthest in escaping the colonial mentality.

McAuley had complained of Australia's citizenry that, 'For it, Plato's a horse, Socrates a dog. Surrounded by its vast domain it sleeps; a pigmy in the iron bed of Og'; but when he grew older he wrote a sequence of suburban poems that gave poetic form to some of the common stuff of Australian life. Social critics also began to give a more sympathetic treatment to the suburbs. A number of autobiographies searched childhood and youth in the 1920s, 30s and 40s, seeking some of the springs of contemporary existence. Australian history had not been taught in the last years of school. Now it was. There had been no courses in Australian history at the universities. Now there were. And books were being written about Australian history

Australian politics had not been studied at the universities, nor Australian writing. Now they both became a regular part of degree programs, and books were being written about them. For a surprisingly long period no sociology had been taught in Australia. Now there were a number of studies of aspects of Australian society. Some of the new books could also interest a general intellectual public. One of the historians, Manning Clark, became, along with Patrick White, a secular prophet.

There was now a great deal more that was 'known' about Australia; the kinds of intellectuals who again had hopes of doing things could seem somewhat more expert about it. After the belabouring received by the 'planners', intellectuals had for many years detached themselves from matters of policy. Now they began to give detailed study to aspects of public affairs. The careful work of an Immigration Reform Group in the 1960s helped change the attitudes of influential people. For a while, economists, singly or in groups, raised a flow of new ideas on tariffs, foreign investment, poverty, social services, national superannuation schemes, taxation, and the economic effects of immigration and 'development' (although they could also retreat into conservative parties). There was increasingly detailed discussion on urban planning, on the environment, on ethnicity, on the position of women. Others gave systematic thought to foreign policy and defence. Even politicians wrote books. Contacts grew between intellectuals outside the Government departments and those inside them. Australia, for so long living on an exhausted political capital, had found a new source of ideas, at least as a potential. It remained to be seen if in a nation in which there was now a release of artistic and intellectual and scientific creativity there could be some equal release in business institutions or a return of creativity to those political institutions that, with their liberalism and their rhetorical concern with equality, had once made Australia seem 'an examplar to the old lands'.

Colin Lancely's 1983 assemblage Where three dreams cross between blue rocks (Blue Mountains) *(left) makes an abstract order from the chaos of junk.*

19. Coming of age: 1950 to 1980s

A revival of pride in Britishness in the 1950s refused to acknowledge that the Empire had virtually gone. Yet Britain was no longer the protector nor the chief foreign investor, even though the Union Jack remained in the corner of the Australian flag. Then, for many, feelings of loyalty extended to the United States – a loyalty that became a matter for bitter division during the war in Vietnam. But the reality was that through immigration Australia was becoming a multicultural society with possibilities of new types of national definition based on ethnic diversity and human tolerance. But as late as the 1980s Australians were still trying to define themselves. In such an atmosphere of apparent racial tolerance the Aboriginal community began to fight determinedly for its rights.

The afterglow of Britishry

As Improvement narrowed down to Development, some of the old values of the age of Authority seemed, again, to strengthen. There was a waning in the more aggressive excesses of the cult of the New Imperialism after its price was paid in the Great War. (Or had the excesses merely been domesticated, in Anzac Day?)

But in its equation of civilisation with Britishness, New Imperialism was strengthened in the 1920s and 1930s; and the acceptance of the British Empire as an economic and strategic unit was not even marked by the kind of occasional public criticisms of British policy by which earlier political leaders had made some of their reputation. The cult seemed full blown, like a dying flower.

Then, in the 1950s, there was an extraordinary revival. Not long after taking over as Prime Minister, despite the clear lessons from the fall of Singapore in 1942, Robert

Two aspects of the British presence: The Courier-Mail *greets Queen Elizabeth on her arrival in Australia in 1954 (above left), and* The West Australian *greets the first British atom bomb explosion in Australia in 1952 (above).*

With the appointment of R.G. Casey as Governor General in 1965, the Liberal Party joined the Labor Party in accepting that governors general should be Australians. Casey himself, inspecting a guard of honour on his last day in office (left), was sufficiently of the old school to carry off the position in the old style.

291

Menzies announced that 'the British Empire must remain our chief international preoccupation', and even when the red had gone from the map some older Liberals still tried to project the 'British Commonwealth' as a political institution. There was an attempt in the mid-1950s to restrict immigrants from Southern Europe; a 'Bring out a Briton' campaign was announced. (It failed.) In this afterglow of Empire, Menzies' annual journeys to London seemed pilgrimages to the Holy Land.

In 1962 even Menzies admitted that 'the old hopes for concerted common policies have gone'. But although the Commonwealth had let Menzies down there was still an attempt to make Britain itself seem the main centre of civilisation. There were ardent proclamations of Britishry ('I am British to the boot heels') and loyalty to Queen Elizabeth ('We are the Queen's men'). Visits to Australia of British royal persons increased from an average of one every two years to up to six a year; when it was announced that Queen Elizabeth's eldest son would spend a year at an Australian school, the Australian High Commissioner in London expressed his pleasure by saying that he felt like jumping over the moon. It was only in 1965 that the appointment of an Australian as Governor General became predictable; while Australians were State governors in New South Wales from the mid-1940s, more than 30 years were to go by before this would become normal in all the States. Vestiges of the Black Hat life of the 1840s continued, and even seemed at times to regain some confidence. The number of royal honours bestowed on Australians increased at four to five times the rate of increase of the total population. There were limits to these excesses. Menzies'

The battle for the flag: *in the 1970s agitation began for a change in the Australian flag. Many designs were prepared: the design (above left) maintains the present colours and the Southern Cross; the design (centre left) is inspired by the Qantas kangaroo; and the design (below left) is inspired by the Eureka flag. The Eureka flag was taken up as a symbol by some Australian republicans. In a demonstration in Melbourne (below) Builders Labourers' Federation members pulled down the Australian flag and put up a Eureka flag.*

In 1975 the Whitlam Government instituted the Order of Australia. The medal of the Companion of the Order of Australia (far below).

Cabinet stopped him from calling the main unit of the new decimal currency the 'royal' and there was derision when, confusing royal with profane love, Menzies welcomed Queen Elizabeth with the lines, 'I did but see her passing by, and yet I love her till I die.' But that side of the Australian style had become one of *tableaux vivants*, seeing the past as if the present were a garden party.

Yet not only had the Empire gone, and the Commonwealth virtually gone: now Australia no longer looked to the British Navy for protection. Britain was no longer the dominant foreign investor in Australia, nor Australia's main source of technological innovation; it was no longer the biggest customer for Australia's exports, nor the second biggest, and with its entry into the European Economic Community its purchases were expected to dwindle further. It was no longer the supplier of most immigrants; London was no longer Australia's only cultural centre; and to younger people the old imperial cult seemed hard to imagine.

But the symbols of Britishry lived on, or if they went, they could be slow in going. When in 1974 a Government-sponsored public opinion poll of 60 000 persons showed that, of 'Advance Australia Fair', 'Waltzing Matilda' and 'Song of Australia', a majority chose 'Advance Australia Fair', Labor Prime Minister Gough Whitlam announced that 'Advance Australia Fair' would replace 'God Save the Queen' as Australia's national anthem. Malcolm Fraser, his Liberal Party successor as Prime Minister, then reinstated 'God Save the Queen'. 'Advance Australia Fair' was accepted as the 'national song' – except that it could be played but not sung, and where singing was required, 'God Save the Queen' would still be played. Bob Hawke, the next Labor Prime Minister, reinstated 'Advance Australia Fair' as the national anthem. Whitlam took the crown off the letter postboxes. Fraser put it back on. It was Queen Elizabeth's portrait that still hung in the officers' messes in the military, and it was she, not the Australian people, who was toasted at dinners and national days. Governments were still spoken of as 'the Crown'. When a South Australian Police Commissioner was asked why he had kept certain information from his Premier, he said, 'I felt my loyalties were to the Crown and beyond elected government.' The Union Jack in the corner of the Australian flag remained a symbol of dependence to some, and, to others, a symbol of honour. When an organisation, Ausflag 88, was formed, with the object of gaining a more distinctively Australian flag by 1988, the RSL established a National Flag Association to fight the battle of keeping the Australian flag British. For a while, Fraser hoped the Prince of Wales might become Governor General. Except for special issues, the monarch's face went off the postage stamps in 1972; remaining constitutional links (except for the monarchy itself) were being removed; an Order of Australia was instituted by Whitlam and for the Labor governments it replaced the British Orders (although the conservatives still kept them). That Australia would at last get around to being ready to elect its own head of state was inevitable, and Labor members, including Labor premiers and prime ministers, were now ready to declare that in principle they were republicans. Yet moves in 1984 not to require immigrants to swear an oath to the monarch in naturalisation ceremonies were attacked as treachery.

For a while the excitements of Evatt's foreign policy revived a latent big-headedness, with his hope that Australia might become the conscience of the world, and even after the Liberal victory there remained some dash and independence in Australian diplomacy.

The first Liberal External Affairs Minister was one of the main prompters of the Colombo Plan for economic and technical assistance to South and Southeast Asian countries, and his successor was careful to continue to promote the rhetoric of an Australia newly defined because of its nearness to Asia.

But public attitudes of independence evaporated. When Australia signed the ANZUS Treaty between Australia, New Zealand and the United States, to many Australians this seemed more than the act of a sovereign nation independently entering an alliance. For those seeking a greater comfort than that, it was as if Australia had successfully joined a different empire – that of the United States. Australians knew that it was the United States, not Britain, that had saved them from the Japanese (they were

The 'Colombo Plan' was instituted in the 1950s, allowing for the training of Asian students in Australia. The entry of these students represented one of the first weakenings of the infamous White Australia Immigration Policy.

not even resentful of the United States for saving them). Australia was the first nation to send forces to the desolate sweeps of mountains and the rivers and rice paddies of Korea, and while Australian troops there later became part of a British Commonwealth Division it was from the United States that Australia was seeking rewards for its merit; even its forces in Malaysia and Singapore were seen as part of an offering to maintain US interest in Southeast Asia; and when Australia sent a battalion to South Vietnam, and then a task force, introducing selective conscription to man it, Queen Elizabeth was required to issue medals to Australians for fighting in a war of which the British Government had no part. It seemed significant that the event that was celebrated from the war against the Japanese was not the defeat of the Japanese by the Australians at Milne Bay – the first land defeat of the Japanese – but the United States victory over the Japanese in the Battle of the Coral Sea. For a period, Coral Sea Week became one of the symbolic ceremonies of the year, culminating in a Victory Ball at which, among the red, white and blue decorations the Australian kangaroo was now joined not with the British lion, but the American eagle.

Politics and ideas of what kind of a nation Australia was were debilitated by transferring to 'the American alliance' the older excesses of loyalty to Empire. Instead of being defended merely as a prudent arrangement in an uncertain world, the relation with the United States was treated with much of the sacredness that had been so disastrous in dealings with Britain in the 1920s and 1930s. Menzies had announced in 1950 that 'we cannot survive a surging Communist challenge from abroad except for the cooperation of powerful friends', but keeping in with powerful friends moved from caution to something close to sycophancy. Publicly there was never any Australian disagreement on any aspect of United States policy and privately the Australian Government carried the principle of loyalty to the extreme of assuming that the US could not be reckoned on as an ally in even the most serious circumstances unless Australia did what it was told on even minor occasions. Menzies maintained this inner humility with some outward dignity – his public acting of the loyal Briton provided a diversion from the realities of the new alliance – but his successor, Harold Holt, transferred to the United States the public adulation that had previously been

Two aspects of the United States presence: *A special stamp was issued in 1955 (left) to commemorate the building of the United States Memorial in Canberra. Women demonstrate against the United States 'Defence Space Research' installations at Pine Gap (far left), established in 1969.*

For a season, between the prime ministerships of R.G. Menzies and E.G. Whitlam, Australian prime ministers made an annual 'pilgrimage' to the White House, where the climax was a presidential dinner. When Prime Minister William McMahon's wife, Sonia, wore a split dress to the 1971 White House dinner (right), the dress made front page news in the United States Press.

A bill to ban the Communist Party was put to a referendum in 1951, and defeated. Both sides lobbied enthusiastically – for (centre right) and against (far right).

saved for the British. He proclaimed to President Johnson that Australia would go 'all the way with LBJ'. One of his colleagues said, 'Where America goes, Australia goes.' Holt's two successors each carried the ANZUS Pact to Washington for blessing as if it were a magic charm instead of a mere document signed by human hands. The annual pilgrimage of Australian prime ministers to the White House, with guards of honour, the firing of salutes, bands playing in the rose garden and large ceremonial dinners seemed, briefly, to have become one of Australia's principal ceremonies of state. When Whitlam became Prime Minister there was concern that he might not be invited by the President to dinner.

For more than 20 years, fear played a part in Australian political life, colouring attitudes to the United States. The nation that in 1948 had shown itself most expecting war found it easy in 1951 to believe Menzies' warning that war could break out at any time within three years. In 'the Movement' and among some of the 'Groupers' it was already 'ten minutes to midnight'. Estimates were made of how long Australia had to go. ('I give us four years,' was a common prediction in the 1950s.) For two decades

cataclysm was always just around the corner. It was as if, with so much apparent cohesion and success at home, Australians looked increasingly to the outside world for that sense of threat that could give texture and difference to politics and poignant purpose to life. (Nevertheless, just as in World War I Australians had twice voted 'No' to conscription, in 1951, when the Cold War was at its height, Australians voted 'No' – if narrowly – to a proposal to ban the Communist Party.)

So far as Menzies' warlike warnings were concerned, a gap separated words from actions; he announced he would put Australia on a semi-war footing, then he let military expenditure slide down to a level lower than in almost any other nation. Until the 1960s, when President Sukarno's 'confrontations', domestic criticism, and private United States pressure, forced an increase in military expenditure, in their trance-like dissociation between the images of threat and the realities of business-as-usual, the Liberals could move from warnings of imminent danger to assurances that expenditure on 'national development' rather than the armed forces was really the best form of defence. The result was a corruption of political life by a sometimes hysterical

With the defection of the Soviet diplomat Vladimir Petrov in 1954, there began tensions within the Australian political system that were to last for many years. The most theatrical event in the Petrov affair came when Mrs Petrov was led on to an aircraft in Sydney by Soviet officials (above), but then herself defected when the plane arrived in Darwin.

Catholic organisation: B.A. Santamaria

Concern about the shortcomings of capitalism, which 'had precipitated the Great Depression, bringing universal misery in its train', caused a group of Melbourne Catholic intellectuals in the 1930s to form Catholic Action. However, after the Spanish Civil War communism began to seem the arch-enemy. The Cold War period, with the increasing number of battles between Communists and their opponents for control of Australian trade unions diverted Catholic Action's attentions from the failings of capitalism.

A young law student, Bartholomew Augustine (Bob) Santamaria, was an early member of the Catholic Action movement. In January 1938, aged 22, he was appointed for a two-year term as director of a new National Secretariat established by the Catholic hierarchy, a position he held for over 40 years.

Santamaria's parents were poor emigrants from the Aeolian Islands north of Sicily. Among his motivating influences were the European peasant virtues of religious belief, hard work, family ties and rural values, and also the intensely religious, political, Irish attitudes of Melbourne's famous Archbishop Mannix.

As head of a secret Catholic organisation code-named 'the Movement', Santamaria became influential in the Labor Party, although never a member of it. When the existence of the Movement was disclosed, the Labor Party split, disastrously, and took many years to recover. (The Democratic Labor Party emerged from the break.) Santamaria, a man with a social conscience and a yearning for social justice, had been caught in a political conflict which made him and many of his allies heirs to the sectarian conflict and the divisions between faith and scepticism that had always been a part of the Australian way.

use of language that did not prompt action (except vote-getting): Australians were urged to fear, but not to self-reliance. Not long after Menzies was forced into some rearmament, he resigned.

At first, as part of the period of Cold War, there was a general concern that what was still an international Communist movement under Soviet influence would prove even more expansionary than the Nazis. To Australia this world threat was given extra meaning by seeing Southeast Asia as 'the most unsettled region of the world'. Then a more particular sense of threat emerged – from China. To Australians who had so recently known Japan attack from the north it seemed possible that history could be repeated, especially when President Sukarno's theatricalities turned Indonesia into an ally of China. At election times red arrows appeared on maps with exhortations to stop the Chinese at the border between North and South Vietnam. One election advertisement showed the Chinese in occupation of the Sydney Harbour Bridge.

Much of Australia's sense of danger was shared by large parts of the rest of the world, and its fears, when expressed in their more moderate forms, could be seen as making as

sensible a basis for action as any other. But behind specific fears there often lurked a more general and absurd, but degrading, terror of *all* Asia, as if it were one political entity whose faceless hordes would swoop down on Australia like huns from the Steppes wanting more room for their horses.

Australia enjoyed the greatest – and perhaps the last – of its imperial moments after Harold Holt was drowned during a Sunday morning swim in December, 1967. From this quick death, symbolic of Australia's pursuit of innocent happiness, there arose an imperial funeral. The President of the United States announced that he would fly to Australia to give the occasion meaning, and Asian presidents, prime ministers and foreign ministers took to their aircraft to be near him. Australia had received the greatest honour for its imperial loyalty: the presence of the emperor himself. For a day Melbourne had fulfilled an old dream. With processions of presidents, princes and prime ministers passing through its streets it seemed an imperial city.

But a few months later the President would announce that he abdicated his power. The 'anti-Vietnam' movement had destroyed Lyndon B. Johnson's acceptability as

With changing times, the styles of war artists also changed. Ivor Hele's Medical Air Evacuation 1953 *(left), and Ken McFadyen's* Diggers Sitting on APC on Patrol, Phuoc Toy Province *(below left).*

During the presidency of Sukarno in Indonesia it became routine for Australian politicians to visit Jakarta. The Australian Postmaster General, C.W. Davison, is photographed with the President (above right).

'Anti-Vietnam': *division over the Vietnam War brought one of the recurrent periods of bitterness to Australian politics. US President Lyndon B. Johnson's visit to Australia in October 1966 sparked demonstrations against involvement in Vietnam and conscription (centre right).*

With the death from drowning of Prime Minister Harold Holt in December 1967, Australia saw its first 'international' funeral, with four presidents and many other world statesmen. It was the decision of United States President Lyndon B. Johnson to fly to Australia for the funeral which caused the others to come. Johnson leads Holt's grandson by the hand at the funeral (below right).

Democratic candidate at the next presidential election. It had even touched him in Australia, which he had visited in 1966 to help Harold Holt win that year's election, when, as well as the cheers of hundreds of thousands in the streets of Melbourne and Sydney, the balloons and ticker tape, the unscheduled stops with their hand-shaking and distribution of souvenir ballpoint pens, and the presidential cries of 'I love ya, Australia', there were the anti-Vietnam protestors, chanting, 'Hey, hey, LBJ, how many babies did you kill today?' In Sydney they threw themselves in front of the imperial limousine.

The eight-year anti-Vietnam movement was one of those radicalising movements, like the Anti-Transportation League in the late 1840s and early 1850s that could, for some members of a generation, become the formative experience of their political lives, later remembered as days of innocence and hope. As with other protest movements, it had begun, and continued, mainly in protest forms first worked out in the United States, such as the 'demo' itself, street theatre, the 'vigil', the 'sit-down', the 'teach-in'. It was at one of the first teach-ins, in July 1965, that the movement gained some of that middle-class respectability

that can lend credibility to reform movements in Australia, when the best-selling author Morris West spoke in Canberra. Further respectability came when Gordon Barton, carrying all the prestige of a self-made businessman, ran an advertisement in *The Sydney Morning Herald* featuring an open letter to President Johnson and received so many letters that he formed a Liberal Reform Group that ran candidates, partly on an anti-Vietnam policy, in the 1966 elections. Further respectability came with 'Project Vietnam' in which, among other things, 58 Australian writers opposed sending conscripts to Vietnam, and again in 1969 when public support was given to the Melbourne-based Draft Resisters Union (which was running an underground network for some of the more militant of the 13 000 young men who had evaded the call-up); the support came in the form of the 'Committee for Defiance of the National Security Act' which collected signatures to a statement illegally calling for defiance of the draft. Among the 8000 signatures was that of Patrick White, in one of the first of many acts in which he was to lend his prestige to 'protest'. Protest forms grew – in folk songs, posters ('OUT NOW!'), badges, stickers, the burning of United States flags and Australian draft cards. In Sydney there was set up a Draft Resistance Advisory Centre. The protests reached their theatrical climax in the rallies of the first 'Moratorium' in 1970, most notably in Melbourne where a crowd of between 70 000 and 100 000 people sat down in the streets and chanted 'We want peace'.

There had never before been quite such a public challenge to conventional thinking about Australia's habit of displaying its loyalty by sending off expeditions to the causes of great and powerful friends. There had been some protests against the Boer War, but nothing like this, and although there was more bitterness in 1916 and 1917 – not least because there were so many more Australians dying – the campaigns then were against conscription rather than against the war itself, and in any case were restricted by the Government's wartime powers of arbitrary police raids, arrests, censorship and bannings.

But when 'anti-Vietnam' was all over, not all that much seemed to have changed. Whitlam acted out a greater style of independence, but things remained much the same; Fraser saw the Chinese as friends, but seemed at times to project a direct Soviet threat to Australia. When he was in Washington, the new Labor Foreign Minister, Bill Hayden, reversed the earlier symbolism and tried to encourage the United States to play down the importance of ANZUS: but when, as Prime Minister, Bob Hawke made his first trip to Washington, he said, 'We will be altogether forever.'

The real change had come when the newly elected President Nixon announced a new doctrine, in 1969, in which he called on nations like Australia to do more for themselves in their defence strategies. After that there was some talk about how Australia should, for the first time in its existence, arrange its own defence. The talk was related to continuing Defence Department assurances that it was not 'ten minutes to midnight' after all, and that Australia was removed from immediate threat. But although intellectuals could write about it, and some of the people in the Defence Department could talk about it, building up a genuine Australian defence force that could itself handle low-level threats seemed beyond Australian political skills.

A multicultural Australia

One of the oldest divisions among Australians was now fading – the bitterness between Protestants and Catholics. The Irishness of the Catholic Church had been taken away, and even if the Church remained more sensitive to the Vatican than many other national churches, its clergy and hierarchy became Australian.

As late as 1929 Archbishop Mannix could still say, 'The more deeply they breathe the Irish atmosphere the stronger and more vigorous will be the Australian faith.' But in the 1930s Australian-trained priests were moving in and a few were made bishops; in 1937 one of them became Archbishop of Hobart, another, Norman Gilroy – so Australian that he had been a telegraph messenger boy and had then served at Anzac Cove – became Archbishop of Sydney in 1940 and was later made a cardinal. Other appointments followed. By the late 1950s some Catholic intellectuals were beginning to break out of their self-perceived 'ghetto' but, although better represented among the well-to-do and the university-educated, Catholics still seemed to challenge cohesion with the exclusiveness that had marked them since Pius IX. To

some, their talent for conspiracy could seem to threaten the very basis of society. The Catholics' own sense of persecution eased when, to get Catholic votes, Liberal governments in the 1960s began to subsidise Catholic schools, partly returning to the policies of a hundred years before, the abandoning of which had caused so much bitterness. General community attitudes to Catholics changed when Pope John and the Second Vatican Council began to look for the Christianity in other churches. In 1965 Catholic priests were allowed to join other clergymen in the official Anzac Day celebrations. When Pope Paul spent 65 hours in Australia in 1970, presiding over two Masses in St Mary's Basilica and a Mass for a quarter of a million at Randwick racecourse, he joined Protestant clergy in Sydney's Town Hall in the Lord's Prayer, an occasion that would have astounded the Town Hall's founders.

The old declared hatred of immigrants also faded. By 1960 a fifth of Australian children were either immigrants or the children of immigrants. The proportion increased: by the 1980s more than one fifth of all the Australians were immigrants; in Melbourne and Adelaide immigrants were more than a quarter of the population; in Sydney almost a

PLACE OF BIRTH	1947	1981
AUSTRALIA	90.2%	79.2%
UNITED KINGDOM AND IRELAND	7.1%	7.9%
OTHER PARTS OF EUROPE	1.5%	7.6%
NEW ZEALAND	.6%	1.2%
ASIA AND PACIFIC ISLANDS	.3%	.3%
AMERICA	.2%	.7%
AFRICA	.1%	.4%
TOTAL POPULATION	7.6 mill	14.8 mill

Immigrant make-up: *from 1947 to 1981 the percentages of immigrants from parts of Europe other than the United Kingdom and Ireland, and from Asia, increased considerably.*

Whenever the 'migrant ships' arrived in Australia, newspaper reporters looked for an angle. When this family arrived in Sydney in 1966 (left) there was no difficulty: there were four generations.

For many Australians, one of the greatest symbols of a new tolerance was the enthusiasm with which Pope Paul VI was received when he came to Australia in 1970 (below).

quarter; in Perth, almost a third. What was even more remarkable was that only about 40 per cent of them were British. The 'displaced persons' had been mainly East Europeans but they were followed by large migrations from Italy, Greece and Yugoslavia, Germany and the Netherlands. By the late-1960s Australia was looking for immigrants from Spain and Portugal, Turkey, Lebanon and Egypt; then there were openings up with Latin America and Southern Asia. Australia was now a society of multi-national origin, with Turks as well as Dutch, Chileans as well as Germans, Singaporeans as well as Poles. Their spread was uneven; the non-British gathered more in the cities than in rural areas, and of the cities, while Melbourne had 18 per cent and Sydney and Canberra 15 per cent, Brisbane had only seven per cent of non-British immigrants. In the two biggest cities non-British immigrants provided half the small shopkeepers and most of the restaurateurs. The contents of Australian delicatessens became the most varied in the world. In some inner suburbs immigrants formed minority national colonies; in some outer suburbs they outnumbered the natives. Many worked in heavy industry, manufacturing, building and construction, doing much of

Discussion on Australian 'multi-culturalism' became one of the new talking points in the popular Press and in intellectual journals such as Social Alternatives *(above).*

Old racial prejudices were stirred among some Australians when Indo-Chinese refugees ('the boat people') were brought to Australia. There was a strong reaction when a boatload of Indo-Chinese arrived directly in Australia, at Darwin, in 1978 (above right).

After many predictions that Papua New Guinea would not gain even home rule this century, Australia suddenly granted its colony independence. Prince Charles presided over the Independence Day celebrations (right) in the presence of Governor General John Kerr.

Australia's dirtiest work, some in business or skilled trades or the professions; as owners of restaurants, art galleries, specialty shops, they helped smooth out the affluent life. Although immigrants were not well represented in official life, they gave Australian cities a much greater diversity and richness of texture, and as ambitious families they provided children who had a much greater propensity to 'do well' than the children of the Australian-born.

The Australian dislike of admitting that strangers were entering their country that had earlier made them call immigrants 'emigrants', now produced the euphemism 'migrants'; but fears proved false that ordinary Australians would turn their historic intolerance on the 'migrants'. With low unemployment until the 1970s, 'migrants' provided no economic threat – especially since they were handling the most boring jobs – and the balance of nationalities was well-proportioned, with no dominant nationality making a critical challenge. Whether or not native-born Australians loved their new neighbours, they learnt to tolerate them. But beneath the increasingly open tolerance in the public culture there were many discriminations against 'migrants': they had many disadvantages in the work force; the education system did not allow for the difficulties of their children; the medical, welfare and legal services did not allow for their special problems; and the official policy of 'assimilation' was designed to strip them of their customs while at the same time not providing even efficient English language instruction.

Some more new ideas came in from the United States: first, the idea of 'integration' rather than assimilation, with policies designed to allow immigrants to fit into the society without being brutally absorbed by it, and then the ideal of 'ethnic pluralism' – that they had a right to preserve some aspects of cultural identity (contrasted with the 'anglo-conformism' that was intended to make them British). Unlike other movements that came from the United States, which were taken up by 'the people' (viz middle-class liberals, radical unionists and students) against the system, the moves towards what became known as 'multiculturalism' largely worked up within the system itself, especially in the universities and then among politicians (some of whom would excuse their new idealism by saying there were votes in it). But once the new idea of 'ethnic' was beginning, a number of 'ethnics' became visible and they seemed to recognise in this the chance they had been waiting for. The Whitlam Government took up the new 'multiculturalism', with its joint concern to limit discrimination and to foster some cultural diversity; the Fraser Government took it up with such vigour that some members of the Labor Party began to suspect that after all there might be something wrong with it. There were many dangers, especially those of tokenism: that Latvian folk dances were put on in a shopping mall did not mean that there was not still discrimination in work places; that Serbo-Croatian was accepted as a 'community language' in schools did not mean that immigrants did not still have special difficulties in welfare agencies. But the greatest danger lay in the signs of a backlash from those who wanted to keep Australia 'British'. By the mid-1980s this backlash began to re-appear in the public culture.

Australia seemed to shed its colony of Papua New Guinea almost without noticing. The whole island of New Guinea had seemed such a rampart, defending Australia, that late in the 1950s the Australian Government had strongly supported the Netherlands in trying to keep the eastern part of the island Dutch: when President Sukarno mounted a 'confrontation', Australia, baffled that the United States was not supporting Australian policy, gave in. Nevertheless, the Australian territories could still seem Australian forever. The External Territories Minister had said in 1951 that it would only be 'in the generations to come' that the natives might be 'required to manage their own affairs to a greater degree', and although by the mid-1960s there was beginning to be some talk of home rule there was still such caution, even among the Papua New Guinea politicians in the recently created House of Assembly, that when one of them said that Papua New Guinea might soon be independent he was expelled from his party. Papua New Guinea was independent by 1975.

Although there had been student protests against the White Australia immigration policy in Melbourne in the early 1960s, there was not much concern with the White Australia policy when the great period of protests began, perhaps because it was not the kind of campaign for which there were ideas to draw on from 'Overseas'. The anti-apartheid campaign of 1971, against the all-white South African rugby team, was more familiar: trade unionists, students and concerned citizens put on such a mighty show, with a thousand arrests, that the sporting authorities decided that South African teams were more trouble than they were worth. The reform of the White Australia policy began, however, among the politicians themselves, with a liberalisation in 1966 under Holt, a year after the Labor Party had finally removed from its platform an overt

Aboriginal protest: *the Aboriginal land rights movement became associated with a number of important symbolic events. Among these were a strike by the Gurindji Aborigines in the Northern Territory from 1966 to 1967, the erection of the Aboriginal Tent Embassy in Canberra in 1972, and the design of the Aboriginal flag.*

declaration of the support for the White Australia policy. By the beginning of the 1970s about 10 000 non-Europeans and part-Europeans were entering Australia each year; in 1971 the Liberal Prime Minister, John Gorton, declared that Australia might become 'the first truly multiracial society with no tensions of any kind' and Chipp said he would like to see 'a stage in the 1980s when Australia is becoming the only truly multiracial country in the world'. The loudest protests came from a former Labor leader who wanted to protect 'red-blooded Australians' from Asians who 'bred like flies': nevertheless it was Whitlam's Government that finally dismantled what was left of the policy. Although avoiding the kind of speech-making that might have urged Australians to be proud of these achievements, Fraser presided over an increase in the proportion of Asian immigrants. Amongst other immigrants, 60 000 Indo-Chinese refugees were accepted into Australia during his prime ministership, with relatively little friction. As with multiculturalism, however, a backlash had begun.

Even with the Aborigines, things had begun moving. While at Government conferences in 1951, 1961 and 1965 there were increasingly refined definitions of the

'assimilation' that Aborigines were supposed to be moving towards so that they would cease to be Aborigines, the Aborigines themselves were beginning to provide their own answers. A new range of Aboriginal organisations were using new protest techniques and new approaches to publicity – at first modestly, with struggles for the return of land that had previously been leased to them, or for the retention of reserves (with appeals to the United Nations and petitions written on bark to the House of Representatives); then in association with white students, in an anti-discrimination 'Freedom Ride' bus tour of a United States kind through northern New South Wales; then, most spectacularly, in a strike at the Wave Hill cattle station in the Northern Territory, which culminated in a long march to Wattie Creek, in what had been the territory of the Gurindji tribe, which they now claimed back as their own, wishing to turn it into a cattle station. In the next year the Aborigines at Yirrkala went to court to claim back from an aluminium company what they said were tribal lands at Gove. The struggle for 'land rights' had now begun.

On Australia Day, 1972, an Aboriginal Tent Embassy went up outside Parliament House, and it was not pulled

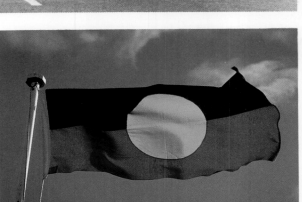

Two Northern Territory Aborigines went to Sydney in 1966 to go on a fund-raising speaking tour (left). After six months, police dismantled the Aboriginal Embassy in Canberra (above left). Aboriginal land rights protest marchers carry the Aboriginal flag along Macquarie Street, Sydney, to Parliament House (above). The Aboriginal flag (right): red for the land, black for the people, yellow for the life-giving sun which unites people and land.

Two attempts through stamp issues to pay symbolic respect to the Aborigines were the Albert Namatjira stamp from the 1968 Famous Australians series (above), and the Truganini stamp from the 1975 Famous Women series (top).

down by the police until six months later. New Aboriginal groups formed; for a while there was talk of 'black power'; Whitlam opened a large spending program as a token of esteem; legal aid services and other devices to assist urban Aborigines began in some of the cities (where a large minority of Aborigines were now settling); there was a cultural revival (the Australia Council set up an Aboriginal Arts Board) and concern with sacred sites; an Aboriginal flag was devised; there were new programs for Aboriginal health services (which did not show much success) and for a while a movement to redress past grievances by signing a treaty with the Aborigines. Above all, there was the movement for land rights. It gained momentum first in the Northern Territory, where almost a third of the land went to Aborigines, and in South Australia where about 20 per cent went to Aborigines. In both cases it was land of little or no farming value – but it interested mining companies.

Enormous resentments built up against the Aborigines amongst some whites, even going so far as to suggest that (like 'dole bludgers') they were a privileged group. The Aborigines still suffered many such insults and grievances, but they were now beginning to gain confidence.

In the early 1960s there began to be talk about Australia's national identity. Some Australians saw this concern as a mere chauvinism that was claiming for Australian society superiorities over other societies that did not exist.

To some, Australia's self-definition and self-importance came from its being British: not recognising that clinging to Britishness had been the principal form of Australian chauvinism (in its heyday not only claiming superiority but justifying world dominance), they saw claims to separate Australian identity as provincial-minded. Others, mainly on the Left, preferred the cosmopolitanism of an 'overseas' (that in fact did not exist). Another possible reaction to talk of a 'national identity crisis' was, however, to express surprise that the change had been so long coming. National identities are not made up for fun. Since humans belong to nation-states, they define them. And if things change, there is likely to be a struggle to change the definitions, to provide new bases for thought and action.

For some of those for whom 'Britishness' remained as the key definition of Australia, it became a code word that

Black rights lawyer: Pat O'Shane

At primary school in Cairns in the 1940s, Pat O'Shane defended herself from racial taunts with her fists; by the time she was in secondary school she was able to defend herself with words. She became school captain, State swimmer, Queensland's first Aboriginal woman teacher, Australia's first Aboriginal lawyer, a senior public servant in several New South Wales departments, and in 1983 she was appointed Head of the New South Wales Department of Aboriginal Affairs.

Always a fighter against racism, and quick to reject suggestions that she was 'different' from other Aborigines, Pat O'Shane was the eldest of five children of an Aboriginal mother and an Irish cane cutter. When her father was on strike her parents went without food so that their children could eat enough to keep them alert at school. The driving force was to get an education and thereby escape poverty.

After ten and a half years' teaching in Queensland schools, married with two children, she suffered a nervous breakdown. While recovering in Sydney, her marriage finished, she worked for the Black Rights Movement and started a law course at the University of New South Wales. The late 1960s and early 1970s were heady political days; a range of people expressed confidence in their powers to lead Australia. But Pat O'Shane was initially a curiosity, if not a threat, to black male radicals who had to accommodate themselves to a black woman who not only put forward ideas, but was able to develop suitable programs for implementing them.

provided a polite way of implying distrust for 'continentals'; it could even politely signify white racism. Others rejected such extreme expressions of a colonial mentality, but transferred them to ideas such as 'the United States alliance' and 'foreign investment'. For them, although they no longer saw material significance in the British connection, there was symbolic significance in maintaining the monarchic link: it provided a polite reassurance about Australia's essential insignificance. But for those Australians who wanted to feel they belonged to something bigger than themselves, there were now new opportunities.

From their earliest days, although seeing themselves above all as British, Australians had also the opportunity of seeing themselves as part of the Pacific Ocean. In their ambitious moments they could plunder the islands of the Southwest Pacific; in their less assured moods they could fear the Pacific as the ocean of some conqueror. But by 1970 Australia had become a Pacific Ocean nation in another sense: its economic prosperity now depended above all on a three-way economic relationship between Australia, Japan and North America, the three most 'modern' areas of the Pacific. By 1970 Australia was getting more than two-thirds

of its imports of machinery and equipment from the United States and much of its foreign capital; at the same time, just as Australia's prosperity had once been attached to the rapid expansion of Britain, it had now become attached to the rapid expansion of Japan, the world's fastest-growing economy. Japan had become Australia's best customer, the United States its second best. And, while in its relationship with Japan and the US Australia was small, its wealth was almost equal to that of all the Southeast Asia which it adjoined. Those Australians who wanted to, could imagine Australia as a Pacific Ocean power of some significance, in itself, and in its link with Japan and the United States.

There was another way Australians could imagine themselves as of some importance. In the early days some Australians had seen themselves as 'Austral-Asian', South Asian. In the great days of Empire this self-definition withered, but with the destruction by the Japanese of the European colonies, Australians could again begin to realise that they were near some of the countries of Asia. The idea of Australia as a power in Southeast Asia began to be welcomed in the 1950s by External Affairs Ministers. Their Department (later re-named the Foreign Affairs Department

Australian identity: *part of the celebrations to mark the bicentenary of the landing of Cook in 1770 included a re-enactment of Cook being rowed ashore at Botany Bay in a long boat (above).*

Perhaps one sign of Australian maturity was that concepts of Australian 'identity' were becoming more diverse. For a season, to many television viewers 'the typical Australian' became Norman Gunston (below left), a neurotic character with an overweening inferiority complex that forced him into a succession of outrageous acts. In films, as well as bush epics there were now also movies of urban life such as Love Letters From Teralba Road *(above left), starring Brian Brown and Chris McQuade, and based on a series of letters found in a deserted house.*

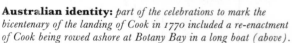

A China connection: *as part of Australia's wider public perspectives, as well as the ritual visits to London and Washington, prime ministers now made ritual visits to China. Malcolm Fraser visits the Great Wall in 1976 (above right) and Bob Hawke is welcomed in Peking in 1984 (right).*

to emphasise Australian independence) became, for a period, one of its main prophets. At this time, of Australia's 68 missions around the world, most of those coveted by diplomats wanting to make their mark were in Asian countries, and in the politics of Australia's immediate neighbourhood they showed increasing skill and subtlety in finding a path through the intricacies of relationships between Indonesia, the Philippines, Singapore and Malaysia. The view of 'Asia' involved in this was, however, a narrow one and in any case the Department's institutional confidence began to fade.

There was a similar development among some Australian intellectuals. At a time in the late 1950s and early 1960s when many European intellectuals were finding novelty in the idea of the 'African', a number of Australian intellectuals saw liberation in the idea of the 'Asian'. Moods changed with protests against the Vietnam War in the second half of the 1960s, but an increasing number of academics and journalists grew to know more about a number of Asian countries. Coverage of these areas in radio, television and Press increased considerably for a period (and then slackened); some Asian countries became increasingly

popular to tourists; some young people preferred to get their 'overseas' experience there rather than in London; many executives had contacts with some Asian countries; technical assistance programs and cultural tours led Australians into areas where they could be confident. There seemed to be a slow but accelerating movement towards new horizons by many groups and thousands of individual persons. Overall, there were enough adjustments to maps and statistical tables for Australians, if they wanted to, to imagine themselves not only as a Pacific Ocean power of significance but also as a nation of European origin adjoining an Asian area and therefore able, in hundreds of ways, to show how a 'white' nation could seek the humanity common to different races, gradually merging its own whiteness, and how a nation of one culture could cross-fertilise with many different cultures.

Even those Australians who still wanted to see themselves as a European nation (and that was most Australians) now had wider choices. A society of such diverse multi-national origin could imagine itself as European in a much less parochial sense than when it saw itself as British. There had always been some understanding of other European

cultures; it now became wider and deeper. And although in 1970 there was a 200th anniversary of the 'discovery' of Australia by Captain Cook ('It is truly here at Botany Bay, April 29, 1770, that Australia began') with Queen Elizabeth presiding, and with the Aborigines' National Tribal Council putting on a counter-demonstration in which they displayed the names of the 700 Aboriginal tribes destroyed since 1770, there was nevertheless, at least in the public culture, the beginnings of that understanding of the presence of the Aborigines in Australia without which 'multiculturalism' could become just another expression of white racism. Multiculturalism could become a 'national ideal' – a claim to national identity both programmatic and symbolic used by most of the people who perform in the public culture.

Counterposed to the chauvinism of being British had been the chauvinism of the bush – itself a declaration of the colonial mentality, if of a different kind. (If all that mattered about being Australian were gumtrees and bushmen, why did Australia matter?) The bush could be simply a metaphor for an Australia that knew its place in the world as a somewhat primitive society important mainly

The rise of the 'Ocker': *most famous of the 'Ockers' was Paul Hogan who first achieved fame in launching Winfield cigarettes – in front of a symphony orchestra (above). There was still a lot of money to be made from commercialisation of the bush; koalas and wildflowers decorate a tea towel (above left). Another commercial outburst of patriotism came with the Advance Australia campaign, which extended to patriotism the techniques of football-fan paraphernalia (far left above).*

Australia advancing where?: *the puzzles of what it might mean to be an Australian were shown in the stamp issues of the mid-1970s. Was it to be an Australia in which Louisa Lawson (far left centre) as a pioneer feminist, could now seem more important than her son Henry? Or was it still the Australia of 'National Development' (centre)? Or had it become an Australia of scientific achievement (far left below)? Was it still an Australia noted for wildflowers and sporting stars (centre below)? Or was it an Australia of a new cultural awakening, represented by the Sydney Opera House (centre) with a new interest in its past (left below)?*

for its export of primary products to more mature countries and for its unique contributions to the world's zoos and, feeling this, the new sophisticates combatted it in a variety of forms, from programs for urban renewal to short stories about intellectual life among the converted terraces. Although the bush was still there, whether in abstract expressionist paintings, or in films like *The Man From Snowy River*, or in folk songs sung by tourists in restaurants in old colonial buildings, or merely in sugar gums planted in suburban gardens, it was now being reduced to *chic*: in the souvenir stalls there were Bullocky Bill dolls and Waltzing Matilda tea towels. Declarations about Australia as a primitive society important mainly for its exports of primary products now came from another source: they were now being made more convincingly in one form of the new sophistication – in boasting about the development of minerals. Some of the most moving icons in television documentaries and even television commercials became oil rigs, earth-moving equipment, men in hard hats. In the first round of what became known as 'the new nationalism' much of the boasting was simply that Australia had a lot of minerals.

Another aspect of the bush cult – an assertion of male toughness as the characteristic Australian attribute, also found in the cities in the turning of the larrikins into romantic figures – had a revival in the idea of the 'ocker', an assertive, no-nonsense, ignorant male presented as the true Australian. Unlike his predecessors, the 'ocker', a noisy individualist, was not softened even by the earlier fraternal and equalitarian assertions of mateship. The cult of the ocker reached one of its peaks in the television public character of Paul Hogan, a Sydney Harbour Bridge rigger, who in 1972 was hired to give a note of genuine Aussie character to the launch of a new brand of cigarettes, and then became a popular television entertainer.

The habit of typifying the Australian as a rugged male was to produce patriotic songs in nationalist television commercials such as the beer commercial 'I feel like a Tooheys' and the World Series cricket commercial 'C'mon Aussie, c'mon'. To this was added a great deal of straight flag-flapping and the paraphernalia of an 'Advance Australia' campaign, launched in 1979, with its accompanying 'Advance Australia' ties, T-shirts, lapel badges, cuff links and plastic drinking cups. Big corporations, some foreign, illustrated their Australian-ness with patriotic slogans and icons of oil rigs and rugged ranges of iron ore. This kind of loyalty to Australia was hard to distinguish from loyalty to a sporting team: with the winning of the America's Cup in 1983, the two coincided.

Apart from the imperial vision and the vision of the bush, the other way of looking at Australia had been that of Improvement, which at one of its heights had seen Australia as an 'exemplar to the old lands' in social reform, and in another had seen Australia as the most prosperous society on earth. Both forms of Improvement had failed. In the way in which these things were measured, Australia had entered the 1960s ranking as the world's fifth most prosperous country; it entered the 1980s ranking 15th. And insofar as Improvement suggested a concern with equality, by the 1980s in the land of mateship incomes were becoming more, not less, unequal; while the unemployed had been vilified as 'dole bludgers', the revelations of massive tax evasion among the rich were more likely to produce respect for those who were able to get away with it. For a time Whitlam had spoken the language of Improvement; but his downfall was interpreted by political wiseacres as the price he paid for speaking of it.

Something of the old spirit of Improvement remained. There was still a kind of free-floating self-confidence and an innocent hopefulness, looking for something better (or believing it was already there). But while, as Improvers, many Australians had some of the United States belief that man could master anything, as a society founded in an age of scepticism they could settle for less. They did not see either man or the machine as God; they merely expected that things would go on changing for the better – although they could be lackadaisical in helping change along. When American self-belief cracked in the late 1960s, the self-belief of ordinary Australians still seemed to survive. It had not set itself such high standards. Perhaps they didn't know what was going on.

To some of its own intellectuals Australia could appear superficial. This was even seen as a reason for a lack of depth in its arts. In some cases this came from comparing some work of modest aims with the work of Rembrandt, Shakespeare or Mozart but, superficially, Australia *did* appear 'superficial'. Apart from the assaults on Aboriginal society, its past had been more peaceful than that of almost every other country, and the search for innocent happiness among its people was an affront to a student of history.

When, after a night of thunder, drunkenness and lovemaking, a thousand or so people assembled among the red gums to hear Phillip announce the birth of what seemed a small and remarkably ill-favoured colony, there was no sense of mission, either religious or secular. The foundation of New South Wales was a matter of convenience and such individual senses of mission as first emerged were among those Emancipists who desired to achieve respectability or those old hands who scorned it. A recurrent theme was the conflict, often within the one person, between the contrary tendencies later personalised as the larrikin and the suburbanite.

The extension of Australia's frontiers was tedious rather than heroic, producing sardonic wit more than high hope, and with an emphasis on luck as an element of success rather than on hard work (which could seem merely the penalty of failure). When a public sense of mission came, it was that of the age of Improvement – the 19th-century optimistic materialism of which could be an affront to the intellectual standards of the second half of the 20th century. All this could make Australia seem trivial or even repellent to those Australians who through their acquired culture had learnt of other things; but this did not make Australia superficial – it merely confronted Black Hats, churchmen, the Protestant work ethic, and intellectual bearers of an acquired culture. There was no denying it. It was Australia. But so were they.

Images of Australia in Australian films: Careful, He Might Hear You *(above left) 1983;* Man of Flowers *(above right) 1984;* Starstruck *(right) 1982;* Breaker Morant *(below) 1980;* Gallipoli *(below left) 1981.*

World context

It can be disastrous to the understanding of Australia to look at it as if it existed in itself. The most ambitious account of Australia's place as an area of influence of contradictory strands in European civilisation is to be found in C.M.H. Clark, *A History of Australia*, vol. I (1962). Of particular importance to the themes of my book (and partly affecting them) are Asa Briggs, *The Age of Improvement* (1960) and Heinz Gollwitzer, *Europe in the Age of Imperialism* (1969). E.P. Thompson, *The Making of the English Working Class* (rev. 1968) is worth looking at, along with studies of the growth in England of particular institutions that were transplanted to Australia. Louis Hartz in *The Founding of New Societies* (1964) puts up a general argument on the different kinds of 'fragments' of European societies that provided the European colonies in the Americas and Australia. (He sees the Australian 'fragment' as radical.) Histories of the United States would seem essential reading, but some acquaintance with two classics on the US, Alexis de Tocqueville's *Democracy in America* and F.J. Turner's *The Frontier in American History*, is equally important since so many Australian commentators either directly or at second or third hand received their views of Australia from these two works.

Detailed studies of particular aspects of relations with Britain in the early period are J.J. Auchmuty, 'The Background of the Early Australian Governors' in *Historical Studies*, vol. 6, no. 23 (1954); J.C. Beaglehole, 'The Colonial Office 1782–1854' in *Historical Studies, Selected articles, Second Series* (1967); Peter Burroughs, *Britain and Australia 1831–1851. A Study in Imperial Relations and Crown Lands Administration* (1967); J.J. Eddy, *Britain and the Australian Colonies 1818–1831. The Technique of Government* (1969); John M. Ward, *Earl Grey and the Australian Colonies 1846–1857* (1958); A.G.L. Shaw, *Great Britain and the Colonies* (1970); David S. Macmillan, *Scotland and Australia, 1788–1850* (1967).

General reference

The great work that dominates the field, both through its length and in its imaginative power (which is like that of a large Victorian novel) is the six-volume *A History of Australia* by Manning Clark. As a useful background to how this was written, see Clark's Boyer Lectures, published as *A Discovery of Australia* (1976). Of the short histories, the most widely known is also by Clark, *A Short History of Australia* (new illustr. ed., 1983). Other short histories include: Russel Ward, *Australia Since the Coming of Man* (illustr. 1982); Douglas Pike, *Australia, the Quiet Continent* (1962), useful as a reminder of regional history; R.M. Crawford, *Australia* (4th ed., 1979). Somewhat longer short histories include R.M. Younger, *Australia and the Australians* (1970); and F.K. Crowley (ed.), *A New History of Australia* (1974). For a French perspective, there is Robert Lacourt-Gayet's *Histoire de l'Australie* (1973), translated as *A Concise History of Australia* (1976). Histories that tell part, or most, of the 19th century story include Geoffrey Blainey, *A Land Half Won* (1980), a clearly written account of the economic 'development' of Australia in the 19th century; David Denholm, *The Colonial Australians* (1979), which did a new job of bringing the 19th century to life; and K.S. Inglis, *The Australian Colonists* (1974), an exploration of the national imagination of colonial Australians. The modern story is told in a conventional (and mainly political form) in Fred Alexander, *Australia Since Federation* (1967) and *From Curtin to Menzies and After* (1973); Russel Ward, *A Nation for a Continent: the History of Australia, 1901–1975* gives a labour view; Humphrey McQueen, *Social Sketches of Australia, 1888–1975* (1978) gives a radical view. For browsing, and for reading about matters the short histories may miss, there are Richard Appleton (ed.), *The Australian Encyclopedia* (4th ed., 1983) and Douglas Pike (ed.), *The Australian Dictionary of Biography*. For ruminations on where Australian history-writing is going and how it is changing, see G. Osborne and W.F. Mandle, *New History: Studying Australian History Today* (1982).

Of special interest are Arthur W. Jose, *History of Australia*, first published in 1899 and Ernest Scott, *A Short History of Australia*, first published in 1916 and revised many times since. These were the first serious attempts at short histories of Australia and were to represent just about all that two generations of Australians were likely to know of the history of their country.

Special perspectives

Works attempting to throw up some special perspectives have been rare in Australian history-writing. W.K. Hancock, *Australia* (1930), was most influential of the Tocqueville-style interpretations; Russel Ward, *The Australian Legend* (1958), was the best of the applications of F.J. Turner's 'Frontier Theory' to Australia's special conditions; R.M. Crawford, *An Australian Perspective* (1960), can be read to offset Hancock and Ward because of its emphasis on non-democratic as well as democratic trends in Australian history, the recognition of which can make present Australian society more intelligible, and with this might be read Hugo Wolfsohn, 'The Ideology Makers' in Henry Mayer (ed.) *Australian Politics: A Second Reader*. Geoffrey Blainey, *The Tyranny of Distance* (rev. 1982) provided many Australians with a fresh introduction to their history. Humphrey McQueen, *A New Britannia* (1970) successfully popularised some of the new directions of Australian history-writing and provided a sharp attack on some of the positions of more traditional Left historians. R.W. Connell and T.H. Irving, *Class Structure in Australian History* (1980), attempted a history of class conflict in Australia. Special perspectives can also be found in S. Encel, *Equality and Authority: A Study of Class, Status and Power in Australia* (1970); Richard White, *Inventing Australia: Images and Identity 1688–1980* (1981); Sydney Labour History Group, *What Rough Beast? The State and Social Order in Australia* (1982); A.G.L. Shaw, 'Violent Protest in Australia's History' in *Historical Studies* no. 60 (1973). Of special relevance to some of the themes of dependence in *The Story of the Australian People* is S. Alomes, 'The Satellite Society' in *Australian Studies* no. 9 (1981).

Australian classics

Australian history-writing did not broaden out until after World War II. The earlier histories, such as G.W. Rusden, *A History of Australia* (3 vols, 2nd ed., 1897) or H.G. Turner, *A History of the Colony of Victoria* (2 vols, 1904) have little to interest the modern reader. The earliest real achievement was T.A. Coghlan, *Labour and Industry in Australia* (4 vols, 1918, reissued 1969), now coming back into fashion, as can be seen in the comments on it by E.C. Fry in *Historical Studies* no. 55 (1970) and S.J. Butlin, *Australian Economic History Review* vol. xi, no. 1 (1977). Another survivor still worth reading is W. Pember Reeves, *State Experiments in Australia and New Zealand* (2 vols, 1902, reissued in 1969) which attempted to provide an overall picture of the colonies as vehicles of Improvement. Apart from Hancock's works there was little of significance in general histories. There were, however, some specialist studies, now become classics: Edward Shann, *An Economic History of Australia* (1930); S.H. Roberts, *History of Australian Land Settlement* (1924, reissued 1968); S.H. Roberts, *The Squatting Age in Australia, 1835–1847* (1935); Eric O'Brien, *The Foundation of Australia* (1937, 2nd ed. 1950); R.B. Madgwick, *Immigration into Eastern Australia 1788–1851* (1937) – see also the comment on this by R.J. Shultz in *Historical Studies* vol. 14, no. 54 (1970); G. Arnold Wood, *The Discovery of Australia* (1922, reissued 1969); R.C. Mills, *The Colonisation of Australia, 1829–42* (reissued 1974). Of the 'classics' the two histories most relevant to *The Story of the Australian People* are Brian Fitzpatrick, *British Imperialism and Australia 1788–1833* (1939) and *The British Empire in Australia 1834–1939* (1949, reissued 1969).

19th century contemporary accounts

J.T. Bigge, *Reports* (1822, 1823), which provided the first attempt at a comprehensive account of Australian society has been edited by John Ritchie as *The Evidence of the Bigge Reports* (2 vols, 1971). The two most widely read accounts for the early period are P. Cunningham, *Two Years in New South Wales* (1827, reissued 1966) and 'Alexander Harris', *Settlers and Convicts* (1847, reissued 1969). A number of visitors gave their impressions: of these the best known are the chapters on Australia in Charles Darwin, *The Voyage of the Beagle* (1845, reissued 1972); C.W. Dilke, *Greater Britain: A Record of Travel in English-speaking Countries during 1866 and 1867* (1868); Anthony Trollope, *Australia and New Zealand* (1873, Australia section reissued 1967); R.E.N. Twopeny, *Town Life in Australia* (1883, reissued 1973); J.A. Froude, *Oceana* (1886); A.G. Austin (ed.), *The Webbs' Australian Diary 1898* (1965); Mark Twain, *Following the Equator* (1897); Joseph Conrad, *The Mirror of the Sea* (1906). Perhaps the best of them all is A. Métin, *Le Socialisme sans Doctrines* (1901), translated by Russel Ward and published as *Socialism Without Doctrine* (1977). In *Australia in Western Imaginative Prose Writings* (1967) Werner P. Friederich provides an anthology of pieces about Australia in European and American writing.

Of the impressions of residents in the second half of the 19th century, the most interesting are Francis W.L. Adams, *Australian Essays* (1886) and *The Australians: A Social Sketch* (1893); John Stanley James, *The Vagabond Papers* (abridged ed., 1969); and *The Letters of Rachel Henning* (ed., 1963 by David Adams).

Selections of documents

For those who would just like a taste of how it seemed at the time, C.M.H. Clark, *Sources of Australian History* (1957) and *Select Documents in Australian History*, vol 1 1788–1850 (1950), vol 2 1851–1900 (1955), provide an illuminating run through, with a rich bonus in the editor's prefatory notes to each section. An idea of the development of city life can be got from Alan Birch and David S. Macmillan, *The Sydney Scene* (1962); and James Grant and Geoffrey Serle, *The Melbourne Scene, 1803–1956* (1957); and of what it was like to be an explorer from Kathleen Fitzpatrick, *Australian Explorers, A Selection from Their Writings* (1958); and C.C. MacKnight, *The Farthest Coast. A Selection of Writing Related to the History of the Northern Coast of Australia* (1969). Contemporary accounts are collected in Russel Ward and John Robertson, *Such Was Life: Select Documents in Australian Social History, 1788–1850* (1969). Its difference in emphasis makes it interesting to compare with the earlier Helen Palmer and Jessie MacLeod, *The First Hundred Years of Australia as seen by the people who lived it* (1954). Some of the heights of Australian rhetoric are found in Ian Turner, *The Australian Dream* (1968). R.N. Ebbels (ed. L.G. Churchward), *The Australian Labor Movement, 1850–1907* (1960) gives extracts from contemporary documents of the working-class movement. There are samples of intellectual life in B. Smith (ed.), *Documents on Art and Taste in Australia, 1770–1914* (1975); J. Barnes (ed.), *The Writer in Australia, 1856–1964* (1969); and A.M. Moyal (ed.), *Scientists in Nineteenth Century Australia: A Documentary History* (1976). There have been several collections of documents on women in Australian history, including Beverley Kingston, *The World Moves Slowly* (1977); Ruth Teale (ed.), *Colonial Eve* (1978); and Kay Daniels and Mary Murnane (eds), *Uphill all the way* (1980). F.K. Crowley's *Documentary History of Australia* (three volumes on colonial Australia and two volumes on modern Australia) provide a kind of scrapbook presentation of how, to some people, things seemed at the time.

Special topics

ABORIGINES

A study of the creation of Australia is to be found in Charles Laseron and Rudolf Brunnshweiler, *Ancient Australia* (rev. ed. 1984); D.J. Mulvaney, *Prehistory of Australia* (1969) was the first attempt to report on the state of knowledge of this subject. Geoffrey Blainey, *Triumph of the Nomads* (1975) was the first attempt to 'bring to life' Aboriginal society before the coming of the British. The first significant attempt to give an historical account of relations between Aborigines and whites was C.D. Rowley's trilogy, *The*

Destruction of Aboriginal Society (1970), *Outcasts in White Australia* (1971) and *The Remote Aborigines* (1971). Two of the best efforts to fill in more detail have been Henry Reynolds, *The Other Side of the Frontier* (1981), which gives an active rather than a passive view of Aboriginal responses to the European invasion; and Lyndall Ryan, *The Aboriginal Tasmanians* (1981), which refuted the comforting myth that the Aboriginal Tasmanians had been exterminated (a myth that ignored their mixed-race descendants). In Alan Frost, 'New South Wales as *Terra Nullius*: the British Denial of Aboriginal Land Rights' in *Historical Studies* no. 77 (1981), there is a useful study of why the British treated the native Australians as a people without claims to their own territories. There is a short history of black responses to white dominance in Richard Broome, *Aboriginal Australians* (1982); and most of A.T. Yarwood and M.J. Knowling, *Race Relations in Australia* (1982) is also concerned with black-white relations. In Geoffrey Dutton, *White on Black* (1974), there is a pictorial examination of how Aborigines have been seen in European art.

ARTS, ENTERTAINMENTS, MEDIA

In *From Deserts the Prophets Come: The Creative Spirit in Australia 1788–1972*, Geoffrey Serle attempted a general intellectual history, which does not really come off; there does not seem enough feeling for the material itself. In literature, Geoffrey Dutton (ed.), *The Literature of Australia* (1976) has greater intellectual interest than the extremely restricted view of Leonie Kramer (ed.) *The Oxford History of Australian Literature* (1981). Neither of them goes beyond verse, fiction and drama, however, and neither is really a history of writing in Australia. In painting, the ground work was laid by Bernard Smith, *Place, Taste and Tradition* (1945) and his *Australian Painting 1788–1970* (1971) remains the standard text. Daniel Thomas, 'Australian Art' in James Mollison and Laura Murray (eds), *Australian National Gallery: An Introduction* (1982), gives a brief overview. Richard Haese, *Rebels and Precursors* (1981) concentrates on the 1940s, the decade of new directions. There are, of course, a number of collections of the work of individual painters. On music, Roger Covell, *Australia's Music* (1967) provides a sense of social background to its subject. For the theatre, there is Margaret Williams, *Australia on the Popular Stage* (1983); for radio, Jacqueline Kent, *Out of the Bakelite Box: The Heyday of Australian Radio* (1983); and K.S. Inglis, *This is the ABC* (1983); for films, John Tulloch, *Legends on the Screen, 1919–1929* (1981), and David Stratton, *The Last New Wave: The Australian Film Revival* (1980); for architecture, J.M. Freeland, *Architecture in Australia: A History* (1968); for censorship, Peter Coleman, *Obscenity, Blasphemy, Sedition* (1962), and Geoffrey Dutton and Max Harris, *Australia's Censorship Crisis* (1970). Among the studies of 'popular culture' there are P. Spearritt and David Walker (eds), *Australian Popular Culture* (1979) and Susan Dermody et al. (eds), *Nellie Melba, Ginger Meggs and Friends* (1982). All that is available on the print media are R.B. Walker's, history of NSW newspapers, the two-volume *Newspaper Press in New South Wales, 1803–1920* (1976) and *Yesterday's News* (1980); however, Gavin Souter has written an excellent history of the Fairfax Company in *Company of Heralds* (1981). Domestic living, on cooking there are Michael Symons, *One Continuous Picnic* (1982); and Anne Gollan, *The Tradition of Australian Cooking* (1978). Apart from the booklet Victor Crittenden, *The Front Garden: The Story of the Cottage Garden in Australia* (1979), on housing the 'classic' is Robin Boyd, *Australia's Home* (1952).

ECONOMICS

Apart from the 'classics' by Shann and Fitzpatrick already mentioned, there are not many overall economic histories of Australia. For a time the ground was seen as covered by S.J. Butlin, *Foundations of the Australian Monetary System, 1788–1851* (1953); and N.G. Butlin, *Investment in Australian Economic Development 1861–1900* (1964). Since then, there have been published W.A. Sinclair, *The Process of Economic Development in Australia* (1976); R.V. Jackson,

Australian Economic Development in the Nineteenth Century (1977); E.A. Boehm, *Twentieth – Century Economic Development in Australia* (1970); Colin Forster (ed.) *Australian Economic Development in the Twentieth Century* (1970); N.G. Butlin, A. Barnard, J.J. Pincus, *Government and Capitalism* (1982). Geoffrey Blainey, *The Rush that Never Ended* (1964) provides a history of the mining industry; no one has written a matching history of the farming industry. For beginners, although meant mainly as a textbook, James Griffin (ed.) *Essays in the Economic History of Australia* (1967).

EDUCATION

There are few general histories of education. Useful are A.G. Austin, *Australian Education 1788–1900* (1961); C. Turney (ed.), *Pioneers of Australian Education. A Study of the Development of Education in New South Wales in the Nineteenth Century* (1969); Alan Barcan, *A Short History of Education in New South Wales* (1965); Derek Whitelock, *The Great Tradition: A History of Adult Education in Australia* (1974); Rupert Goodman, *Secondary Education in Queensland 1860–1960* (1968); S. Murray-Smith, 'Technical Education in Australia – a Historical Sketch', a chapter in E.L. Wheelwright (ed.), *Higher Education in Australia* (1965); and J.J. Auchmuty and A.N. Jeffares, 'Australian Universities: the Historical Background', and E.L. French, 'The Humanities in Australian Education', chapters in A. Grenfell Price (ed.), *The Humanities in Australia* (1959).

ETHNIC PREJUDICE AND IMMIGRATION

There is an overall treatment in the three volumes of F.S. Stevens, *Racism the Australian Experience* (1971, 1972, 1977); and in A.T. Yarwood and M.J. Knowling, *Race Relations in Australia* (1982); and there is a special perspective in Ann Curthoys and Andrew Markus (ed), *Who Are Our Enemies?* (1978). M. Dugan and J. Szwarc, *There Goes The Neighbourhood* (1984) provides a well-written and well-illustrated popular history. There are useful ideas in William W. Bostock, *Alternatives of Ethnicity: Immigrants and Aborigines in Anglo-Saxon Australia* (1977). Kenneth Rivett (ed.) *Immigration: Control or Colour Bar?* (1962) was extremely influential among intellectuals in articulating criticisms of the White Australia Policy and some of the story of the dismantling of the policy is told in Kenneth Rivett, *Australia and the Non-White Migrant* (1975). Since then, there have been studies of individual ethnic groups. Geoffrey Sherington, *Australia's Immigrants 1788–1978* (1980) is useful as an overall history. On a special theme there is Douglas Cole, 'The Crimson Thread of Kinship: Ethnic Ideas in Australia, 1870–1914' in *Historical Studies* no. 56 (1971).

ENVIRONMENT

For overall accounts, there are Geoffrey Bolton, *Spoils and Spoilers* (1981); and J.M. Powell, *Environment Management in Australia, 1788–1914* (1976). Eric Rolls gives a nicely written account of introduced pests in *They All Ran Wild: The Story of Pests on the Land in Australia* (1969). Of edited collections there are George Seddon (ed.), *Man and Landscape in Australia* (1976); Amos Rappoport (ed.), *Australia as Human Setting* (1972) and H.F. Recher, Daniel Lunney and Irina Dunn, *A Natural Legacy: Ecology in Australia* (1979). For a special study, there is M. Williams, 'The Making of the South Australian Landscape' in *Australian Economic History Review*, 15:2, 1975.

FARMING

Edgars Dunsdorfs, *The Australian Wheatgrowing Industry 1788–1948* (1956) opened up a possibility for industry-by-industry studies that, unfortunately has not been followed up. Frances Wheelhouse, *Digging Stick to Rotary Hoe* (1966) tells a story of Australian industrial innovation, in the development of agricultural machinery; and D.W. Meinig, *On the Margins of the Good Earth* (1962) provides a valuable region study in farming development, on the South Australian wheat frontier. B.W. Davidson, *European Farming in Australia* (1981) is useful (in parts) for the general reader.

LANGUAGE

Sidney J. Baker, *The Australian Language* (rev. ed. 1966) is as valuable (perhaps more valuable) for its social comments as its philology, in showing the nation-defining use of language. Academic studies include G.A. Wilkes, *A Dictionary of Australian Colloquialisms* (1978); W.S. Ramson *Australian English* (1966); and W.S. Ramson (ed.), *English Transported – Essays on Australian English* (1970).

REGIONAL

New South Wales: W.K. Hancock, *Discovering Monaro* (1972); L.T. Daley, *Men and a River: Richmond River District 1828–1895* (1966); G.L. Buxton, *The Riverina 1861–1891* (1967); Brian Kennedy, *Silver, Sin and Sixpenny Ale: Broken Hill 1883–1921* (1978). Queensland: Rose Fitzgerald, *From the Dreaming Time to 1915* (1982); G.L. Bolton, *A Thousand Miles Away: North Queensland to 1920* (1962). South Australia: J.B. Hirst, *Adelaide and the Country 1870–1917* (1973); Douglas Pike, *Paradise of Dissent 1829–1857* (1957). Tasmania: L.L. Robson, *A History of Tasmania* (1983). Victoria: Geoffrey Serle, *The Golden Age. A History of the Colony of Victoria 1851–1861* (1963) and *The Rush to be Rich* (1971); Les Blake, *Wimmera* (1973); Ian Wynd, *Geelong the Pivot* (1971); J.C. Angus and H.W. Forster, *The Ovens Valley* (1970); J.M. Powell, *Lucky City. The First Generation of Ballarat. 1851–1901* (1979); Michael Cannon, *Land Boom and Bust* (1972). Western Australia: C.T. Stannage, *A New History of Western Australia* (1981); F.K. Crowley, *Australia's Western Third* (1960). New Zealand: W.H. Oliver and B.R. Williams (eds) *The Oxford History of New Zealand* (1981); W.H. Oliver, *The Story of New Zealand* (1960); Austin Mitchell, 'A Political scientist looks at New Zealand history', a chapter in *Politics and People in New Zealand* (1969).

RELIGION

The most interesting general studies have been by and about Catholics. Of these, the most readable and comprehensive is Patrick O'Farrell, *The Catholic Church and Community in Australia* (1977). See also T.L. Suttor, *Hierarchy and Democracy in Australia, 1788–1870* (1965); John N. Molony, *The Roman Mould of the Australian Catholic Church* (1969); Michael Hogan, *The Catholic Campaign for State Aid* (1978). James G. Murtach, *Australia: The Catholic Chapter* (1969) is interesting as an expression of the pieties of what used to be the traditional Catholic view of the labour movement. Most readable of all is Edmund Campion, *Rockchoppers: Growing Up Catholic in Australia* (1982). Henry Mayer, *Catholics and the Free Society* (1961) is interesting as an example of the kind of debate going on when Catholic intellectuals saw themselves as emerging from their 'ghetto'. On religion more generally, there are: Jean Woolmington, *Religion in Early Australia* (1976); A.M. Grocott, 'Convicts, Clergymen and Churches' in *Historical Studies* no. 77 (1981); W. Phillips, 'Religious Profession and Practice, NSW 1850–1901' in *Historical Studies* no. 59 (1972); Hans Mol, *Religion in Australia* (1971).

SPORTS

The field of sport history is now being developed. Examples are W.F. Mandle, 'Cricket and football in England and Victoria in the late nineteenth century' in *Historical Studies* no. 60 (1973), 'Cricket and Nationalism in the Nineteenth Century' in T.D. Jaques and G.R. Pavia, *Sport in Australia* (1976) and the chapter 'Sport and Australian Nationalism' in W.F. Mandle, *Going It Alone* (1977); Leonie Sandercock, *Up Where Cazaly?* (1981); Keith Dunstan, *Sports* (1973); W.F. Mandle, *Winners Can Laugh* (1974) and relevant chapters in R. Cashman and M. McKernan (eds), *Sport in History* (1979) and *Sport: Money, Morality and the Media* (1982).

URBAN HISTORY

This is another area of history-writing that has only recently opened up. The emphasis began with Sean Glynn, *Urbanisation in Australian History* (1970), the first attempt to throw up general theories on Australia's high rate of urbanisation, followed by 'Urbanisation in Australia', a special issue of *Australian Economic History Review* (1970). In the same year there came out Hugh Stretton, *Ideas for Australian Cities*, a work with a number of historical observations – and also a radical defence of suburbia. Since then there have been a number of works, including: Graeme Davison, *The Rise and Fall of Marvellous Melbourne* (1978); Peter Spearritt, *Sydney Since the Twenties* (1978); Max Kelly (ed.) *Nineteenth Century Sydney* (1978); a review of these and other urban history works, 'The New City Histories', *Historical Studies* no. 74 (1980); Leonie Sandercock, *Cities for Sale* (1975); J.W. McCarty and C.B. Schedvin (eds) *Australian Capital Cities* (1978); Jill Roe (ed.) *Twentieth Century Sydney* (1980); G.C. Curr, 'Liberalism, Localism and Suburban Development', *Historical Studies* no. 74 (1980).

UNIONS

There are not many overall histories of the union movement. Two useful short histories are Ian Turner, *In Union Is Strength* (1976); and Bede Healey, *Federal Arbitration in Australia* (1972). The 'classic' text is Brian Fitzpatrick, *A Short History of the Australian Labor Movement* (1940, reissued 1968). J. Harris, *The Bitter Fight: A Pictorial History of the Australian Labour Movement* (1970); John Iremonger, John Merritt and Graeme Osborne, *Strikes* (1973); and Noel Ebbels (ed.) *The Australian Labour Movement* (1960) give some of the 'feel' of the labour movement.

WELFARE

The field used to be dominated by T.H. Kewley, *Social Security in Australia, 1900–72* (1973). To this has now been added Jill Roe (ed.) *Social Policy in Australia, 1901–75* (1976); and the more radical Richard Kennedy (ed.) *Australian Welfare History* (1982). For an earlier perspective, see R.A. Cage, 'The Origins of Poor Relief in NSW: An Account of the Benevolent Society, 1809–62' in *Historical Studies* 20:2 (1980).

WOMEN

There should not, of course, be a separate section labelled 'women' unless there is also one labelled 'men', but writing on women in Australian history at present has generally corrective effects that can provide a common interest. The year in which this process began was 1975, which saw the publication of Anne Summers, *Damned Whores and God's Police*, Beverley Kingston, *My Wife, My Daughter and Poor Mary Ann*, Jan Mercer (ed.), *The Other Half: Women in Australian Society* and Edna Ryan and Anne Conlon, *Gentle Invaders: Australian Women at Work* (1975). Since then, among others, there have been: Miriam Dixson, *The Real Matilda* (1976); Helen Heney, *Australia's Founding Mothers* (1978); Elizabeth Windschuttle, *Women, Class and History: Feminist Perspectives on Australia 1788–1978* (1980); Margaret Bevege, Margaret James and Carmel Shute, *Worth Her Salt: Women at Work in Australia* (1982); Ann Game and Rosemary Pringle, *Gender At Work* (1983); Megan McMurchy, Margot Oliver and Jeni Thornton, *For Love or Money: A Pictorial History of Women and Work in Australia* (1983). See also Elizabeth Windschuttle, 'Discipline, Domestic Training and Social Control: The Female School of Industry, Sydney, 1826–47' in *Labour History* no. 39 (1980); A. Hyslop, 'Temperance, Christianity and Feminism: The Women's Christian Temperance Union of Victoria, 1887–97' in *Historical Studies* no. 66 (1976).

Period studies

Part 1: the age of Authority

THE FIRST YEARS

There is a profusion of contemporary accounts. Some of the earliest are collated in John Cobley (ed.), *Sydney Cove 1788* (1962), *Sydney Cove 1789–1790* (1963) and *Sydney Cove 1791–1792* (1965). Most popular at present is W. Tench (ed. Fitzhardinge), *Sydney's First Four Years* (1961). There are also the accounts of Hunter, Bradley,

Southwell, Bowes, King, White, Clark, Collins and Scott. Ged Martin (ed.), *The Founding of Australia* (1978) summarises historians' debate about why the colony was founded.

GENERAL HISTORIES AND BIOGRAPHIES

O'Brien's *The Foundation of Australia* and Fitzpatrick's *British Imperialism and Australia* (1939) now give way to C.M.H. Clark, *A History of Australia*, vol. 1 (1962) and vol. 2 (1968). The best known early period biographies are G. Mackaness, *The Life of Vice-Admiral Bligh* (1931); M.H. Ellis, *Lachlan Macquarie, his Life, Adventures and Times* (1947), *Francis Greenway* (1949) and *John Macarthur* (1955); and H.V. Evatt, *Rum Rebellion* (1938). Hazel King, *Richard Bourke* (1971) gives a picture of Australia's first vice-regal Improver. Other useful biographies are Margaret Kiddle, *Caroline Chisholm* (1950); and Ruth Knight, *Illiberal Liberal* (1966), a biography of Robert Lowe that also provides a general picture of the times. More recent biographies include A.T. Yarwood, *Samuel Marsden: The Great Survivor* (1977); S.G. Foster, *Colonial Improver: Edward Deas Thompson* (1978); and A.G.L. Shaw, *Sir George Arthur, Bart* (1980).

EARLY SOCIETY

What was left of old illusions about the convicts seemed to be cleaned up in L.L. Robson, *The Convict Settlers of Australia* (1965); and A.G.L. Shaw, *Convicts and the Colonies* (1966); but then J.B. Hirst, *Convict Society and its Enemies* (1983) added a new perspective, in which the convicts are shown playing a less passive part. For recent studies of the convicts as protesters, see George Rudé, 'Protest and Punishment, The Study of the Social and Political Protesters Transported to Australia, 1788–1860' in *Historical Studies* no. 74 (1978), and 'Early Irish Rebels in Australia' in *Historical Studies* no. 62 (1974); and Alan Atkinson, 'Four Patterns of Convict Protest' in *Labour History* no. 37 (1979). On drunkenness, see A.E. Dingle, 'The Truly Magnificent Third. An Historical Survey of Australian Drinking Habits' in *Historical Studies* no. 75 (1980); and N.G. Butlin, 'Yo, Ho, Ho and How Many Bottles of Rum?' in *Australian Economic History Review* XXIII-1 (1983). On female convicts: A.J. Hammerton, 'Without Natural Protectors: Female Immigration to Australia, 1832–36' in *Historical Studies* no. 65 (1975); J. Williams, 'Irish Female Convicts and Tasmania' in *Labour History* no. 44 (1983); and Michael Sturma, 'Eye of the Beholder, The Stereotype of Women Convicts, 1788–1852' in *Labour History* no. 34 (1978). For an overall view, taking in this period and later there is Donald Denoon, 'Understanding Settler Societies' in *Historical Studies* no. 73 (1979). There are interesting small studies in M. Roe, 'Colonial Society in Embryo' in *Historical Studies*, vol. 7, no. 26 (1956); Ken Macnab and Russel Ward, 'The Nature and Nurture of the First Generation of Native born Australians' in *Historical Studies*, vol. 10, no. 39 (1962); L.A. Whitfield, *Founders of the Law in Australia* (1969); Kelvin Grose, 'William Grant Broughton and National Education in N.S.W., 1829–1836' in E.L. French (ed.), *Melbourne Studies in Education* (1965); J.A. La Nauze, 'The Collection of Customs in Australia: A Note on Administration' in *Historical Studies*, vol. 4, no. 13 (1949); Hazel King, 'Some Aspects of Police Administration in New South Wales, 1825–1851' in *Journal of the Royal Australian Historical Society*, vol. 42, part 5 (1956). On different aspects of the frontier the following are valuable: T.M. Perry, *Australia's First Frontier* (1963); H.C. Allen, *Bush and Backwoods* (1959); John M.R. Young, *Australia's Pacific Frontier* (1967); M. Roe, 'Australia's Place in the Swing to the East, 1788–1810' in *Historical Studies*, vol. 8, no. 30 (1958); and Geoffrey Blainey's emphasis on the sea frontier in *The Tyranny of Distance*.

ECONOMIC

S.J. Butlin, *Foundations of the Australian Monetary System, 1788–1821* (1953) has already become a classic. G.J. Abbott and N.B. Nairn (ed.), *Economic Growth of Australia, 1788–1821* (1969) provides a good, comprehensive run through. D.R. Hainsworth, *Builders and*

Adventurers (1968) clears up some old mysteries about how a convict settlement quickly became a get-rich-quick society and presumably ends old historians' squabbles about the Rum Corps. G.M. Dow, 'Samuel Terry the Botany Bay Rothschild' in *Australian Economic History Review* XVI-2 (1974) shows one builder and adventurer in action. Other studies, all in the *Australian Economic History Review*, include W.A. Sinclair, 'Was labour scarce in the 1830s?' (XI-2, 1970); E.A. Beever, 'The Pre-Gold Boom in Australia, 1843–51' (XIX-1 1970); and G. Wotherspoon, 'Saving Banks and Social Policy in NSW, 1832–71 (XVIII-2, 1978). Margaret Kiddle, *Men of Yesterday, A Social History of the Western District of Victoria, 1834–1890* (1961) and Marnie Bassett, *The Hentys, An Australian Colonial Tapestry* (1954) give human accounts of the squatting age. Special aspects of the wool rush are taken up in E.H. Beever, 'The Origin of the Wool Industry in N.S.W.' in *Business Archives and History*, vol. 5, no. 2 (1965); K. Buckley, 'Gipps and the Graziers of N.S.W.' in *Historical Studies*, vol. 6, no. 24 (1955) and vol. 7, no. 26 (1956); D.W.A. Baker, 'The Squatting Age in Australia' in *Business Archives and History*, vol. 5, no. 2 (1965). Some of these test some of the approaches in S.H. Robert's *The Squatting Age in Australia*.

THE COMING OF IMPROVEMENT

A new interest was given to the second quarter of the nineteenth century (long neglected, except for rural life) by George Nadel, *Australia's Colonial Culture* (1957); Michael Roe, *The Quest for Authority in Eastern Australia, 1835–1851* (1965); and John Barrett, *That Better Country. The Religious Aspect of Life in Eastern Australia 1835–1856* (1966). All three – referred to in Paul F. Bourke, 'Some Recent Essays in Australian Intellectual History' in *Historical Studies*, vol. 13, no. 49 (1967) – help solve the puzzle of the connection between then and now. In fact it was only after reading Roe's book that I realised that it was possible to write this book. L.J. Hulme, 'Working Class Movements in Sydney and Melbourne before the Gold Rushes' in *Historical Studies, Selected Articles, Second Series* (1967) gives another example of the transplant to Australia of English institutions of Improvement. Glimpses of some aspects of Australian intellectual and social life are provided by J. Normington-Rawling, *Charles Harpur, An Australian* (1962). A.C.V. Melbourne, *Early Constitutional Development in Australia* (1963) gives an overall framework, and Margaret Kerr, 'The British Parliament and Transportation in the Eighteen Fifties' in *Historical Studies*, vol. 6, no. 21 (1953) gives the background to the crisis with Britain; but Ruth Knight, *Illiberal Liberal. Robert Lowe in New South Wales, 1842–1850* (1966) brings it all splendidly to life and Terry Irving and Baiba Ferzins, 'History and the New Left: Beyond Radicalism' in Richard Gordon (ed.), *The Australian New Left* (1970) makes an attempt at comprehensive theory. For studies in immigration, see A.J. Hammerton, 'Without Natural Protectors: Female Immigration to Australia 1832–36' in *Historical Studies* no. 65 (1975) and *Genteel Poverty and Female Immigration, 1830–1919* (1979); and Alan Beever, 'From a Place of "Horrible Destitution" to a Paradise of the Working Class: The Transfer of British Working Class Attitudes to Australia, 1841–1851' in *Labour History*, no. 40 (1981).

Part 2: the age of Improvement

GOLD AND MELBOURNE

The gold rushes are no longer seen as decisive in Australian history as they were in *The Eureka Centenary Supplement, Historical Studies* (1954). Useful sidelights are given in G. Blainey, 'Gold and Governors' in *Historical Studies*, vol. 9, no. 36 (1961) and 'The Gold Rushes: The Year of Decision' in *Historical Studies*, vol. 10, no. 38 (1962); Bruce Kent, 'Agitations on the Victorian Gold Fields, 1851–4' in *Historical Studies*, vol. 6, no. 23 (1954); and D.R.G. Packer, 'Victorian Population Data' in *Historical Studies*, vol. 5, no. 20 (1953); but full accounts are given in Serle's *The Golden Age* and Blainey's *The Rush That Never Ended*. Charles Bateson, *Gold Fleet for California* (1963) describes the rush out of Australia. For the continuing story of Melbourne, see the excellent chapter 'Melbourne, a Victorian Community Overseas' in Asa Briggs, *Victorian Cities* (1963); and for Melbourne's downfall Michael Cannon, *The Land Boomers* (1966).

ECONOMIC

Much background analysis is given in N.G. Butlin, *Investment in Australian Economic Development 1861–1900* (1964), a book that liberated thinking about economic development in this period, not least in the importance of urban development. Other background can be found in Alex Hunter (ed.), *The Economics of Australian Industry* (1963); and F.G. Davidson, *The Industrialisation of Australia* (1957, second ed. 1960). Special studies can be found in Helen Hughes, *The Australian Iron and Steel Industry, 1848–1962*, (1964); Alan Barnard, *Visions and Profits. Studies in the Business Career of T.S. Mort (1961)*; Alan Birch and David S. MacMillan (eds), *Wealth and Progress. Studies in Australian Business History* (1967); A.H. Morris, 'Echuca and the Murray River Trade' in *Historical Studies*, vol. 4, no. 16 (1951). On wool: Alan Barnard, *The Australian Wool Market 1840–1900* (1958). D.W.A. Baker, 'The Origins of Robertson's Land Acts' in *Historical Studies*, vol. 8, no. 30 (1958), and N.G. Butlin, '"Company Ownership" of N.S.W. Pastoral Stations, 1865–1900' in *Historical Studies*, vol. 4, no. 14 (1950), both raised new theories about old subjects.

EDUCATION

The annual publication *Melbourne Studies in Education* (M.S.E.) shows continuing interest in this period. For the long fight over the system of education: A.R. Crane, 'The New South Wales Public Schools League, 1874–1879' in *M.S.E. 1964*; Kenneth E. Dear, 'Bishop Perry and the Rise of National Education in Victoria, 1848–1873' in *M.S.E. 1965*; Mary Raphael Leavey, 'The Relevance of St. Thomas Aquinas for Australian Education' in *M.S.E., 1963*. For something of the quality of education: G.E. Saunders, 'Public Secondary Education in South Australia – The Nineteenth Century Background' in *M.S.E., 1968–1969*; A.M. Badcock, 'The Vocational Fallacy in State Secondary Education in Victoria, 1900–1925' in *M.S.E., 1965*; C. Turney, 'The Rise and Decline of an Australia Inspectorate' in *M.S.E., 1970*. For the general secularist background: J.S. Gregory, 'Church and State in Victoria, 1851–72' in *Historical Studies*, vol. 5, no. 20 (1953).

CLASS

For two estimates of the extent of poverty and the existence of an 'underclass', see Alan Mayne, 'City back-slums in the land of promise: some aspects of the 1876 report on overcrowding in Sydney' in *Labour History* no. 38 (1980); and S.H. Fisher, 'An Accumulation of Misery' in *Labour History* no. 40 (1981). A particularly valuable perspective on the development of working-class respectability can be found in J. McCalman, 'Class and respectability in a working-class suburb: Richmond, Victoria, before the Great War in *Historical Studies* no. 78 (1982). For the rise of a middle class, see J. Rickard, *Class and Politics, 1890–1910* (1976), which displays a well-developed, non-Marxist view; Brian Dickey, 'Colonial bourgeoisie – Marx in Australia? Aspects of a Social History of N.S.W. 1856–1900' in *Australian Economic History Review*, XIV-1 (1974); C.N. Connolly, 'The middling-class victory in N.S.W., 1853–62' in *Historical Studies* no. 70 (1981). In Denis Rowe, 'The Robust Navvy: the railway construction workers in Northern N.S.W.' in *Labour History* no. 39 (1980) special attention is given to one working-class group. For a general round-up, see Stuart Macintyre, 'The making of the Australian working class: an historiographical survey' in *Historical Studies* no. 71 (1978).

LABOUR MOVEMENT

The story of what until recently was one of the most significant unions in Australia is told in Robin Gollan, *The Coalminers of New South Wales. A History of the Union, 1860–1960* (1963). More general accounts are given in Robin Gollan, *Radical and Working Class*

Politics. A Study of Eastern Australia, 1850–1910 (1960); Ian Turner, *Industrial Labour and Politics. The Labour Movement in Eastern Australia 1900–1921* (1965); and B. Nairn, *Civilising Capitalism: the Labour Movement in N.S.W. 1870–1890* (1973). There are special studies in Helen Hughes, 'The Eight Hour Day and the Development of the Labour Movement in Victoria in the Eighteen Fifties' in *Historical Studies*, vol. 9, no. 36 (1961); N.B. Nairn, 'The Role of the Trades and Labour Council in New South Wales, 1871–91' in *Historical Studies*, vol. 7, no. 28 (1957); L.G. Churchward, 'The American Influence on the Australian Labour Movement' in *Historical Studies*, vol. 5, no. 19 (1952); N.B. Nairn, 'The 1890 Maritime Strike in N.S.W.' in *Historical Studies*, vol. 10, no. 37 (1961); A.A. Morrison, 'The Brisbane General Strike of 1912' in *Historical Studies*, vol. 4, no. 14 (1950). J.A. Merritt, 'W.G. Spence and the 1890 Maritime Strike' in *Historical Studies* no. 60 (1973); J. Tampke, 'German literature on the Australian labour movement and social policy, 1890–1916' in *Labour History* no. 36 (1979). For the general 'feel' of the more respectable side of the labour movement, L.F. Fitzhardinge, *That Fiery Particle, Vol. 1 of a political biography of W.M. Hughes* (1964) is useful; and in W.M. Hughes, *The Case for Labor* (1910, reprinted 1970) can be found specimens of the writings of one of the movement's most talented articulators. Some of the story of Catholic influence in the labour movement is told in Patrick Ford, *Cardinal Moran and the A.L.P.* (1966); Celia Hamilton, 'Irish Catholics of N.S.W. and the Labor Party 1890–1910' in *Historical Studies*, vol. 8, no. 31 (1958), and 'Catholic Interests and the Labor Party: Organised Catholic Action in Victoria and N.S.W. 1910–1916' in *Historical Studies*, vol. 9, no. 33 (1959). The story of the unsuccessful export of Australian utopianism to Paraguay is told in Gavin Souter, *A Peculiar People; The Australians in Paraguay* (1968). A counterblast on traditional views of the nature of the labour movement (or what he alleges them to be) is found in Humphrey McQueen, *A New Britannia* (1970).

POLITICS

The groundwork of finding system in the apparent mess of the faction period in politics was provided by A.W. Martin, 'Henry Parkes and Electoral Manipulation, 1872–1882' in *Historical Studies*, vol. 8, no. 31 (1958); and P. Loveday and A.W. Martin, *Parliament, Factions and Parties; The First Thirty Years of Responsible Government in N.S.W. 1856–1889* (1966). Sidelights on this period are provided in Brian Dickey, *Politics in New South Wales 1856–1900* (1969). The story is continued in Joan Rydon and R.N. Spann, *New South Wales Politics, 1901–1910* (1962). It is brought together in P. Loveday *et al.* (eds), *The emergence of the Australian Party Systems* (1977). Cyril Pearl, *Wild Men of Sydney* (1958) gives an idea of how tough Australian politics could be. There are several particular studies: J.M. Main, 'Making Constitutions in New South Wales and Victoria 1853–1854' in *Historical Studies, Selected Articles, Second Series* (1967); Joy E. Parnaby, 'The Composition of the Victorian Parliament 1851–1881' in *Historical Studies, Selected Articles, Second Series* (1967); Bruce Mansfield, *Australian Democrat: William O'Sullivan* (1965). An extraordinary sidelight on fringe politics is found in Henry Mayer, *Marx, Engels and Australia* (1964).

NATIONALISM AND IMPERIALISM

For the best account of the Britishness of federated Australia, See G. Souter, *The Lion and the Unicorn: The Initiation of Australia, 1901–1919* (1976). The main paintings of the 1890s school can be found in Alan McCulloch, *The Golden Age of Australian Painting* (1969). There is a background to the uses of bushrangers as proto-Australians in R.B. Walker, 'Bushranging in Fact and Legend' in *Historical Studies*, vol. 11, no. 42 (1964). Vance Palmer, *The Legend of the Nineties* (new ed. 1963) is interesting as an example of what was once believed. For metropolitan studies of the metropolitan development of the bush legend, see P. Corris, 'The Bush Ethos in the 1890s' in *Historical Studies* no. 58 (1972); and Graeme Davison, 'Sydney and the Bush: an urban context for the Australian Legend'

in *Historical Studies* no. 71 (1978). For the rather different matter of the development of the idea of 'pioneers', see J.B. Hirst, 'The pioneer legend' in the same issue. K.S. Inglis, 'Australia Day' in *Historical Studies*, vol. 13, no. 49 (1967) is relevant to Australians' difficulties in deciding what they were going to be nationalist about. B. Mansfield, 'The Background to Radical Republicanism in New South Wales in the Eighteen Eighties' in *Historical Studies*, vol. 5, no. 20 (1953) records a failed movement. It should be read in conjunction with Charles S. Blackton, 'Australian Nationality and Nationalism: The Imperial Federationist Interlude 1885–1901' in *Historical Studies, Selected Articles, Second Series* (1967). For other imperialist episodes, see Marjorie G. Jacobs, 'Bismark and the Annexation of New Guinea' in *Historical Studies*, vol. 5, no. 17 (1951), and 'The Colonial Office and New Guinea' in *Historical Studies*, vol. 5, no. 18 (1952); B.R. Penny, 'The Age of Empire: An Australian Episode' in *Historical Studies*, vol. 11, no. 41 (1963), and 'The Australian Debate on the Boer War' in *Historical Studies*, vol. 14, no. 56 (1971); C.N. Connolly, 'Manufacturing Spontaneity: The Australian Offers of Troops for the Boer War' in *Historical Studies* no. 70 (1978). For English attitudes and the relation of defence to federation there is Luke Trainor, 'British Imperial Defence Policy and the Australian Colonies, 1892–96' in *Historical Studies*, vol. 14, no. 54 (1970). For the collapse of nationalism, Charles Grimshaw, 'Australian Nationalism and the Imperial Connection 1900–1914' in *Politics and History*, vol. 3, no. 2 (1958). On immigration policy: A.T. Yarwood, 'The "White Australia" Policy: A Re-interpretation of the Development in the Late Colonial Period' in *Historical Studies*, vol. 10, no. 39 (1962); and Myra Willard, *History of the White Australia Policy to 1920* (1923).

FEDERATION

Why the Australian colonies federated still tends to mystify historians. There was an attempt to raise new issues in R.S. Parker, 'Australian Federation: The Influence of Economic Interests and Political Pressures' in *Historical Studies*, vol. 4, no. 13 (1949); but the quick reply by Geoffey Blainey, 'The Role of Economic Interests in Australian Federation' in *Historical Studies*, vol. 4, no. 15 (1950) seemed to end the discussion until A.W. Martin (ed.), '*Essays in Australian Federation*' (1969). However, a significant biography of the man most notably associated with articulation of the new nation came out in that period: J.A. La Nauze, *Alfred Deakin*, 2 vols. (1965). Deakin's own account, *The Federal Story*, was not published until 1944. Since then, there has been a selection of his newspaper dispatches in Alfred Deakin, *Federated Australia. Selections from Letters to the Morning Post 1900–1910* (1968). That he was anonymously acting as Australian political correspondent to a newspaper in London while he was Prime Minister, even commenting on his own actions, gives Deakin a unique niche in the world history of stagecraft. A contemporary account of the beginnings of the Federal Parliament is provided in Henry Gyles Turner, *The First Decade of the Australian Commonwealth* (1911). Some of the political rhetoric of the time has been put together in Scott Bennett, *Federation* (1975) and *The Making of the Commonwealth* (1971). After the constitutional crisis of 1975 the whole history of the making of the Constitution came to be reconsidered. The first new look of this kind came with Richard Hall and John Iremonger, *The Makers and the Breakers* (1976); and Hugh Anderson (ed.) *Tocsin. Radical arguments against Federation, 1897–1900* (1977).

Part 3: the age of Development

STATE OF THE NATION

Of the modern 'state of Australia' books, the first was John Douglas Pringle, *Australian Accent* (1958). This was followed by Robin Boyd, *The Australian Ugliness* (1960); Peter Coleman (ed.), *Australian Civilisation* (1962); Donald Horne, *The Lucky Country* (1964, rev. several times but the best edition to give a picture of the period is the first rev. ed., 1965); Craig Macgregor, *Profile of Australia* (1966); Donald Horne, *The Next Australia* (1970); and Ronald Conway, *The*

Great Australian Stupor. An Interpretation of the Australian Way of Life (1971). Of those that followed, the most distinctive were Maximillian Walsh, *Poor Little Rich Country* (1979); Humphrey McQueen, *Gone Tomorrow. Australia in the 80s* (1982); and Greg Crough and Ted Wheelwright, *Australia: A Client State* (1982). With the publication of A.F. Davies and S. Encel, *Australian Society* (1965) there developed a new, sociological genre, of which four examples would be Donald Edgar, *Introduction to Australian Society* (1980); John Higley *ed al.* (eds) *Elites in Australia* (1979); R.W. Connell, *Ruling Class Ruling Culture* (1977); and John S. Western, *Social Inequality in Australian Society* (1983). Of the autobiographies that became fashionable in the 1960s the most useful for social insights are Jack Lindsay, *The Roaring Twenties* (1960); Hal Porter, *The Watcher on the Cast Iron Balcony* (1963) and *The Paper Chase* (1966); Donald Horne, *The Education of Young Donald* (1967); and George Johnston, *My Brother Jack* (1964) and *Clean Straw for Nothing* (1969). Belonging to the same class is Vincent Buckley, *Cutting Green Hay* (1983). Egon Kisch, *Australian Landfall* (1937, reissued 1969 with a foreword by A.T. Yarwood), and H.G. Wells, *Travels of a Republican Radical in Search of Hot Water* (1939) bring together many of the moods and discontents of the 1930s. The most widely quoted account is D.H. Lawrence, *Kangaroo* (1923). A source book of many of the criticisms of Australians is J.B. Bryce, *Modern Democracies* (1921). Not much has yet been written about the period of social change from the mid-1960s to the mid-1970s apart from Donald Horne, *Time of Hope* (1980). Richard Gordon (ed.), *The Australian New Left* (1970) projects some of the aspirations and analyses of the time, and Jack Mundey, *Green Bans and Beyond* (1981) is an account from one of the principal actors. The most sustained expression of the new type of criticism is found, perhaps, in Dennis Altman, *Rehearsals for Change* (1980). There is a splendid evocation of intellectual life in the period of the rise and fall of Whitlam in Frank Moorhouse (ed.), *Days of Wine and Rage* (1980).

ECONOMIC

The various volumes of E.L. Wheelwright and Ken Buckley, *Essays in the Political Economy of Australian Capitalism* provide among other things, background interpretation of this period. Particularly related to some of the themes of *The Story of the Australian People* are David Clark, 'Australia: Victim or Partner of British Imperialism' (in vol. 1); Sol Encel, 'Capitalism, the Middle Classes and the Welfare State' (in vol. 2); M. Beresford and P. Kerr, 'A Turning Point for Australian Capitalism: 1942–52 (in vol. 4); and W. Armstrong and J. Bradbury, 'Industrialisation and Class Structure in Australia, Canada and Argentina: 1870 to 1980' (in vol. 5). Overviews are to be found in N.G. Butlin *et al.* (eds), *Government and Capitalism. Public and Private Choice in Twentieth Century Australia* (1982); and Colin Forster (ed.) *Australian Economic Development in the Twentieth Century* (1970). There is growing reading matter on the Great Depression, including C.B. Schedvin, *Australia and the Great Depression* (1970); L.J. Louis and Ian Turner, *The Depression of the 1930s* (1968); Judy Mackinolty, *The Wasted Years* (1981); Wendy Lowenstein, *Weevils in the Flour* (1978); Keith Amos, *The New Guard Movement* (1976). For examples of contemporary expression of moods of disillusion with economic development there are W.D. Forsyth, *The Myth of Open Spaces* (1942); B.R. Davidson, *The Northern Myth* (1965); and Peter Thompson, *Power in Tasmania* (1981). Perhaps the most readable biography of a businessman is Geoffrey Blainey's biography of Essington Lewis, *The Steel Master* (1971). The best study of a government economist is H.C. Coombs' study of himself and his times in *Trial Balance* (1981). In R. Manne (ed.), *The New Conservatism in Australia* (1982) there is a chapter, 'Elites in Australian History' by W.D. Rubinstein, that investigates the weaknesses of capitalists in Australia.

BIOGRAPHIES

The three biographies that best give the feel of public figures and their times have not been written by professional historians: David

Marr, *Barwick* (1980) may be the best biography written by an Australian; Graham Freudenberg, *A Certain Grandeur. Gough Whitlam in Politics* (1977) and Blanche d'Alpuget, *Robert J. Hawke* are both informative studies of public leaders in action. Kylie Tennant, *Evatt, Policies and Justice* (1970) is over-generous, but informative in the view it gives of what people wanted Evatt to be. Don Watson, *Brian Fitzpatrick. A Radical Life* (1979) captures some of the feeling of Melbourne radicalism.

FOREIGN POLICY

T.B. Millar, *Australia in Peace and War, 1788–1977* (1978) provides an overall ivew of external relations. W.J. Hudson, *Billy Hughes in Paris* (1978) provides a view of Australia's first active (if one-man) diplomacy and his *Towards a Foreign Policy, 1914–41* (1967) gives a quick run over a mainly inactive period. There is a debate on the degree of activity in J.R. Poynter, 'The Yo-Yo Variations' in *Historical Studies* no. 55 (1970) and W.J. Hudson's comment on this in *Historical Studies* No 55 (1970). E.M. Andrews provides a special study in 'The Australian Government and Appeasement' in *Politics and History* XIII-1 (1967). Australia-United States relations are considered in Raymond A. Esthus, *From Enmity to Alliance, 1931–41* (1964); Roger J. Bell, *Unequal Allies. Australia-American Relations and the Pacific War* (1977); and Norman Harper (ed.) *Australia and the United States* (1971). In Desmond Ball, *A Suitable Piece of Real Estate* (1980) there is a discussion of United States installations in Australia. Of the post-war period, three different views are given in Alan Watt, *The Evolution of Australian Foreign Policy* (1967); Alan Renouf, *The Frightened Country* (1979); and Malcolm Booker, *The Last Domino* (1976). Bruce Grant, *The Crisis of Loyalty* (1972) examines the traditional mentalities of Australian strategic thinking; and David Martin, *Armed Neutrality for Australia* (1984) challenges them.

POLITICS

V.G. Childe, *How Labour Governs* (1923, reissued 1964) is an example of a certain kind of contemporary disillusion. Bernie Schedvin, 'E.G. Theodore and the London Pastoral Lobby' in *Politics*, vol. vi, no. 1 (1971) give a fascinating vignette of how British pressure could be applied to Australian politics; and Miriam Dixon, 'Ideology, the Trades Hall Reds and Lang' in *Politics*, vol. vi, no. 1 (1971) provides an example of shifts between faction and ideology. To this can be added Robert Cooksey, *Lang and Socialism* (1971). B.D. Graham, *The Formation of the Australian Country Parties* (1966), Ulrich Ellis, *A History of the Australian Country Party* (1963) and L.F. Crisp, *The Australian Federal Labour Party* (1955) are useful both for their special subject and a general background to the times. Of the Labor political biographies L.F. Crisp, *Ben Chifley* (1960); Irwin Young; *Theodore, His Life and Times* (1971); and Lloyd Ross, *John Curtin* (1977) are the most worth reading. Heather Radi and Peter Spearritt (eds), *Jack Lang* (1977) is a useful study of one of Australia's more interesting political phenomena. W. Denning, *Caucus Crisis* (reprinted 1982) is a contemporary account giving the feel of the Scullin Government. J.C. Horsfall, *The Liberal Era* (1974) and the relevant sections of W.F. Mandle, *Going It Alone* (1978) provide an introduction to the Menzies period. D. Horne's *The Lucky Country* looks at the period from a different perspective. On Menzies himself nothing very satisfactory has yet been provided: Cameron Hazlehurst, *Menzies Observed* (1979) is of some use. Menzies' own *The Forgotten People* (1943) is a fascinating reminder of his rhetorical power. Marian Simms, *A Liberal Nation* (1982) is a stimulating account of the nature of the Liberal Party. Robert Murray, *The Split: Australian Labor in the Fifties* (1970) runs through the civil war in the Labor Party that helped keep Menzies in power. A new kind of political writing (or a continuation of the kind of writing pioneered by Denning in *Caucus Crisis*) began with Alan Reid, *The Power Struggle* (1969), a description of John Gorton's rise to power. Reid himself followed this up with *The Gorton Experiment* (1971). Others have included: Laurie Oakes and

David Solomon, *The Making of an Australian Prime Minister* (1973); C.J. Lloyd and G.S. Reid, *Out of the Wilderness: the Return of Labor* (1974); Michael Sexton, *Illusions of Power: The Fate of a Reform Government* (1979); Alan Reid, *The Whitlam Venture* (1976); Allan Patience and Brian Head, *From Whitlam to Fraser* (1979); and Paul Kelly, *The Hawke Ascendancy* (1984). E.G. Whitlam's dismissal has produced a whole sub-literature of its own.

WARS

There are descriptions of the anti-conscription battles preceding World War I in L.C. Jauncey, *The Story of Conscription in Australia* (1935, reissued with a foreword by P. O'Farrell, 1968); and John Barrett, *Falling In* (1979). C.E.W. Bean (ed.), *Official History of Australia in the War of 1914–1918*, 12 vols (1921–37) includes one volume on the home front by Ernest Scott. There is a useful potted history in C.E.W. Bean, *Anzac to Amiens. A Shorter History of the Australian Fighting Services in the First World War* (1946). K.S. Inglis, 'The Australians at Gallipoli' in *Historical Studies*, vol. 14, no. 54 and vol. 14, no. 55 (1970) gives an account of the beginning of the Anzac Legend. Bill Gammage, *The Broken Years* (1974) tells the story in the words of the Anzacs themselves; and Kevin Fewster, *Gallipoli Correspondent: The frontline diary of C.E.W. Bean* (1983) provides the first-hand reactions of the greatest single literary creator of the idea of the Australian as 'Digger'. Ian Turner, *Sydney's Burning* (rev. 1969) describes the wartime actions of the IWW and their treatment. Two books by Michael McKernan, *The Australian People and the Great War* (1980) and *Australian Churches at War* (1980) give some of the feel of the home front. Geoffrey Serle, *John Monash* (1982) gives the story of Monash at war and in peace. There are contrasting views of the enigma of W.M. Hughes in L.F. Fitzhardinge, *The Little Digger* (1979) and Donald Horne, *In Search of Billy Hughes* (1979). Of the 22 volumes of *Australia in the War of 1939–1945*, the volumes on civil affairs are Paul Hasluck, *The Government and the People, 1934–41* (1952) and *1942–45* (1970); S.J. Butlin, *War Economy, 1939–42* (1955); and D.P. Mellor, *The Role of Science and Industry* (1958). For an overall picture of Australian society at war, see Michael McKernan, *All In! Australia During the Second World War* (1983). For an overall view of the war, see John Robertson, *Australia Goes to War, 1939–45* (1984). For the Korean war see the various volumes of Robert O'Neill, *Australia in the Korean War* (1981); and for an initial treatment of Vietnam, Peter King (ed.), *Australia's Vietnam* (1983).

Sources of illustrations

(Abbreviations: a = above, b = below, c = centre, l = left,
r = right, t = top)

Adelaide Advertiser 267a; *Adelaide News* 251ca; *Age* 115bl, 242a, 266al,
294br, 295bl; Alexander Turnbull Library 76a; Allport Library &
Museum of Fine Arts 83al; Angus & Robertson 247b, 303l; *Argus*
227ar; Art Gallery of New South Wales 34al, 41a, 80a, 99l, 108ar,
112, 149, 169a, 173ar, 176al, 209t, 213, 241l, 289a, 290; Art
Gallery of South Australia 43l, 66, 113a, 157a, 172r; Art Gallery of
Western Australia 143a; Associated Press of America 303b; J.J.
Atkinson 170br; 'Ausflag 88' 292al, cl, bl; Australian Archives
184ar, br; Australian Consolidated Press 227b, 232, 243l, 255b,
264tl, 272bc, bl; Australian Council for Social Security 270al;
Australian Information Service 180, 284al, 292br, 299ar;
Australian Institute of Aboriginal Studies 301b; Australian Labor
Party 211, 274l, cl; Australian Museum, Mint Collection 42br;
Australian National Film & Sound Archive 234r, 235a, bl, 244l;
Australian National Gallery, Canberra 81t, 136c, t, 173b, 176bl, r;
216, 229, 237, 253al, bl; ANZ Travel 276tr; Australian News &
Information Bureau 222ar; Australian War Memorial 131a, 194r
neg no H11567, 195a neg no A769, 195br neg no C6667, 196l neg
no H16396, 196r neg no H11572, 197al neg no V34, 197r neg no
V38, 199ar neg no A3376, 200al neg no E829, 200r neg no E711,
201a no 7545, 201br, 204br, 205, 206l, br, 243r, no V6723, 244ar
no 98, 244br no 40, 246ar no 16, 246br neg no 122422, 247a no
V52, 248r neg no 14028, 248ar neg no 14211, 248br neg no 14082,
249a no 44, 249bl neg no 12627, 249br neg no 11544, 251al no
V332, 251br neg no 43968, 252l no 8, 252r cat no 26, 253ar, br,
296a cat no 290, 296b cat no 27; Australian Unesco Committee for
Man and the Biosphere, Commonwealth of Australia 286l;
Australian Wine and Brandy Corporation 75bl; Bendigo Art
Gallery 96al; BHP 221; Professor G.C. Bolton 184l; Brisbane
Courier-Mail 276ct; Brotherhood of St Lawrence 269, 270br, ar;
271br; CBS Records Australia Ltd 265b; Central Highlands
Regional Library Service 95a; Channel 7 Sydney 277r; CSR 139tl;
CSIRO Archives 224; Constitutional Museum of South Australia
113bl; Noel Counihan 228r; Crawford's Film Production 262b;
Department of Crown Lands & Survey, Victoria 131b; Dixson
Galleries 1, 19, 30al, 35, 36l, 40a, 41b, 45, 56, 57b, 77c, 78al, bl; 81cl,
83ar, 89, 103l; Dixson Library 12a, b, 13a, 22ra; Max Dupain 2,
212ar, 256l; Esso Australia 268l; Education Department of New
South Wales 40bl, 54ar, l; John Fairfax & Sons Pty Ltd 140r,
226ar, 228bl, 231br, 255a (*SMH* 1949), 260bl (*Australia II*), 266ar,
br; 271ar, 275, 278, 280tl (*Nation Review*), 281bl, 283, 287al, ar;
297c, 300a; Gas & Fuel Corporation of Victoria 42bl; GMH 258al,
bc; 277a; *Girls' Own* 281ca; Government Printer, New South Wales
145a, 156br, 162bl, 169b, 214, 219al, ac; GTV Channel 9,
Richmond 261al; Herald & Weekly Times Ltd, Melbourne 226br,
233l; Hobart *Mercury* 227al; Horne Family Album 165bl, bc, br;
208; Housing Commission of New South Wales 256r; International
Newsreel 199bl; Bob Irving 209c; Sir John Jess 137ca, ra, cb, rb; La
Trobe State Library of Victoria 57a, 64, 77br, 90, 91, 93a, 103br,
116bl, 120, 147ar, br; 158b; Josef Lebovic 236r; Department of
Leisure, Sport & Tourism 258a; Michael Leunig 280ca; Liberal
Party of Australia 274cl, r; Library Board of Western Australia
142r, 190a; Library Council of Victoria 101; Norman Lindsay
251br (*Bulletin*); Malaysian Airline System 276cl; Manly Art
Gallery and Museum 164, 165al; Melbourne *Herald* 293; Middle
Head Action Group 285bl; Mitchell Library 6, 8, 9, 13a, b, 14b, ra,

15, 16tr, al, bl, br, 17a, b, 18t, c, b, 20One Pound Promissory Note,
Rum Mug, Bill of Exchange, 21, 22al, 24, 25 26bl, cb, 28al, bl, r,
29l, r, 30ar, b, 32bl, 33a, b, 34bl, ar, 36ar, 37, 38al, bl, r, 39a, c,
40br, 42cl, ar, 43r, 44br, 46ca, cb, 48a, b, 49, 50a, b, 51al, ar, b,
52ca, cb, r, 53b, 55al, bl, r, 59, 60a, 61a, c, b, 62a, b, 63, 65al, ar,
b, 67a, b, 70a, b, 71l, r, 72a, b, 74al, bl, r, 75a, 76bl, br, 77t, bl,
78ar, br, 79l, ar, br, 80b, 81cr, bl, br, 82a, b, 83b, 85, 86al, ar, b,
88al, bl, 92l, 94, 95b, 96bl, r, 97ar, 98br, 99r, 100a, b, 102, 104bl,
ar, 105a, 106, 107, 108al, cb, br, 109al, ar, b, 111b, 115br, 116al,
br, 117a, 118, 120a, 121a, 122al, b, 124, 125, 126ar, b, 127t, c, 128,
129bl, 130, 132ar, 133r, 134bl, 139r, 140l, c, 142al, bl, 145bl, lr,
146, 148bl, 150, 151ar, br, 152l, ra, 154ar, bc, 155, 157bl, br, 158al,
159t, 161l, 162a, 166r, 167l, rb, 170al, ac, 173al, 174r, 175l, 178r,
179l, 181al, 181ar, 182b, 185r, 188l, br, 191ar, br, 194al, 198, 199l,
206ar, 209bl, 210l, 222ac, 235r, 236ca, bl, 238; David Moore
258br, 277l, 298; Museo de Naval, Madrid 26t; Museum of Applied
Arts & Sciences 105br, 119br, 171; Museum of English Rural Life,
University of Reading 46al; National Gallery of Victoria 126al,
135, 136b, 160, 172l, 177, 192, 193, 204al, 223, 262a, 288b, 289;
National Library of Australia 115al, 144bl, 166l, 174l, 190br, 191al,
197bl, 201bl, 219ar, b, 231al, 250b; National Library of Australia
Rex Nan Kivell Collection 14rb, 22bl, rb, 23bl, 31l, tr, cr, br, 34br,
36br, 39b, 52l, 69a, b, 98ar, 110r, 111a, 116ar, 122ar, 161r, 179al,
182a, 185l, 186ar; Neil T – Towels 304tcl; Thomas Nelson 270bl;
Newington College 129a; New South Wales Public Library 23al, r,
44ar, 46bl, ar, br, 47al, bl, r, 58a, 87b, 93bl, br, 104al, br, 108bl,
113br, 115ar, 117bl, br, 133l, 141r, br, 148al, bc, br, 151al, bl,
154al, 156al, ar, 159bl, 162br, 178al, bl, 179br, 186l, br, 187,
188ar, 195bl, 199br, 202, 203, 207l, 209br, 210r, 212al, br, 215,
218l, 222al, 226l, 230, 231bl, 233c, r; News Ltd 154al, 231al, 236al,
246r, 254, 260al, br, 261bl, ar, 263, 264bl, br, tr, 265al, ac, ar,
268r, 270ca, 272al, ac, 273, 276bl, 279tl, bl, tr, br, 280cb, br, 281al,
ar, br, 282, 285al, ar, 287bl, bc, br, ar, 291bl, 292ar, 294al, 295al,
ar, 297b, 299al, br, 301al, 302l, br, 305; John Oxley Library 97al,
139cl, bl, 148ar, 159br; PBL Marketing Pty Ltd 260ar; Pelaco
Australia 241r, Penguin Australia 279cbl; Phillips Cons Co.
Northbridge New South Wales 276br; private collection 84a, b,
190bl; Queen Victoria Museum and Art Gallery 53a, 68c, b, 87t;
Queensland University 299bl; Queensland Museum 138; Reader's
Digest 20: Five Shilling Promissory Note, Holey Dollar, front of
Dump, back of Dump, French Écu, Dutch Guilder; Reserve Bank
189la, lb; Rigby Publishers 281bc; St Joseph's College, Hunter's
Hill 129br; Sanyo 257r; Anne Schofield 92br; Semmens Collection,
University of Melbourne Archives 97br; Seven Seas Stamps 132,
175, 189ra, rb, 217, 240l, 294ca, 301ar, br, 304cl, c, cr, bl, bcl, bcr,
br; Bernard Smith 242l; *Smith's Weekly* 234al, bl; Snowy Mountains
Hydro-Electric Authority 266bl, 284ca; South Australian Archives
183; Peter Spearitt 207r, 228ca; State Library of South Australia
123, 153; State Rail Authority of New South Wales 42al, 103ar;
State Library of Victoria 97bl, 98bl, 119bl, 240r; Sunbeam 257l;
Sunday Telegraph 271l, 291al; Sydney Institute of Education 156bl;
Talma Studios 178c; Les Tanner 280bl; Tasmanian Museum and
Art Gallery 32al, 68a, 168; Telecom Australia 163a; *Tribune* 300b;
Tyrrell Collection 167ar; United Nations 250a; UPI 294cb, 297a,
303ar; University of Melbourne 134a; University of Sydney
Archives 54b; Victa Mowers 259; Victorian Racing Club 144a;
Victorian Railways 163b; Steven Wallace 302ar; *West Australian*
181bl, 291r; West Australian Government Printer 143b; White
Wings 166ca; Wilderness Society 284ar; WD & HO Wills 166cb;
World Travel 261br.